LIFTING THE VEIL

LIFTING THE VEIL

British Society in Egypt
1768–1956

ANTHONY SATTIN

J. M. Dent & Sons Ltd

London

This book is set in Bembo
Printed in Great Britain at The Bath Press, Avon
for
J. M. Dent & Sons Ltd,
91 Clapham High Street, London SW4 7TA

British Library Cataloguing in Publication Data

Sattin, Anthony
Lifting the veil: British Society in Egypt 1768–1956.
1. Egypt, Britons. Social life, 1768–1956.
I. Title
962'.00421

ISBN 0-460-04750-7

CONTENTS

ILLUSTRATIONS

ACKNOWLEDGEMENTS

I first went to Egypt for a holiday, familiar only with Harriet Tytler's account of travelling overland from Alexandria to Suez on her way out to India in the 1840s, and returned a few years later, having edited the letters Florence Nightingale wrote when she went up the Nile in 1849. My conviction then was that while there had recently been a glut of books about the experiences of foreigners and particularly the British in India, Africa and many other parts of the world, very little had been written about foreigners in Egypt. Of course there are excellent political histories, but few books on the social history. What struck me most forcibly when I went up the Nile was not just the antiquity of the ruins and towns, but the fact that people had been coming to visit them for a very long time – the graffiti on the temple walls is proof of that. So I set out to tell the story of how and why these visitors came.

In the introductory chapter of *Passenger to Teheran*, Vita Sackville-West quotes one of her favourite authors who states that 'A writer expresses himself in words that have been used before because they give his meaning better than he can give it himself, or because they are beautiful or witty, or because he expects them to touch a chord of association in the reader, or because he wishes to show that he is learned or well-read.' I hope I will be indulged for recalling so many voices from the past, but some of them are beautiful or witty or moving and I hope that together they bring this recent past in Egypt to life. It is hard not to hear their echoes in Egypt even now.

I am grateful to the following people for allowing me to quote from works still in copyright: The Bodley Head on behalf of Putnam & Co as the publisher of *Out Of Africa* by Karen Blixen; Condé Nast Publications Ltd for James Cameron's article *Egypt* from *Travel in Vogue*; Gerald Duckworth & Co Ltd for *When the Going Was Good* by Evelyn Waugh; Faber & Faber Ltd for *The Alexandria Quartet* by Lawrence Durrell; Victor Gollancz Ltd for *Gods, Graves and Scholars* by C. W. Ceram; Michael Haag Ltd for *Alexandria, a History and a Guide* by E. M. Forster; Robert Hale Ltd for *A Family in Egypt* by Mary Rowlatt; Hamish Hamilton Ltd for *Inside Africa* by John Gunther; John McPherson for *The Man Who Loved Egypt* by Bimbashi McPherson; John Murray Ltd for *Oriental Spotlight* by Major C. S. Jarvis, *Egyptian Service* by Sir Thomas Russell Pasha and *The Coast of Incense* by Freya Stark; A. D. Peters &

Co Ltd for *Places* by Jan Morris; the Estate of Alan Moorehead for *African Trilogy* and *The White Nile*; and Titus Wilson Ltd for *Boyle of Cairo* by Clara Boyle. *The Middle East Diary* is copyright 1944 the Estate of Noël Coward and is republished by arrangement with Michael Imison Playwrights Ltd, 28 Almeida Street, London N1 1TD. Permission to quote from *Passenger to Teheran* by Vita Sackville-West was granted by Curtis Brown Ltd, London, on behalf of the author's estate.

I am also grateful to the following for the loan of illustrations: the Thomas Cook Archive, 45 Berkeley Street, London W1; The Fine Art Society, 148 New Bond Street, London W1; Patrick Connor and the Martyn Gregory Gallery, 35 Bury Street, St James's, London SW1; and Priscilla Wrightson of Henry Sotheran Ltd, 80 Pimlico Road, London SW1.

In Egypt, I owe thanks to the staff of the Alexandria Sporting Club, the British Council, in Cairo, the Cairo Press Centre, Gezira Sporting Club and the Cataract, Marriott, Mena House, Shepheards and Winter Palace Hotels. In Cairo, Mr Ahmed Artif allowed me access to the archives of the *Egyptian Gazette*, Professor Halim Grace of the Anglo-American Hospital shared his memories with me, Mr Salah El Derwy of EGAPT helped me organize my travels and Sir Alan Urwick, Her Britannic Majesty's Ambassador, kindly spared the time to take me through the British Embassy and its history – to all of them I am most grateful. Shyam Bhatia of the *Observer*, Hassan El Geretley, Suzy Naga of the Cairo Marriott Hotel and Dr Mursi Saad El Din all offered advice and provided entertainment and hospitality. In Alexandria I was helped by Mr Mohammed Amiri of the Cecil Hotel and Mr Photios Photaros of the Union Restaurant and I am also indebted to Mr Peter, the Cook's No. 1 guide in Luxor for sharing his memories with me.

In England, I am grateful to the able staff of the British Library, the London Library and the Royal Geographical Society's library for their assistance, to Peter Mansfield for his guiding advice, to Edmund Swinglehurst for allowing me access to the Thomas Cook Archive, and to Mr Samir Darwish and Dr Siham Khalil of EGAPT, Mr Gallal of the Egyptian Press Office and Mr M. Kader of Egyptair who helped me plan my journey. Finally, I owe grateful thanks and much more to the many people who provided books, encouragement and hot meals; to my agent, Mike Shaw of Curtis Brown, and my editor, Peter Shellard, who have guided me from the start, to my brother Richard for his photography, to my parents for providing me with a pencil so that I could write, and to Belinda Rowland, who came with me on my first visit and who suffered the birth of this book.

FOR BELINDA ROWLAND, WHO CAME WITH ME

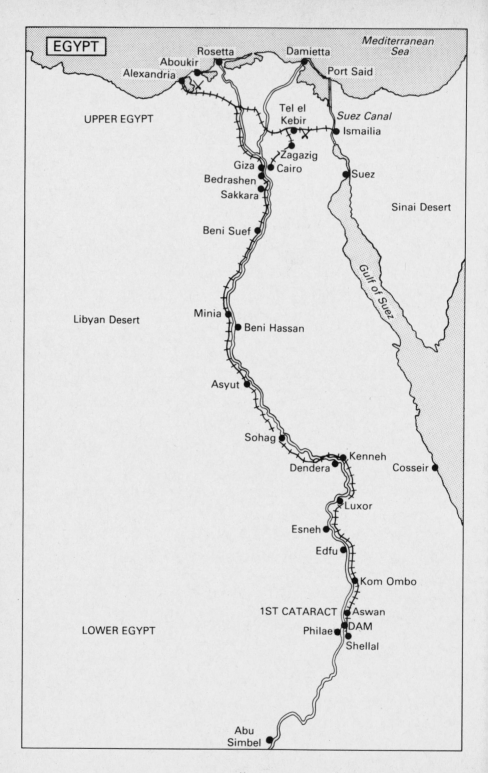

EGYPT

Mediterranean Sea

Rosetta
Aboukir
Alexandria
Damietta
Port Said

UPPER EGYPT

Tel el Kebir
Suez Canal
Ismailia

Zagazig
Giza
Cairo
Bedrashen
Sakkara
Suez

Sinai Desert

Beni Suef

Gulf of Suez

Libyan Desert

Minia
Beni Hassan

Asyut

Sohag

Kenneh
Dendera
Cosseir

Luxor

Esneh

Edfu

Kom Ombo

1ST CATARACT
Aswan
LOWER EGYPT
Philae
DAM
Shellal

Abu Simbel

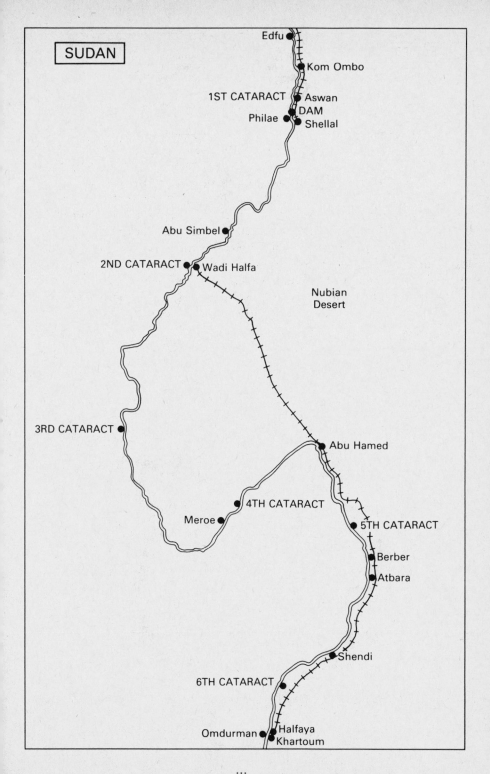

SUDAN

Edfu

Kom Ombo

1ST CATARACT · Aswan

DAM

Philae · Shellal

Abu Simbel

2ND CATARACT · Wadi Halfa

Nubian
Desert

3RD CATARACT

Abu Hamed

4TH CATARACT

Meroe

5TH CATARACT

Berber

Atbara

Shendi

6TH CATARACT

Omdurman · Halfaya
Khartoum

'Upon ancient dynasties of Ethiopian and Egyptian kings – upon Greek and Roman, upon Arab and Ottoman conquerors – upon Napoleon dreaming of an Eastern Empire – upon battle and pestilence – upon the ceaseless misery of the Egyptian race – upon keen-eyed travellers (Herodotus yesterday, and Warburton today) – upon all and more this unworldly Sphynx has watched... And we, we shall die, and Islam will wither away, and the Englishman straining far over to hold his loved India will plant a firm foot on the banks of the Nile and sit in the seats of the Faithful, and still that sleepless rock will lie watching and watching the works of the new busy race, with those same sad earnest eyes, and the same tranquil mien everlasting. You dare not mock at the Sphynx.'

A. W. Kinglake, *Eothen*, pp. 223–4

PREFACE

'They talk of you and me behind the veil
But if the veil be lifted, where are we?'

The Rubaiyat of Omar Khayyam

On the first morning of our first visit to Cairo, my companion and I left our hotel on the southern tip of Gezira and, employing a basic Arabic vocabulary to decline the offer of a taxi – *la shokran* – walked along the riverbank and across Tahrir (Liberation) Bridge. The Nile was still high and moved swiftly, breaking up into dark, powerful eddies behind the legs of the bridge and we leaned against the railings for a while to watch the water flow, turning our backs on the solid jam of cars and carts and on the crowd of Egyptians crossing the river. It was only ten o'clock on an April morning, but it was already hot enough for us to perspire and the power of the sun made our skin tingle on this first exposure after a long, hard, northern winter. It was both comforting and stimulating. I kept rubbing my exposed arms and the back of my neck. Belinda, who is blonde and fair skinned, felt the heat even more. When we continued our walk across the bridge, we noticed – idly, and without deliberation – four or five Egyptian girls coming towards us. They were all dark skinned, with pharaonically wide and dark-brown eyes, and black hair, dressed in jeans and long-sleeved cotton shirts buttoned at the neck. They walked alongside each other and almost filled the pavement, so we moved to one side to let them pass, but as they reached us, two of the girls ran their hands up and down my bare, white arm and said something in Arabic to which the others laughed.

Later, when we had passed through the chaotic centre of the city and reached the tenth-century mosque of Al Azhar, we left our shoes outside amongst rows of sandals and slippers watched over by a squatting, old man, and were about to enter through the worn and battered wooden doorway into a cloistered courtyard when another, younger man stood in our way.

'You cannot enter like this,' he said, pointing at Belinda's uncovered head. He handed her a long, broad piece of faded, blue and white cotton. 'Here you must wear a veil,' he said. When he had finished arranging the disguise, all that could be seen of her were a few tufts of blonde

1

hair, her sky-blue eyes and her nose. The rest was completely, shape-lessly hidden.

The veil separated Egyptians from foreigners. A hundred years ago, both used to wear a veil, although for entirely different purposes. Muslim women adopted it as an aid to modesty, as the Prophet had ordered that they should hide themselves from the view of men; while western women visiting Egypt were also advised to wear a veil – not as a matter of decency, but to protect themselves from the climate. In 1891, for instance, Murray's *Handbook for Travellers in Lower and Upper Egypt* recommended that 'Coloured-glass spectacles with gauze sides afford great relief to the eyes from the glare of the sun, and a blue or green veil is useful for the same purpose.'

Egypt is a country of particular extremes and this is especially so as regards its climate, for while it is overpoweringly hot in the south, it can be cold, wet and windy on the northern coast. While days in the desert are withering, the night brings a chill that will make you shiver. The weather dominates everything. While it burns the desert sands, it also nourishes the fertile land along the river – what Kipling called a narrow strip of market garden – which usually produces enough food to support the population. The climate also dictated the activities of foreigners who came to Egypt, forcing them to adopt new manners and customs. Some embraced the change eagerly, glad to be rid of what they viewed as the constraints of living in polite European society. Others, however, resisted. The British in particular were often reluctant to give up their habitual ways of living and out of the clash between their old ways and the new ones they encountered in Egypt came some excitement and understanding, and a great deal of humour – one Englishwoman in Egypt in the 1860s wrote, 'It is all a dream. You can't think what an odd effect it is to take up an English book and read it and then look up and hear men cry, "Yah Mohammad."' This meeting of the ways changed the face of Egypt and, at the same time, changed the foreigners, too. Somehow it didn't seem quite as difficult for the French or Italians, the Germans or Americans, as it was for the British, and the French traveller Gérard de Nerval mockingly observed in the 1840s that, 'Above all it is the English who are perfect and they never fail to cause the greatest amusement. Imagine a gentle-man on a donkey with his long legs almost reaching the ground. His round hat is covered with a thick piece of white cotton; an invention which is supposed to protect him against the sun by absorbing its rays.'

There were other inventions as well. An English traveller called Levinge developed a new use for mosquito netting in the first half of the nineteenth century when he fixed it to a pair of sheets which were already sewn together. The net, which was intended to cover the upper part of the body, was then suspended from the ceiling to create a small, individual tent. The entrance, in the side of the sheets, could then be sealed by tying up the draw-string. Levinge's invention was immediately popular and was soon recommended by guide books and travellers alike. The British, like other people unused to the climate, also needed protection from the sun during the day and, in addition to their face veils, they were recommended to bring along parasols to provide shade when they were out walking or riding. When they were on the river, the sun decks of their Nile boats, whether dahabiehs or steamers, were always covered by an awning from end to end. And what with their puggarees and sun-glasses, gloves, coats and range of hats from 'wide-awakes' to solar topis, it is hard to say whether they or the Egyptians were the most completely hidden.

Lucie Duff Gordon, who lived in Egypt in the 1860s, was rare among foreigners in that she was able to strike up friendships with Egyptians which were not based on official obligations; she was in Egypt to recover her health. She was therefore well placed to observe the way Egyptians lived and to consider the nature of the country. In 1863 she wrote that 'This country is a palimpsest, in which the Bible is written over Herodotus, and the Koran over that. In the towns the Koran is most visible, in the country Herodotus.' Here were three facets of Egypt – Herodotus and the ancient civilization, the Biblical world, and the living, Islamic culture. Through their own private involvement with the country and, later, through their official contact under the 'Veiled Protectorate', Lucie and the many other foreigners who came out to Egypt before and after her created yet another facet. What I have set out to do in this book, with the help of their own accounts of their lives as well as the more tangible things that they have left behind which are now their own monuments, is to unveil this most recent, western inscription on the Egyptian palimpsest.

PART ONE

COMPOSING OUR BOWL

' "What will you do at home? You are not an India
merchant?" I said, "No." "Have you no other trade nor
occupation but that of travelling?" I said, "That was my
occupation." "Ali Bey, my father-in-law," replied he, "often
observed there was never such a people as the English; no
other nation on earth could be compared to them, and none
had so many great men in all professions, by sea and land:
I never understood this till now; that I see it must be so,
when your king cannot find other employment for such a
man as you, but sending him to perish by hunger and thirst
in the sands, or to have his throat cut by the lawless
barbarians of the desert.'
Mahomet Bey Abou Dahab to James Bruce, Cairo, 1773

For a young man in search of fame and fortune in the middle of the
eighteenth century, some of the best opportunities were to be found
in the Indian colonies. Egypt, although nearer, was certainly not considered to be a promising place to start, for although there was rich
potential in trading with Egypt, the country was considered to be too
unpredictable; one year the Egyptians made encouraging noises, while
the next they were either banning Christian ships from their ports on
the grounds that they were too close to the holy places in Mecca and
Medina, or inhibiting Muslims from making their pilgrimage. To the
English, Egypt still appeared to be very much like the country described
in the *Tales of the One Thousand and One Nights*, which had first appeared
in English in 1706–8 in what was known as the Grub Street edition.
While these tales had a wide appeal as fiction, few Englishmen would
have willingly chosen to live in such a society. Certainly James Bruce
showed no desire to visit the country in his youth.

Bruce was the eldest son of a large and noble Scottish family and
although they were wealthy, their fortune was not considered sufficient
to support him in 'respectability' and it was decided, therefore, that
he would have to find a suitable occupation for himself. He was first
sent to Harrow and then entered Edinburgh University with a view
to sitting for the Scottish Bar. But he had a weak chest and fears that
he might contract consumption if he stayed in Britain led him to abandon
his studies and consider going abroad. India caught his imagination.

'The splendid fortunes with which several adventurers had returned to Britain about that time,' Bruce's first biographer explained, 'appeared ... more than sufficient to balance the dangers, the hazard, and the toils with which they had been procured.' In 1753, at the age of twenty-two, Bruce decided to go to London and to obtain the permission of the Directors of the East India Company to go out to India as a free trader. But before he had even had an interview with the Court of Directors, he was diverted from his intended course by another of the city's attractions – Bruce met and fell in love with a young woman called Adriana Allan, whom he married in 1754.

The Allan family were well-established in London in the wine trade and, as often happens to young men when they marry, Bruce put away all ideas of foreign travel. Instead, he settled down to a happy and distinguished family life and was made a partner in the Allan business. In view of what he was to achieve, it seems almost impossible that he would have been satisfied with this life for long. But Bruce never had to make the choice between London and foreign travel; it was made for him when, in the first summer of their married life, Adriana contracted tuberculosis. On her doctor's advice, she went to Bristol to take the waters and breathe the drier air, but this did not effect her cure and so, as the summer ended, she decided to travel to France with the idea of wintering in Provence with her mother and husband. The climate would be better for her. But the Bruces got no further south than Paris, where her condition deteriorated and she died at the beginning of October.

Because she was a Protestant, and therefore was seen as a heretic, Adriana was pursued by Paris's proselytizing Catholic clergy during the days of her illness – 'many of the Roman Catholic clergy hovering about the doors,' Bruce wrote to his father afterwards, 'myself unable to find any expedient to keep them from disturbing her in her last moments.' They then hounded Bruce after she was dead and, in order to bury her according to her own religious beliefs, he was driven to adopt the most extraordinary procedures. He was given permission to inter her in the British Ambassador's own burial plot and, he wrote, 'having ordered the mournful solemnity, with as much decency as is allowed in that country to heretics, at midnight, between the 10th and 11th ult. accompanied only by the chaplain, a brother of my lord Foley's, and our own servants, we carried her body to the burying ground, at the Porte St Martin, where I saw all my comfort and happiness laid with her in the grave.' That night, immediately after the funeral, Bruce rode to Boulogne, desperate to be out of the country.

If he was not to have happiness or comfort, Bruce decided that there might at least be some consolation in learning and adventure. Fourteen years after Adriana's death, having travelled widely through Europe, witnessed the battle of Crevelt, learnt Arabic and educated himself broadly in Oriental studies, as well as having served as British Consul in Algiers, Bruce was a fit and healthy man, who at six feet four inches tall and with bright red hair was, in his own words, 'in the prime of life, of no ungracious figure.' In 1768, he left for Egypt in the company of an Italian artist, Luigi Balugani, ready for the journey for which he had now so diligently prepared himself – to discover the true source of the Nile.

*

The Egyptian part of Bruce's journey, although hazardous and uncomfortable, was not considered particularly remarkable. British travellers and traders had been going there for centuries and their journals had given some idea of what he could expect. They were attracted by the things which continue to fascinate tourists today – they marvelled at the mosques, were horrified by the poverty and dirt in the city, were moved by constant reminders of a glorious past and were delighted by crocodiles, hippopotamus, bananas, palm trees and many other things they had never seen before. Each account went a little further in its understanding of the people and their past and, by the beginning of the eighteenth century, Europeans were aware that there was proof in the Bible story that Egypt had once been a great and advanced civilization, although they would not have placed it on the same level as Greece or Italy in terms of enlightenment. But in the 1720s and 1730s, all this was to change.

Until that time, few foreigners had ever travelled further south in Egypt than Cairo. They had been to Alexandria and Cairo, had seen the pyramids at Giza and Sakkara, and some had crossed the eastern desert to Suez or to the monastery on Mount Sinai and to the Holy Land. Then, in 1721, the chaplain of the British settlement in Algiers, the Rev Thomas Shaw, travelled to Egypt and wrote in his *Travels, or Observations relating to Several Parts of Barbary and the Levant* that 'No diversion can be attended with greater pleasure than travelling upon the Nile.' This was certainly not the accepted opinion of Egypt. In the same year as Shaw, another Englishman, Colonel William Lethieullier, also travelled up the Nile as far as Cairo. While Shaw stimulated interest in Egypt through his writings, Lethieullier took back to England with him a collection of antiquities, including figures of a number of Egyptian gods and a mummy intact in its coffin.

In the following decade, three Europeans travelling independently of each other – a Danish sea captain called Frederick Norden, who was sent to Egypt by King Christian VI of Denmark, the Rev Richard Pococke and a Dr Charles Perry – all sailed up the Nile as far as Aswan. Norden went even further up the river and reached Derr in Nubia, but there he was attacked and was obliged to escape back down the river to save his life. All three travellers published accounts of their travels and Norden, unprejudiced by his experiences, wrote that it would now be necessary to re-evaluate the opinions of Ancient Egypt held in Europe. 'Let them talk to me no more of Rome; let Greece be silent . . . What other nation ever had the courage to undertake work so surprising!'

The result of the publication of these accounts was twofold. More English men and women now came out to Egypt, among whom were a number of young men on the Grand Tour, who extended the traditional itinerary and crossed the Mediterranean. When they went back to England, they usually took souvenirs in the form of antiquities, so that sizeable collections were built up and an Egyptian Society was founded in London in 1841, with a 'sheich' as its president and Frederick Norden amongst its 'philoaegyptian' members. Then in 1753 the British Museum was initiated through the bequest of Sir Hans Sloane. Among his collection of antiquities were 150 pieces from Egypt.

*

James Bruce wrote, in dedicating his account of his own *Travels* to King George III, that he lived in 'a golden age, which united humanity and science'. By the time he reached Alexandria on 20 June, 1768, he had probably seen the collection of antiquities in the British Museum – which now also included the mummy that Colonel Lethieullier had brought back from Sakkara. He had certainly read a great many accounts of travel in Egypt, including Shaw, Pococke and Norden – 'every other year has furnished us with some account of it, good or bad,' he wrote – as well as the classical historians like Herodotus, Juvenal, Homer, Pliny and Strabo. 'The study and knowledge of the globe,' Bruce concluded, 'for very natural and obvious reasons, seem, in all ages, to have been the principal and favourite pursuit of great Princes; perhaps they were, at certain periods, the very sources of that greatness.'

Bruce was impressed by the appearance of Alexandria as he approached it from the Mediterranean in June 1768, but as soon as he landed he realized that what had appeared to be fine buildings around Pompey's Pillar and the ornate mosques were in fact 'ill-imagined, ill-constructed, and imperfect buildings.' Nor did his further acquaintance with the city alter this impression. The port had two harbours, but the larger and deeper one was forbidden to Christian ships. The town, which had only recently been opened up after a severe bout of the plague, as a desolate place and Bruce did not like it. Like many travellers since, he was eager to leave Alexandria and, on 30 June, he and his assistants departed on horseback for Rosetta and Cairo. The journey across the desert he reported as being 'reputed dangerous ... people travel burdened with arms,' but Bruce had already sent most of their arsenal on ahead with the heavy luggage and they only carried pistols in the belts of their Arab clothes. Instead of a show of force, he trusted to their disguises to protect them and in this he was right: when they met another group coming towards them, about three miles out of Aboukir, they ignored them and the leader of the other group pronounced with contempt, *Bedowé!*, peasants.

They reached Rosetta without incident and Bruce described the town as 'a favourite halting-place of the Christian travellers entering Egypt ... There they draw their breaths, in an imaginary increase of freedom, between the two great sinks of tyranny, oppression, and injustice, Alexandria and Cairo.' He explained that Rosetta was known for the mildness of its inhabitants, 'but I must say,' he wrote, 'that, in my time, I could not discern much difference.' He continued on his way to Cairo.

By the time he reached the capital, in the beginning of July, his Arab disguise was totally convincing and he records himself as being known as 'a Fakir, or Dervish, moderately skilled in magic, and who cared for nothing but study and books'. His facility with the language and knowledge of local customs allowed him to pass freely through the city. Apart from ensuring his safety, the disguise also helped him to conceal the true purpose of his journey to Egypt since, he explained, Egyptians regarded the Nile with some jealousy and a 'regular prohibition' had been imposed on foreign travellers, which meant that if he was known as such, he would have to obtain a special dispensation from the Pasha before he could leave. But in spite of his secrecy, 'This intention was not long kept secret (nothing can be concealed at Cairo): All nations, Jews, Turks, Moors, Cophts, and Franks, are constantly upon the inquiry, as much after things that concern other people's business as their own.'

But Bruce was fortunate in the timing of his journey to Egypt, for a new Mameluke ruler called Ali Bey had seized power and ousted the Pasha who had been appointed by the Sultan of Turkey, the official sovereign of Egypt. Ali Bey, who had styled himself Sherif of Mecca, Sultan of Egypt, and King of the Mediterranean and Red Seas, was eager to encourage contact with Europe, for this was one way in which he could consolidate his position and distance himself from Constantinople. As Bruce wrote, 'The instant that I arrived at Cairo was perhaps the only one in which I ever could have been allowed, single and unpro-tected as I was, to have made my intended journey.'

As a result of the new régime, the foreign trading community in Egypt had begun to grow and the French especially were well estab-lished. Bruce, putting his own prejudices against the French aside, wrote,

> The part of Cairo where the French are settled is exceedingly commodious, and fit for retirement. It consists of one long street, where all the merchants of that nation live together. It is shut at one end, by large gates, where there is a guard, and these are kept constantly close in the time of the plague.
> At the other end is a large garden tolerably kept, in which there are several pleasant walks, and seats; all the enjoyment that Christians can hope for, among this vile people reduces itself to peace, and quiet; nobody seeks for more.

When the ruler Ali Bey heard about Bruce's intentions, he had him moved to the Greek convent of St George, to the south of the city, near the site of ancient Babylon and near the mosque of 'Amr. From here, at nine o'clock one night, Bruce was summoned to the Pasha's palace, where he found the young Ali Bey 'sitting upon a large sofa, covered with crimson-cloth of gold; his turban, his girdle, and the head of his dagger, all thick covered with fine brilliants; one in his turban that served to support a sprig of brilliants also, was among the largest I have. ever seen.' The scene is reminiscent of tales from the *Arabian Nights*. The Bey, believing that Bruce's knowledge of science would enable him to see into the future, asked him his opinion of the likely outcome of the war between the Turks and the Russians. When Bruce told him that the Turks would be beaten but that Constantinople would be spared, the Bey said, 'That will be sad indeed! but truth is truth, and God is merciful.' Bruce was given coffee and sweetmeats, guaranteed protection and sent back to the monastery.

Several nights later, he was again summoned by Ali Bey, this time because the young ruler thought he had been poisoned. Bruce sensed he was being trifled with and told the Bey that he had probably just overeaten. He recommended a cure of green tea, to be followed by a good shot of alcohol.

'Spirits!' Ali Bey complained. 'Do you know that I am a Mussul-man?'

'But I, sir,' Bruce replied in a tone which rings out again and again through his narrative, 'am none. I tell you what is good for your body, and have nothing to do with your religion, or your soul,' to which

Ali Bey replied, 'He speaks like a man!'

Force of personality, a natural cunning and a strong sense of purpose were Bruce's most obvious characteristics and they enabled him to pursue his journey. With letters of recommendation from Ali Bey, he hired a 100-foot canja on the Nile and left the dock at Boulak on 12 December, 1768. 'There was nothing so much we desired as to be at some distance from Cairo on our voyage,' Bruce wrote. 'Bad affairs and extortions always overtake you in this detestable country.' But if he thought that he had outstripped them by taking to the river, he was mistaken, for soon after leaving Boulak Bruce discovered that his rais, or captain, Hassan Abou Cuffi, who claimed to be a sherif descended from the Prophet himself, a Haji (he had made the pilgrimage to Mecca) and 'half a saint besides', was extremely unsaintly in his devotion to alcohol and had missed their sailing. At night he had to be on his guard against robbers who swam silently alongside the boat and stole whatever they could lay their hands on while the owners were sleeping. He also discovered that many Nile villagers were unhappy with his presence on their river – shots were fired at him when he tried to land at Antinous to see the ruins of Hadrian's town. (Bruce of course fired back until the villagers 'slid away', and he called out after them, 'Infidels, thieves, and robbers!')

At Mallawi, however, he was received with greater hospitality by Sheikh Mahomet Aga, who sent his respects along with a gallon of brandy, honey-preserved oranges and lemons, and a whole lamb. Just before Dendera, Bruce sighted his first crocodile, always an important event, and at Thebes, among the 'magnificent, stupendous sepulchres' in the Valley of the Kings, he discovered the tomb of the Pharaoh Rameses III, which is still known as 'Bruce's Tomb', or the 'Tomb of the Harper', because of the wall paintings of harpists – 'I was rivetted, as it were, to the spot by the first sight of these paintings, and I could proceed no further,' he later wrote.

Copying these paintings was a long and laborious process and, as he sat in the tomb with his servants holding up lights around him, the sun set behind the Theban Hills. The servants then explained that the valley was notorious as a hide-out for robbers and suggested that they should all leave the valley before nightfall. When Bruce told them that he would be happy to stay there overnight, the servants made it quite clear that if he did stay, he would be doing so alone – 'they made dreadful illuminations of tragical events' – and, at this, Bruce decided to return to the river with them. But as they left the entrance to the tomb, large rocks rolled down the hillside around them. It might have been an accident, but the servants were sure it was the work of the robbers, whom Bruce rather dryly calls 'troglodytes'. While his servants wished to run for it, their master wanted to stay and fight. Handing his horse over to one of the men, and sending them all on ahead, Bruce waited for his pursuers to arrive. It was dark in the valley now – twilight is brief in Egypt – and although he could not see them, he heard footsteps. He fired his pistols and a blunderbuss in the direction of the sounds, evidently with some success, as he reported hearing people crying out with pain.

But Bruce's tussle with the 'troglodytes' did not end there. Having reached the canja in safety, he made his way across the river to Luxor, where he stayed the night. The next morning, Bruce heard that the thieves had vowed vengeance on him and would follow him along the river, even as far as Aswan if they had to. Bruce replied that if they pursued him, he would 'exterminate' them. 'After this,' Bruce explains, 'we heard no more of them.'

From Luxor, Bruce sailed up the Nile to Aswan, but decided not to follow the river through Nubia and the Sudan to its source. Norden's experiences further up-river had not been good, as Bruce explained to a sheikh at Aswan: 'a Danish gentleman some years ago, going up thither, with orders from the government of Cairo, was plundered, and very nearly assassinated.' Having already faced this prospect down-river, it is strange that he should have stopped here. But he did, and he turned his boat and floated back down-stream to Kenneh where, on 16 February, 1769, he joined a caravan of Arabs from the Libyan desert, and Turks from Mount Taurus, to cross the desert to Cosseir on the Red Sea.

By June, he had sailed south to Jeddah, where he met an English sea captain called Thornhill, who ran the route between Jeddah and Bombay in his ship the *Bengal Merchant*. With Thornhill and Captain Price of the *Lion*, also from Bombay, Bruce reached agreement that if he could get Ali Bey's permission for British ships to sail to Suez, then they would run a regular shipping service between India and Egypt. All this must have seemed very far-fetched at the time; Bruce had yet to undertake the most dangerous part of his travels, into the Abyssinian highlands in search of the source of the Nile. When he left Jeddah, on 8 July, the English ships in the harbour all saluted him, perhaps not expecting to see him again.

But Bruce was seen again – he reached Aswan more than three years later, on 29 November, 1772, believing that he had indeed found the source of the Nile. He alone; not Alexander, not the great kings and generals in history who had searched in vain for the origin of the great river, but he – James Bruce, an independent, God-fearing, King-loving Briton – had found it first. He was, however, mistaken in this belief for he had been on the wrong river – the true source of the Nile is considered to be the White Nile at Lake Victoria, far to the south – and had even failed to arrive at the true source of the tributary Blue Nile, at Lake Tana. Worse still, he was not even the first European to stand on the spot he had reached: a Portuguese priest named Pedro Paez, whose claims Bruce dismisses as hearsay, had drunk from the same waters of the Little Blue Nile at Ghish in April 1618, over 150 years earlier. But even if he had been aware of Paez's journey, and therefore that he was not the first European at Ghish, Bruce knew that reaching it himself was a great achievement. He wrote in his account of the journey that 'I triumphed here, in my own mind, over kings and armies.' Considering that thousands of private Britons today regard themselves as adventurous for managing the air-conditioned ascent of the Nile as far as Aswan, Bruce's journey more than 200 years ago was indeed a magnificent achievement.

The final stage of his journey to Aswan had taken him through the Nubian desert. During the eleven days he spent crossing with his caravan, he suffered badly from swollen, bleeding feet. During the nights they were in danger of being robbed by nomads. By day they were scorched by the sun and literally assaulted 'by an army (as it seemed) of sand pillars'. Bruce wrote that 'An universal despondency had taken possession of our people.' It took possession of himself as well. 'That desert, which did not afford inhabitants for the assistance or relief of travellers, had greatly more than sufficient for destroying them.' Two days before they reached Aswan, he thought that he could go no further: 'Nothing but death was before my eyes.' The camels had been unable to rise that morning and they had slaughtered two of them for their flesh and their water reserve. His Italian companion Luigi Balugani had died of dysentery long ago. One of his guides had lost an eye. Another was very sick. Bruce's feet were so swollen that he could only walk with difficulty and, most upsetting of all to him, without the camels he was obliged to leave behind all his notes, records and sketches. All his hopes were gone and it seemed unlikely that they would escape with their lives.

But he did make it back and, at Aswan, the Aga, who was less than friendly to begin with, eventually provided him with food and the means to return to the desert to retrieve his records and equipment. On 11 December Bruce sailed for Cairo, which he reached one month later, tired, ill, barely able to walk, and initially unrecognisable to the brothers of the Convent of St George, where he had stayed more than four years earlier.

When he had convinced the brothers of his identity, Bruce was given a room to rest in, but he had no sooner settled down and drifted off to sleep than he was disturbed. Two messengers came into the room and, unable to rouse him any other way, reached forward to shake his arm.

'Keep your distance, you insolent blackguard,' Bruce shouted at the man as he woke. 'Remember I am an Englishman.'

No doubt he meant this profession of nationality as a warning to the man, but the messenger persisted and Bruce was persuaded to get up to meet the new Pasha of Egypt, Mahomet Bey Abou Dahab, the son-in-law of Ali Bey. Outside the convent, the messengers had asses waiting for him and, at a trot through the streets of Cairo, they rode together the three miles from the convent. At the palace, Bruce found the Bey reclining on a divan. 'Though it was late, he was in full dress, his girdle, turban, and handle of his dagger, all shining with the finest brilliants, and a finer sprig of diamonds upon his turban than what I had seen his father-in-law wear, once when I was with him.'

The rooms were so brightly lit and richly decorated that Bruce suddenly became aware of the state he himself was in, of the dirt on his feet, of the coarse brown woollen waistcoat and old trousers he was wearing, like a peasant. The Bey was clearly shocked at his appearance and expressed his desire to help, but Bruce only asked that he be allowed to sit down, since his feet were hurting him so much.

At the end of the interview, Bruce was led into an ante-chamber where a servant offered him an orange from a large basket he was carrying. A present from the Bey, the servant told him, to oblige him. 'Put your hand to the bottom, the best fruit is there.' When Bruce did as he was told, he found a gold purse full of money. His surprise was only exceeded by that of the servant when Bruce, with all due gratitude and respect, refused to accept the gift. The servant was unsure of what he should do next and took Bruce back to the Bey, who was obviously impressed by the foreigner's behaviour; the refusal of a gift of money was a rare thing indeed. Bruce explained that he had no need for the money, while he was sure that there were plenty of people in the city who would be very grateful to receive it.

' "This being so," says the Bey, with great looks of complacency, "what is in my power to do for you?" '

Bruce remembered his agreement with the captains Thornhill and Price at Jeddah and asked the Bey to allow British ships to operate between India and Suez, and for British merchants to trade across Egypt.

'Why, let it be so,' said Mahomet Bey Abou Dahab, and in February 1773 a *firman* was drawn up which decreed: 'Let this order be obeyed with the assistance of God in all parts, which is written from the Divan of Cairo the fortified, and which contains an agreement with the esteemed Captains and Christian merchants, who are famed for their honesty, may they have a good end ... I make you sure, therefore, that you may come to Suez with your ships with good profit ... and that you may come to Cairo itself, and trade for money, or barter, as suits you best, without restraint from any one ...'

★

Bruce left Egypt at the beginning of March 1773, and went first to France, where he was received by Louis XVI, and then to Italy, for his health, where he saw Pope Clement XIV. There was much interest expressed in his journey. When he finally returned to England, in June 1774, he presented his own drawings and those of Luigi Balugani to the Royal Collection. Their acceptance, and his subsequent election as a Fellow of the Royal Society, were no doubt very gratifying, but the stories he told of the things he had done were treated with some incredulity. Some of them were indeed incredible, as for instance his account of a banquet he attended in Abyssinia where meat was cut from living cows, which were then sent back out to graze. In part, the fact that he had seen so many extraordinary things made Bruce an easy target to mock. But he also invited criticism by his own inaccuracies in recounting these events, as Mr Murray, who prepared the second edition of Bruce's *Travels*, explained in his preface: 'A few apparent exaggerations in description, and some casual mistakes in matters of inferior consequence, gave occasion to the envious to depreciate Mr Bruce's character ... and to excite suspicions unfavourable to the general credit of his narrative.' One of the people who was suspicious of Bruce's stories was Dr Johnson, who was considered an expert on Abyssinian matters after the publication of his translation of Father Lobo's *A Voyage to Abyssinia* and of his own novel *Rasselas*. Although Johnson had never actually been to Abyssinia, one of Bruce's biographers quoted Dr Johnson as saying that 'when he first conversed with Mr. Bruce, the Abyssinian traveller, he was very much inclined to believe he had been there, but that he had afterwards altered his opinion.'

Bruce was not a man who could accept criticism and the public mocking of his accounts of his travels offended him. He returned to his Scottish estates and married a woman twenty-four years his junior, decided against writing up his travels and lived, instead, the life of a country squire. And so things might have ended, but, just as he had been spurred on to travel in the first place by the death of Adriana, so the death of his second wife in 1788 persuaded him to console himself with the writing of his adventures. The result, the five-volume *Travels to discover the Source of the Nile, in the years 1768, 1769, 1770, 1771, 1772, and 1773, by James Bruce of Kinnaird, Esq. F.R.S.*, was published in 1790 and, even though it was dedicated to King George III, it too attracted criticism and disbelief, which might in part be explained by the tone of Bruce's narrative. Here is a passage from the dedication: 'From Egypt I penetrated into this country, through Arabia on one side, passing through melancholy and dreary deserts, ventilated with poisonous winds, and glowing with eternal sunbeams, whose names are as unknown in geography as are those of the antidiluvian world.' He described the countries he had passed through as containing 'all that is terrible to the feelings, prejudicial to the health, or fatal to the life of man,' and yet he had returned to tell the world about it. His audience would have to believe that he was either a hero or a liar. Many still chose to believe that he had invented his narrative and Bruce's vanity and egotism were again offended. After publication, he withdrew once more to his Scottish estates.

There was no vindication during his lifetime. One evening, four years after the publication of his *Travels*, Bruce was entertaining at his house in Kinnaird when, escorting a friend to her carriage, he slipped and fell down the last six or seven steps, an unfortunate domestic accident for a man who had survived so many hazards abroad. By the following morning he was dead. He was buried in the churchyard at Larbert in Stirlingshire and his tombstone included the following inscription:

> 'His life was spent in performing
> useful and splendid actions;
> He explored many distant regions,
> He discovered the fountains of the Nile,
> He traversed the deserts of Nubia.'

Although Bruce never had the satisfaction of seeing his achievements properly recognised, the effects of his travels were far-reaching. He had focused English attention on the Nile, and one question in particular occupied the energies of a number of remarkable men for the next hundred years: if Bruce had not found the true source of the Nile, where was it? Richard Burton, Speke and Grant, Sir Samuel and Lady Florence Baker, Dr David Livingstone and Henry Stanley all kept the search for the source of the great river constantly in front of the public. Their tales of hardship and remarkable exploits became common lore. Not only did the British public have a seemingly limitless appetite for narratives of events and descriptions of life in Africa, but they now considered the discovery of much of it, this great unknown, as an exclusively British occupation. As Bruce had written in dedicating his *Travels* to George III, 'I humbly hope I have shewn to the world of what value the efforts of every individual of your Majesty's subjects may be . . .'

Apart from increasing interest in the river Nile itself, Bruce's travels also drew attention to the achievements of the ancient and lost civilization that had existed in Egypt and to the monuments and relics that had survived. The drawings which he and his artist-companion Balugani made in the Valley of the Kings at Thebes, especially of the harpists in the tomb of Rameses III, were, Bruce insisted, 'an incontestible proof, stronger than a thousand Greek quotations, that geometry, drawing, mechanics, and music, were of the greatest perfection'. But as with the rest of his assertions, his comments on the achievements of the ancient Egyptians were also treated with scorn, and Horace Walpole considered the 'Theban harp, as beautifully and gracefully designed as if Mr. Adam had drawn it for Lady Mansfield's dressing room.'

What is most important about the reaction to Bruce's work, unfortunate though it was, is that it shows how Egypt had become a suitable and widespread topic for public discussion. Throughout the eighteenth century, Egyptian relics and antiquities, brought back to England by travellers and collectors, had been exhibited and discussed. One of the more remarkable aspects of ancient Egypt – at least as far as Europeans were concerned – was the extent to which it had disappeared. There were only the accounts left by Herodotus and the other 'fathers' of history on which to base opinions. All understanding of the language of the ancient Egyptians and of the way it was spoken was lost and therefore their own accounts of their history and beliefs, as told by the inscriptions on their monuments, and on papyri in tombs and mummy pits, were undecipherable. The extent of the achievements of the ancient Egyptians became a matter of great debate; as the British estimation of their own culture grew, Britons enjoyed the opportunity of comparing themselves with one of the great civilizations of antiquity.

★

Six years after James Bruce returned from Egypt, the twenty-three-year-old Eliza Fay left England for India in the company of her newly wedded husband, Anthony, in the hope of making their fortune in Calcutta. What is unusual about their journey is that they decided not to sail around the Cape but to travel across Europe, even though England was at war with France at the time, and then to cross overland from Alexandria to Suez, where they would board a boat for Calcutta. From the outset it was clear that the young husband Anthony was one of that breed of Englishmen who really should never have been permitted to leave their homes. 'They were both of them', according to E. M. Forster, 'underbred and quarrelsome and he was a fool to boot.' Eliza, however, was also a determined and capable woman.

The Fays reached Alexandria on 23 July and Eliza, like Bruce before her, thought it made 'a fine appearance from the sea on near approach'. On closer inspection, however, she was less enchanted and she wrote to her 'dear friends' at home that 'This once magnificent City, built by the most famous of all Conquerors, and adorned with the most exquisite productions of art, is now little more than a heap of ruins.' But they only stayed in Alexandria for a couple of days before they continued on to Cairo. They were intending to cross the desert to the Nile, but they heard that it was 'notorious for the robberies and murders committed on it', and decided instead to take a boat around the coast and up the Nile. But they were mistaken in thinking that the river-route would be any safer for no sooner had night fallen than 'we were alarmed by perceiving a boat making after us, as the people said, to plunder, and perhaps, to murder us ... You may judge,' she wrote home, 'in what a situation we remained, while this dreadful evil seemed impending over us. Mr Fay fired two pistols, to give notice of our being armed. At length, thank God, we out-sailed them...' Her friends in England must have been horrified at the events that the young Eliza was describing to them. But the danger did not end that night, for although the party reached 'Grand Cairo' in safety, they still had to cross the desert to Suez.

The Fays arrived in Cairo on 29 July 1779, and were hoping to pass straight on through to Suez. As soon as Mr Fay made contact with George Baldwin, the East India Company's Agent in Cairo, plans were made for them to join a caravan which, Eliza recorded, 'was to set off in three hours'. But they were still in Cairo a month later, at the end of August. By this time they had caught an 'epidemical disease,' which had all the symptoms of the plague but which proved not to be fatal. They had also seen some of the sights, with Eliza dressed in the local fashion of trousers, leather half-boots and over-slippers, a loose wide-sleeved gown which was pulled in at the waist by a sash, a short-sleeved robe over this and, on her head, a coloured turban which dangled more than two feet down her back. 'This,' as Eliza pointed out, 'is the dress for the House; but as I was going out, she [the maid] next put on a large robe of silk ... and then covered my face with a piece of muslin ...; over all, she threw a piece of black silk, long and wide enough to envelop the whole form ...' This was her outfit for the height of summer in Cairo.

Eliza Fay did not like Cairo – 'Grand Cairo by no means answers to its name at present, whatever it may have done formerly. – There are certainly many magnificent houses, belonging to the Beys and other rich individuals, but as a city, I can perceive neither order, beauty, nor grandeur; and the contrast between the great, who seem to wallow in splendour and luxury, and the people at large, who appear to want the common necessaries of life, is not more striking, than disgusting.' But however much they wanted to leave, they were obliged to delay their departure from Cairo when they heard that another caravan of foreigners had been attacked in the desert. Twelve Europeans and an Arab guard, carrying goods said to be worth £40,000, had left Suez on 14 June and were attacked twenty miles into the desert. The men were stripped and robbed of their merchandise, their private possessions and their camels. 'My heart sickens,' Eliza wrote, 'my hand trembles as I retrace this scene.' Only five of the Europeans chose to return those twenty miles to Suez, where they all arrived safely. The other seven, ill-equipped, decided to continue to Cairo, but only one of them reached the city alive. This, perhaps, would not have been enough to deter the Fays from crossing the desert straightaway. But something did make Eliza miss the departure of the caravan on 29 July, and they heard the next day, while they were still in Cairo, that it too had been seized. Eliza was in Mr Baldwin's parlour when the news was received. Other Europeans rushed to the consul's house. This time they expected a general attack on Christians and they came armed. A gallant Frenchman, the lone survivor of the June attack, who had reached Cairo, turned to Eliza and said, 'Oh Madam, how unhappy you are in having come to this wretched place.' We must assume that the young English-woman agreed with him. Nothing did happen to them then, although two more ships were seized at Suez on 10 August and their Christian passengers were brought to the capital, and by the end of the month the Fays were ready to move on.

It took them three days to cover the eighty-four miles from Cairo to Suez, a journey, as Mr Fay wrote, 'over a most dreadful Desert, where every night we slept under the great canopy of Heaven, and where we were every hour in danger of being destroyed, by troops of Arabian robbers.' Amongst their caravan was a small group of 'English gentlemen, and servants,' all well armed. Under the command of a Major Baillie, the Fays 'marched the whole way in order of battle, and though we could frequently see superior numbers, they never dared to molest us.'

It is not surprising that, after her adventures in Egypt, Eliza wrote less enthusiastically about the country as she sailed away down the

Red Sea than she had done when she first sighted Alexandria. 'This is the Paradise of thieves, I think the whole population may be divided into two classes of them; those who adopt force, and those who affect their purpose by fraud.' She was not at all surprised that the Biblical children of Israel had been so keen to leave the country after what she had seen of it during the eight weeks they had taken to cross from Alexandria to Suez. But she still found some of its charms irresistible, even during those tense days in the desert under constant threat of attack, when one of the Englishmen fainted and fell from his horse, when the other horses groaned and throat-rattled in the heat and the dogs that were accompanying them collapsed in the sand and were immediately butchered by the Arabs. Even then, Eliza decided, it would be impossible not to be struck by the 'exquisite beauty' of the stars at night.

As for the terrors she had survived, they must have seemed less terrible to her when she reached the town of Calicut on the Malabar Coast, for there, because he was in conflict with the British in India, the local ruler imprisoned all of the English passengers. Eliza and her husband were held from 5 November 1779 – 'to me ever memorable' – to 17 February of the following year.

★

The caravan that was attacked crossing the desert from Suez to Cairo was of special interest to James Baldwin, the East India Company's Agent in Cairo, for he had invested heavily in the £40,000 venture. After the Fays left Egypt, Baldwin managed to persuade the new Pasha to send men out in search of the culprits. But this was not the Pasha, Mahomet Bey Abou Dahab, with whom Bruce had reached his agreement. His successor was a man of entirely different temperament and although a troop of 100 soldiers was sent into the desert and the goods were recovered, Baldwin and the other foreigners involved in the venture were then arrested for breaking the Turkish ban on Christian ships sailing up the Red Sea. This incident caused outrage in Europe and the British government demanded the release of its subjects. All of them except Baldwin and another Englishman by the name of Skiddy were released, but these two were held as security against reprisals. The British government protested again but, before it had time to take further action, Baldwin escaped from prison and slipped out of the country.

It would have been understandable if he had decided never to return to Egypt after that, but in 1786 he arrived in Cairo as the newly created British Consul-General, having persuaded the British government that he could secure an agreement with the new Pasha for the safe passage through Egypt of British and Indian trade and passengers. The British had agreed to let him try, but they had only given him one year to secure the treaty; after that, he would be relieved of his post. Nine years later, Baldwin had still not succeeded in his plan – politics in Egypt were too unsettled – but he had succeeded in bringing ships from England and from India, and in safely passing their cargoes overland through Egypt. On one occasion, when the two caravans had met in Cairo, Baldwin wrote that 'We composed our bowl of the Ganges, the Thames, and the Nile, and from the top of the pyramid drank prosperity to England.'

Life for English traders in Egypt was not always so hard and one traveller a few years earlier had observed that they lived a charmed life 'agreeably enough among themselves . . . and in a plentiful country they do not want whatever may make life pass agreeably. The morning being spent in business, the remainder of the day is often passed in riding out to the fields and gardens to the north of Cairo . . . sometimes the whole day is spent in diversions that way.' But on 8 February 1793 a despatch was sent from London dismissing Baldwin from his post; Baldwin claimed that he never received it and continued to act as the British representative for several more years. Officially, though, the British had no consul in Egypt from 1793. As Baldwin wrote later in his *Political Recollections*, 'The Reader will rather suspect, from the improbability of the thing, that the letter must have been a forgery.'

Baldwin never had any doubts that the trading route through the Red Sea and overland through Egypt would eventually succeed and he insisted that if the British did not have control of it, the French would take it and would therefore threaten Britain's growing empire in the East. The French would then be able to send troops out to India in a fraction of the time it would take British soldiers to sail around the Cape. Indeed, a French consul arrived in Cairo to renew diplomatic relations only nine days before Baldwin's letter of dismissal was sent from London. In 1796, Baldwin noted, a Frenchman by the name of Tinville – 'brother of the notorious Public Accuser' – arrived in Cairo 'to inveigle the Beys of Egypt into the designs of the French, and particularly to obtain consent to their project of passing an army through Egypt, to the East Indies, by the Red Sea, in order to strengthen Tippoo, and finally to annihilate the British Dominion in the East Indies.' The British, of course, paid no attention to the consul they had dismissed until one moonlit night, with the Nile glowing silver and the Pyramids throwing long shadows across the valley, when a French army under Napoleon Bonaparte arrived in Egypt. But by then Baldwin was a failed old man, had finally left his post in Egypt and had gone into an unrewarded retirement.

SEIZING EGYPT

'It was asked, "What is the wish of the blind?" "A basket full
of horns," they replied, "if he does not see, he may like butting."'
Arabic proverb reported by Jean Louis Burckhardt

A few miles along the coast from the centre of Alexandria is Agami
Beach, where smart Cairene families come for the summer. It is a
busy, built-up place now, where the sand is fine on the big stretch
of beach and sea breezes cool the long summer days. Early on the
morning of 2 July 1798, the twenty-nine-year-old French general,
Napoleon Bonaparte, landed at Agami with the vanguard of his Army
of the East. At three o'clock that morning, by the light of a bright
moon, he reviewed the first few thousand soldiers just up from the
beach. With this army he was – in his own words – 'about to undertake
a conquest whose effects on the world's civilization and trade are incalcu-
lable.' But in the words of Sheikh Abdel Rahman el Djabarty, who
witnessed the French invasion, 'it was the beginning of a series of great
misfortunes.'

There was an element of crusade as well as conquest about the French
arrival in Egypt in 1798; Bonaparte came with a group of *savants* as
well as his army of soldiers. The *savants* were scholars who were brought
to fulfil the noble part of the expedition, to rediscover and save the
wisdom and civilization of ancient Egypt. But a greater motivation
was the French desire to disturb or destroy the remarkable growth
of Britain's eastern trading empire. In the end, the army failed to stop
the development of Britain's trading links but the *savants* did draw attention to the importance of Egypt. More people in Europe fell for the
lure of the East.

By eleven o'clock on Bonaparte's first Egyptian morning, his conquest of the East had already begun: that Alexandria fell was due more
to the lack of preparations on the part of the Egyptians than to any
great martial skill exhibited by the French. Less than three weeks later,
on 21 July, Bonaparte was engaged in one of his finest victories, at
what one romantic called the Battle of the Pyramids – the Pyramids
of Giza were in fact some five miles from the scene of the fighting,
but the Battle of Embaba, as it could have been known, did not have
the same ring to it. El Djabarty, who witnessed the battle, thought
sadly that 'Never had Egypt seen so many horrors. Never have we

seen such things in the history of nations; to hear is not to see.' The official French report of the battle, perhaps not the most impartial of sources, listed the French as having lost twenty-nine men – one for each of Bonaparte's years. The combined armies of the Mamelukes, Arabs and Egyptians, they thought, had suffered more than 2,000 casualties. However inaccurate the figures, the engagement was undoubtedly an unhappy one for the rulers of Egypt.

On 24 July, Bonaparte made a victorious but relatively understated entry into Cairo. Egypt was his, he believed, and the East – particularly the wealth of India – was now within his reach. The prospect of forming the greatest empire the world had ever seen appeared to be becoming a reality. From the palace of Mohammed Bey el Elfi, in the square of the Ezbekieh, Bonaparte considered his progress and wrote: 'Glory is stale when one is twenty-nine; I have exhausted everything...' These thoughts, bred in the sudden calm which followed his great victory, were soon interrupted. On 1 August, Nelson and the English fleet finally tracked down the French and were in the midst of their own famous victory, the Battle of the Nile – in fact at Aboukir Bay, more than twenty direct miles from the Rosetta mouth of the Nile – where only three French fighting ships from their entire fleet escaped destruction or capture.

Without his fleet, Bonaparte and his army were cut off from France. He insisted that now 'we shall have to recreate the Egyptian Empire', which would provide him with a secure base. The following year, with the French in control of Lower Egypt, Bonaparte defeated a liberating Turkish army, also at Aboukir Bay. In 1801, with the French general long back in France and considering campaigns elsewhere, Sir Ralph Abercromby landed an English army of 17,000 troops in the same bay. Such places invite the making of history: from the same spot, later that year, the remainder of Bonaparte's defeated Army of the East embarked for home.

At almost the same time as the French detachment was leaving Cairo for the coast, in the scorching heat of an Egyptian July, some 5000 British soldiers and Indian sepoys arrived in the capital. Like James Bruce, they had used the Red Sea port of Cosseir and marched with full packs across the Arabian desert, before following the Nile downstream. But they arrived at the capital too late to be of any use: the French campaign in Egypt was over; the English campaign against the French in Egypt was over. Only the Turks, who had been outfought on all sides, remained to govern in their own way. But although Constantinople still officially ruled Egypt, it was a long way away and in Cairo there were now two factions fighting for the right to exercise power: the established Mamelukes, among them the wealthy Elfi Bey whose palace had been used as the French headquarters, and who were favoured by the British; and the Albanian mercenaries who had been sent by the Turks to fight Bonaparte and who, under their new leader Muhammad Ali, were in turn supported by the French.

When the British returned to Egypt in 1807 with a small army of 5000 troops, they were not trying to emulate the French. Their intention was to exert influence, not to conquer, and they thought that with their intimidating presence Elfi Bey and the Mamelukes ought to be able to consolidate their claim to power – in this, the British were not the last to underestimate the ability of Muhammad Ali. Their own force was ill-trained and badly led; their allies, the Mamelukes, were more renowned for indolence than fighting. In a way which had become commonplace in Egypt, and which added much to its reputation, the Mamelukes suddenly lost their figureheads when both Elfi Bey and his supporter Bardissy were mysteriously poisoned. In the pitiful military encounter that occurred between their followers and the Albanians, Muhammad Ali's army killed over 1000 British soldiers – those who were captured alive were reported to have been marched into Cairo carrying the heads of their dead comrades. The British army left Egypt soon after and the British government was now obliged to support the Albanian mercenary; there was no one else to back. Even the Turkish sultan now confirmed Muhammad Ali's title of Pasha, although he might have intended this as an empty gesture, since Egyptian pashas had a habit of dying young or of suddenly leaving for foreign parts. But Muhammad Ali founded a dynasty which lasted longer than anyone at that time expected.

In less than a decade, then, at the turn of the century, the Egyptians had been fully 'visited' by Europe and had experienced the blessings of its advanced cultures. In this case, the flag had followed trade, but what Bruce, Baldwin and Bonaparte had all fought for had failed to come about: neither England nor France were in control of the country or of a route through to India. Still, Egypt was firmly in the public mind. Nelson's popular reward for his victory at Aboukir, for instance, was a peerage with the title of Lord Nelson of the Nile, although when Emma Hamilton heard the news she declared that 'If I was King of England I would make you the most noble, puissant Duke Nelson, Marquis Nile, Earl Alexandria, Viscount Pyramid, Baron Crocodile, and Prince Victory, that posterity might have you in all forms.' But she was not King of England, and Nelson was more simply known as 'of the Nile'.

For several years after the campaigns, British soldiers and sailors returned home with wounds, souvenirs, plunder and stories of the fantastic land of the Nile. The well-informed Robert Southey wrote in his *Letters from England* that what was now an identifiable Egyptian influence was very noticeable in London. 'At present, as the soldiers from Egypt have brought home with them broken limbs and opthalmia, they carry an arm in a sling, or walk the streets with a green shade over their eyes. Every thing must now be Egyptian: the ladies wear crocodile ornaments, and you sit upon a sphinx in a room hung round with mummies, and with the long black lean-armed long-nosed hieroglyphical men, who are enough to make the children afraid to go to bed.'

Stories circulated in English drawing rooms and drinking establishments of atrocities committed by the Turks, Albanians and Egyptians – they seemed to merge into a single image of a cruel, depraved barbarian – of the horrors and sinful pleasures of this strange, fallen land, and even of God-fearing Christians being forced to convert to Islam. No doubt there was some truth in the earlier stories; the third claim, of conversion, was certainly true and in this way a few Britons came to live in Egypt. A tale is told by the traveller Alexander Kinglake, of a Scottish soldier called Donald Donald, who was known as Osman Effendi, whom Kinglake met in plague-stricken Cairo in 1835. As Kinglake wrote in *Eothen*, an extraordinary account of his travels, 'Osman's history is a curious one. He was a Scotsman born, and when very young, being then a drummer-boy, he landed in Egypt with Fraser's force [1807]. He was taken prisoner, and according to Mohammedan custom, the alternative of Death or the Koran was offered to him. He did not choose Death, and therefore went through the ceremonies necessary for turning him into a good Mohammedan. But what amused me most in his history was this – that very soon after having embraced Islam he was obliged in practice to become curious and discriminating in his new faith – to make war upon Mohammedan dissenters, and follow the orthodox standard of the Prophet in fierce campaigns against the Wahabees, the Unitarians of the Mussulman world.'

Luckily for Osman, he was on the winning side this time. The Wahabees were defeated and the new convert returned to Egypt. In 1814, the British MP, Thomas Legh, met Osman in Minieh and, since he was not a free man, offered to buy him out of service so that he could reject Islam and return home. 'At one time,' Legh explained, 'his master had agreed to give him his liberty for 2,000 piastres; but a few days previous to our departure we were informed the Bey had married him to one of the women belonging to his harem, and we heard no more of him.'

Osman did well to stay, though, for whereas in Scotland he was a poor man, in Egypt he flourished and was respected, starting his own business providing accommodation in Cairo for visiting Europeans, and became himself an effendi, or gentleman. Legh thought that 'he had never shown much anxiety about obtaining his liberty,' and had rejected his homeland and heritage. Kinglake, however, viewed the matter differently:

> the strangest feature in Osman's character was his
> inextinguishable nationality. In vain they had brought him
> over the seas in early boyhood – in vain had he suffered
> captivity, conversion, circumcision – in vain they had passed
> him through fire in their Arabian campaigns – they could
> not cut away or burn out poor Osman's inborn love of all
> that was Scottish; in vain men called him Effendi – in vain
> he swept along in Eastern robes – in vain the rival wives
> adorned his Harem; the joy of his heart still plainly lay in
> this, that he had three shelves of books, and that the books
> were thoroughbred Scotch – the Edinburgh this, the
> Edinburgh that – and, above all, I recollect he prided himself
> upon the 'Edinburgh Cabinet Library.'

★

That Muhammad Ali was an Albanian and not an Egyptian does not matter now; after all, the British pride themselves on the many achievements of the eighteenth-century Georgian monarchs without troubling too much about their Hanoverian origins. So Egyptians look back upon the reign of Muhammad Ali as a period of great advancement, which it undoubtedly was. He is seen as the father of modern Egypt, even if the birth was attended by a great deal of bloodshed and cruelty. Muhammad Ali's rivals were the Mameluke Beys, the allies of the British during their 1807 campaign; but instead of confronting them, the new Pasha showed great tact and courtesy towards them. He even made a point of inviting them to attend the celebrations for his son Tusun, who was off to lead an army against the Wahabees – the war in which the Scotsman Donald Donald fought – since, after all, the Mamelukes believed in the Prophet and had ruled Egypt from as far back as the thirteenth century. Muhammad Ali proved on that day, 1 March 1811, that Eastern hospitality really was as dangerous as many British soldiers had claimed. He trapped his Mameluke guests in the citadel at Cairo and murdered them all – 470, according to some accounts. Legend has it that one Mameluke Bey did escape by riding his horse over the citadel's ramparts, but this probably owes more to lore than to fact. That night, many hundreds more Mamelukes were murdered in the town, but some 300 managed to escape along the river with their wives and children and settled in Nubia beyond the First Cataract. But from now on, they were an insignificant, if irritating, force.

After this carnage, Muhammad Ali was secure in Cairo, for a while at least, although memories of the massacre continued to outrage people for many years to come. Nearly forty years later, for instance, Florence Nightingale visited the scene and remembered that 'he counted them at break of day, and when the sun set where were they? He sleeps now close to the murdered chiefs; and people can forget that murder, and laud Mehemet Ali!' Her outburst was deeply felt and not unique, but in spite of this revulsion at his methods, Muhammad Ali was praised for bringing order and stability to the country and thereby making it possible for people like Miss Nightingale to travel to Egypt and to sail up the Nile in safety.

Egypt's new-found stability was in direct contrast to the goings-on in Europe where Bonaparte was now exercising his genius. This proved to be to Egypt's advantage, for just a few years after the ignominious European withdrawal, travellers and Grand Tourists found themselves unable to follow their traditional itineraries and looked to the Holy Land and Egypt for their pleasures and education. The team of intellectuals that Bonaparte had brought with him to Egypt to explore the country had done their work well. The *Description de l'Egypte* was just what it claimed to be, a complete description of the country. With its extensive range of plates, it helped to stimulate the appetite for the study of ancient Egypt and for travel on the Nile and, in the second decade of the nineteenth century, a number of extraordinary Europeans arrived to further the study of ancient and modern Egypt.

Jean Louis Burckhardt was born in Lausanne, Switzerland, in November 1784 and, at the age of twenty-five, was commissioned by the African Association in London – a society dedicated to the exploration of Africa – to travel into the interior of Africa and to discover the source of the river Niger. The Association had already sent out a number of expeditions to this end, including Mungo Park's, and all had ended unfortunately, in death or failure. Burckhardt was instructed to join up with an Arab caravan, which would follow the Nile south into the continent. To do this he would have to disguise himself as an Arab, for as a European he would not have been allowed to join the caravan, or would probably have been robbed or killed on the way.

Burckhardt reached Egypt by travelling overland from Antioch and Aleppo – where he stayed with the British consul John Barker, later consul in Alexandria from 1825 – and on through Syria and the Holy Land, all the time perfecting his disguise, living as he found the natives of the country living, and losing his European characteristics. At a monastery in Nazareth, Burckhardt met the celebrated Lady Hester Stanhope, soon to be acknowledged as Queen of the Desert, who took an instant dislike to the young man and, in a letter home, dismissed him as having gone 'God knows where into the desert . . .'

Maybe God did know where Burckhardt was going, but certainly no westerner could have known, for on the way to Egypt he 'discovered' the city of Petra, lost to the western world since the time of the Crusades. It continued to be lost for a considerable time after its rediscovery, too, for Burckhardt had convinced his unwilling Arab guide that he wished to sacrifice a goat on the site and was only able to spend a few hours there. Burckhardt wrote to his masters in London that 'I regret that I am not able to give a very complete account: but I know well the character of the people around me; I was without protection in the midst of a desert where no traveller had ever before been seen; and a close examination of the works of the Infidels, as they are called, would have excited suspicions that I was a magician in search of treasures.'

Burckhardt left Petra immediately after this and never returned to it. Instead he headed across the northern side of the Sinai desert. It was August and the heat was overwhelming. Reading the accounts of early travellers in the East, one marvels at their determination to exchange comfortable and secure lives in Europe for the hardships of travel amongst hostile, dangerous people and in countries and climates to which they were unsuited. Burckhardt crossed the desert in the hottest month of the year, but he would no sooner have considered waiting for a cooler month to travel than some of his patrons at the African Association would have considered travelling themselves to the scene of their telescopic philanthropy.

Burckhardt arrived in Egypt in 1812, the year after the Mameluke assassination. By then his disguise and his new identity – as Sheikh Ibrahim Ibn Abdullah – was so convincing that the British Agent in Cairo, Mr Aziz, failed to recognize that he was a European. At that time, the senior British representative, the Consul-General Colonel Edward Missett, lived in Alexandria, where Muhammad Ali also had a palace, for Cairo, although full of magnificent mosques and palaces, was a wild, dirty city of narrow tracks and hemmed-in houses. Donkeys, horses and camels were ridden through the streets; on the surface, little had changed here for hundreds of years. The people in the city clung to old customs and behaviours. Not for nothing had an English lady visiting Cairo at the time referred to it as 'that sink of iniquity'. Clearly Cairo was not a place to expect to find polite society.

Burckhardt, who was not necessarily looking for any such refinements, did not stay long in Cairo. Travelling first by donkey and then by camel, he made his way along the Nile with his guide, passed Aswan and the cataracts, and went on into Nubia. One day he saw a boat travelling down-stream with some foreigners in it – the scholar and MP Thomas Legh and his companion the Rev Charles Smelt, both Grand Tourists par excellence who, unable to tour in Europe because of the Napoleonic wars and avoiding Turkey because of its plague, had arrived in Egypt rather as a last resort. They had already been up the Nile as far as Ibrim, beyond Derr, with their American captain, but they had decided not to go further in case they met the survivors of Muhammad Ali's Mameluke massacre.

When Burckhardt hailed their boat, they ignored him. 'The fear of the Mamelukes still operating upon the minds of our crew,' Legh explained, 'we rowed to the other side of the Nile.' When he hailed them a second time, they recognized him, with some surprise, as the man they had seen in Asyut looking healthy, well and dressed 'after the Turkish fashion'. Now he 'had all the exterior of a common Arab, was very thin, and upon the whole his appearance was miserable enough. He told us he had been living for many days with the sheiks of the villages through which he had passed on lentils, bread, salt and water, and when he came on board, could not contain his joy at the prospect of being regaled with animal food.'

Burckhardt could have travelled in the style of a European, but had chosen not to. He might have looked ill-fed and haggard to Legh and Smelt, but he was clearly more resilient than them, a quality which was more important to the traveller than to the tourist. While the English tourists had stopped at Ibrim, Burckhardt went further up the Nile and reached Ipsamboul – Abu Simbel – on 22 March 1813. Here he saw the great temple which Rameses II had built in memory of his wife, which was to become as famous among Egyptian monuments as Shah Jehan's Taj Mahal was among Mogul works. Just as Burckhardt had revealed the lost city of Petra to the western world, so now he rediscovered Abu Simbel, unrecorded by western eyes since the Graeco-Roman era, although the entrance to the great temple was concealed by the weight of sand blown up against it over many centuries and all he could see of it was the head, breast and part of the arms of one of the colossal images of Rameses II, the broken head of the second, and the crowns of the third and fourth. The entrance lay more than thirty feet below him.

The thrill of a second discovery was great indeed, but as at Petra, Burckhardt could do little more than merely record the existence of the temple. Excavation would be done by those he was sure would follow in his footsteps. From Abu Simbel, Burckhardt joined a caravan of slave-traders and continued along the river into the Sudan as far as the great market town of Shendi – Khartoum, to the south, was not founded until 1820 – and then headed east to the Red Sea: he had now decided to make the pilgrimage to the holy cities of Mecca and Medina, since he believed that only as a Haji, a man who had made the pilgrimage, would he be thoroughly convincing as Sheikh Ibrahim on his journey south into Africa. It seems that whatever he did at this time, his mission was always in his thoughts; if he delayed his departure in search of the source of the Niger, it was because no suitable caravan was expected.

At Medina, Burckhardt suffered from a bout of dysentery – so severe that there were fears he would die – which obliged him to travel more slowly. When he had recovered, he returned to Egypt, but at Suez he heard that there was plague again in Cairo. He waited for it to pass, living with a Bedouin tribe at an oasis in the Sinai desert. When he did finally reach the capital, on 24 June 1815, the plague was dying out and Europeans were beginning to open up their houses again.

In the same month of June, a Paduan-born circus strongman by the name of Giovanni Belzoni arrived in Alexandria with his English wife and an Irish 'lad', James Curtain. Belzoni was a large man – over six foot six inches tall – who had earned a living and a reputation as a latter-day Samson. Among his circus acts was one where he created a human pyramid, walking around the ring with a dozen people supported by a harness around his waist. But Belzoni became bored with the circus and was attracted, instead, to Egypt, where he arrived with the intention of persuading Muhammad Ali of the viability of an hydraulic water pump – much more efficient than the shaduf, with which Egyptians had been irrigating their fields for centuries, and surely of great potential in a country where water was so abundant but where most of the land was desert.

When the Belzonis left their ship in Alexandria the plague was still active; tradition had it that it would end on the feast of St John, 24 June, the day of Burckhardt's arrival in Cairo. Until then, quarantine was the only solution but Belzoni wrote that 'The necessity of putting ourselves into a voluntary prison; the caution we were obliged to take, not to touch any person, or suffer any one to touch us; the strict order to be observed in receiving any thing that came from out of doors; and the continual perfumes with which we were regaled, to prevent the plague, as they say, were extremely strange to a novice in the customs of the country.'

The customs of the country were soon to thwart him for a second time: when he had fixed up his ox-drawn hydraulic pump at Shubra, he invited Muhammad Ali and his advisers to a demonstration. All was going according to plan and the pump was working excellently, even though there was some dispute about exactly how much water it was drawing. But then the Pasha asked to see it worked by men instead of oxen. This experiment was not so successful and, in the ensuing catastrophe, young James Curtain had his thigh broken. Any deal that Belzoni had hoped to make fell through. 'The Turks,' he wrote almost understandingly, 'have a belief, that, when such accidents happen in the commencement of any new invention, it is a bad omen.'

But even before this, Belzoni had had a chance to see just what sort of country he had come to. Riding his ass, a frequent if unfamiliar form of transport for Europeans in Egypt, through the narrow, twisting streets of Cairo, he saw a fully laden camel making its way towards him from the opposite direction. There was just enough space for the two animals to pass. But then a bimbashi – an army officer – also came along the road towards him at the head of his troop of men. Although Belzoni was in their path, there was not enough room for him either to turn around or to move out of the way. The bimbashi was obviously put out by this and when he saw that it was a foreigner who was blocking the road, he lashed out and struck the Italian in the stomach. Now Belzoni was a tall, strong man and not at all the sort of person to tolerate such behaviour. He retaliated by taking his whip and striking the bimbashi across his naked shoulders. 'Instantly,' Belzoni related, 'he took his pistol out of his belt; I jumped off my ass; he retired about two yards, pulled the trigger, fired at my head, singed the hair near my right ear, and killed one of his own soldiers, who, by this time, had come behind me.' Seeing that he had missed, the bimbashi pulled his second pistol on Belzoni, but he was overpowered by his men before he could fire it. At this point a crowd began to form, guards rushed to the scene and Belzoni wisely concluded that his company was no longer desired. This unusual episode gave him a clear idea of the sort of country he had come to. 'Such a lesson was not lost upon me,' he confessed, 'and I took great care, in future, not to give the least opportunity of the kind of men of that description, who can murder an European with as much indifference as they would kill an insect.'

Soon after the failure of his hydraulic pump demonstration, Belzoni began looking around for other work. 'My principal object,' he noted, 'was not antiquities at that time,' although he had already met the new Consul-General, Henry Salt, as well as Jean Louis Burckhardt, with whom he was very impressed. ('But what can I say,' Belzoni wrote in his *Narrative*, 'of the late Sheik Burckhardt, who was so well acquainted with the language and manners of these people, that none of them suspected him to be an European? His account of the tribes in these countries is so minutely correct, that little or nothing remains for observation in modern Egypt and Nubia.') With Burckhardt, he had discussed the possibility of moving antiquities, and in particular the colossal bust of the Young Memnon, Rameses II, which lay on the ground by the Ramesseum at Thebes, back to England. Belzoni had already suggested to Muhammad Ali that the bust should be sent to the Prince Regent as a present, but the Pasha, according to Belzoni, thought it 'too trifling an article to send to so great a personage'. So Burckhardt and Henry Salt decided to send Belzoni to remove the bust – the Italian found it 'smiling on me, at the thought of being taken to England' – which they would then present to the British Museum (where it can still be seen).

Reading Belzoni's *Narrative of the Operations and recent Discoveries within the Pyramids, Temples, Tombs, and Excavations, in Egypt and Nubia*, a cool and restrained account of his four-year stay in Egypt with Mrs Belzoni and James Curtain, it is necessary sometimes to remind oneself of the excitement he must have felt at making his discoveries for, although he was lucky enough to uncover things which had been hidden for centuries, Belzoni records little of his emotions, perhaps because he knew that a large number of critics was waiting to read his account of his work. In Egypt he had to overcome not only the intricacies of negotiating with local cacheffs [governors] and sheikhs, but also the rivalry of the French-backed explorers. A French team, for instance, had already tried and failed to remove the head of Rameses II from the Ramesseum and, under Bernadino Drovetti, did all they could to stop Belzoni from succeeding. Later they even went as far as damaging statues, so that the British would not want to take them. Or so Belzoni claimed. The Egyptians played one side off against the other, sometimes to delay work which they thought was inexplicable or evil, and sometimes to extract more presents, or larger payments for their labour. 'The greatest difficulties I had to encounter,' Belzoni complained, 'were not in the discovery of antiquities, which I consider the smallest part of my task, but in controlling the complicated intrigues of my enemies and false friends.'

But Belzoni did succeed in 'the smallest part' of his task, to a remarkable degree. Where his patron 'Sheik' Burckhardt had first travelled,

Belzoni returned, to open tombs and temples and to excavate statues and mummies. His successes are all the more remarkable considering the incomplete information he started out with, often relying on guess-work and hunches. The Rosetta Stone – the basalt slab found near Rosetta by the French Captain Bouchard in 1799, which had identical inscriptions carved on its surface in Greek, hieroglyphic and demotic (the popular and more simple Egyptian script), from which hieroglyphics were eventually deciphered – was still being studied and the language of the ancient Egyptians was still a mystery. Belzoni therefore had to rely on the later historical accounts of Herodotus, Pliny, Strabo and the other Graeco-Roman historians in his research, since he had no access to earlier, contemporary accounts of life in ancient Egypt. It is not surprising, therefore, that he puts much of his success down to good fortune and his own perseverance.

The Ramesseum, the mortuary temple of Rameses ii, had been built on the lower slopes of the Theban hills, on the eastern side, and some distance away from the Valley of the Kings where Bruce had encountered the troglodytes. To move the colossal bust – 'I will not venture to assert who separated the bust from the rest of the body by an explosion,' Belzoni later wrote, implicating his French rival Drovetti – he had brought fourteen poles, four ropes of palm leaves and four rollers. With these, he and his Egyptian labourers levered the bust onto a wooden platform and rolled it down to the river.

Belzoni began the operation on 23 July by having all of his and his wife's things brought from their boat, as the temple was too far from the river for them conveniently to make the journey each day. He chose a likely spot within the temple for them to live. 'A small hut was formed of stones, and we were handsomely lodged. Mrs Belzoni had by this time accustomed herself to travel, and was equally indifferent with myself about accommodations.' But within a couple of days the heat had overpowered him and he complained that 'The place I had chosen in the Memnonium was worse than any, as the whole mass of stones was so heated, that the hands could not be kept on it.' By the following evening he was ill and 'began to be persuaded that there is a great difference between travelling in a boat, with all that is wanted in it, and at leisure, and the undertaking of an operation, which required great exertions in directing a body of men.' The next day he was too ill to walk, and had 'all our household-furniture, beds, kitchen-pottery, and provisions' taken back to the boat. Mrs Belzoni, he records with some envy, 'had tolerable health all the time.'

By 1 August, however, Belzoni was on his feet again and ready to complete the operations. It was an arduous task, though, and on a good day they were able to drag the bust only 400 yards. It took them seventeen days to reach the banks of the Nile, but Belzoni was pleased with the rate and wrote of his labourers that 'I am at a loss to conceive how they existed in the middle of the day, at a work to which they were totally unaccustomed,' especially since it was Ramadan, which meant that they were forbidden to eat or drink during the day, and, being July and August, this was also the hottest season of the year.

When they reached the Nile, Belzoni was unable to find a boat to take the bust down-river to Cairo and it was not until that December that arrangements were made and the bust was rolled down the river bank and loaded onto a boat. Relieved at the completion of his work, Belzoni watched the boat move off along the river. '"Thank heaven!" I exclaimed, and I had reason to be thankful.'

Belzoni returned to Thebes in February 1817 and since he was now conducting excavations on both sides of the river, he lived either in the house (later known as the French House) belonging to Mr Salt, on top of the temple of Luxor, or in the tombs in the Valley of the Kings, where he made great discoveries. The tomb of Tutankhamun may now be the star attraction in the valley, but the most important tomb is still known by the name daubed in black on the wall just inside its entrance – Belzoni – which originally belonged to the Pharaoh Seti I and is the largest in the valley, stretching nearly 500 feet into the rock, and dropping 150 feet on the way in. The stir caused by its discovery was perhaps as great in its way as Tutankhamun's, more than a century later, even though it contained no great store of treasure; the only thing he did discover inside it was a beautiful carved alabaster sarcophagus – empty of course – decorated with scenes from the Book of the Gates.

News of Belzoni's find spread quickly along the river and, as often happens, each re-telling distorted the facts, so that when Hamed, the Aga of Kenneh and commander of the eastern side of Thebes, heard about it, he travelled for thirty-six hours non-stop to be with Belzoni. The Italian, who had not liked Hamed on their previous meeting, was more than a little surprised to see him at the tomb. When the Aga greeted him 'very cordially', Belzoni realized that something was up; he invited the Aga into the tomb and had torches lit so that he could see the exquisite wall paintings. The Aga, however, had little time for the art show. Instead he and his followers searched each of the chambers with great care, and ended up in the one containing the sarcophagus. Here he seated himself in front of the Italian.

'Pray,' he asked calmly, 'where have you put the treasure?'

'What treasure?' Belzoni replied, understanding all at last.

'The treasure you found in this place,' was the Aga's reply.

Belzoni smiled at this; the Aga was convinced that there was treasure hidden somewhere inside the tomb. 'I have been told,' he added, 'by a person to whom I can give credit, that you have found in this place a large golden cock, filled with diamonds and pearls. I must see it. Where is it?'

There was no such thing, Belzoni insisted – not even a mummy – and, after much discussion, he managed to convince the Aga of this. The Aga decided that at least the tomb would make a good place for a harem – 'the women would have something to look at' – and with that, he and his men left Belzoni alone. But if there was no golden cock, there was something else of great value that Belzoni had his eye on. The Egyptians, he realized, only considered gold and precious stones to be worth taking – they believed, for instance, that Belzoni had discovered the bust of Rameses II to be full of jewels or gold, for why else would he bother to move it? Disappointed at not having found any treasure for himself in the tomb of Seti I, the Aga had sat down in front of the sarcophagus, which was brilliantly worked and in perfect condition. Belzoni showed great control as he watched the man, for he was afraid that the Aga might take it into his head to smash the alabaster to see whether it concealed any gold. But the Aga did not look twice at it. Later, Belzoni had it shipped back to London where, after the British Museum had turned it down, it was bought by Sir John Soane for £2,000 and is still one of the main attractions in the Soane Museum in Lincoln's Inn.

In other places, however, Belzoni was not so delicate with the ancient remains he discovered. While the kings of Egypt were buried singly in deep mortuary chambers, the less regal citizens of Thebes were lowered into mummy pits or stacked in caves in the surrounding valleys. The entrances to the pits were narrow and for several hundred feet it was only possible to crawl. For Belzoni the confinement must have been very trying. In one pit, he arrived eventually at a place where he thought it would be possible for him to sit up and here, by the light of a candle, flickering and spluttering in the rarified air, he noticed that he was surrounded by mummies. They were everywhere; even the Arab guides with him, covered in dust, seemed to him like living mummies. At one time, when he sat down, 'When my weight bore on the body of an Egyptian, it crushed it like a band-box. I naturally had recourse to my hands to sustain my weight, but they found no better support; so that I sunk altogether among the broken mummies, with a crash of bones, rags, and wooden cases, which raised such a dust as kept me motionless for a quarter of an hour, waiting till it subsided again.' But with each step he took, he crushed another mummy. Heads rolled against him; the dust of bodies choked his throat. Belzoni crawled on, searching the mummies for the papyri which were wrapped against what was left of their bodies, across their chests, under their arms or along their legs.

Belzoni returned often to Thebes during his four years in Egypt. Unlike James Bruce, who had been in the valley forty years earlier, Belzoni was not attacked by the Arabs who lived in the hills, for by then the sight of foreign visitors was common enough. Belzoni did, however, find them 'superior to any other Arabs in cunning and deceit, and the most independent of any in Egypt.' When they discovered why he had come to the valley, they were eager to keep him away from the tombs since they, too, made a living out of finding and selling antiquities. But with familiarity came acceptance. These Arabs, Belzoni reported, 'live in the entrance of such caves as have already been opened, and, by making partitions with earthen walls, they form habitations for themselves, as well as for their cows, camels, buffaloes, sheep, goats, dogs &c.' While he was working in the valley, he slept in the entrance to one of the tombs where sheep were usually kept. Above the doorway were broken Egyptian figures. On either side of the opening, there was a figure of Anubis, the jackal, god of the Dead. Here the Arabs brought antiquities for him to buy which they had found in the valley, or in the tombs nearby. Here also they brought him a bowl of milk and bread for his dinner or, at other times, a pair of fowl baked in an oven heated with pieces of mummy cases, or with the mummies themselves. Then, with a lump of sheep's fat burning as a nightlight in a niche in the tomb-wall above him, Belzoni stretched out on his mat on the rock floor. 'It is no uncommon thing to sit down near fragments of bones,' he wrote later; 'hands, feet, or sculls are often in the way; for these people are so accustomed to be among the mummies, that they think no more of sitting on them, than on the skins of their dead calves. I also became indifferent about them at last, and would have slept in a mummy pit as readily as out of it.'

Egypt had turned into a glorious treasure hunt for Belzoni, who was ahead of his competitors for much of the time. Apart from moving the bust of Rameses II and opening six new tombs in the Valley of the Kings, he also uncovered the great temple at Abu Simbel which his one-time patron Burckhardt had first glimpsed four years before. In this he was again sponsored by the British Consul-General, Henry Salt. Accompanied by William Beechey, who was Salt's secretary, a Greek servant, a janissary, an Arab cook, the five-man crew and two British naval captains – the Honourable Charles Irby and James Mangles

– Belzoni set off up river. They stopped at Philae where they celebrated the birthday of King George III: at midday on 4 June 1817 with the Union Jack flying from the highest pylon of the temple, they solemnly fired a 21-gun salute. 'At night,' Belzoni remembered, to the delight of his British readers, 'we repeated our rejoicings, and frightened all the natives round, who could not imagine why we wasted so much powder without killing somebody.' The zealous display was not just motivated by patriotism, though, for in this way the villagers along the Nile came to hear that the travellers on board the boat were well armed and their safety was thereby ensured.

When they reached Abu Simbel, they had great difficulty in getting labourers to work for them; when they did work, they worked badly and often stopped to demand presents or more money. In the end, the two captains, the secretary, the Greek servant, the janissary and Giovanni Belzoni dug the sand away themselves, working from first light until nine in the morning and then from three o'clock in the afternoon until the sun set. Stripped to the waist, to the amazement of their reluctant labourers, Belzoni's party worked through the heat of a Nubian July and in twenty-two days they cleared more than thirty-one feet of sand from the temple-front; on 1 August, with mud and stones and date-trees propping up the sand-hill to stop it sliding back over the entrance and burying them inside, they were ready to enter the temple. What they saw left them speechless. 'Our astonishment increased,' Belzoni recorded, 'when we found it to be one of the most magnificent temples.' But it was so hot that they found it impossible to draw, for the perspiration from their hands made their sketching books wet.

Having opened the temple, they did not stay long at Abu Simbel, for they were having great difficulty in obtaining food – another ploy of the local cacheff to hinder their progress. Captain Irby wrote that when two men came from the nearest village, they were amazed to find that they had succeeded in clearing away the sand. 'They appeared to think the temple would make a good hiding place for their cattle, &c., whenever the Bedouins came to rob them.' The Englishmen made no comment on this, just as the villagers said nothing about the magnificence of the temple's architecture.

*

While Belzoni was opening the temple at Abu Simbel, Burckhardt, one of his sponsors, was ill in Cairo, where he had taken a house in the Turkish quarter. The dysentery he had contracted during his pilgrimage to Mecca had returned and, although he was a sturdy and resilient young man, he suffered badly. There seemed to be little that doctors could do for him, since the cause of the disease was still unknown. Although he was only thirty-two years of age, he looked older, for the sun had lined his face and his illness had taken away his strength. In his house, Burckhardt was looked after by his faithful Egyptian servant, Shaharti, and by Osman Effendi – the converted Scotsman Donald Donald – who acted as his dragoman. In addition, he owned one slave who looked after his asses and another who ran the house.

When he heard that Belzoni had moved the head of Rameses II and that it was on its way to London, Burckhardt felt proud. At least he had achieved something. He had the good news, too, of the opening of the temple which he had found at Abu Simbel. But just as Henry Salt was preparing to take Lord Belmore and his physician Dr Richardson up the river to see the newly uncovered temple, Burckhardt's condition deteriorated. Salt went to see him one afternoon and found a crowd outside the house, for Burckhardt was greatly respected in the community as a sheikh, a scholar and a haji – his illness was a matter for public concern.

That afternoon, Burckhardt dictated his will to Salt and expressed his disappointment at not being able to complete the mission that he had been sent on in the first place – that of discovering the source of the Niger. Then he told Salt that when he died, 'The Turks will take my body, – I know it, – perhaps you had better let them,' and Salt did. As Sheikh Ibrahim, he was given a Muslim funeral and buried in a tomb just outside the city walls beyond the Bab el Nasr, the Gate of Victory. But his influence was felt even after his death. According to his will, Osman was bequeathed 2,000 piastres (about £100) as well as the two slaves and the scant contents of the house – with this, and with the knowledge he had acquired from his master, Osman established himself as a dragoman in Cairo, where he lived and worked – as Kinglake saw – until the severe plague of 1835.

On the afternoon that Burckhardt died, Henry Salt wrote to Sir Francis Darwin that 'It is a terrible blow to the African Association, which had built all its hopes, and with justice, on him; he was enterprising, yet cool and prudent, had been ten years preparing himself, had become a perfect Arab, and in two months intended to set out, through Fezzan, to Tombuctoo [sic]: God has otherwise disposed it.'

★

Belzoni returned to Cairo in the beginning of 1818 and, in March of that year, he found the entrance into the Pyramid of Chephren, the second Pyramid of Giza. The following year, he and his wife left Egypt and travelled to Italy and then on to England. On 1 May 1821, he opened a remarkable exhibition of Egyptian antiquities – aptly enough, in the Egyptian Hall in Piccadilly – in which he also showed a full-size reconstruction of the now-famous tomb of Seti I, 'Belzoni's tomb,' as well as details of parts of the temples at Philae and Abu Simbel and of the second Pyramid. The exhibition was a great success and gives an idea of the popularity of Egyptiana for, on the first day alone, nearly 2,000 people visited the Egyptian Hall; and, since they each paid an entry fee of half a crown, it seems that the undertaking was also a rewarding one for the Belzonis. The exhibition ran for a year. After the publication of his *Narrative* in 1820 and the accompanying *Plates* in 1822, the number of tourists and travellers turning their sights to the Nile increased once again. Also, in 1822, the French scholar Jean Francois Champollion announced his system for deciphering hiero-glyphics. It was a breakthrough that meant it was at last possible to be certain who the pharaohs were, to discover what they called their gods, and when they had lived.

The field of Egyptology was now wide open, but Belzoni decided not to return to Egypt. He had been fêted in London, but he had not parted amicably with Henry Salt in Cairo. The first point of contention between the two men was whether Salt had actually employed Belzoni to transport the bust of Rameses from Thebes, or whether he had merely suggested that he do so. Belzoni insisted that 'I positively deny that I was ever employed by him in any shape whatever, either by words or writing.' However, Giovanni d'Athanasi, who was employed by Salt as an interpreter at the British Consulate, claimed that Belzoni and his wife, 'who with tears in her eyes began a recital of all the hardships her husband had suffered,' had been employed from the out-set. The second point, which seems a clearer issue, was whether Belzoni was right to claim to have sponsored the opening of the Second Pyramid at Giza. Belzoni said that he did pay for it himself. But d'Athanasi, who called Belzoni 'impatient and intractable', claimed that money was advanced by the British Consulate in Salt's absence, and that he himself had obtained a firman for the work from Muhammad Ali in Henry Salt's name. 'Belzoni,' wrote d'Athanasi, 'would never have been able to have struck a single axe into the ground about the pyramids without the name of Mr. Salt.' 'It is really very melancholy,' the interpreter went on, 'that in the absence of all modesty, he could have supposed that the truth could remain forever concealed, without one day bursting through the veil with which he wished to cover it.'

D'Athanasi also claimed that rather than deciding to give up his work in Egypt, Belzoni was finally dismissed by Salt, but whatever the truth of that assertion, it was clear that Belzoni would have found it difficult to return to Egypt after his exhibition in London. Belzoni was in search of fame above all else and it had upset him that, 'On my arrival in Europe, I found so many erroneous accounts had been given to the public of my operations and discoveries.' Looking around for something else to occupy his prodigious energies and abilities, Belzoni hit upon the idea of pursuing Burckhardt's ambition of finding the source of the river Niger. There would certainly be lasting fame in that achievement and Burckhardt had been one of the few Europeans in Egypt for whom Belzoni had shown a genuine respect. There seems, therefore, to have been an element of homage also in his decision to travel into the African interior. But the journey to the Niger proved to be Belzoni's least successful venture and, like Burckhardt, he contracted dysentery. Weakened by the heat and worn out by his exertions, Belzoni died on 3 December 1823, in Gato, Benin.

Four years later, the British Consul-General Henry Salt, described by his biographer as 'nearly in the prime of his life', died in Egypt. The three men responsible for removing the massive bust of Rameses II – which Thomas de Quincey described as having 'the most diffusive and pathetically divine [smile] that the hand of man has created' – had all died before their time: Burckhardt at thirty-two, Belzoni at forty-five and Salt at forty-seven. Had there been a gutter press such as flourishes now, it might well have found something unusual about this.

PASSING THE LIFELINE

'In another ten years such wonders will there be,
We shall go and dine in Egypt and then come home for tea.'

Sarah Terry, 1853

In December 1839, Harriet Tytler, an eleven-year-old English girl who lived in India – her father was a medical officer in the East India Company's army – was sent home to England for her education in the sailing ship *Seringapatam*. She travelled with her younger brother and sister in the care of a friend of the family, a Mrs Birch. The captain of the *Seringapatam* was a certain Mr Hopkins, nicknamed 'the Bengal Ayah' and 'noted for his care of the little ones sent home in his charge,' Harriet wrote. This was the first time that she or her siblings had travelled on a large ship and the novelty helped to calm the thoughts which troubled her: would she ever see her father or mother again? what if something happened to her while she was in England? Why, she had never before even seen the aunt and uncle she was going to stay with – what if they were unpleasant or didn't get on? Still, Mrs Birch was attentive, and Captain Hopkins did his best to entertain the children. Although he did not allow them on shore with the adults when the ship docked at Cape Town, he did let them look through his telescope to see the line when they reached the Equator – 'we did not know till afterwards,' Harriet remembered, 'how he had traded on our simplicity by fastening a hair across the lens.' Also at the Equator a sailor dressed as Neptune paraded around the ship and tarred and feathered anyone who had not crossed the line before. But children were exempted and, as the adults had all crossed the line on their way out to India, it was only the novice sailors from Calcutta who suffered.

The journey was slow and tedious, they were often becalmed – 'Now children,' Captain Hopkins told them, 'whistle for a wind.' – and it was spring, more than four months later, before they sailed up the Channel. At that time there were more than 40,000 Britons in India and the number was increasing all the time. Beyond India, the British empire was spreading, too, and as Australia, the Seychelles and Mauritius, Singapore and Burma came under British rule, the need arose for a regular and efficient shipping service between England and the colonies, not just for trade and communication, but also for this growing number of passengers. Of the routes to the East, the Overland Route via Egypt had an advantage over travelling via the Cape of Good Hope since it was considerably shorter and would cut down the time needed for the journey. James Bruce knew this and argued the case for setting up a regular link between England and the East through Egypt. The Consul George Baldwin knew it, too, and, tiring of the lack of response to his official despatches, he even went as far as publishing a book, in 1801, putting forward his views on the benefits that would follow, not only from trading with the East but also with Egypt which he called 'the resort of all the traders of the world'. Although Baldwin was a trader himself, at this point he was probably overstating his case, and very little changed until the development of steam transport and the advent of a young British naval officer called Thomas Waghorn.

Waghorn was born at the start of the nineteenth century, joined the Royal Navy at the age of twelve and had passed the lieutenancy examination before his eighteenth birthday. But eighteen was too young to be commissioned as a lieutenant in the navy, so Waghorn served with the Bengal Pilot Service instead and saw action in the First Burmese War of 1824–6. No doubt he would have had a distinguished career in the navy, but his imagination was caught by the substantial 'prizes' being offered by the Calcutta Steam Committee, set up to encourage the development of a steamer service to England. If he could prove the efficacy of his route, the Committee would back him.

Although he began by supporting a steam route around the Cape, Waghorn was quick to realize how difficult it would be to establish that line. Steamers needed coal and coal came from Britain. To set up a steamer route, coaling stations would need to be built at regular intervals along the line and supplied with coal brought out in sailing ships. The costs would be high and when the British Post Office, whom Waghorn was counting on as his major customer, fixed the rate of postage to India below his own estimate, Waghorn realized the impossibility of this plan. Returning to India to talk to his supporters on the Steam Committee, Waghorn decided to travel via Egypt. This was not an idle choice on his part, for he had a rival in another Englishman, James Taylor, who had already decided to promote the route through the eastern Mediterranean and via Suez.

James Taylor was well on his way to Egypt when Waghorn left London on 28 October 1829, carrying letters for Sir John Malcolm, the Governor of Bombay. Waghorn crossed the Channel, travelled overland via Paris and Milan to Trieste, and then sailed on to Alexandria. In Egypt he rode by camel from Cairo to Suez and reached the Red Sea, over the desert, in three days, intending to meet the steamship *Enter-*

prize, which was expected from India. But when Waghorn reached Suez, the ship had not yet arrived and, unable to wait, he found a small sailing boat and pushed out, alone, into the brilliant waters of the Red Sea. This was a rash undertaking; the Red Sea might look beautiful, but it is difficult to navigate and its winds and currents are notoriously dangerous. And even if he had survived the heat and the sea, he was too good a target to be left untouched by the less honest sailors along the coast. But Waghorn was determined to reach India before Taylor, whom he knew had left Suez just before him. He must have believed, as the wind caught his sails and pushed him away from the Suez seafront, that the contract could still be his.

Waghorn reached Jeddah in safety, a remarkable achievement in itself, and found that he had been right not to wait for the *Enterprize*, for it had met with an accident and had never even left Bombay. Spurred on by this, but displaying a little more wisdom than he had at Suez, he decided that his little boat could not take him all the way to India and instead he chartered a large sailing ship. It seems that he hired the ship more with an eye to the speed with which it could leave harbour than the reliability of its crew, for they had not been underway for long when it became clear that the crew would be troublesome. They must have thought he was a rich man, and a stupid one for travelling alone. They demanded more money and threatened to leave him if he did not provide it. Of course Waghorn refused to give them more but, fearing for his safety, he kept an armed vigil on board ship. It was a relief to him, then, when he spotted the Bombay Marine's brig-of-war *Thetis* under Commander Moresby, which was sailing back to Bombay from Suez, where it had just set up a coaling station. Waghorn decided to leave his mutinous sailors and continue on Moresby's ship – it would be quicker, and certainly safer. He then discovered that James Taylor was also on board and that the two men were going to reach Bombay together; the only consolation Waghorn had was that his journey had been much quicker. The day before their arrival in Bombay on 20 March 1830, the steamer *Hugh Lindsay* left Bombay for Suez, running off the coal that the *Thetis* had left for it, and the Red Sea steamer route was open.

All Waghorn's attempts to control the Overland Route seemed to be in vain. He was an intelligent and energetic man, and his determination to play a part in carrying the mail along this route to India was unshakable. Later, towards the end of 1844, William Thackeray, staying at the Hotel d'Orient, recorded that, 'The bells are ringing prodigiously; and Lieutenant Waghorn is bouncing in and out of the courtyard full of business. He only left Bombay yesterday morning, was seen in the Red Sea on Tuesday, is engaged to dinner this afternoon in the Regent's Park, and (as it is about two minutes since I saw him in the courtyard) I make no doubt he is by this time at Alexandria, or at Malta, say, perhaps, at both. *Il en est capable*. If any man can be at two places at once (which I don't believe or deny) Waghorn is he.' But there was a difference between operating a courier service (as he later did) and controlling the Overland Route – even with his rival, Taylor, dead, Waghorn's hopes of running the route were unrealistic. He had neither the resources to build the steamers, nor the constant support at both ends of the route to guarantee his influence. When other competitors appeared, Waghorn gave up all hope of winning the Steam Committee's contract.

Not all was lost, though, for in 1835 Waghorn advertised that he was setting himself up as an 'East India' agent for the transit of Egypt. He would see passengers, their luggage or their letters through Egypt in safety. Just as Muhammad Ali had encouraged the use of the Overland Route, knowing that it would then be subject to his continued consent, so Waghorn knew that whoever had control of the practical arrangements for crossing a difficult, if now much safer country, like Egypt, would also become indispensable. He was proved right when the British Post Office appointed him as their official Agent in Egypt.

Unfortunately, as with his original plans for the Overland Route, Waghorn was not the only East India Agent. Two other Englishmen by the names of Hill and Raven had already set up a regular line of transport through Egypt and opened a hotel in Cairo to accommodate transit passengers. At the same time as Waghorn, they began to build a hotel at Suez and again Waghorn was out-manoeuvred: Messrs Hill & Raven had greater financial backing and received £1,000 a year from the Bombay Steam Committee. The Committee then sent a Colonel Barr from India to supervise the construction of a series of post or rest houses across the desert from Suez to Cairo, and these also were put at the disposal of Hill & Raven.

Passengers arriving at Suez from India were now approached by agents from both Waghorn's and Hill & Raven's organizations. The choice they had to make was this: either they could pay £6 to Messrs Hill & Raven who would take them across the desert as far as Cairo and could offer them exclusive use of the desert rest houses on the way, or they could pay £13 to Waghorn for a rather hot journey with nowhere to cool off, but which included transportation right through to Alexandria, connecting with the steamer service in the Mediterranean. Waghorn's advantage over his rivals was that he invariably had a monopoly on the wagons and horses and camels along the route, which he had put to good use carrying British coal from Cairo to Suez for the Red Sea steamers, bringing the price of coal in Suez down from £10 to £3 per ton in the process.

Providing both of these transport companies with customers was the newly incorporated Peninsular and Oriental Steam Navigation Company, which had won the contract to run the British mails to India. By 1842 the P&O, as it was soon known, had regular steamer services on both sides of the isthmus of Suez. In 1839 the British had invaded Aden and, as well as in Ceylon on the Indian Ocean side, and Malta and Gibraltar in the Mediterranean, the P&O built coaling stations to keep their steamers running. With the backing of the British government and the kudos of their royal charter, the P&O succeeded where Waghorn had failed and, as he had guessed, the rewards were great indeed.

In 1841, Arthur Anderson, one of the founders of the P&O, arrived in Alexandria to sort out the rivalry between the two transport agencies. Under pressure from Anderson, Waghorn was 'encouraged' to sell his business to his rival and the naming of the new company – Hill & Co – suggests that there was little role left for Waghorn. Mr Hill then employed another Englishman, Samuel Shepheard, of whom we shall hear more later, to run his hotels. While Anderson was still in Egypt, he also had an interview with Muhammad Ali and discussed the idea of building a canal between the Mediterranean and the Red Sea. It was not in his company's interests to have to break the journey at all; an all-sea route via a canal would obviously benefit them considerably.

The Overland Route developed quickly: while in 1839, 275 people had travelled that way, the number increased to over 3,000 in only eight years. Refinements were made to ease the journey across the desert for the growing number of passengers. Seating arrangements in the carriages were made beforehand so there was no longer any need to scramble for places. The six stations or rest houses along the route were well stocked with food and drink, and wells were dug at each of them which were filled with water brought from the Nile. One Englishman who made the crossing in the 1840s described Station No 2 as 'a building containing a large saloon, with divans and a long table, three sleeping rooms, kitchen, etc., and here we found a good supper laid out, consisting of smoking dishes of Irish stew, cold turkeys and fowls, and eggs *à discretion*.' There was also beer and ale at a shilling a bottle and what he called 'a modest looking *"carte des vins"'* which satisfied most travellers, although he had heard that one young officer making his way out to India for the first time had ordered champagne and complained when it was served warm. 'I never found any one *returning*,' the English-man added, 'make any unreasonable objections of this kind.' The organi-zation of the crossing was improved as well and the carriages usually stopped at one of the stations during the heat of the day. Because Suez was an unappealing place for passengers to spend any amount of time in, a semaphore signalling system was then set up between Cairo and Suez so that eastbound passengers could stay in the greater comfort of the capital until their steamer for India was ready. The complexity of the operation which was run for these travellers by the transit organi-zations is suggested by the number of animals they used on the desert route between Cairo and Suez – 3,500 camels, 440 horses and 46 carriages – and by the four steamers which now made the journey along the Nile and the Mahmoudieh Canal between Cairo and Alexandria.

*

Leaving England and her Birmingham aunt, a particularly unpleasant woman whom she rather understatedly called 'one of the old school,' the freshly educated seventeen-year-old Harriet Tytler set out to return to India in October 1845. This time she was put in the care of Mrs Moresby, wife of the captain of the *Thetis* – Thomas Waghorn's saviour back in 1830 – who was now captain of one of the P&O's flagships, the *Hindostan*, a 250-foot paddle steamer which ran regularly between Suez and Calcutta.

The P&O also ran two steamers – the *Oriental* and the *Great Liverpool* – between England and Egypt and it was on one of these that Harriet Tytler embarked at Southampton docks. No sooner had the steamer slipped its berth than the band struck up and the dancing began. This, Harriet suggests, was to help the 260 passengers overcome their sadness at leaving England; Harriet, of course, felt nothing but relief and excite-ment at her own escape, but sadness at leaving her younger sister behind in her aunt's care. The next aid to recovery was dinner at the 'princely tables', where the best food and wine was served – champagne flowed on Thursdays and Saturdays. 'On these occasions I took especial care as to whom I danced with.'

After more than five years of what amounted to deprivation and almost total captivity at her aunt's house – she had been allowed out once a day to play in the cemetery, what she called her 'early training amongst the graves' – life on board the P&O steamer was fun for Harriet. She danced twice a day, played cards and ate heartily. At Gibraltar she stopped to see the fortifications and in Malta she did some shopping. When she reached Alexandria, Harriet stayed in what she called 'Shep-heard's Hotel', one of the hotels belonging to the new Egyptian Transit

Administration which had taken over Hill & Co's operation in 1845, after Muhammad Ali had agreed a postal convention with the British Post Office guaranteeing the security of the Overland Route: the new administration had encouraged Samuel Shepheard to continue running the hotels on the route. While in Alexandria, Harriet had time to do some sightseeing – Cleopatra's Needle, Pompey's Pillar and some of the royal palaces – before boarding one of the P&O steamers up to Cairo. Alexandria was now linked to the Nile by the Mahmoudieh Canal, built by Muhammad Ali at the suggestion of the English banker Samuel Briggs. According to one near-contemporary report, 23,000 people had died during the first ten months of the building operations, since the labourers – fellahin forced into working on it – were supplied with neither food nor equipment. If they had none of their own, they literally scooped out the canal with their hands, and worked until they died.

At Cairo, Harriet Tytler did not stay long enough to see the sights, since Mrs Moresby, her chaperon, was anxious to meet her husband in Suez. As a sort of privilege, therefore, they were included in the first convoy of six horse-drawn carriages, each of which held six passengers, while those who had to wait behind went off to see the Pyramids. 'I do not now recollect whether it was eighteen or twenty hours that we took doing the eighty miles,' Harriet explained, 'all I do remember is that it was an awful journey.' In some places the tracks were very rough and passengers were banged about in the carriages as the wheels crushed the bones of horses and camels which had died along the way. In other places, though, the going must have been more comfortable because, as night fell across the desert, Harriet drifted off to sleep and her head rested on the firm and discreet shoulder of her neighbour, Mr Wiltshire, 'a very nice young fellow, a tea taster going to China.' Later, when Harriet's sister left her Birmingham aunt and went back out to India, she travelled with Mr Wiltshire's brother who confessed that the tea taster had had the greatest difficulty in restraining himself from kissing an English girl who had fallen asleep on his shoulder in a dark carriage in the Egyptian desert.

On the *Hindostan*, with Mrs Moresby reunited with her husband, they stopped at Aden – 'as God-forsaken a place as any on earth' – and also at Point de Galle in Ceylon, where she again disembarked. 'It was necessary to go on shore at all the places we stopped at, as the coaling was very disagreeable.' By this time, though, Harriet had learned of the death of her father – her anxiety at leaving India had been justified – and when she finally reached Calcutta, she discovered that her mother and the younger children were all set to return to England.

Harriet had gone from Southampton to Calcutta in under two months, less than half the time it had taken her to reach England, sailing via the Cape, only five years before. Thomas Waghorn who, more than anyone else in his day, had brought about this transformation, was still active in the Overland route. At the same time as Harriet Tytler arrived back in Calcutta, Waghorn reached London carrying despatches from Bombay which it had taken him only twenty-nine days to deliver. And he was sure that he could knock a few more days off that time. As William Thackeray, on his P&O courtesy tour in 1844 wrote, Bonaparte had performed wonders in Egypt,

> But what are his wonders compared to Waghorn? Nap
> massacred the Mamelukes at the Pyramids: Wag has
> conquered the Pyramids themselves; dragged the unwieldy
> structures a month nearer England than they were, and
> brought the country along with them . . . O my country! O
> Waghorn! *Hœ tibi erunt artes.* When I go to the Pyramids
> I will sacrifice in your name, and pour out libations of bitter
> ale and Harvey Sauce in your honour!'

*

The smooth operation of the Overland route was an obvious inducement for travellers to visit Egypt and, as the Empire grew and touring became more popular, the type of person likely to pass through Egypt changed. When Baldwin and Salt were the British consuls, the travellers they looked after were invariably wealthy and educated, often people on the Grand Tour who were forced to change their traditional itineraries through France, Italy and Greece because of hostilities in Europe – in the 1810s, for instance, Thomas Legh had explained that he was obliged by his 'exclusion from Europe . . . to direct his steps to the shores of Egypt'. But the progress in transport brought other types of travellers and, even as early as 1837, Captain C. Rochfort Scott noticed that 'the Franks [Westerners or Christians] are rapidly on the increase, and of all the varieties of the human species that throng the narrow streets of Cairo, they are the most disreputable in appearance, as well as – I believe I may safely add – in their dealings.' In 1850 Florence Nightingale complained that 'Cairo is overflowing with Franks.' They were not just English, either, but the French – never far away – and Italians, Greeks, Dutch, Americans, Germans and even Russians. The route had become too popular for some travellers, who thought that the place was spoiled. The Ezbekieh area in particular was crowded and one visitor in 1856 dubbed it 'the St James's Park of Cairo, though considerably smaller.'

Bonaparte did not stay long in Egypt, but he and his team of *savants* left a legacy of observations and suggestions for the development of the country, many of which were pursued in the following century. Bonaparte had understood the importance of Egypt for the domination of the East – he had called it the most important country in the world – and events proved that his assessment was right. As the transit of Egypt became the easiest link between Europe and the East, so quicker and simpler ways of crossing it were looked for. The idea of digging a canal across the isthmus of Suez or, alternatively, of linking up the Nile with the Red Sea, and thereby making it possible for ships to move straight through from the Mediterranean to Arabian waters, had considerable attractions. The idea was hardly new; there had been a canal between the Nile and the Red Sea in pharaonic times. The Roman Emperor Trajan extended the canal, which then ran from the Roman fortress of Babylon to somewhere near present-day Suez. Later, the canal was re-opened by the general Amr so that wheat for Mecca could be taken by ship directly from Cairo to Jeddah. One hundred and thirty years later, the Caliph al Mansur had the canal blocked in order to stop the supply of grain to the other holy city, Medina, which was in revolt. When Bonaparte invaded Egypt with his Army of the East he had actually been instructed by the Directory in Paris 'to cut a canal through the isthmus of Suez'. The canal would be a French undertaking and would ensure that French troops could strike with speed at India.

But the report of Bonaparte's engineer, Le Père, put an end to this plan. Working in less than ideal conditions, Le Père made fundamental errors in his survey of the proposed canal site and confirmed the ancient tradition that the Red Sea was considerably higher – Le Père made it thirty feet – than the Mediterranean. Under those circumstances a canal was not possible and no more was done by the French at that time. The canal scheme was still theirs, though. For a number of reasons, including their own hostility towards anything French, Britain opposed the building of a canal – not only was it not possible, they claimed, but it was also not desirable – and instead they promoted their own cause, a British-made railway. Muhammad Ali, who wanted whatever was best for himself and his country, encouraged both schemes.

But if the official representatives of France had abandoned the plan for a canal, private individuals had not. While Thomas Waghorn was rushing from London to Bombay and Calcutta to prove the efficacy of the route through Egypt, the disciples of Claude Henri, Comte de Saint-Simon, were actively pursuing their intention of cutting a canal.

The Comte himself had died in 1825, having spent his life championing a number of worthy, visionary or sometimes just far-fetched schemes. One of these was the connecting of the Atlantic and Pacific Oceans and he had even gone as far as proposing his prototype Panamanian canal to the Viceroy of Mexico, although without much success. His suggestion probably would have been greeted with more enthusiasm by Muhammad Ali, but the Comte was less interested in Egypt.

However, after the death of their founder, the Saint-Simonians, as his disciples were called, continued to promote visionary schemes and their new leader, Prosper Enfantin, was attracted to Egypt. Like Bonaparte before him, he saw it as the meeting place between what the Saint-Simonians considered to be the masculine vigour of the West and the feminine receptivity of the East – what is seen today as being exploitative aggression and a vulnerability brought about by underdevelopment. The Saint-Simonians wanted 'to make the Mediterranean the nuptial bed for a marriage between the East and the West and to consummate the marriage by the piercing of a canal through the isthmus of Suez' (Enfantin). All very symbolic, but unfortunately their arrival was greeted with something less than excitement by the French consul who had to exert his influence to stop the Pasha from sending them straight back to France.

Enfantin and his followers were entertained in Cairo by a number of sympathizers, including Soliman Pasha, commander of the new Egyptian army. Soliman was a French artillery officer – Colonel Sève – who had fought at Waterloo and who, having converted to Islam (a practice not reserved solely for Britons), was employed by Muhammad Ali to train his new army. But while Enfantin and his followers, including the engineers Fournel and Lambert, kept their idea of the canal alive through their 'marriage' plans, a British engineer called J. A. Galloway was advising Muhammad Ali to build a railway from Cairo to Suez instead. What could be simpler, the railroaders insisted? There were no ditches to dig, less labourers were needed, the British would supervise the construction and Arthur Anderson, the director of the P&O who had been in Cairo two years before, had even offered to help fund it. But in 1835, when railway construction materials started being unloaded in Alexandria, Galloway Bey – as he was now known – died and neither his scheme nor the Saint-Simonian canal were allowed to progress any further. People in Cairo still remembered the state of near-anarchy in Egypt only thirty years before, as well as the blood shed by English and French and Turkish and Albanian soldiers – a few of them even remembered the ban on Christian ships in the Red Sea above Jeddah and in one of the ports at Alexandria – and they considered that everything was moving too quickly. The Pasha's declining health – both physical and mental – was seen as reason enough to slow the process down and not until Muhammad Ali's grandson came to the throne in 1849 did these changes continue.

Abbas was the eldest son of Ibrahim Pasha, who had only survived Muhammad Ali by a few months. Abbas was considered to be an Anglophile, encouraged in this by the congenial British Consul-General Charles Murray, a man of taste, refinement and learning. Although Abbas was a conservative man and was generally opposed to the modern changes his grandfather had introduced, he was prepared to listen to Murray. Where Muhammad Ali had favoured French advisers, Abbas replaced them with English ones. Muhammad Ali built schools and factories; Abbas closed them. Muhammad Ali had strengthened the army; Abbas reduced its size but increased taxation. But encouraged by Murray, who could speak both Arabic and Turkish, Abbas proceeded with the railway and signed an agreement on 12 July 1851, by which Robert Stephenson – son of George Stephenson, the inventor of the *Rocket* locomotive – was paid £56,000 to build a track between Cairo and Alexandria, the first in the East. The fee was obviously attractive because Stephenson and his eighteen British engineers began work two months after the agreement was reached and the line was opened in 1854. With Stephenson as Chief Engineer of the Egyptian Railways, Abbas appointed a British army officer from India called Richards as its first director. Richards had arrived in Egypt during the reign of Muhammad Ali and served as an interpreter at the British Consulate. Deciding to convert to Islam, he adopted the new name of Agha Abdallah, or Hagh Abdallah, but he was more commonly known as El Inglisy. Under Stephenson and El Inglisy, Egypt's railway system was inaugurated. There were twelve stations built along the line from the 'Station of the Pasha', near the port and the new Ras el Tin palace in Alexandria, to the terminal at Cairo, built on its present site in Rameses Square. The year the line was fully opened, Abbas's successor, Said Pasha, imported a luxury saloon car from England for his own personal use which was eighteen feet long, divided into three interconnecting rooms, each separated by double doors, and with an open terrace in the middle. The regular train operated just one service a day to begin with, on which there were three classes of carriage – an open wagon for third class, a covered one for second and a luxurious first class, which was described by one Englishman who went on it in 1856 as 'handsomely fitted up by Messrs Wright of Birmingham . . . the movement on the rail,' he reported, 'is as smooth and fluent as any railway I have travelled upon.'

The second leg of the railway, connecting Suez with Alexandria – the line from Cairo to Suez – was completed in 1858, but even before then the British had begun to benefit from the speed with which it was now possible to cross Egypt. In 1857 the mutiny broke out among the sepoys in the East India Company's Bengal Army and, to help restore British rule, the India board in London sent British troops out via Egypt. By the end of that year, the railway to Suez had been completed as far as what was known as Station No 12, fifty-eight miles from Cairo. Here, in the middle of the desert, the track ended, the old road ran on, and like Harriet Tytler before them, British soldiers were taken across the last stretch of the desert in horse-drawn vans. With the help of the railway, by March 1858, 5,000 British troops had been sent out, taking just over two days to travel from Alexandria to Suez, and just over five weeks from London to India.

William Howard Russell, a special correspondent of *The Times*, who had won great fame for his coverage of the Crimean War, was sent out to cover the Indian Mutiny in 1857, and he travelled by the same route as the troops. Russell landed at Alexandria on the P&O ship *Valetta* and was encouraged to disembark straightaway – ' "As soon as you can for shore, ladies and gentlemen, the train is just off!" ' After a short boat trip to the pier, he then rode two miles through the crowds to the railway station, 'a big white flag, of the usual architecture invented for those structures'. As soon as he arrived, he heard that the train was indeed ready to leave – 'Why this haste was manifested, only those in the secrets of the Transit Mal-Administration can guess,' Russell complained, 'but of a surety we were pressed and rammed into first and second class carriages, and, swollen by the passengers of the *Pera* from Southampton, who had just landed before us, we filled a most formidable train.'

Russell had already handed in his P&O voucher and had received two tickets in return – one for the train and another for refreshments along the line. Since the train did not leave straight away, Arab boys selling oranges appeared at the windows or in the doorways, calling out, ' "I say, John! – Buy orange? buy orange? – I say, Backsheesh!" ' and not even the fierce beatings they received from the policemen in the station deterred them.

Although it left the station soon enough, Russell's train was obliged to stop halfway to Cairo to let the Pasha's special train pass. They waited on the track for two hours before 'the Pasha sent word by electric telegraph to say he was not coming, and a messenger on foot carried the message from some distant station to the conductor.' Then, when they reached the Nile, they stopped to eat what Russell described as a 'Barmecide banquet', which was named after a prince of Baghdad who, in one of the *Tales of the One Thousand and One Nights*, places a succession of empty dishes in front of a beggar, pretending that they are all filled with delicious food, a pretence which the beggar keeps up. Russell also kept up the pretence at his 'banquet' although the setting was far removed from the Arabian Nights, under the sign of '"Mat Jackson – Entertainment – Ale, Porter, Tobacco – Gin and Whiskey – English Cheese."'

In Cairo, Russell was supposed to spend the night in Samuel Shepheard's hotel, but he was told at the station that it was full, because passengers from the steamer which had docked before the *Pera* – and who were supposed to have already embarked at Suez – had been kept in Cairo since the Red Sea steamer had broken down. At the same time, passengers from India who had just arrived in Suez had 'with that precision of mal-administration which distinguishes the transit through Egypt', also been sent on to the capital. Eventually Russell found a room at the Hotel du Nil, which he discovered 'well deserved the name, for we could get nothing to eat'.

After a night punctuated by the activities of the mosquitoes with which he shared his room, Russell was woken at 5 a.m. by the sounding of a bell. The train, he was told, would leave the station at 6.30 – so he had better get up. Soon after this he was disturbed a second time to be told that the train had now been delayed until 9.30 a.m. Not wishing to waste these precious few hours allowed him in Cairo, Russell decided to visit the city's famous markets. 'The great advantage of seeing the Bazaar at this early hour is that you can get nothing to buy, as the shops are all shut.'

The desert impressed him with its 'barren grandeur and primaeval antiquity', but the single line of track laid by French engineers, brought in to complete the line, was unnecessarily uneven. At regular intervals there were coaling stations, 'helpless, hot, ovenlike erections generally eked out by old Crimean wooden huts, within the shade of which may be seen an undoubted Englishman, smoking his pipe.' At Station No 12 the train stopped; this was the end of the line and stretching out ahead, as far as Russell could see, were the camps of the Arab 'navvies' working on the last stretch of the line. Here they were served a dinner of 'hot joints of recondite animals, papier-mâché chickens, and lignite vegetables ... it had come all the way from Cairo – so had the wine, and beer, and spirits.' After eating what he could of the dinner, Russell prepared to complete his journey to Suez in one of the seven or eight vans which were waiting for the train's passengers – 'resembling Brighton bathing-boxes laid longitudinally on wheels, to which were attached creatures of an uncertain number of legs, resembling very much Scarborough ponies at the end of the season.' But of course there were too many passengers – enough for five times as many vans – and they were obliged to draw lots to decide who would go first. Russell fought his way into a seat in the last van.

Out in the desert, the leading vans but a cloud of dust up ahead of them, the sun setting in 'one great bath of purple cloud', the darkness around them complete, Russell was thrown around the little carriage by the unevenness of the road. The little paper lantern he had bought to brighten their passage did not ease matters much, but then 'a kind young moon', rising over the sand dunes, allowed them to see that they had now left the track and were lost. When the driver realized his mistake, he disappeared into the darkness, supposedly to find out where they were and to see if he could find the road. Their unease and mistrust of the country and its people quickly surfaced. The desert was quiet and empty, its outlines softened by the dull moonlight. Then they saw another light – a group of men coming towards them carrying torches. Were they going to attack them? Was this a trap to rob them? They had all heard of such things, of course, of this less romantic side of Egypt which Eliza Fay and so many other poor abused travellers had seen in this desert. But this was Egypt in 1857, not 1785 – Bonaparte and Muhammad Ali had been and gone, and the Arabs – who might even have been working on the railway line – knew that there was a safer piastre to be made by helping the Franks to get back onto the right track than there was in robbing them then.

Russell and his fellow-passengers reached Suez at 11.30 that night to find that they were staying in a place which reminded Russell – who had only been back from the Crimea for less than a year – of a barracks more than a hotel. In the morning, he woke to find a man holding a razor to his throat – a native barber was trying to shave off his beard. He was alarmed, of course, but he wrote that 'I have since learned that it is the *chef d'oeuvre* of Asiatic tonsorial art to shave one whilst he is asleep and without awakening him.' Russell, with some relief, had been approached by something less than a master of this art. All around him in the hotel – in lobbies, rooms, on staircases – the other inmates of the 'barracks' were preparing themselves for the day ahead.

Outside the hotel was the Red Sea and a young Arab boy calling, ' "I say, I give change for sovren – nineteen bob and a tizzy," ' which led the English journalist to observe that this was 'Wonderful proof of the spread of the English language, and of a just appreciation of the principles of commerce!' Outside, also, there was a long line of camels making their way to the wharf with their luggage. There were so many passengers and so much luggage that Russell doubted whether they would all fit onto the single steamer that lay at anchor in the harbour, but at midday they all assembled on the wharf, ready to be taken out to the India-bound ship. However, their agents had let them down once again and at two o'clock they were still waiting on the wharf. It was hot and bright, and the local boatmen had been pestering them to let them take them to the steamer for two hours now; so they gave in and allowed themselves to be poled and rowed across the glittering sea at the start of the final leg of their journey to India.

Here we leave them – more of the Queen's soldiers followed them out to India soon afterwards – with Russell wondering, 'Shall I seek then to give a faint notion of the wretchedness of the seven days' passage down the Red Sea in a steamer which contained the passengers destined for two boats of the same size as that which carried the double burthen?' He thought that he would be all right, for he had reserved a cabin, but just before the steamer disappeared over the horizon the ship's purser, 'with the air of a man who was collecting for a charity sermon', did the rounds of the deck and asked all the gentlemen if they would kindly give up their berths for the cabinless ladies from the other steamer. 'I knew it, sir,' one angry old India-hand shouted at him, 'I knew it. They never dared to ask such a thing round the Cape.'

*

Abbas might have been a popular pasha with the British – although Florence Nightingale thought that 'It really seems to matter so little whether an Abbas or an Ibrahim reigns, a swine or a jackal' – but he was clearly as unpopular with the fellahin as he was with the French: in the summer of 1854 he was murdered – some say stabbed, others that he was strangled – by two of the servants at his palace in Benha, an appropriate setting near the point at which his new railway crossed the Damietta branch of the Nile. In a macabre attempt to pretend that the Pasha was still alive – to give Abbas's son, then being educated in Europe, time to return and stake his own weak claim to power – his supporters bundled the corpse into a closed carriage and took it for a drive around town. But seeing is not always believing and news of his death was accepted widely.

Abbas was succeeded by his uncle Said Pasha – according to the law of succession, power passed to the eldest heir of Muhammad Ali – whom Florence Nightingale approvingly labelled 'an excellent man, an educated man, and a gentleman'. This might have been true, but it was not all of the truth; Said was also compliant and gullible. He trusted people on instinct, but his instincts let him down. Muhammad Ali is reported to have told one visitor that, 'I know that among fifty men who come from Europe to offer me their services, forty-nine are only to be compared to false stones. Without testing them, I cannot discover the only genuine diamond that may be among them. I begin by buying them all and when I discover the one, he often repays me by a hundred-fold for the loss I have incurred by the others.' Said could not really afford to incur the loss brought on by testing the foreigners who came to him for help.

In the 1810s, Jean Louis Burckhardt had noted that there was a saying which was popular in Cairo at that time: 'The riches of Egypt are for the foreigners therein.' It would have been just as popular in the 1850s, when Said filled the viceregal divan. His family, friends, advisers and even the foreign consuls could all obtain audiences with him for foreign merchants, speculators and schemers, many of whom met with unexpected success. If that was the case with strangers, imagine how far an insider could go if he was an old friend of the Pasha, if he had been invited to Egypt by Said himself and if he had a scheme that was grand and full of the prospect of glory.

Mathieu de Lesseps had been a popular and successful diplomat at the French Consulate in Egypt during the early years of the nineteenth century and Muhammad Ali is supposed to have said of him that he was 'a great personage when I was a very small one.' When his son Ferdinand de Lesseps was sent to Egypt in 1832 by the French government, he too was greeted with warmth by Muhammad Ali. It was through his intimate contact with the Pasha that de Lesseps came into contact with one of his younger sons, Muhammad Said, who was being educated according to French principles. By the time he left Egypt five years later, de Lesseps had been made Consul-General and was a firm friend of this younger son. It might just have been good fortune that created their friendship in the first place: Said loved to eat and was a fat child – he grew into a twenty-five-stone man – and Ferdinand de Lesseps was on hand to feed him at the French Consulate. There is little reason to suspect any ulterior motive on de Lesseps's part at this time, since Said was not then in direct line to succeed Muhammad Ali. Later, of course, when de Lesseps was in retirement and Said became Pasha of Egypt, the Frenchman was quick to send a letter of congratulation. He wrote, as he explained to his friend the Dutch Consul-General in Egypt, 'that political considerations at home had given me the leisure which would permit me to present my respects to him in person as soon as he would let me know the date of his return from Constantinople.'

But de Lesseps wanted to present more than his respects. Since his first arrival in Egypt in 1832, when he read the report prepared by Bonaparte's engineer, Le Père, concerning the proposed canal from the Mediterranean to the Red Sea, de Lesseps had been inspired by the scheme. He had even contacted Enfantin and the Saint-Simonians about it, who rather simply believed that de Lesseps wanted to further their own plan. De Lesseps, however, was determined that if the canal was to be built, he would be the one to build it.

As for Said, perhaps he wanted to be – or wanted to be seen to be – decisive. Perhaps he really was as gullible as he sometimes appears. Perhaps, then, he did not consider it a matter of much importance who owned or controlled or even built the canal which de Lesseps wanted to dig across the Suez isthmus. Or maybe he believed in the prophetic note that de Lesseps sent him, assuring him that 'The names of Egyptian rulers who built the Pyramids, those monuments of human vanity, remain unknown. The name of the Prince who will have opened the great maritime canal will be blessed from century to century until time shall be no more.' Perhaps he wanted to believe it would be true, and thought that the Frenchman could make it happen. Certainly he did not guess how much it would cost his country in terms of money and men to build it, nor how little they would get back for that trouble, nor how it would focus the attention of the western powers on his country with such disastrous effects. Nor could he have known that he would not be that 'Prince' who would open it. And he would certainly, also, have been unhappy with his share of that promised immortality – the name of a port at the northern end of the canal, of which an Englishman earlier in this century observed, 'In 1860 it did not exist, but by 1890 it had achieved the distinction of being called the wickedest town in the East, and vice and evil were rampant in its streets. It was always used by writers of sensational novels as the setting for Oriental romances . . .' All that, thankfully, lay well in the future.

According to de Lesseps, an energetic, egotistical, forward-thinking man, he was invited on his arrival in Egypt to accompany Said to the Western Desert to witness military manoeuvres. Said was a young Pasha, thirty-two on his accession, and enjoyed his involvement with the Egyptian army. He placed great value on a man's martial qualities and, during the trip into the desert, de Lesseps was presented with several opportunities to exhibit these. Needless to say he did not waste them and he was complimented by the Pasha for his horsemanship and the accuracy with which he could shoot.

On 16 November 1854, only a few months after Said became Pasha, de Lesseps woke in the desert camp and stepped outside his tent. Above him there was a brilliant rainbow which arched from east to west. Here, surely, was a sign from heaven that his project must go ahead. Moved by the beauty of the rainbow, and by its biblical associations, de Lesseps decided that this was the day on which he must broach the subject of the canal with Said. By sundown that evening he had put forward his proposal, the Pasha had thought it over for a moment or two and de Lesseps had heard the magical reply – *'entendue; vous pouvez compter sur moi.'* The matter was hardly settled then, for there were the objections of the British and Turkish and even the French governments to overcome. There was also the matter of funding to arrange – the Suez Canal Company was eventually capitalized at FF. 200 million, while in the end the canal cost FF. 453,645,000 – as well as the supply of labourers to cut, dredge or drag away the estimated 97 million cubic yards of sand, mud, silt and rocks which would become the canal.

The British government objected to the canal because it was unnecessary – what was wrong with the railway? The Ottoman Sultan disapproved because it would cut him off from Egypt – still officially part of his empire – and would expose Mecca and Medina to direct contact with Europe. The French government disapproved because they thought that de Lesseps was using their name to further his own ends, which he was. But in spite of all these objections, digging finally started on 25 April 1859, initially with 12,000 fellahin forced from their lands, who, as with the digging of the Mahmoudieh Canal, were neither properly paid for their work nor adequately equipped or provided for. Four years later Lucie Duff Gordon noticed, after spending less than two months up-river at Thebes, that 'Everyone is cursing the French here. Forty thousand men always at work at the Suez Canal at starvation-point does not endear them to the Arabs.' Ten years after starting their work the fellahin were still cursing, but people from all over the world had come to Egypt to cheer de Lesseps and his brilliant achievement.

The Suez Canal was officially opened on 17 November 1869. Since the British government had expended so much energy in trying to stop it being built, it was only natural that British royalty stayed away from the opening ceremonies; the ambassador from Constantinople, Mr Henry Elliott, came instead. However, the Prince and Princess of Wales, with William Russell of *The Times* amongst their entourage, had toured the eastern Mediterranean earlier in the year and, for Said's successor, Ismail, who had travelled widely through Europe in the previous years to encourage support for the opening ceremonies, looking after them was like a test run for the November festivities. Egypt had been transformed since Russell was last there – roads had been built, whole new areas of European-style houses had been developed in Cairo and Alexandria, and the capital now even had an opera house, built along the same lines as the great houses of Europe and visited by French and Italian singers and theatre companies.

The Prince and Princess of Wales were met at Alexandria by the Khedive's special train which took them straight into the special plat-form at the Kasr el Nil palace in Cairo, where Ismail was waiting to greet them. After a stay in Cairo they were sent off up the Nile for six weeks on the khedival dahabieh and were generally indulged and displayed. Everywhere the Prince and Princess went they were impressed by the scale and grandeur of the entertainments which Ismail had organized for them. And when they finally visited the canal, eight months before it was due to be opened, they were amazed by the scale of the works. Port Said and Suez, at either end of the canal, were bustling towns and Russell thought that Port Said was similar to Venice. Its streets, he noted, 'are straight and regular enough to fill the heart of M. Haussman with pleasure – shops, cafés, hotels, and stores, a Health Office, a Life-Boat station, a Light-House, a considerable length of detached supra-villa-like houses facing the sea.' Suez surprised him just as much. When he had passed through in 1858 on his way to India, the town had had 3,000 inhabitants, a few ships waiting in the harbour, and the barrack-like hotel. In eleven years its population had grown to 20,000, the port was crowded with passenger steamers, troop ships and cargo vessels, and dinner in the hotel 'was worthy of one of the best hotels in Europe'. But neither Port Said nor Suez impressed him as much as Ismailia, linked to Cairo by rail and a halfway point between the two seas. Here, in the middle of the desert, 'you would be tempted, as you hear the click of the billiard-balls and the rattle of the dominoes, and look in through the gauze blinds and see the smoking crowds, to imagine that you were in some country quarter of La Belle France.'

In November, with the Prince and Princess of Wales safely back in England, the Empress Eugenie of France arrived in Egypt to open the canal. This time the celebrations were so spectacular that one guest wisely observed that Ismail's guests were eating up Egypt. No mention was made, then, of the British opposition to the work. All that was left for speculation and history: the canal was a fact, recognized by Thomas Cook, who took his first group of tourists to Egypt to see the inauguration of what his *Excursionist and Tourist Traveller* magazine called 'the greatest engineering feat of the present century'. The cele-brations themselves were a feat worth recording. Ismail had imported

500 chefs and 1,000 servants from Europe to cater for his guests. The list of titled and distinguished Europeans who arrived is long and included the Prince and Princess of Holland, the Emperor of Austria and the Crown Prince of Prussia. At Ismailia, on opening day, the French artist Eugene Fromentin remembered that there were 'Fireworks in front of the Viceroy's Palace. Open house everywhere. In one marquee there was a dinner party for five hundred guests, in another for two or three hundred... Luxurious dinners, vintage wines, exquisite fish, partridges, wild duck. Seven or eight thousand people sitting down to dinner in the middle of the desert. It was,' he decided, 'like something out of the Arabian Nights,' although Ismail had announced that, with the opening of the canal, Egypt was now a part of Europe.

A week after the canal was opened, the Empress Eugenie steamed north to Port Said in her yacht *L'Aigle*. She had never met Thomas Waghorn, pioneer of the route to the East through Egypt which had just been so lavishly celebrated. Twenty years before, Waghorn had been forced by his financial situation into writing begging letters to the British government, demanding recognition and some recompense for his work – for the honour of it, he insisted, and also to help him pay off the heavy costs which had built up while he promoted the route via Egypt. Parliament granted him a pension, but the sum was derisory and, only a year after the first payment, Waghorn died heavily in debt. But he was not forgotten. On 24 November 1869, Eugenie paid tribute to him by unveiling a bust of him, which is still in place, overlooking the harbour of Port Said.

EFFENDIS AND OTHERS

'The theory is that the English traveller has committed some sin against God and his conscience, and that for this the Evil Spirit has hold of him, and drives him from his home like a victim of the old Greek Furies, and forces him to travel over countries far and strange, and most chiefly over deserts and desolate places, and to stand upon the sites of cities that once were, and are now no more, and to grope among the tombs of dead men. Often enough there is something of truth in this notion . . .'

A. W. Kinglake, *Eothen*

In 1773, Mahomet Bey Abou Dahab, lounging on his divan with the brilliant jewels of his turban sparkling in the candlelight, questioned James Bruce on his return from Abyssinia and on his search for the true source of the Nile. What would Bruce do now, the Pasha wished to know. He was not in business of any sort, so surely there was no reason for him to continue travelling? Bruce told the Pasha that travelling *was* his business. To the Egyptian, this was a matter of wonder. To travel in order to perform the Haj at Mecca was something he could understand. To travel for trade or to make war, or on an embassy to a foreign prince, were also comprehensible. But to travel just to look, merely for the sake of having been somewhere? His wonder was similar to Karen Blixen's, 150 years later. The Danish writer was camping in the Ngong Hills up above Nairobi where the land falls away into the Great Rift Valley. Along the ridge of the hills, the grass was short and a well-defined path led along the heights. 'One morning,' she wrote, 'I came up here and walked along the path, and I found on it fresh tracks and dung of a herd of eland. The big peaceful animals must have been up on the ridge at sunrise, walking in a long row, and you cannot imagine that they had come for any other reason than just to look, deep down on both sides, at the land below.' Mahomet Bey interpreted Bruce's journey in similar terms. The English, he concluded, must be a very great nation if they could afford to send a man of Bruce's obvious qualities 'to perish by hunger and thirst in the sands, or to have his throat cut by the lawless barbarians of the desert' – and all that just to find out where the Nile came from, to see the exact spot.

Maybe, like the eland, Bruce did come just to look, as he said, and to report back. But there were other Europeans behind him, eager to follow his lead, who usually came to do things other than to look; their influence changed the country. Within a hundred years, mainly through their activities, the Suez Canal had been cut, Egypt was opened up by new roads and railways, the old towns were rebuilt along European lines and new ones had been established, with European shops, offices and factories, the ancient sites had been dug up and more modern ones cleared. Egypt might not have been, as the Khedive Ismail wished it to be, a part of Europe, but it was markedly different from its African neighbours.

★

The ruins along the Nile, as we have seen, caught the imagination of a certain group of people in Europe right at the start of the nineteenth century. The more popular side of this interest was less concerned with deciphering hieroglyphics, establishing the true list of kings and rewriting the history of ancient Egypt. The Bible held a central role in the make-up of Victorian values and attitudes and biblical codes of conduct were the ones by which people tended to be judged. Egypt and the Holy Land, especially in their 'fallen' state, were living proof of the wisdom of the teaching in the scriptures – look what had happened to these sacred lands. With each new discovery in Egypt, it was believed that another part of the Bible was being authenticated. The artists who travelled in Egypt later in the century endorsed this popular view: David Roberts might have returned to England in 1839 with more of an architectural than a religious perspective, but William Muller, travelling in the same year, wrote that 'Egypt is full of scriptural subjects, and a Holy Family is found in every Arab village'. Frederick Goodall claimed that his sole reason for going to Egypt in 1859 'was to paint Scriptural Subjects'. The work of these and other artists in this field added to the impact of the collections of antiquities which had been brought back to Europe earlier in the century. Even the Egyptologists had a 'scriptural' streak to them.

While some British travellers went just to look at the sites and monuments of ancient Egypt, others hoped to pick up a few antiquities on the way, either *in situ* or in the Egyptian markets, although by the middle of the nineteenth century travellers were complaining about the difficulty of finding figures or anything else that could be easily removed from the tombs and temples. Some enthusiastic amateurs even tried to organize their own digs in search of new sites in the hope of finding something worth taking home. In 1833 Alexander Hoskins set off up the Nile into Sudan to study the sites between Abu Simbel and Khartoum. In 1837, Colonel Richard Vyse found the entrance to the third Pyramid – of Mycerinus – at Giza. In 1842, the Prussian government sponsored Richard Lepsius and a team of scholars and artists, among them the Englishmen Joseph Bonomi and James Wild, to examine the ruins of the Nile as far as Meroe in the Sudan. Then, in 1850, the French Egyptologist Auguste Mariette was sent out to Egypt by the directors of the Louvre. Mariette's first season's dig uncovered the Serapeum at the old capital of Memphis, the burial place of the sacred Apis bulls and source of many of the Egyptian antiquities now on show in the Louvre. Throughout the century the Egyptian earth was turned, yielding up prehistoric burial pits, new tombs and stone implements – pieces of a lost history which threw light on the development of western civilization.

In Egypt, private collections built up by amateurs like Henry Abbott and the merchant Anthony Harris were open to visits from travellers and Florence Nightingale wrote from Alexandria on 29 November 1849 that 'Yesterday Dr. Abbott showed us his antiquities; he has adopted the Turkish dress and married an Armenian wife . . . one thing I should very much like to have understood, – a funeral papyrus, but it has never been read.' On Easter Monday, 1850, having travelled up the Nile as far as Abu Simbel, Florence Nightingale was in Alexandria again. 'We went before breakfast,' she wrote to her family with some satisfaction, 'to Dr. Abbott's museum, to look at his funeral papyrus, which we could now understand a little about. The different transformations of the dead, different trials, and subduings of successive vices under the form of beasts, like the labours of Hercules, are all there.' Again and again the Victorians found parallels with their own ethics in the works of the ancient Egyptians.

After Mariette's arrival in 1850 and the success of his initial excavations, Said Pasha appointed him as Conservator of Egyptian Monuments and Keeper of Egyptian Antiquities. Until this time there had been no official Egyptian organization for supervising or collecting antiquities. For instance, both Harris's and Abbott's museums were privately owned and run from their own houses, and both of their collections were sold outside Egypt after their deaths: Harris's was bequeathed to his adopted daughter Selima, who sold it in the 1870s to the British Museum, while Abbott's was taken to the United States, exhibited in New York in 1853 and eventually sold to the New York Historical Society. Not even the Egyptian Society, of which Harris was president in 1836, was officially sanctioned: Bonaparte's impetus, which had resulted in the creation of the Institut d'Egypte, had not been sustained by Egypt's rulers. But in appointing Mariette, Said Pasha made a sounder choice than when he signed de Lesseps's canal agreement. Mariette insisted that there should be a government-run museum of antiquities in Egypt and to this end he secured part of an old post office building at Boulak. The present site and building of the Egyptian Museum was not settled upon and opened until 1902. In front of the present building there is a monument to the fathers of Egyptology – to Champollion, Lepsius, Maspero and others – and in its centre is a bust of Mariette.

Before Mariette's appointment, people who wanted to dig for relics in Egypt were supposed to obtain a firman from the Pasha. This was a haphazard affair and some people began digging without official authority – payment of baksheesh usually kept dissenters quiet. Most people did apply to the Pasha for permission to undertake larger works – when Belzoni was ready to start excavating at Thebes, the British Consul-General Henry Salt obtained a firman from Muhammad Ali for himself and appointed the Italian as his contractor, which later caused much bitterness on the part of the explorer. But there had been little difficulty in obtaining the necessary permission since at that time Egyptians showed little interest in the rediscovery of their past and, so long as no treasure was being taken away, foreigners could do more or less as they liked.

At the start of the nineteenth century, foreigners involved in the exploration of ancient Egypt accounted for a large proportion of travellers in the country. But by the time Florence Nightingale travelled, or the Suez Canal was opened, Egyptologists were clearly outnumbered by sightseers – their area of interest increasingly spilled over into the more popular one of tourism. John Gardner Wilkinson, an Englishman who spent twelve years in Egypt – some of them in a mud-brick house he built in the Theban hills – published his scholarly and hugely successful *Manners and Customs of the Ancient Egyptians* in 1837, which for the first time gave some insight into the way the ancient Egyptians had lived. Only six years later, though, he published what was in effect the first guide book to the country entitled *Modern Egypt*. This was a useful handbook for tourists in Egypt. But Wilkinson was a scholar not a tour operator and his readers were not let off lightly; along with the detailed description of the sites, and advice on the most comfortable way to see them, he also gave a list of useful things to do in Egypt which included excavating the temple at Heliopolis, clearing the Sphinx and copying 'the *whole* series of the sculptures and hieroglyphics of one *entire* tomb' in the Valley of the Kings at Thebes.

★

The categories into which foreigners can be divided are not intended to be exclusive, for some travellers were driven by a number of reasons at the same time, often also by the 'Evil Spirit' that Kinglake had written about. For instance, Wilkinson, in the end, was as famous for his work on modern Egypt, which became the basis for the popular and indispensable Murray's guide-book, as he was for his *Ancient Egyptians*. In the same way, Amelia Edwards was more noted for her travel writing than she was for founding the Egypt Exploration Fund, and E. A. Wallis Budge reached a wider audience by writing the *Cook's Handbook for Egypt and the Sudan* than he did with his work as keeper of Egyptian antiquities at the British Museum.

Edward Lane, who arrived in Egypt in 1825, four years after John Gardner Wilkinson, had initially intended to train as an engraver in London, but he contracted typhus and was forced to give up his apprenticeship and to travel abroad for his health. But with a lively and energetic mind, Lane was not the sort of man to travel just for the pleasure or the therapy of it. He studied Arabic before he set off for the East and when he landed at Alexandria, the twenty-four-year-old Englishman wrote that 'I was not visiting Egypt merely for my own amusement, to examine the pyramids and temples and grottoes ... I was about to throw myself entirely among strangers, among a people of whom I had heard the most contradictory accounts; I was to adopt their language, their customs, and their dress; and in order to make as much progress as possible in the study of their literature, it was my intention to associate almost exclusively with the Muslim inhabitants.'

By this time, Bruce, Belzoni, Burckhardt, Irby and Mangles and, among many others, even the Vicomte de Chateaubriand, had published volumes on their travels and observations. More important, Jean François Champollion had published his understanding of the hieroglyphic system in his *Lettre à M. Dacier* three years before, but no one had yet attempted an objective and systematic study of Egypt since Bonaparte's *Description de l'Egypte*. There was new ground to be covered now that hieroglyphics could be read. In addition, the whole field of Arab learning had yet to be charted. Burckhardt's collection of *Arabic Proverbs* which he had compiled while living in Cairo as Sheikh Ibrahim had provided new insight into this field. James Bruce's account of his residence in Egypt – what was believed of it – also added to the accepted view. But it was Lane's work which provided a thoroughly researched basis for an understanding of Islamic society.

It was as well that Lane was not a superstitious man – as Belzoni, to his cost, had found the Arabs to be – for his journey to Egypt was particularly inauspicious. The brig *Findlay* in which he had taken his passage was overtaken by a hurricane off Tunis and the captain, a weak man by Lane's account, was completely unnerved by it. He begged the young scholar to guide the ship himself and, lashed to the wheel to stop him from being swept overboard, steering by the flashes of lightning and later, when the storm passed, by the light of the moon, Lane brought the brig through the hurricane. That was not the end of it. When the ship reached Malta, the crew mutinied – 'seemingly not without reason,' Lane's great-nephew and biographer, Stanley Lane Poole, observed – an event which was communicated to the young Englishman by a pistol shot piercing the pillow on which he was resting.

In Alexandria, Lane stayed with Henry Salt before travelling with the French engineer and explorer, Louis Linant de Bellefonds, up to Cairo. Here again he stayed in the British Consul's house until, through the services of the Scotsman, Osman Effendi, he found a house to rent near the Bab el Hadeed, not far from the present site of Cairo's Rameses Station. Within five days of his arrival in Cairo, Lane was installed in the house and had adopted the local dress. It will be obvious by now that Lane was no ordinary tourist; he applied himself whole-heartedly to whatever he undertook. When he went to the Pyramids at Giza, soon after his arrival, his fleeting tour was not as idle as it appeared to the Arabs there. Two months later, he was back with food and bedding, sketch-books and camera lucida, a new invention consisting of a box with a prism on the front which threw the image of whatever was being observed onto a sheet of paper on its back plate, where it could be traced. The principle was developed into our present-day camera.

With his equipment, Lane found a tomb near the Pyramids which had already been divided into two rooms, each eight feet square. 'In this tomb,' he wrote, 'I took up my abode for a fortnight, and never did I spend a more happy time, though provided with fewer articles of luxury than I might easily and reasonably have procured.'

Lane had two servants with him, an Egyptian and a Nubian whom he had taken on in Cairo, and together they cleaned out the tomb and spread out the mats and mattresses on the rock floor. Lane hung his weapons from a peg in the wall and lit a candle and his pipe. Then, he remembered, 'I looked around me with complacency and felt perfectly satisfied.' During the day he sketched and made notes of his observations of the Pyramids; in the evenings, he sat outside the tomb, smoking his pipe and looking across the valley to Cairo and the Mokattam Hills. 'My appearance corresponded with my mode of living; for on account of my being exposed to considerable changes of atmospheric temperature in passing in and out of the Great Pyramid, I assumed the Hirám (or woollen sheet of the Bedawee), which is a most convenient dress under such circumstances; a part or the whole being thrown about the person according to the different degree of warmth which he may require.' Lane also did away with his shoes and although initially his feet were easily cut, he found that they soon became tougher and that it was easier to climb up and into the Pyramids in bare feet as the local Arabs did. Obtaining food from the neighbouring villages, and joined by a young Bedouin deserter from Muhammad Ali's army who needed somewhere to hide, the two weeks passed quickly for Lane.

If he enjoyed the solitude he had found out at the Pyramids, Lane did not avoid the company of other Europeans in Cairo. Wilkinson and Bonomi, Linant de Bellefonds and Robert Hay were all involved to some extent in the study of the remains of ancient Egypt. If they were not in Cairo, they would meet each other along the river. In March 1826, for instance, Lane hired a dahabieh and sailed up into Upper Egypt and met Hay at Thebes. Then at Philae he met Linant de Bellefonds. Everywhere, though, he studied, sketched and observed. If there were no monuments in sight, he watched the boatmen or the fellahin at work, saw their women come down to the river from the villages to draw water, or young boys lead oxen to the river to drink; he had decided to include this modern aspect of Egypt in his work as well. Lane made two more trips up the Nile before returning to England in 1828 to complete and publish his work.

Although there had never been an attempt to write a complete account of 'known' Egypt, both ancient and modern, Lane found that his manuscript was not greeted with the enthusiasm that he had expected. To embellish the text, Lane had made over a hundred drawings with his camera lucida, but to include these in the book, he was told, would make it a very expensive proposition indeed. Lane, of course, was adamant; his *Description* must include the illustrations. But he was an unknown and untried writer and, unlike Belzoni or Salt, his book did not give first-hand accounts of well-known events, such as bringing to England a popular piece of sculpture. He found it impossible to persuade a publisher to take the risk and this work has therefore never appeared in print. But the effort was not entirely wasted, since the Society for the Diffusion of Useful Knowledge in London showed an interest in publishing the section of the book which described the modern Egyptians. Lane was happy with this – it was something at least – and, with a view to expanding and perfecting it for publication, he arrived back in Egypt in 1833.

He was now thirty-two years old, the age at which Burckhardt had died, and he was more eager than ever to make something of his work. Plague had broken out a few days before his arrival and twenty-three people had already died, although the worst was thought to be over. In Alexandria, Lane stayed with Anthony Harris, a merchant, commissariat official and collector of antiquities. Harris's house backed onto the same garden as Henry Salt's, where Lane had stayed on his first visit to Egypt: 'A part of this garden,' Lane wrote in his diary, 'is converted into a burial-place for the English. Mr. Salt is buried here.' (Salt, who had died in Cairo on 29 October 1827, had been brought back to Alexandria for burial. The monument over his grave included the following inscriptions, which were the basis for the famous Shatby cemeteries: 'His only child, Georgina Henrietta, has been permitted to appropriate this Garden to the interment of European Christians'; in Arabic it said, 'Profane not this sacred ground, where the bodies of believers in Jesus rest in sure and certain hope of a blessed Resurrection.').

Lane's initial reaction on his return to Egypt was one of surprise. He found Alexandria dirty, the villages squalid, the people miserable. Cairo, he noticed, was swarming with prostitutes, the wives or lovers of men pressed into the Pasha's army, who were left with no other way of supporting themselves. 'I see scarcely one good-looking young woman among a hundred, or scarcely one where I used to see a score; and almost all are in rags.' Even Muhammad Ali no longer rode through the streets with a large number of servants and runners. The grandeur was gone and all he could find to cheer him was that the city seemed a little cleaner.

As soon as he reached the capital, he visited 'my old friend 'Osmán,' who had found him a house next door to his own. Of his new home Lane wrote, 'It's situated in the most healthy part of the town, near the N.W. angle; and, to me, who have suffered from ophthalmia, it is a desirable residence, as it has glass windows.' No sooner was he installed than old friends began to arrive – like the 'sheykh Ahmad (or *seyd* Ahmad, for he is a *shereef*) . . . He has resumed his old habit of visiting me almost every day; both for the sake of getting his dinner or supper, or at least tobacco and coffee, and to profit in his trade of bookseller.'

For the next two years Lane lived among the Arabs of Cairo and studied their ways for his book. On the last day of the 'Eed, at the end of Ramadan, 12 February 1834, Lane wrote in his diary that 'This day I accompanied my neighbour 'Osmán to visit the tomb of the sheykh Ibraheem, in the cemetery of Báb en-Nasr, on the north of the city, to see that the monument was in good repair, and to pay to the memory of the lamented traveller that tribute of respect which is customary on the occasion of the 'Eed.' At the cemetery they had to force their way through a crowd of children playing on swings and adults watching conjurors and dancing girls, but 'we soon arrived at the tomb of the sheykh Ibraheem. It is a plain and humble monument of the usual oblong form, constructed of the common, coarse, calcareous stone of the neighbouring mountain range of Mukattam, with a stele of the same stone, roughly cut, and without any inscription, at the head and foot.' Here, as was customary, they paid a fakir to recite passages from the Koran – 'He did it very rapidly, and without much reverence, seated at the foot of the tomb' – and a palm branch was then broken up and laid over the tomb. The scene might have passed unnoticed at the time, with others paying their respects at nearby graves, but it is worth pausing to consider it now. Here, chanting the Koran with an Egyptian fakir, was a young scholar from Hereford and a drummer-boy from Scotland. Both were dressed in Arab costume, both now looked 'eastern', and both travelled under assumed names – Lane as Mansour Effendi and Donald as Osman Effendi. They were praying their adopted prayers at the grave of a Swiss traveller who had died young and who had also travelled in disguise and under an assumed name. In a way they were imposters, and yet Lane and Burckhardt did more to further awareness of the way in which the Arabs lived than almost anyone else in the century.

Osman, as Sheikh Ibrahim's faithful servant, did well to bring Mansour Effendi to his master's tomb and he was equally right to give him Ibrahim's certificate of pilgrimage to Mecca, an odd-sounding document, 'the greater part occupied by a representation of the temple of Mekkeh,' Lane wrote, 'drawn with ink, and ornamented with red, yellow, and green, and with silver leaf.' The document stated that 'The respected Hágg Ibraheem hath performed the pilgrimage, according to the divine ordinances, and accomplished all the incumbent ordinances of the Prophet, completely and perfectly. And God is the best of witnesses.' The significance of the gesture goes beyond friendship – Lane was Burckhardt's successor in many ways.

On his thirty-third birthday, seven months after the visit to Burckhardt's tomb, Lane wrote that 'I have completed, as far as I can see, my notes on the manners and customs of the Muslims in Egypt. I have only to look over them . . .' Another three months later, at the beginning of the new year 1835, and he had begun to write out a fair copy. But the plague spread from Alexandria to Cairo and, the day after the first death was reported in the capital, of a Maltese from Alexandria, Lane hired a boat to take him into Upper Egypt. Three days later, on 8 January, he left the dock at Boulak with a Mr Fresnel for company.

At Thebes he had intended to live in a tomb 'which had been converted into a convenient dwelling by Mr. Wilkinson and Mr. Hay. We found Mr. Gosset occupying one apartment of it: I have taken possession of another apartment . . . and Mr. Fresnel has settled in a tomb just below, which was occupied by Bonomi and other artists in the employ of Mr. Hay.' Lane paid a man called 'Owad who looked after the tombs – probably on his own authority and initiative – fifteen piastres a month as rent. However, far from being safe there, the plague spread along the river settlements, carried by boatmen and travellers and the inevitable rats, and on Good Friday Lane reported that a man had died in their own valley. By this time the Englishman was getting worried: he was not ready to die. Since the man who died of the plague was a relation of the guard, Lane sent the guard away and put himself into quarantine. Others did the same, and the French Consul-General, who was staying at Luxor at the time, banned all communication between the two sides of the river except for the delivery of food from the east bank every two days. Not even this worked, though. On 20 April, three days after the first death in the valley, Lane recorded a second fatality. He put himself in total quarantine, which meant that he saw and touched no one for the next three weeks, and this seemed to work for, by 9 May, there had been no further incidents and the whole settlement gave up its quarantine and waited for better news from the north.

Lane did not leave Thebes until the end of June, but when he got back to Cairo he found that the city had been devastated. The plague, he recorded in his diary 'has destroyed a third, or more of the population of the city, about 80,000 persons; chiefly young persons, between 10 and 25 years of age: and most of these females. It has also been particularly fatal to Franks and other foreigners.' The traveller Alexander Kinglake, who had arrived in Cairo during the plague, had met Osman Effendi, whom he thought seemed afraid of having any contact with him in case he was infected. 'The fear of the Plague,' Kinglake wrote sadly, 'is its forerunner. It is likely enough that at the time of my seeing poor Osman the deadly taint was beginning to creep through his veins, but it was not till after I had left Cairo that he was visibly stricken. He died.'

Lane had a similar fear of the plague. He had been too ill as a young man to risk putting himself into contact with the plague. There were also too many earlier travellers who had died before their time. His manuscript was now ready and, in August, a few weeks after his return to Cairo, he left Egypt for England. The following year his first book,

An Account of the Manners and Customs of the Modern Egyptians, was published, and the subsequent new editions of 1837, 1842 and 1846 are confirmation of its success. The book is still in print. What Lane captured in his *Modern Egyptians* was a final flourishing of a centuries'-old culture, one which had enchanted Burckhardt before him. Lane refers many times in his own book to the value of Burckhardt's perception of Arabic customs and to his collection of *Arabic Proverbs*. 'I write these words in Cairo,' Lane explained, 'with his [Burckhardt's] book before me.' The editor of the fifth edition of *Modern Egyptians* was E. Stanley Poole, Lane's nephew, who noted that 'Mr. Lane wrote his account of the "Modern Egyptians," when they could, for the last time, be described. Twenty-five years of steam communication with Egypt have more altered its inhabitants than had the preceding five centuries.'

*

Among the steadily growing number of passengers who took advantage of steam communication with Egypt, many were on their way between England and India. Of these, some had no time to visit the Pyramids and the other attractions around Cairo, but hurried on to Suez or Alexandria to board their steamers, while others broke their journey in Cairo and headed off up-river. An alternative to crossing from Suez to Cairo was to leave ship at the Red Sea port of Cosseir, from which James Bruce had set off into the Red Sea.

Henry Fane arrived in Cosseir in 1840, fresh from his post as aide-de-camp to the Commander-in-Chief in India. He found it an unprepossessing town. Fane had left Bombay on 1 January on board the East India Company's steamer *Zenobia* with about twenty other passengers, all bound for England. As they steamed up the Red Sea for Suez, the captain offered to stop at Cosseir if anybody wished to land there. Since Fane had described his cabin on the steamer as a 'dog-hole' he was only too glad of the chance to get off early. He and three others decided to make their way overland to Luxor and sail down to Cairo from there.

When they landed at Cosseir they were met by what Fane called the British agent, 'a fat native gentleman', who took them to his house from where they made their arrangements for the trip to Thebes. Agents at this time were very often unofficial and unpaid, but had acquired their 'agency' by having a reputation for being able to help out and to organize transport. Fane called Cosseir 'a filthy hole – wretched in the extreme, perhaps holding a thousand inhabitants, whose means of subsistence it would be very difficult to determine.' He and his three fellow-travellers left the following morning.

There is little but desert between Cosseir and Luxor. Apart from the life around oases, the wind blows nothing but sand over sand. Perhaps because he had just come from India and had been on active service in Afghanistan, Fane was undaunted by the desert journey. Certainly they were well enough equipped. They borrowed a tent, which had been sent to Cosseir by the East India Company for the use of travellers across this desert, and hired the rest of their equipment. With three 'fellows' to pitch the tent, one French-speaking servant and a cook, they set off on a dozen camels with another dozen donkeys following behind laden with cooking implements, tea cups and cutlery. 'With this set-out,' Fane wrote in his journal, 'and the addition of some fresh water, potted soups, and some eggs, chickens, wine, and beer, we made our exit from Cosseir, bidding adieu to our civil friend the agent, who first begged out of us a silver spoon and fork.'

On their first day, they covered twenty-six miles, half of it on foot for some unexplained reason. 'The whole of today's route,' Fane reported, 'put me much in mind of the worst part of Affghanistan,' except that he thought the Egyptian desert had less watering holes. On the fourth day of their travels, they came across the Nile valley. The desert had bored Fane – nothing happened and there was little that he found worth seeing. He dismissed it in what became a recognizable manner by deciding that it was 'only fit for camels and Arabs'. The joy of leaving the desert was sweet indeed. 'Instead of barren and wretched country, such as that we had now happily left behind us, we now looked down upon a rich and varied scene, the noble river running through huge sheets of cultivation, mixed with villages, and in the distance the ruins of the great city of Thebes.'

Fane and his party arrived at Karnak on 22 January 1840. The crops were high in the fields. The river was fast-flowing. He thought the temple complex at Karnak was probably the largest structure that man had ever built and considered Luxor, where they pitched their tent, to be a 'wretched hole, chiefly remarkable for dirt and pigeons'. Strangely enough, for this was prime touring time, they met no other Europeans on the east bank that day, although there was evidence in the form of grafitti that certain Smiths and Thompsons had been there recently. The following day, however, when they returned from the west bank and the Valley of the Kings, they met an American couple and, during their dinner, 'an Englishman, a Mr. D., paid us a visit, he being on his way to the cataracts of the Nile. He seemed by no means cut out for a traveller; he was well packed up in a Mackintosh, and complained grievously of the cold night air.'

Fane's journey through Egypt has a remarkably modern aspect to it – speed. He rushed across the desert in four days, which is understand-able, spent only another four days looking over Karnak, Luxor and Thebes and then, instead of heading up-river to Philae, he went down to Cairo: more like a 1980s American Express tour than an early Victor-ian journey. He liked much of what he saw, though, including the temple of Dendera – 'magnificent' – and he enjoyed the Turkish bath at Asyut – 'not to be despised' – but cared less for the rock tombs at Beni Hassan, although like the present-day travellers who make the journey out there he eventually conceded that 'altogether, I did not regret having gone.' But there is a note of relief in his writing when he finally reaches Cairo and checks into the hotel of Messrs Hill & Raven, the rivals of Thomas Waghorn. 'Found the house very comfor-table and clean,' Fane reported, 'and, as usual in a place where so many English congregate, not without meeting an acquaintance or two.'

Fane spent a week in Cairo, seeing the sights – the citadel, the tombs of the Mamelukes, Dr Abbott's collection of antiquities, Muhammad Ali's 'English' garden at Roda, which was tended by a Scottish gardener, and, of course, the Pyramids. Here he climbed the Great Pyramid which he confesses was 'one of the most fatiguing jobs I have ever had the misfortune to try,' went into the two opened Pyramids and then had tiffin in a nearby tomb, before setting off back to the hotel.

In Alexandria Colonel Hodges, the British Consul-General, took Fane and 'a tolerably numerous party, mostly Englishmen' to see Muhammad Ali. Visiting the Pasha was an important part of a certain type of tourist itinerary, and if you were not invited to an audience you felt slighted. Fane and the rest of the group rode to the Pasha's palace, were shown right in – like all good tours – straight up a flight of stairs and into a marble hall. 'From this,' he wrote, 'we entered another, surrounded with divans and hung with bad prints of men-of-war, in the left corner of which was seated Mehemet Ali, Pasha of Egypt. He acknowledged our introduction by a slight bend of his head.' For the next halfhour, Colonel Hodges talked with the Pasha, while the tourists looked on and made notes. Then they left without more ado.

After a full week in Alexandria, Fane paid his hotel bill and boarded the steamer *Megaera* and, nearly seven weeks later, had 'the inexpressible pleasure' of seeing the white cliffs of England and Falmouth harbour. He had been five and a half weeks in Egypt, from being dropped off in Cosseir to boarding in Alexandria. During this time he had seen some of the finest sights that the country had to offer and had not been so very badly inconvenienced while doing so. All in all he thought that the transit had been a good one, and it had only cost him just over £20 – with maybe another £6 or so for the boat from Thebes to Cairo. Apart from the shortage of water crossing the desert to Thebes, 'no difficulty of any kind occurs,' he concluded, with a recommendation for his readers that 'coming *from* India, it is a route I should strongly recommend to all overland travellers.'

Most overland travellers, however, chose not to take Fane's recommendation, preferring instead to follow in the footsteps of Eliza Fay by crossing from Alexandria to Suez. The novelist William Thackeray arrived in Egypt on his P&O 'promotional tour' four years after Fane had sailed for home, in 1844. From the Alexandria steamer, he raced into Cairo on a donkey, crossed the gardens of the Ezbekieh and arrived at a 'fine new white building with HOTEL D'ORIENT written up in huge French characters . . . As a hundred Christian people, or more, come from England and from India every fortnight, this inn has been built to accommodate a large proportion of them, and twice a month, at least, its sixty rooms are full.' Almost all of these 'Christian people' whom Thackeray was observing were travelling between Alexandria and Suez because it was quicker and safer than heading up the Nile and then crossing to Cosseir. It was such a well-worn route, now, that he joked that 'The road between Cairo and Suez is *jonché* with soda-water corks. Tom Thumb and his brother might track their way across the desert by these landmarks.'

Installed in his 'overland' hotel in Cairo, Thackeray noticed that 'the court is full of bustling dragomans, ayahs, and children from India; and poor old venerable he-nurses with grey beards and crimson turbans, tending little white-faced babies that have seen the light at Dumdum and Futtyghur.' In one sense, now, the East did not start until they were outside their hotels, for inside everything was so familiar. At six o'clock that evening, for instance, the dinner gong was struck and 'Sixty people sit down to a quasi-French banquet: thirty Indian officers in moustaches and jackets.' The rest were civilians, among whom he particularly appreciated the bare-shouldered ladies with hair arranged in ringlets, who had pale complexions and a penchant for pale ale. After dinner, during which he believed he had finally discovered the fleshpots of Egypt – but was that donkey-flesh he had just eaten, he wondered? – the ladies retired to another room and the men passed round the pale French brandy.

What did they say to each other, these Englishmen abroad? Perhaps the only thing they had in common with each other was their nationality and the fact that they were all away from home. The differences between them would have been more striking. We take so much of our travelling for granted now. It would not surprise anyone to meet a Japanese on the Nile or an Englishman in the Maldives. But then, only seven years after Victoria became Queen of England, when travel for anyone other than explorers, traders and soldiers was a novelty and entirely unpredictable, these Englishmen seem to have thought it no more remarkable that they should all be sitting around a table in Cairo than if they had been in their clubs along Pall Mall. 'One of the Indians offers a bundle of Bengal cheroots,' Thackeray reported, 'and we make acquaintance with these honest bearded white-jacketed Majors and military commanders, finding England here in a French hotel kept by an Italian, at the city of Grand Cairo, in Africa.'

★

The excitement of Cairo's streets, the elaborate intricacies of the Oriental mind, the unsolved mysteries of the Pyramids and the riddle of the Sphinx, the contrasts that were to be seen everywhere in Egypt – Flaubert wrote that 'splendid things gleam in the dust' – these were powerful and romantic attractions. They took hold of Europeans and Americans in search of escape from the march of industry or society in their own countries. The lure was indiscriminate – there was no scheme to those who were caught in it. John Barker, the British Consul-General from Henry Salt's death until 1833, was clearly excited by the country. A man of fine sensibility, he gathered together an important collection of antiquities during his time in the East, although his attitude towards the relics of Egypt's past was not always reverential. Whereas George Baldwin, Consul before him, had drunk a toast from the top of the Pyramid, Barker went one or two steps further: on 29 June 1829 he wrote that 'we were amused in our trip to Cairo, by a view of the Pyramids, on the top of the largest of which my daughter danced a quadrille.' Clearly the sanctity of the ancient burial tombs did not press down upon him with too much force. There seems to be something irresistible about these monuments; generation after generation use them as a backdrop for their own activities and each is dwarfed by the magnificence of the Pyramids.

At the same time as John Barker was representing the British government in Egypt, a young Englishman by the name of Maze arrived in the East. He was the son of a Bristol merchant, well-known in the Levant, who operated from Smyrna (the modern Izmir in Turkey) where Barker had also acted as Consul. Maze travelled from England to Egypt in March 1831 apparently with just a single portmanteau which later, upon examination, was found to contain one change of linen and a watch. Whoever the young man fell into conversation with on the way from Alexandria to Cairo remembered that his sole topic of conversation was the Pyramids. He was clearly obsessed with the idea of them, as many are, and his excitement as he approached Cairo was obvious.

Admirers of the Pyramids – in fact all but the most dull-minded – find the view towards the monuments from Cairo a stirring one. For Maze it must have been overwhelming. He was here at last and, leaving the city, his sights fixed upon the plateau of Giza, he made his way across the Nile by ferry and then rode through the fields to the edge of the desert where the Pyramids stood, as though they had been waiting for him. As he approached the monuments, he was greeted, inevitably, by a group of Arabs. They would help him climb up to the top of the Great Pyramid, for the building of which Herodotus relates that the Pharaoh Cheops prostituted his own daughter and on the top of which, more recently, Barker's daughters had danced their quadrille. No doubt they told the young English tourist that the view from the top was beautiful – very fine. No doubt they also told him that it was safe, that no one had ever come to any harm when they had been around.

Maze accepted their help and soon reached the broad flat platform at the summit where the apex stones have been worn and stripped away by nature and man in concert. From here, he would have been able to see to the west where the desert stretches across the African continent and forms a buffer between the northern and southern hemispheres. To the east lay the fields and palm trees of the Nile valley, burning now as the summer approached. And beyond the valley, desert again. But even if he had studied the view, it was not in the scenery that his interest lay. He had come to Egypt to climb the Great Pyramid and then to throw himself off it. According to Barker the Arabs with him did whatever they could to stop him from doing so, but he was not to be denied: he jumped and was dead when they found him below.

Maze's death shocked the foreign communities in Egypt. There was no doubt that it was suicide, of course, since, as Barker wrote, 'there is no instance of the kind in the traditions of Egypt that a person has ever fallen off the Pyramids'. He could have been pushed, but presumably that possibility had been explored and dismissed. But the idea of someone coming all the way out from England with the sole intention of throwing himself off a Pyramid was clearly absurd. Barker's son Edward, who later became Consul himself, concluded that Maze must have been insane and have wanted to achieve immortality by linking his name with that of the Pyramids. If that was the young Englishman's intention, to a certain extent he succeeded.

Some of John Frederick Lewis's friends and relations thought that he, too, was a little insane, but he was looking for something other than immortality in Egypt: he came to sketch and paint. David Roberts had spent less than five months in the country, during the winter of 1838–9, and returned to England with sketches, notes and paintings, convinced – and rightly so – that he had collected material that 'will serve me for the rest of my life'. Even before Roberts produced his masterly *Egypt and Nubia*, the Oriental subject in painting, as in literature and drama was popular. After the extraordinary success of Roberts's work, Egypt was even more important for European artists and, during the next decade, Vernet, Wilkie, Richard Dodd, Edward Lear and Narcisse Berchere all came to paint. As William Thackeray noticed in 1844, 'There is a fortune to be made for painters in Cairo, and materials for a whole Academy of them. I never saw such a variety of architecture, of life, of picturesqueness, of brilliant colour, and light and shade. There is a picture in every street, and at every bazaar stall.'

Lewis travelled to Egypt, like Edward Lane, to study and record modern Egyptians. He was less interested in the biblical aspect of the subject. As Lane produced his account of the modern Egyptians' manners and customs in his prose, so Lewis intended to capture it in oils and watercolours. Two of his great strengths as an artist were his sustained attention to detail and his interpretation of colour. The Egyptian scenes he chose for his larger works – 'the Mid-day Meal, Cairo', for instance, which he based on a scene in the upper gallery of his own house in the city, and 'The Hhareem' – rely on these qualities. The subject matter – the elaborate carvings of the mushrabiyeh screens or the patterns of the fabrics on clothes and divans – demanded great care; Lewis's representation was faithful. In all daytime subjects, there was the power of the sun to take into consideration and Lewis observed the way in which it drained all colours of their strength – fabrics especially bleached in sunlight.

If the Egyptian subject suited Lewis's painting skills, the way of life suited his temperament just as well. He found a freedom which he had longed for in England. During his tour of the country, William Thackeray, who had been a friend of Lewis's in London, paid a visit to the painter's house, 'far away from the haunts of European civilization, in the Arab quarter'. The entrance to the house was down a shaded alley and Thackeray, leaving his donkey with a servant at the gate, entered a courtyard with galleries all around it. A camel was resting on the grass. Chickens and pigeons pecked in the dust. As he looked around at the windows, the writer saw a pair of eyes staring at him from behind a screen in an arched window. They were large, dark, beautiful eyes – undoubtedly feminine. Now why, Thackeray wondered, was there a woman hiding in the house?

Thackeray was then led into another part of the house where he expected to see his friend but where, instead, he was led by a grey-bearded servant, in a blue robe with a broad red sash around his stomach, into a great hall about forty feet long and twenty feet high. Here he was invited to sit on a divan while the servant went away to bring him a pipe to smoke. Left alone again, Thackeray studied the carved and gilded ceiling, the frieze with its Arabic inscriptions, the great bay window and the garden outside. While he was taking all this in, another man entered the hall. This one was wearing a yellow robe and a red tarboosh wrapped round with a white turban. His long, dark beard was flecked with grey – his head had been shaved. 'It was some time,' Thackeray remembered, 'as the Americans say, before I could "realise" the *semillant* J – of old times.' Lewis kicked off his outer slippers, sat on the divan, clapped his hands and summoned his servant Mustapha, and then began at last to remind Thackeray of his London companion – 'his Oriental coolness and langour gave way to British cordiality'.

The two friends talked about England and Egypt, then and over a dinner prepared by Lewis's Egyptian cook, which Thackeray relived on the page: 'We had delicate cucumbers stuffed with forced-meats; yellow smoking pilaffs, the pride of the Oriental cuisine; kid and fowls à l'Aboukir and à la Pyramide: a number of little savoury plates of legumes of the vegetable-marrow sort: kibobs with an excellent sauce of plums and piquant herbs. We ended the repast with ruby pomegranates, pulled to pieces, deliciously cool and pleasant. For the meats, we certainly ate them with the Infidel knife and fork; but for the fruit, we put our hands into the dish and flicked them into our mouths in what cannot but be the true Oriental manner.' As if in jest, he then adds that he asked if the cook could rustle them up a lamb cooked with pistachio nuts, and then perhaps some cream tarts *au poivre*, but these were not served.

After the dinner, which was washed down with a few bottles of beer 'prepared by the two great rivals, Hadji Hodson and Bass Bey', Thackeray at last managed to broach the subject which had been bothering him throughout his visit and which was even in part responsible for his coming to Egypt. Lewis, the writer insisted, was a London-bred man. He belonged in society, was still expected at his club, was missed by his family who were more than a little disturbed by the news that their darling John Frederick was seen rushing around a strange and heathen city with a long beard, blue embroidered suit – 'a pair of trousers, which would make a set of dresses for an English family'

– and a scimitar pushed into his sash. To do it for a while, rather like living out a prolonged fancy-dress ball – that was just about all right. But Lewis had been away for nearly five years now. What did he think he was playing at? '. . . Home, London, a razor, your sister to make tea, a pair of moderate Christian breeches in lieu of those enormous Turkish shulwars,' Thackeray suggested, 'are vastly more convenient in the long run.' Or was there some attachment of a more personal nature, of which Lewis's family and friends were unaware? Who was the lady with the large, dark eyes who had stared at Thackeray in the courtyard?

Thackeray, Lewis insisted, had misunderstood his motives. The dark eyes belonged to an Egyptian woman who was his cook – she had prepared their dinner – and, upon his honour, there was nothing more to it than that. What he loved about Egypt and what kept him there was the 'dreamy, hazy, lazy, tobaccofied life'. He had leisure. There were no dinner parties he had to go to. He did not have to wear white kid gloves or starched shirts. Across the city in Shepheard's Hotel, for instance, they were probably dressing for dinner at that moment, but Lewis wanted to get away from all that. Even his reclusive life in Cairo was a little too public for him sometimes. His friends, or the acquaintances of his friends, indeed anyone who had even the faintest connection with him or the remotest pretext to visit, seemed to call as they passed through the city. Then, with his time no longer his own, Lewis would long to be in the desert where he was excused from all social obligations. In the desert there was little to do but sit in his tent, smoking, or ride through the sands on a fine Arab mount. There were no crowds there. He could be free. The desert was a place apart.

What must Thackeray have thought of all this? His reaction is probably only partly stated in his *Notes of a Journey from Cornhill to Grand Cairo*. As a go-between from the London clubbers to their desert-won outcast, he had found himself in the Arab quarter of Cairo, sitting on a divan with his old friend – 'venerable and Bey-like' – and with a 'Turkified European' who had arrived during dinner. On the way back to the Hotel d'Orient, with darkness around him, two guides running ahead with lanterns, he was touched by the silence in the city. It was complete and restful, broken occasionally by a prayer from a mosque, or the challenge of a sentry or night watchman, and by the 'howling and singing' of a man in the madhouse. Trapped by bars, but believing himself to be a Prince, he is 'one poor fellow still talking to the moon,' which seems to be not entirely different an opinion from the one Thackeray held of his own dear Lewis, indulging himself in

James Bruce (1730–94), the Nile explorer (from his own *Travels to discover the source of the Nile*, 1768–73)

Bruce's canja under sail (from Bruce's *Travels...*)

Giovanni Belzoni (1778–1823), the Italian entrepreneur who opened the Second Pyramid at Giza and the Great Temple at Abu Simbel (*Hulton Picture Library*)

Henry Salt (1780–1827), the British Consul–General who, with Jean Louis Burckhardt, presented the head of Rameses II to the British Museum (*Mary Evans Picture Library*)

David Roberts's painting of the entrance to the Temple of Luxor after the French had removed one of its two obelisks (*Henry Sotheran Ltd*)

Thomas Waghorn (1800–50), pioneer of the Overland route from England to India (*Hulton Picture Library*)

The Mahmoudieh Canal, completed in 1820, which linked Alexandria with the Nile (*Private collection*)

Khedive Ismail (1830–95). At the opening of the Suez Canal in 1869, he announced that 'Egypt is henceforth part of Europe, not Africa.' (*Hulton Picture Library*)

Khedive Ismail's dahabieh, loaned to the Prince and Princess of Wales during their visit before the opening of the Suez Canal (*The Fine Art Society; by William Simpson*)

The first boats through the Suez Canal in November 1869 (*Hulton Picture Library*)

The British royal family did not attend the opening of the Suez Canal, but many British visitors were there for the celebrations (*Hulton Picture Library*)

The Opera House in Cairo, built by the Khedive Ismail, where Verdi's *Aida* was first performed (*Private collection*)

After the riots that followed the British bombardment of Alexandria in 1882, many buildings in the European quarter were left in ruins (*Royal Geographical Society*)

his Arab house with his dark-eyed cook and his venerable servants, just 'like a languid Lotus-eater'.

*

In 1850, the year before Lewis left Cairo for England – his painting of 'The Hhareem' had been widely acclaimed when it was exhibited at the Old Water Colour Society in London – a twenty-eight-year-old Frenchman and an Englishwoman one year older than him, both travelled up the Nile as far as Abu Simbel and then returned to Cairo on their way back to Europe. They did not travel together and there is no definite record that they ever met each other. The only connections they have are that they both wrote letters to their families at home, recording their journey on the Nile, and that within seven years they were both famous: Florence Nightingale for her pioneering nursing activities in the Crimea, and Gustave Flaubert as the notorious and prosecuted author of *Madame Bovary*. Both were tourists travelling for distraction – Miss Nightingale to escape English 'society' and her sadness at having rejected a proposal of marriage from someone she loved, in the hope of becoming something other than a wife; Flaubert in order to amuse himself, to consider the criticisms levelled at his fantasy *The Temptation of Saint Anthony* and on account of his health – and both joined the expeditions of their friends.

Flaubert arrived in Alexandria on 17 November, 1849, in the company of one of his closest friends, the much travelled Maxime Du Camp, and a servant called Sassetti, an ex-dragoon. 'I gulped down a whole bellyful of colours, like a donkey filling himself with hay,' he wrote to his mother from the port. But he was soon dismissing Alexandria as being too European, far too familiar, where his trousers were let out by a French tailor, his financial arrangements were made with a French banker, and his security was guaranteed by the great Soliman Pasha, the French Colonel Sève in command of the Viceroy's army. A few days later he and Du Camp, who was on an official mission for the Institut de France, to photograph the monuments and inscriptions he encountered in Egypt, were dressed up in white tie and tails to see the Egyptian Minister of Foreign Affairs and the French Consul.

Two days after Flaubert and Du Camp disembarked in Alexandria's harbour, Florence Nightingale arrived in the East with her maid, Trout, and her two companions, the well-known travellers Charles and Selina Bracebridge – 'and oh!' she wrote to her family, 'that I could tell you the new world of old poetry, of Bible images, of light, and life, and beauty which that word opens'. But she also found Alexandria too

83

European, too cosmopolitan. She and her companions were looked after by the English community. Mr Gilbert, the British Consul, called to pay his respects within an hour of their landing; they stayed in the Frank Square and went to the Anglican Church where, after the service, they talked to the priest, the Rev Winder.

Flaubert's travels in Egypt have been called 'a sensibility on tour' by the editor of his letters and notes, Francis Steegmuller. Flaubert was in Egypt to enjoy himself and to be inspired. 'I live like a plant,' he wrote to his mother from Cairo, 'filling myself with sun and light, with colours and fresh air. I keep eating, so to speak; afterwards the digesting will have to be done, then the shitting; and the shitting had better be good! That's the important thing.' He tried to lose himself in Egypt and soon did away with his too-tight trousers, his white tie and tails. 'I am wearing a large white cotton Nubian shirt, trimmed with little pompoms ... My head is completely shaved except for one lock at the occiput (by which Mohammed lifts you up on Judgment Day) and adorned with a tarboosh which is of a screaming red and made me half die of heat the first days I wore it. We look quite the pair of Orientals.' But he noticed that he was paid more respect when he dressed as a European than as an Egyptian or Turk and so, for safety's sake, he decided to control what he called his 'sartorial splurges'.

On 25 November 1849, early in the morning, a little steamer towed a boat out of Alexandria along the Mahmoudieh Canal towards Cairo, and it seems likely that both Florence Nightingale and Gustave Flaubert were on board. Florence makes no mention of any French passengers on the boat, but Flaubert refers to 'an English family, hideous; the mother looks like a sick old parrot (because of the green eyeshades attached to her bonnet) ...' Was he referring to Selina Bracebridge? Since Florence said 'we have hardly any English, no Indians, for luckily it is not transit week,' it is possible that they were the four English people whom Flaubert mistook for a family.

When they reached Atfeh they all transferred to a boat on the Nile, Florence with the Bracebridges in a cabin below, Flaubert and Du Camp up on deck. From her cabin window, that evening, Florence watched the moon set and the stars shine. The water glistened around them. At six o'clock Venus, the morning star, rose while Flaubert and Du Camp dozed in their camp beds in the open air. It was the first night that any of them had spent on the Nile and, as tourists, they were inspired. Flaubert recited poetry, thought of Cleopatra, and also watched the stars shine. 'Such rapture!' he wrote. The great river did not disappoint them and, when they woke the following morning, there were the Pyramids to their right, and the citadel and Muhammad

Ali's mosque over to the left. It was an impressive introduction to Cairo; the less impressive part of arrival – the considerable delays and struggles they suffered at the harbour of Boulak, which one now encounters at Cairo's Heliopolis Airport – was soon lost beside the wonder and excitement of the larger monuments. But within an hour of their arrival at Boulak, they were on their way along the avenue of acacias which led to the gates of Cairo. With their bags strapped onto camels, Arab runners clearing the way ahead of them, they made their way into the European quarter of the city, to Ezbekieh Square where, fifty-two years before, Bonaparte had taken up residence in the palace of Elfi Bey, where the travellers now went to their respective hotels: Florence and the Bracebridges to the Hotel de l'Europe and Flaubert with Du Camp to the Hotel d'Orient.

Touring in Egypt was a more refined affair by the middle of the century. In Alexandria and Cairo, the hotels and cafés, societies and meeting-houses established for foreigners were flourishing. The inheritors of Muhammad Ali's divan ruled from Alexandria and Cairo but attempted to keep just as tight a check on Upper Egypt as the founder of the dynasty had – the corvée and conscription were unpopular but they were also the most obvious way for a pasha to exhibit his authority. Egypt was a public country in that what went on at one end was soon known about at the other. The river carried everything with its flow. News would arrive in Cairo with a boatload of slaves or skins from Aswan. Information was received up-river with the latest detachment sent to guard the border with Sudan. Flaubert was attracted to Egypt because it matched his own preconceived images of what the East ought to be, of the magical Orient. That there were temples and tombs to look at, and for Du Camp to photograph, was all well and good, but there were also villages to explore along the river, markets, singers and dancers and above all for him, there were prostitutes. Some of the most memorable passages in Flaubert's extraordinary letters describe his experiences with the almehs, with La Triestina, 'a small woman, blonde, red-faced' – with the famous Kuchuk Hanem at Esneh, 'a tall, splendid creature, lighter in colouring than an Arab' – and with Azizeh in Aswan, 'tall, slender, black'. The almehs were supposedly named from the Arabic word *awaleim*, which as Flaubert happily noted 'means "learned woman," "blue-stocking," or "whore" – which proves, Monsieur, that in all countries women of letters . . . !!!' Flaubert was captivated by the open sensuality of the almehs, by the way that Kuchuk Hanem danced to the music provided by a one-eyed old man and a child, both of whom play the *rebabah* – 'Kuchuk's dance is brutal. She squeezes her bare breasts together with her jacket. She puts on a girdle fashioned from a brown shawl with gold stripes, with three tassels hanging on ribbons. She rises first on one foot, then on the other – marvellous movement ... I have seen this dance on old Greek vases.' This was perfect material for Flaubert's romantic vision and the sights he records with feeling – the poor village life, the mournful chants of the boatmen, the burnt-out sun setting behind the western hills – all reaffirm this view. And while the temples were magnificent, they 'bore me profoundly. Are they going to become like the churches in Brittany, the waterfalls in the Pyrenees? Oh necessity! To do what you are supposed to do; to be always, according to circumstances (and despite the aversion of the moment), what a young man, or a tourist, or an artist, or a son, or a citizen, etc. is supposed to be!' Flaubert wanted freedom, not just of movement, but of thought and of feeling as well, and he found it in Egypt.

Florence Nightingale was looking for a very different kind of freedom. There were no almehs or dancing girls for her; instead there was time on the dahabieh, named the *Parthenope* after her sister, for her to think and read and to write her letters home. There was peace and solitude in the desert – as Lewis had found – and as Florence discovered at Abu Simbel where 'I saw nothing, met nothing, that had life, or *had had* life, but the whitened bones of a poor camel ... the golden sand, north, south, east, and west, except where the blue Nile flowed, strewn with bright purple granite stones, the black ridges of mountains ...' She was glad, too, to be away from society and to be watching instead the Nubians leading camels along the river bank, women bringing a flock of sheep to drink at a pool beside the river, which made her 'think of Rebekah and the Hebrews' task'. But most of all she was struck by the ancient monuments, proof of a past greatness. She enjoyed learning about the beliefs of the pharaonic Egyptians and compared it with learning a language, one in which she was quite fluent by the time she returned to Cairo.

The modern Egyptians delighted her with their more picturesque qualities, but horrified her with the poverty and squalor in which so many of them lived. '... No European,' she informed her parents, 'can have the least idea of the misery of an African village; if he has not seen it, no description brings it home.' She wanted to be able to do something for them, of course, but she had not yet found a way of doing so – the Crimea and her hospital at Scutari were still four years away. For now she was just a tourist, an onlooker.

Florence and Flaubert were both tourists on the Nile before tourist traffic built up. In their three-cabin boats – Flaubert's blue canja and its crew of nine, the Bracebridges' dahabieh with a sitting cabin painted with green panels and with divans along the walls – they moved with the winds up-river to Abu Simbel and floated back down on the stream, stopping at villages which were still untouched by the growing influence of the West. The towns of Asyut and Kenneh, Luxor and Aswan, showed more of a Turkish than a French or English influence. But soon we shall find tourists from the West rushing up and down the river in a matter of days, in steamers and then in trains, and still writing home about the peace and untouched romance and beauty of the country. But in 1850, when a journey up the Nile took fifteen or twenty weeks, Florence Nightingale could still write in horror from Thebes of having to rush to finish her letter because a steamer was about to leave for Cairo. 'I would not go in a steamer on the Nile,' she insisted, 'if I were never to see the Nile without it.' Tourists in Egypt have been just as demanding ever since then.

★

On 21 November, 1862 – by which time Florence Nightingale was already confined to her bed, a much-loved, cantankerous invalid, still battling against bureaucracy and the backwardness of the British Army – an Englishwoman one year her junior arrived in Egypt to recover her health.

Lucie Austin had married Sir Alexander Duff Gordon in London in 1840 and among their distinguished circle of friends were Alexander Kinglake, author of *Eothen*, Eliot Warburton, author of *The Crescent and the Cross*, and William Thackeray, all of whom had travelled in Egypt. By 1851, with her health already failing, she wrote from their family house in Surrey that 'I look thin, ill, and old, and my hair is growing gray. This I consider hard upon a woman just over her thirtieth birthday.' Ten years later, with her illness confirmed as tuberculosis, she went to Cape Colony for the winter, where she was more comfortable. However, when it became clear that she would have to stay away from England for the coming winters as well, Lucie Duff Gordon chose to go to Egypt instead. It was nearer England, for one thing, and her daughter Janet had married a banker in Alexandria in 1860 and so she would have some family nearby – and Lucie herself had had a lively interest in the country through the tales of her traveller-friends. And the warm, dry climate, especially in Upper Egypt, was thought to be the best for her illness.

She was not the first foreigner to seek refuge in Egypt from the cold, damp winters of Europe and North America, for south of the Mediterranean, where summers tend to be too hot for white-skinned people, the winter months are cooler, like the height of an English summer, and the winds that blow from the north relieve the intensity of the sun. But it was clear even from her earliest letters that if health had brought her to Egypt, it was not the only thing that was going to keep her there. She refused to consider herself an invalid and, a few months after her arrival, she confessed that her husband Alick was right when he suggested that she was 'in love with the Arabs' ways, and I have contrived to see and know more of family life than many Europeans who have lived here for years'. Dispensing with the European comforts of Cairo's hotels and clubs, partly through lack of finance, she hired a servant, Omar – known as Abou el Halla'weh, the father of sweets, because traditionally his family were pastry cooks – and then went to Boulak to rent a boat to live on. The owner of the boat she decided on, Sid Achmet el-Berberi, asked a high price for it since she was a European and therefore must be rich. But he lowered it later when she started to bargain because, she explained, 'if I was not like other Ingeleez in money, I likewise differed in politeness, and had refrained from abuse'.

There was clearly something immediately likeable about this Englishwoman. The Berberi's response was not unique: in the same letter to her mother she described a tall Bedouin woman crossing a field to shake hands with her, to ask questions and to look after her. At a village outside Cairo, other women invited her into their houses so that she could see how they ate and slept – while she looked, they observed her, and outside a man from the village kept the children away. At Beni Suef, the priest from the church invited her to his house to drink coffee – they sat on a raised platform and were soon joined by a crowd of Copts, a Muslim mason, and Girgis, the headman of the village. Omar, her attendant, was never far away. Then cattle and sheep crowded in under the shelter. There was always excitement and interest in her, wherever she visited. Sometimes people brought her water; at one place on the river, when they had been forced to stop the dahabieh to fix the rudder, Lucie wandered off alone and came across a group of women fetching water and on their way back to their homes. 'One beautiful woman,' Lucie wrote, 'pointed to the village and made signs of eating and took my hand to lead me . . .'

Lucie was in no hurry to be up-river, unlike Florence Nightingale, who felt she had to rush along the Nile. When Lucie reached Thebes in December she thought that it 'has become an English watering-place. There are now nine boats lying here, and the great object is to *do the Nile* as fast as possible.' But she also moved on since Upper Egypt was having one of its coldest winters in years – the further south she went, the better she felt. Back in Thebes in February of the following year, she wrote that she was 'really much better' and so she continued north to Cairo with the idea of going home to England for a while. She had passed another winter without her husband or her son and daughter; they had had to rely on the irregular river mail service for news of each other; and she had not even seen her eldest daughter Janet at Alexandria. Clearly it was time for her to be at home again, but when she reached Cairo in March she wrote to her husband: 'The worst of going up the Nile is that one must come down again and find horrid fogs, and cold nights with sultry days.' Hekekian Bey, an Armenian doctor who had looked after her before she went up-river, and De Leo Bey, the Egyptian army's chief surgeon, both attended to her. 'I used to hear Omar praying outside my door while I was so ill,' she wrote to her husband – this same Omar who announced that 'I think my God give her to me to take care of her, how then I leave her if she not well and not very rich? I can't speak to my God if I do bad things like that.'

When she did recover, she returned to England for the summer but was back in Egypt by October, taking on her faithful Omar again and another boat to take them up-river. She left Cairo in December and spent the remainder of the winter in Luxor, and further south in Nubia. For the next five years she repeated this pattern, wintering in the south and making her way northwards to Cairo and Alexandria for the summer. Her husband, Sir Alexander Duff Gordon – the 'Dearest Alick' of her letters – was not a wealthy baronet and relied on his job at the Treasury to support them, which made it impossible for him to be with her. And, anyway, what would he do in Egypt? What sort of upbringing would there be for their children? Alick stayed at home and only visited her once, in October 1864, when he found the climate, the customs of the country and the way Lucie was living all very trying. As she wrote to her mother that December after he had left, 'I think he was amused but I fear he felt the Eastern life to be very poor and comfortless.'

But if she did away with many of her European comforts, she did not seem to miss them too much and appeared as much at home squatting on a rug to eat as she would have been sitting in an upright chair dining in London. Some days brought nothing but pain or boredom, but others were precious: in the severe heat of May, Sittee Noor-ala-Noor (Lady Light from the Light, as the Egyptians called her) was invited to spend the day with Mustapha Aga, the British consular agent at Luxor. There were other Egyptians with them, and of course Omar was by her side. As they sat in a hut made out of wheat stalks and roofed over with palm branches, it began to rain, a rare event in Luxor at any time. 'I laughed,' Lucie wrote to her mother, 'and said I had brought English weather, but the Maõhn shook his head and opined that we were suffering the anger of God.' To help the situation, they sent for a young boy to recite passages from the Koran and then sat around the dinner tray filled with lamb and chicken, vegetables and rice, and a dish of stewed apricots with nuts and raisins, which they scooped up in pieces of bread and covered in lime juice. 'We were very merry, if not very witty.' Then Omar, who came from Cairo and was therefore an outsider up-river, stretched out on the ground and recited an Arabic proverb: 'This is the happiness of the Arab. Green trees, sweet water, and a kind face, make the "garden" [paradise].'

When she was in Luxor Lucie stayed either in her dahabieh or in what was known as the Maison de France, the French house, built close to the river and beside, and partly over, the Temple of Luxor. The house had been built by Henry Salt, the British Consul, in 1815, and Belzoni had lived here for some time. But it was sold to the French government in the 1820s and thereby acquired its name. In 1829, Champollion, the decipherer of hieroglyphics, stayed in the house and, two years later, M.Lebas used it as his base while he removed one of the two standing obelisks of Rameses II from in front of the Temple of Luxor to its new home in the Place de la Concorde in Paris. The house was large and rambling, by all accounts, and built from palm trunks and clay. Amelia Edwards, who visited the house during her first Nile tour of 1874, ten years before it was demolished to expose the temple beneath it, was shocked by the room in which Lucie lived – it shocked Lucie, too, sometimes, as at the end of 1867 when she wrote that half of it had fallen into the temple below. But when Amelia looked out of the window she understood how Lucie had lived here. 'That window,' Amelia wrote, 'which commanded the Nile and the western plain of Thebes, furnished the room and made its poverty splendid.' Lucie sat on the lattice-worked balcony in the evenings and watched the sunset and the boats on the river. She was now as tied to the country by her love of the Arab ways as by the health which Egypt's climate restored to her, and she came as close as anyone to lifting the veil between the English and Egyptians.

Lucie Duff Gordon's letters from Egypt were first published in England in May 1865, three years after her arrival in Egypt, and were reprinted three times before the end of that first year. That summer she returned to England, but not before she had celebrated the feast of Bairam at Luxor and had sat down with 200 men at the great dinner given by Mustapha Aga. Here, with the moon bright overhead, she squatted with four others around a wooden tray, rolled up her sleeve and dipped in her bread. When they had feasted, her fellow-diners said, 'God take thee safe and happy to thy place and thy children and bring thee back to us in safety to eat the meat of the festival together once more.' By the end of 1865 she was again in Egypt – again unwell – hoping that the heat and the desert-dried air would undo the effects of the English climate. Two years later her son Maurice arrived from England and stayed more than eighteen months with her, accompanying her on her annual migration to Cairo for the summer and back to Upper Egypt for the winter.

With the success of her volume of letters, Lucie herself became as much a point of interest for tourists on the Nile as the temple she lived on top of. Friends popped in, too. 'Fancy my surprise,' she wrote to her mother in January 1866, 'the other day just when I was dictating my letters to Sheykh Yussuf . . . with three or four other people here, in walked Miss North (Pop) whom I have not seen since she was a child.' Miss North and her father – 'rather horrified at the turbaned society in which he found himself' – called on her again on their way back down-river. Then Edward Lear came to sketch the French House for Lucie's husband, and other English people, strangers to her, also arrived and introduced themselves. And it was not just Lucie who had become a subject of public interest. That year Sheikh Yussuf noticed that he was being shown a greater respect than he had come to expect from tourists and it was only when an American explained to Mustapha that Lucie had written a book about them all that this change in attitude was understood.

The visits had another side to them, though. By February 1866 Lucie noted that more than twenty boats, mostly carrying Americans, had passed upstream. The following year the Upper Egyptian season started with even greater gusto – barely two weeks after Lucie herself had arrived back in Luxor from Cairo, she complained to her husband that 'The first steamer full of travellers has just arrived, and with it the bother of the ladies all wanting my saddle. I forbade Mustapha to send for it, but they intimidate the poor old fellow, and he comes and kisses my hand . . . Last year five women on one steamer all sent for my saddle, besides other things – campstools, umbrellas, beer, etc., etc. This year I'll bolt the doors when I see a steamer coming.'

Some bothers were worth supporting. By 1869 she was a great celebrity and was visited by the Prince and Princess of Wales on their tour of Egypt. On 22 February Mrs William Grey, a lady-in-waiting to the Princess, wrote in her diary that the Prince went to visit Lucie on his own on her boat just north of Aswan. Two weeks later, both the Prince and the Princess, with the Hon Mrs Grey and Sir Samuel Baker, crossed the river to visit the ailing Englishwoman. They drank coffee and smoked pipes in the Oriental manner and were back on their own boats by five o'clock. 'He was most pleasant and kind,' she wrote to Alick in June. 'She is the most perfectly simple-mannered girl I ever saw ... They were more considerate than any people I have seen, and the Prince, instead of being gracious, was, if I may say so, quite respectful in his manner ...'

Health seekers flocked to Egypt as the nineteenth century wore out. They were attracted to the country by the life Lucie had described to them, although very few of them chose to look too hard for it, and by the understanding she had shown – and taught them to show – towards Egyptians. It did not matter that the health she rediscovered in Egypt was such a transient thing; she probably lived longer there than she would have done had she stayed in England. But more important than her demonstration of the compatibility of the Egyptian climate was the compassion with which she had described the lives of the modern Egyptians, placing herself in the footsteps of Burckhardt and Edward Lane.

By the time her son Maurice left for England, in June 1869, just five months before the opening of the Suez Canal, whose construction had caused so much hardship for the Arabs around her, Lucie announced that she was too ill to write any more. Her cough was bad again and she felt very weak. The European doctors in Cairo, and every doctor who happened to pass her on the river, had seen her and suggested whatever they could; her Omar had prayed for her; Abu-l-Hajjaj was supposed to be protecting her, after she was wrapped in the green silk covering from his tomb – 'Never fear, does not God know thee and the Sheyk also?' – and countless other blessings had been heaped upon her head by the Egyptians she lived amongst. But still she grew weaker. 'If prayers could avail a cure,' Lucie told her husband, 'I ought to get well rapidly.' But when she left Luxor in the spring of 1869, she knew that this was a final parting. The Cadi (judge) had prepared space for her in his family tomb. Mohammed at Luxor had cried out, 'Poor I, my poor children, poor all the people,' and Abd el'Haleem, another friend, had sworn that if she lived he would give up drink and hashish – that he would give it up anyway, in fact. And Omar, who had been appointed dragoman to the Prince of Wales, prayed harder for 'the mother he found in the world'. At this point, in the summer of 1869, her husband decided to travel out to see her, but by the time he arrived

Lucie was dead and had been buried in Cairo, away from her people in England and from her other people in Luxor.

★

The nineteenth-century world was set in motion by dreams of empire and the potential of steam power and much of it, at one time or another, passed through Egypt. Tourists, 'lotus eaters', health seekers, students of ancient or modern Egypt, whoever – British and French, the growing number of popular Americans of whom Lucie Duff Gordon wrote, 'The Yankees are always the best bred and best educated travellers that I see here,' as well as Germans and Belgians, and Indians on their way to or from London – Egyptian viceroys from Muhammad Ali to Ismail welcomed them all because they believed that they brought wealth and progress to the country. With it, the Egyptians could fulfill their own dream of empire by securing the part we now call the Middle East from the Turkish sultan. Muhammad Ali had gone a considerable way towards doing this in the 1830s and had even threatened Constantinople, but the European powers had forced him to back down. But for a while the Egyptians held Syria and the Holy Land, Sudan to the south and the Arabian coast to the east. Their influence and prestige was spreading.

Generalizations are always misleading and, because of the variety of foreign travellers in Egypt and of the variety of Egyptians, Turks and Arabs they came into contact with, it would be difficult to point to any specific attitudes between travellers and the people they met in Egypt which would be truly representative. Our own century has shown more clearly than most that a lack of understanding towards other people and their customs can be a very dangerous thing. It was not always so – the Egyptian Bey showed great respect towards James Bruce even though he failed to understand why he had travelled so far from home. There was acknowledgement for his abilities and curiosity towards his country, even though his religion made the Egyptians suspicious. Christianity and Islam seemed to be opposed by tradition, and Muslims in Egypt looked upon the infidels from the West with scorn. Banning Christian ships from their ports was only part of the restrictions imposed to try to keep a distance from what was seen as a corrupting influence. Some Muslims thought that any close contact with Christians was a defilement, and sexual contact was an eternal stain. El-Djabarti, the sheikh whose journal charted the progress of the French in Egypt, tells the story of Zenab, a daughter of the Sheikh el-Bekri. When the French army reached Cairo and Bonaparte entered the city in triumph, the young general was brought a number of Egyptian and Nubian girls for his own pleasure and from all of them, so the story goes, he chose the sixteen-year-old Zenab. Whether her father knew or approved of the liaison is not recorded but, if he did, maybe he was hoping for some advantage or influence for himself. However, no good was to come of it, either for him or his daughter. When Bonaparte left Egypt, he left the daughter behind, too. When the French Army finally evacuated – as is often the way after a war – the natives who had collaborated with the foreigners were called to trial by those who had kept themselves apart or blameless, and so it was with young Zenab. 'The pasha's emissaries presented themselves after sundown at her mother's house,' El-Djabarti wrote ominously. They took Zenab and the Sheikh El-Bekri to the court. 'She was interrogated regarding her Conduct, and made reply that she repented it. Her father's opinion was solicited. He answered that he disavowed his daughter's conduct. Then the unfortunate girl's head was cut off.' It is interesting to compare this story with the accepted image of immorality and vice for which Egypt was infamous.

Egyptians were just as suspicious of the foreigners' interest in their ancient monuments. What did they want with them? Egyptians believed that there must be treasure hidden inside the tombs or beneath the temples, and to a certain extent they were right. Belzoni had had great difficulty moving the head of Memnon from Thebes because the local sheikhs believed it was filled with gold – they had already stopped his fellow-countryman and rival Drovetti, who was working for the French Consul, from moving it from the Ramasseum. If it was not valuable why go to all this trouble to take it away? Certainly not just for the carving of an old statue. There must be treasure. Belzoni encountered the same difficulty at Abu Simbel and Thomas Cook's *Handbook for Travellers* identified the same suspicion as late as 1905: 'That anyone should wish to make excavations,' it noted a little disingenuously, 'for the love of learning is more than they [Mohammedans] can understand, and the older generation regard all who do work of this kind as wicked ones'. Of course, not all foreigners who became involved in the excavations in Egypt were solely interested in the love of learning. As Hollywood, and England's Hammer film company showed, some were motivated by greed or by more mystical forces to go digging at the sites of old cities. As Eliot Warburton concluded after travelling through Egypt in 1843, 'Every Englishman is supposed to possess unbounded medical skills, besides a knowledge of where lies all that buried treasure for which we so often risk our lives in tombs and desert places.'

If Muhammad Ali looked to the West for expertise and new technology, the Khedive Ismail embraced European style and customs as well

– his palaces would not have looked out of place in Italy or France and the rooms he had decorated for the French Empress Eugenie (when she came to open the Suez Canal) in the Gezira Palace (now the Cairo Marriott Hotel) were a reproduction of her own palace in France. The new Cairo opera house and the café singers in the Ezbekieh, the hotels and the number of other amenities which appeared during Ismail's reign, grew out of his desire not to be looked down upon by Europe. He did not want to be seen as the ruler of a backward or primitive nation. In his attempt to make Egypt a part of Europe, not of Africa, he encouraged the activities of the 'colonists' as he called them who would help his country make the necessary changes.

For most Egyptians, however, foreign travellers probably did not represent either advancement or sophistication, good manners or impeccable breeding; to most they just represented an opportunity for increasing their wealth. A traveller needed help with almost everything he did, from getting across Cairo to seeing the sights, taking on a boat and crew and paying off a threatening Bedouin. All of these and the many other services foreigners required resulted in payment, and for every Egyptian who actually did something, there were others who demanded baksheesh merely because they happened to be there. How could they resist asking? These strange people who passed through their country were thought of as magicians where money was concerned. As Alexander Kinglake discovered in the 1840s, by the magic of the banking system 'the wealthy traveller will make all his journeys without carrying a handful of coin, and yet when he arrives at a city will rain down showers of gold'. How it was done mattered little to the poorer people around them. What mattered most was that it was done, and that those in attendance were well covered by the downpour. 'The average Oriental,' *Baedeker* announced in its classic 1929 edition, 'regards the European traveller as a Croesus, and therefore as fair game, and feels justified in pressing upon him with a perpetual demand for baksheesh.' The average European traveller, whether Croesus or not, usually made matters worse by paying up, in the simple delusion that he was buying peace and quiet.

The most persistent demanders of baksheesh, then as now, were to be found at the greatest tourist site, the Pyramids. When the American writer Mark Twain visited Giza in 1867, he arrived with the intention of climbing the Great Pyramid. 'Of course we were besieged by a rabble of muscular Egyptians and Arabs who wanted the contract of dragging us to the top,' he remembered, 'all tourists are. Of course you could not hear your own voice for the din that was around you. Of course the Sheiks said *they* were the only responsible parties.' Of course, too, there was much fighting for their custom – Twain had money and the Egyptians wanted it. At the top of the Pyramid, Twain engaged an Arab to run back down to the bottom, climb the next one and then back up to where he stood in under nine minutes. It was a common wager and Twain offered the man a single US dollar to do it. However, sport was not Twain's only consideration. 'A blessed thought entered my brain. He must infallibly break his neck.' But the runner was experienced and returned in eight minutes and forty-one seconds. Twain then bet him again for another dollar and the man took only five seconds longer. A third time, for a third dollar, he made it back in eight minutes and forty-eight seconds. The loser was getting desperate now and in a final, unsporting gesture, he said, ' "Sirrah, I will give you a hundred dollars to jump off this pyramid head first." ' When the man declined, Twain dismissed him with the judgment that 'the Arabs are too high-priced in Egypt. They put on airs unbecoming to such savages'. But whatever Twain thought of him, the runner had made an extra three dollars from the American, a feat he would no doubt attempt to repeat with the next tourists who engaged him.

*

Whatever went on in Egypt's towns and at the temples along the Nile, life was different in the desert. The barrenness of the country forced the living into new habits. The necessity of having to struggle to stay alive, and the pain of the heat of the sun and the sand-driving winds, changed people's attitudes; but there were some things, as Alexander Kinglake discovered, that would never change. When he was making his way from the Holy Land to Cairo in 1834, he crossed the Sinai Desert with a few European attendants and four Bedouin guides. One day they spotted something moving on the horizon and, by the excitement it caused among his entourage, he guessed that it must be other travellers. As the two groups approached each other, Kinglake saw that there was another Englishman riding towards him wearing a shooting jacket. He had two Arab runners, and a single servant on a camel beside him. The Arabs in Kinglake's party were amazed that anyone would make the journey across the desert with so small a group, for they most certainly would not.

This Englishman, it turned out, was a military man returning to England from duty in India; Kinglake had come straight out from England. They were now midway between their two starting points and both had travelled for many days in the inhospitable desert. But when they approached each other, the sun high overhead and the dry sand crushed beneath their camels' hooves, all they did was to raise their caps at each other and wave. Kinglake had expected the Englishman to say something to him and was quite prepared to be polite and to reply if he was addressed, although he did not really have anything that he wanted to say. Presumably the other man had thought the same of Kinglake, for they passed each other without so much as a hello and it was not until they were some thirty or forty yards apart that Kinglake realized he was alone. His servants had stopped to speak to the stranger's servants. With embarrassment and an acute awareness of the absurdity of his behaviour, Kinglake turned his camel around and rode back to speak to his countryman. 'Seeing this,' Kinglake recalled,

> he followed my example, and came forward to meet me.
> He was the first to speak. Too courteous to address me, as
> if he admitted the possibility of my wishing to accost him
> from any feeling of mere sociability or civilian-like love of
> vain talk, he at once attributed my advances to a laudable
> wish of acquiring statistical information, and accordingly,
> when we got within speaking distance, he said, 'I dare say
> you wish to know how the Plague is going on at Cairo?'
> and then he went on to say he regretted that his information
> did not enable him to give me in numbers a perfectly accurate
> statement of the daily deaths. He afterwards talked pleasantly
> enough upon other and less ghastly subjects. I thought him
> manly and intelligent – a worthy one of the few thousand
> strong Englishmen to whom the Empire of India is
> committed.

Bonaparte, who was right in so many of his predictions on Egypt, believed that to hold that empire, Egypt must be conquered. Successive British governments scoffed at the idea and insisted that they would not invade, but Eliot Warburton sensed that in Egypt 'England is expected,' and even Gustave Flaubert was certain of it when he wrote that 'It seems to me impossible that within a short time England won't become mistress of Egypt.'

PLANTING A FIRM FOOT

'An American lady once said to me that the chief thing which
struck all travelled Americans about us was that "wherever
we go, all over the world, we find you English *at home*."'
E. C. Butcher, *Egypt As We Knew It*

Trading in slaves was prohibited by law in Britain in 1807 and the
owning of slaves was banned in 1833, but there were good markets
elsewhere in the world and British legislation had little effect on slavers
in Africa. During their travels in the 1850s and 1860s, Richard Burton,
John Speke, and David Livingstone each witnessed and made public
the outrages perpetrated by slave traders on the seemingly helpless inhabitants of the Nile headlands and across a broad band of east Africa.
In the 1860s, Samuel Baker and his Hungarian wife Florence saw them
at work in the Sudan. As the historian Alan Moorehead wrote in his
brilliant account of *The White Nile*, 'Probably nothing more monstrous
or cruel than this traffic had happened in history.' In the Sudan, traders
left Khartoum with a few hundred armed men and joined forces with
one southern tribe to attack another rival tribe. Once conquered, villages
were destroyed and their inhabitants rounded up; sometimes the men
were taken, other times they were chased away or killed, while their
women, who fetched a particularly high price and were therefore much
sought after, were led away in chains. A forked pole and crossbar,
called a *sheba*, was fixed across their heads and shoulders, and their
hands were tied in front of them to the pole. Children who could walk
had a chain passed around their necks which was then attached to their
mother's waist. No mention is made of what happened to those children
who were too young or weak to walk. This was business and a small-
time slaver, Alan Moorehead reckoned, could bring 4–500 slaves up
to Khartoum each season and, what with the returns from the villagers'
cattle and ivory, might earn more than £6,000 from a single slaving
trip.

The Sudan was officially the domain of the Khedive of Egypt.
Muhammad Ali's sons Ismail and Ibrahim had established Egypt's right
to rule this inhospitable country through a series of bloody campaigns
in the 1820s. They also founded a new capital, Khartoum, at the junction
of the Blue and White Niles, opposite the village of Omdurman. But

there was a difference between having the right to rule and being able to do so. The Sudanese were fearsome fighters and from the first they resisted. For instance, when Ismail and his officers returned to Shendi, they were invited to a celebration at the palace of the governor, Nimr. But when he had entertained his new rulers for the evening and when they were all tired or drunk, Nimr left them and set fire to his palace, burning them all alive. The Sudanese could not oppose the Egyptians in a pitched battle, but the country was large enough for them to launch attacks on Egyptian garrisons from the provinces. The new rulers, therefore, showed little interest in exerting authority outside the towns and, so long as they were able to extract their dues in the form of men for the army and gold for the pasha, they left the rest of the country to fend for itself. But it would not always stay this way, for the country had wealth; when the Khedive Ismail found himself in need of funds after the extravagance of building and opening the Suez Canal, he employed the explorer Samuel Baker – now Sir Samuel, having discovered and named Lake Albert – to bring the lands below the Sudd, the barrier across the upper reaches of the Nile, under Egyptian control. New lands meant new sources of taxation, new wealth upon which to draw.

Baker was also charged with suppressing the slave trade, although since he only had a force of 1,700 men and a knowledge that was really limited to the river area, he was never likely to be effective in this. But he did succeed in establishing a presence in the upper Nile, or Equatoria as it was now called, and for a while this brought some peace and stability. When Baker and his wife ended their four-year contract and left the province, he felt confident enough about his achievements to write that 'The White Nile, for a distance of 1,600 miles from Khartoum to Central Africa, was cleansed from the abomination of a traffic which had hitherto sullied its waters.' But by the time his replacement had arrived, the province had once again reverted to its violent and lawless state.

Baker had been attracted to the southern Sudan by his previous experiences on the Nile and by the generous salary of £10,000 a year which Ismail had offered. The new Governor-General of Equatoria, Charles Gordon, had never set eyes on the Sudan before, so it was clearly not the place that attracted him. As for the money, he refused the salary that Baker had accepted and suggested that £2,000 a year would do him nicely. It was this, perhaps, which alerted Ismail to the integrity of the man he had employed. Instead of the money, Gordon was attracted by the challenge of crushing the slave trade and by the chance of glory, of doing God's work and being recognized as having done so.

Gordon was forty-one when he arrived in Egypt in February 1874. He had fought in the Crimean War and had also been in China during the Taiping Rebellion when he was given command of the Ever Victorious Army. But for the previous two years he had lived more quietly and less usefully in England as an officer of the Royal Engineers. Gordon was also a devout Christian and a firm believer that Britain, through its Empire, was doing God's work. In Equatoria he saw the chance of starting afresh. It was a place where he could do good, but reading accounts of his approach to the Sudan, it seems inevitable that his Christian superiority would come into conflict with the fervour of the country's predominantly Muslim population.

Amongst the Europeans he took out with him, Gordon enlisted Frederick Russell, the son of William Howard Russell, *The Times* correspondent who had travelled up the Nile with the Prince and Princess of Wales five years earlier. He also took Linant de Bellefonds, the son of the French Egyptologist, as his secretary and interpreter. Gordon and one part of his force left Cairo for Suez on 21 February, 1874, choosing to travel inland from the Red Sea coast, rather than follow the Nile up through Nubia. On this journey across the eastern Nubian desert from Suakin to Berber, above the Fifth Cataract on the Nile, Gordon first learned to ride a camel, an animal with which he is forever associated. Three years later, he rode 3,840 miles around his province on camels.

The country Gordon arrived in was not at all what he had been led to expect. The river was uncharted below Gondokoro, the capital of Equatoria; the natives were hostile; and the Egyptian soldiers in the garrisons were corrupt. The province south of Gondokoro Gordon described in this way: 'A more dreary set of marches you cannot conceive. The country is quite uninhabited – a vast undulating prairie of jungle grass and scrub trees...' It was malarial country as well and, within a few months of their arrival, most of his assistants were suffering from the disease. Gordon himself had to nurse the young Russell back to some sort of health and then sent him down-river to recover. Later Russell chose not to return to Gordon, but entered the diplomatic service and became Vice-Consul in Alexandria.

By the end of his first year in Equatoria, Gordon was ready to move out beyond the lands of the upper Nile. Although Baker claimed to have cleared the slavers from the province, he had really only done so as far as the limits of his area of authority, not that far beyond the river banks. In 1875, Gordon sent Linant de Bellefonds with a small force up towards Lake Victoria, where he was to meet M'tesa, the king of Buganda. Having passed the government stations of Fatiko and Foweira, which Baker had established, Linant was met by messengers from M'tesa who greeted him in the name of the king and with an invitation to the court. They also informed him that another white man was already at the court. This was Henry Stanley, who had come over from Zanzibar, whose name is now as inextricably linked with central Africa as Gordon's is with Khartoum. On June 15, Linant and Stanley met M'tesa. The Bugandan king agreed to ban the selling of slaves and to encourage his traders to do business with the Egyptian government stations on the upper Nile. He even agreed to receive Christian missionaries after listening to the two men's stories of the Creation, the Flood and the life of the Messiah. Stanley then left for the Congo and the west of Africa, while Linant returned to Gordon in Equatoria.

But if there were successes – Gordon managed to control his province and to frighten slavers out of Equatoria; the river was charted; and he had put two steamers on Lake Albert – the overall situation was not so hopeful. Two months after his meeting with Stanley and M'tesa, Linant was killed along with the best of Gordon's men – Baker's old bodyguard, known as the 'Forty Thieves' – in an ill-conceived attack on a small village south of Gondokoro. With fewer and fewer European assistants, Gordon's frustrations grew. Each gain was countered by a greater loss. If he kept the slavers out of his own territories, he soon learned that they were able to trade unhindered in the rest of the Sudan, which was beyond his jurisdiction, ruled by an Egyptian governor-general. He felt increasingly isolated. 'I have been here for nearly three weeks,' he wrote from Gondokoro, 'and never exchange a word beyond a few broken Arabic sayings from morning to night.' The climate began to wear him down as well. When it was hot, it was very hot. When it rained, the country flooded and the air was heavy with moisture. For every beautiful animal he saw, there was a snake waiting to drop on him from a tree or a scorpion ready to creep into his sleeping net and sting him during the night – 'A life in a tent,' he wrote of his own, in July 1875, 'with a cold humid air at night, to which if, from the heat of the tent, you expose yourself you will suffer for it either in liver or elsewhere. The most ordinary fare – *most* ordinary I can assure you; no vegetables, dry biscuits, a few bits of boiled meat and some boiled macaroni, boiled in water and sugar. I forgot some soup. Up at dawn and to bed at eight or nine p.m.; no books but *one* ... All day long worrying about writing orders to be obeyed by others in the degree as they are near or distant from me ... that is one's life.' Thwarted also by his superiors, by the end of 1876 he had returned to Cairo and resigned.

But Gordon was not finished with the Sudan. Ismail summoned him back to Cairo in February 1877 and, during their meeting, Gordon explained why he would not go back to Equatoria. Why should he when the rest of the Sudan was happily accommodating the slave trade to which Gordon – and the Khedive as well, he believed – wished to put an end? In London on January 31, Gordon had written that 'if His Highness will not give me the Province of Soudan I will not go back to the Lakes. I do not think he will give it, and I think you will see me back in six weeks...' But two weeks later Gordon reported of his meeting with Ismail that 'Then I began, and told him all; and then he gave me the Soudan, and I leave on Saturday morning.' Once again he had cut the salary that Ismail offered him, this time from £6,000 to £3,000 a year. Once again he was enthusiastic and energetic and, on arriving in Khartoum with complete authority over a country of 1,000,000 square miles, he wrote, 'I have an enormous province to look after; but it is a great blessing to me to know that God has undertaken the administration of it, and it is His work and not mine. If I fail, it is His will; if I succeed, it is His work.'

This time Gordon knew what to expect from the country and the people. He had allies, was able to recognize his enemies, and believed that the Khedive and God were behind him. He sent those officers and officials he was unhappy with back to Cairo, was careful in his appointment of district governors and had more success suppressing the slave trade. He was an absolute ruler in a country where previous rulers had been interested in little more than their own comfort and wealth. But, unlike his predecessors, Gordon took an interest in what the Sudanese thought and in what they wanted. He took the unprecedented step of putting what he described as 'a box with a slit in the lid for petitions' at the door to his palace. Yet, for all this, he was not really in control. The country was too big and the resources at his disposal were too small to be effective. In October 1877 he wrote that he was feared and respected, but not really liked. Khartoum became oppressive. 'My huge palace is again desolate,' he wrote. 'It is a dreary place. I cannot go out of it without having people howling after me...'

*

'I am an Englishman,' Baron de Kusel wrote at the opening of his *Recollections*, 'born in Liverpool in 1848, and educated at Cheltenham, but I little thought on leaving school that all my life would be spent on land, for in those days I was quite convinced that the sea was the career suitable to me.' At the age of fifteen, however, his father decided that he would not be going to sea, but that he should go to Egypt instead. After he had got over his initial surprise, de Kusel considered the prospect of going east with some relish. 'I no doubt pictured myself as Sultan or something, for the study of Egypt was of no great import- ance in my school's curriculum.' Egypt never did make him a sultan but, looking back over his life, he recognized that it had brought him excitement and adventure.

De Kusel sailed from Liverpool in the ss *Agia Sofia* on 15 September 1863, and arrived in Alexandria fifteen days later, where his own excite- ment seemed to be matched by the crowd of men on the boats and quayside waiting to perform a service for the new arrivals. 'No matter which way I turned, there was something I had never seen before, some- thing that appealed to me, whether it was some splash of colour, vivid and compelling, or simply the newness of my surroundings.' But his first glimpse of the town was brief for, together with a Dr Mustapha, his Egyptian employer, and his wife, de Kusel hurried to the railway station. The train ride was unlike any he had taken in England: they sat in a first-class carriage, ate fruit and bread, drank water from a ghoolah and watched the fertile flatland of the delta pass outside the window. At some stations – two-storey wooden buildings where railway officials both lived and worked – the driver stopped the train and had a coffee and cigarette with his friends. When he was ready, the train started out again.

A hundred miles from Alexandria, having now crossed the Nile, de Kusel, Dr Mustapha and his wife left the train at Benha Junction. They were not going on into Cairo, but were heading twenty miles east to a town called Zagazig, then the terminus of the east-bound railway. But they had missed the only train which ran on the branch line and were obliged to stay the night in Benha and to wait for its return. The station master was a friend of Dr Mustapha and de Kusel spent his first Egyptian night in the assistant station master's office, sharing a divan with an English engineer and his son who were also waiting for the Zagazig train. When they retired for the night, de Kusel could not sleep. It was too hot and there were too many mosquitoes. He stepped outside the office where frogs croaked and in the distance he could hear prairie dogs howling. The moon was bright, the night clear. He walked up and down the deserted platform, feeling the excite- ment of the country and the calm of the night. He stayed out on the platform for some hours and then, just before dawn, a train came down the line from Alexandria towards Cairo. With brakes screeching and steam hissing, it came to a halt in Benha station. It was a goods train and in one of the open wagons de Kusel could see a number of figures standing in silence. Curious, he walked over towards them. 'Some half a dozen women clad in white, and wearing the yashmak or veil, were sitting or lolling upon bales of what I believed to be merchandise, while evidently guarding them were three most villainous-looking ruffians, each with a long scimitar by his side, and a brace of great pistols tucked into his sash.' De Kusel was thrilled. The three men jumped down from the wagon and walked around, while the women remained where they were. When they climbed back up into the wagon, the engine got up steam again and the train pulled out on its way to Cairo. Just then the station master came out onto the platform. Who were they? the Englishman asked him. They were slavers taking Turkish or Circassian women to be sold in Cairo, said the Egyptian. They often passed this way.

Zagazig, where de Kusel and his employer were headed, was a boom town in 1863. The railway was due to be extended through to the Suez Canal; and the American Civil War, now two years old, had increased the demand for Egyptian cotton, the main produce of the Zagazig area. Dr Mustapha, who ran a single-storey cotton-ginning factory, employed de Kusel as a clerk. He began to learn Arabic, bought a donkey so that he could ride out along the Freshwater Canal and watch the gaudy sunsets, and made friends with the other young Englishmen in the town. There was a close English community and, at seven o'clock on the evening of his first Egyptian Christmas, de Kusel joined them at a Greek restaurant in the town to eat a dinner of turkey, duck, plum pudding and mince pies. With wine, beer and whisky, they toasted the Queen, sang the national anthem and spent the rest of the evening singing songs and drinking rum punch. This was home from home.

At the end of the following season, de Kusel was sent to Alexandria on business. There had been an outbreak of cholera and, as he rode in a carriage from Alexandria Station to the P & O Hotel in the Grand Square, there seemed to be a funeral procession around every corner. He asked the coachman if this was the hour for burials, but the man told him that 'There is no special hour, this is going on from sunrise to sunset, and every day.'

The following day de Kusel went to see if the company's boats, which were supposed to be coming down the Mahmoudieh Canal with a shipment of cottonseed, had arrived at the Minet-el-Bassal. This was the area around the cotton exchange, and backing onto the canal, which was the centre of the cotton trade, built, according to E. M. Forster, 'round a pleasant courtyard, with a fountain in its midst. Samples are exhibited. The whole neighbourhood is given up to this, the main industry, of Alexandria; warehouses; picturesque wooden machinery for cleaning the cotton and pressing it into bales; in the season, the streets are slippery with greasy fluff.' Since de Kusel's shipments had not arrived, he was obliged to stay, and by the time his business was sorted out and the seed sold, cholera cases were being reported in Zagazig as well and even Dr Mustapha and his wife had arrived in Alexandria. Finding the P & O Hotel a depressing place, where conversation revolved around the number of deaths that day, de Kusel took rooms in the house of a dentist called Cirioni, where some other young English-men also lived with whom he soon became friends. When the cholera outbreak ended, de Kusel decided to stay in Alexandria; it was more exciting than Zagazig and he had the prospect of a better job. In July 1865, he joined the firm of Barker & Co, merchants and agents, as an Arabic-speaking clerk.

De Kusel was still only seventeen when he joined Barker's, but he lived an independent life in Alexandria. In the evenings, he and the other Englishmen went to the Café de France in the Grand Square, where they played billiards and smoked. He remembered that in the 1860s Alexandria still had 'no paved roads or gas, and many bad char-acters were about. Nearly every night robberies and murders were being committed; and it was necessary to carry a small paper Chinese lantern in order to find one's way.' At night, he and his friends returned to their rooms at Cirioni's.

One of de Kusel's responsibilities at Barker's was to take care of the arrangements with the Rubattino Italian Steamship Company, who ran a regular mail and passenger service from Genoa to Alexandria. It was on one of the Rubattino steamers that he left Alexandria on 15 November 1869, for the official opening of the Suez Canal. He was impressed by the celebrations: Port Said's harbour was crowded, wait-ing for the Muslim ulemas and the Coptic, Greek and Roman Catholic priests to bless the waters. That night, the town and all the ships in the harbour were illuminated; the next day, Wednesday, 17 November, the canal was officially opened and the Rubattino boat followed the royal flotilla down to Ismailia, where the Khedive had built a new palace to entertain his guests. De Kusel was invited to these celebrations and he wrote that 'I shall never forget the magnificence of the ball at the new Khedival palace that evening, for it was one of the most brilliant sights I have ever witnessed, especially the Royal procession, as it passed through the principal ballroom, on its way to supper, which was in itself a thing to be remembered.'

After seven years in Alexandria, de Kusel left his job at Barker & Co and, through the good offices of the British Consul-General, Mr H. Vivian, was appointed chief of the European Department of the Customs Service. In part, his appointment was made possible by the latest developments in Egyptian politics: Ismail's lavish spending – Lord Cromer reckoned that he had overspent by about £7,000,000 a year – had first of all led him to sell his 176,602 shares, a 44% holding, in the Suez Canal Company to the British Government for a mere £4,000,000, and had then obliged him to allow an Anglo-French advisory board to supervise the Egyptian government's financial affairs. Europeans were brought into almost all departments of the Egyptian Service. Baron de Kusel, still only twenty-eight years old on his appointment and married in May 1876 to Elvira, the daughter of an Italian called Cleto Chini who, with his brother, had introduced the first postal service in Egypt in the 1820s, was one of those Europeans who benefited from the new arrangements. He settled down happily to married life and his new posting in Alexandria.

Ismail, however, continued to live beyond his means and to govern in a way which his European advisers considered inept. The governments of England, France, Germany, Austria, Russia and Italy, for once acting in accord, pushed for him to abdicate in favour of his son Tewfik. This suggestion was put to Ismail by the Consuls-General, but of course he refused. Then on 26 June 1879, he received a telegram from the Sultan of Turkey, his official sovereign, which was addressed 'to the ex-Khedive Ismail Pasha.' Ismail sent for his son, who had received a telegram from the same source addressed to the 'Khedive Son Excellence Mehemet Tewfik Pacha', and at 6.30 that evening the artillery battery on the Citadel fired a royal salute in honour of Tewfik's accession.

Four days later, at 11.30 a.m. – times are always recorded precisely at such moments – Ismail left Cairo by train for Alexandria, where he boarded his yacht, the *Mahroussa*, which he had been allowed to keep and which the Hon Mrs Grey, who had sailed in it in 1869 in the suite of the Prince and Princess of Wales, described as 'one mass of silk hangings, Gobelins, gildings, mirrors, tables of Italian marble, mosaic, mother-of-pearl, etc.' Crowds at both railway stations and at the port cheered Ismail. There was a common feeling that he had been hard done by, outmanoeuvred in a game the rules of which he did not understand. One must assume, however, that the crowd who came to cheer and encourage did not know of the million pounds of valuables and cash which he had just loaded on board the yacht.

*

The foreign powers unsettled Egypt more than they had intended when they removed Ismail and replaced him with his more amenable son, Tewfik, and within three years, there was an uprising in army circles. Tewfik attempted to appease the rebels by making their leader, a Colonel Ahmed Arabi, Under-Secretary of War. A little while later he was made Minister of War. Then in March Tewfik made him a pasha. But the problem could not be bought off like this. Egyptians wanted control of their own country and if the Khedive would not fight for it, others in the country would. Arabi had become the figure-head of a powerful nationalist movement. If the foreign powers stayed, so would he.

The thirty-four-year-old de Kusel had lived in Egypt for more than eighteen years now and was sensitive enough to the mood of the country to know that something was very wrong. Rumours were particularly prevalent in the port and what he heard disturbed him enough to send his Italian wife and their young daughter away from Alexandria in April 1882 – first to Beirut, and then to Naples where they stayed until the end of the year. 'There was a feeling of tension all the time,' he remembered, 'as though the steel ropes of peace were being strained to their utmost, and each new movement caused a hum, as though some giant hand was strumming on them, yet when the climax came, it came almost as a surprise; no one seemed ready for it.'

On 20 May, de Kusel stood on top of the Coastguard Office with another Englishman, the Inspector-General of the Coastguard. They watched the British and French fleets come into sight and drop anchor. The battleships were a visible proof, if one was needed, that the foreign powers would not allow Egypt to be ruled by native officers, especially ones of dubious allegiance: Egypt was too important strategically to allow that to happen. Officially, however, they claimed they were there to protect European nationals and their interests, which were threatened by the uprising. But instead of easing the tension, the arrival of the fleets seemed likely to provoke a confrontation, and there was no peace-maker in sight. De Kusel remembered that 'The presence of the Fleet did not in any way calm the air, in fact, rather the reverse, and the European element began to feel slightly alarmed.' And so they should have done, for they were caught between the Egyptian Army and the British Fleet, which consisted of the flagship *Invincible*, six other iron-clads and five gunboats – in all, about 3,500 men and 120 guns – under the command of Vice-Admiral Sir Frederick Beauchamp Paget Seymour.

If there was tension, soon there was also action. The British and French Governments demanded the resignation of the Egyptian Government and the dismissal of Arabi, to which Tewfik, who was not a man of any great resolve or force of character, agreed. Then one week later Tewfik had Arabi reinstated by public demand. European residents, who had no faith in the negotiations being held between the Egyptians and the British and who believed they understood more about the situation than the British admiral, packed up their belongings and headed for Alexandria harbour. Within two weeks of the fleets' arrival, some 14,000 Europeans and their dependents had left Egypt and thousands more were getting ready to go. Then the confrontation took a new turn. Admiral Seymour sent word to Arabi in Alexandria that reinforcements which were being carried out to the town's defences should stop immediately. Arabi denied that they were doing any such thing, but one night a British warship shone its searchlight towards the fortifications and caught the Egyptians at work. In this climate it would only take a little spark to set the whole conflict alight, and that spark came early in the afternoon of Sunday, 11 June.

The previous evening, de Kusel had been invited to spend the weekend with his coastguard friend out in Ramleh, then beyond the city. On the Sunday, they were joined by Captain Molyneux from the British flagship, who arrived in time for lunch. That afternoon the three of them decided to drive into Alexandria to the Public Gardens by the Mahmoudieh Canal where, every Friday and Sunday, smart society turned out to promenade and to listen to music around the bandstand. It was an important social event and it was strange, therefore, that when Molyneux and de Kusel arrived in their Victoria carriage, the only other person they met in the gardens was an engineer from one of the British ironclads. Alarmed, they drove on into town to find out what was happening. The first person they met told them that 'there had been a quarrel in the Maltese quarter between Arabs and Maltese, and that several people had been killed.' As they rode on, they heard people cursing them in Arabic – 'Go on,' they shouted, 'go on, a little faster; the faster the better, you are only going to your death.' In the Grand Square, they drove into the middle of a riot. 'My coachman had just enough time to pull up,' de Kusel wrote, 'and Captain Molyneux, who had stood up and was looking ahead, called out that they were murdering that English officer, and that we had better try to reach the Consulate. Bessie, my mare, helped us admirably, for she reared and plunged, keeping the crowd back as the carriage was turned into a side street; we nearly capsized, but, with luck, broke through the people, and so round to the British Consulate . . .'

'We found the Consulate in a state of indescribable confusion, women and children crowded in everywhere, weeping and terrified,' de Kusel reported. In the rioting, the British Consul, Mr Charles Cookson, had been seriously wounded and the Vice-Consul later collapsed from nervous fatigue. By the time Egyptian soldiers took control of the city, for this was only a civilian demonstration, fifty or so Europeans and many more Egyptians had been killed or wounded in Alexandria. 'As darkness fell,' de Kusel remembered, 'the martial sounds from the streets, the tramp tramp of the infantry and the deep rumbling of artillery were not conducive to the alleviation of the fugitives' fright...' That night and during the following days, more foreigners made their way towards the ships in the harbour, which took them across the Mediterranean to Malta or Spain, Greece or Italy. After they had left, the city settled down to an uneasy peace and foreign officials like de Kusel who remained at their posts found themselves working in a state of almost constant fear. This went on for another month, during which time de Kusel was in sole control of Customs, since the director had already left. Then on 9 July, he too was ordered to leave the city and to embark on the ss *Tanjore*, a merchant ship which usually sailed between Alexandria and Brindisi, which was anchored in the harbour. Being responsible for Customs, de Kusel wanted to take the contents of the Customs safe – about £20,000 – with him. So on Sunday the 10th, he hailed a passing Arab boat and was taken back to the Customs pier.

The Arabs in the Customs House were amazed that de Kusel had come to work. Could he not see that everyone else had run away? Why, even now some of the ships in the harbour were beginning to steam out to sea. De Kusel told them that it was business as usual for him and that therefore, as usual, they would be paying the cash from the safe into the account of the Public Debt Office at the Credit Lyonnais, now operating from one of the French steamers. As a ruse, this was blindingly simple, but de Kusel thought that it might just work. He had the money taken from the safe and put onto his own little boat, but he only got as far as the pier when an Egyptian naval officer and a dozen soldiers came running up to him.

'I arrest you by Arabi's orders,' the officer told him and he was seized. De Kusel was clever enough to continue playing his bluff. Very well, he insisted, if he could not go about his business then, before he would go to see Arabi, he wanted to have the money taken back and locked in the Customs safe. This was done and he was then marched across the city; people in the crowd screamed abuse at him. 'As an Englishman,' he wrote in his unmistakeable tone, 'I do not think the soldiers of the escort could have loved me greatly, but at any rate they saved my life as we marched to the Arsenal.'

At the Arsenal, de Kusel was interviewed by Arabi himself and his council of war. Nothing was wrong, the Englishman insisted; he was just doing his work as usual, and paying the money into the bank. He told them that he failed to see what all the fuss was about. 'We all know you,' Arabi decided, mollified, 'and feel sure that you are a real and true friend of the Arabs. I may add that it is a pity that more officials are not like you.'

De Kusel bowed to the council and was told that he would be called before them again. He left with Arabi's special protection since, as he explained, he was now afraid of the crowd and the uproar outside, and he was escorted back to the Customs House where he carried on working. There were fewer and fewer ships in the habour and at anchor outside the sea walls and it was clear that he would have to hurry if he was going to get back to one of the steamers. But he could not simply leave, and he waited until the early afternoon before he called for his boat again. Then he issued some orders, announced that 'I shall be back at three o'clock,' put on his hat and left the building. When he reached his boat his reserve gave way and he urged his four boatmen to row as fast as they could, for the harbour was almost empty now. He reached the *Tanjore* just before she left the outer harbour. At seven o'clock the following morning, Monday, 11 July, with the French and American forces out of the way and the British admiral's final ultimatum rejected, the British fleet bombarded Alexandria's fortifications. For the next four and a half hours, British guns fired incessantly at Alexandria. De Kusel watched from the *Tanjore*. 'It was rather terrible and awe-inspiring,' he wrote, 'and in spite of myself I trembled with excitement.' By the end of the day, the British claimed six men wounded, while the Egyptians are thought to have lost more than 2,000 men. Arabi withdrew his troops and Alexandria was left to burn. Looters smashed and grabbed whatever they could reach. British troops did not land until two days later, by which time the rioters had done extensive damage.

Foreign property was their prime target. De Kusel, who landed with the first detachments of Marines, was amazed at the destruction in the city. The Grand Square was almost completely ruined. The British, French and Italian Consulates had a few walls still standing, but they had all been gutted. At his own home, in a large block of flats, de Kusel found some baby's clothing just inside the door. 'Jove!' he exclaimed, 'how thankful I was that my own womenfolk had left some time before.' In the stables, he found his coachman Giovanni, an Arab servant and his mare Bessie, all safe, but scared. His flat, however, had been ransacked. 'Everything was smashed, the household glass broken to smithereens – not a whole wineglass left; chairs broken, carpets all ripped to ribbons. I think the drawing-room must have been most offensive to them. It was upholstered in yellow satin, and contained several big mirrors. These had presumably been broken by the fists of the rabble, who had wiped their bleeding hands upon the satin. What had not been broken had been carried off...'

The British action was intended to bring order to Alexandria and as soon as the Marines landed some sort of order was established: looters caught in the act were tried straightaway and some of them were shot in the Grand Square. Order was restored in Lower Egypt during the following month when a British army of some 20,000 troops under General Sir Garnet Wolseley landed from the Suez Canal and finally defeated Arabi's army at the decisive battle of Tel el Kebir on 13 September. British troops were then stationed in barracks in Egypt's cities. Most important, the British were now in control of the Suez Canal and order was also restored in Upper Egypt, although it was not imposed on the Sudan – but even Gordon had dismissed it as a worthless, savage and ungovernable place.

★

If British officials thought they would be able to ignore the Sudan in those early days of the occupation, they were soon to realize their mistake. Since Gordon had left Khartoum after the deposition of Ismail in 1879, the administration he had set up quickly returned to its old ways of bribery, extortion and illegal trading. Egypt had tried to control the country from the garrisons that Gordon had established and over 28,000 Egyptian troops were still stationed in the Sudan, though as one British officer sent to report on them wrote, 'Their general conduct and overbearing manner is almost sufficient to cause a rebellion.' He had chosen his words carefully – when the Mahdi, a religious leader, came out of the desert and claimed to be the reincarnation of the Prophet, the Sudanese rose up and came into conflict with the hopeless Egyptian troops. The Sudan was governed by Sudanese once again and, in a way which has become familiar to us in the late twentieth century, the Mahdi established strict Islamic law. The combination of political resistance and religious fervour was dynamic.

But the political climate in Britain had changed, too, and the public seemed to want no further commitments in Africa if it was going to cost British lives. Gladstone, the Prime Minister, insisted that if the Sudan needed to be controlled it must be done with Egyptian troops, paid for with Egyptian money. In 1883, Colonel Hicks, an experienced soldier from India, led a 10,000-strong Egyptian army into the Sudan with a European staff and a detachment of reporters from newspapers like *The Times* and the *Graphic*. The Mahdi and his army were reported to be in El Obeid, a town some way to the south-west of Khartoum, so Hicks marched south into the desert. He had no experience of such inhospitable countryside or of such ill-disciplined troops. Their morale sank as they were shadowed by Sudanese soldiers and cavalry who engaged them several times, not in battles but, briefly, in skirmishes, so that they had to march in squares. This slowed them down and

111

made the going even more difficult.

There are few eye-witness accounts of the main engagement, but de Kusel thought that the testimony of a slave of Mohammed Bey, an officer with Hicks's army, was reliable: 'It was not yet dhuka (noon),' the slave claimed, 'and we were not far from Elquis. We could see it. We should have been there by noon, and there was an abundance of water ... The guide led us out of the way to a place called Kieb-el-Khaber, instead of taking us straight to Eliquis. It was noon now. Just about this time a rush terrible and sudden, sweeping down like the torrent from the mountain, was made. The Arabs burst upon our front force in overwhelming numbers. It was swept away like chaff before the wind ... A terrible slaughter commenced.' When it was over, Hicks, his European colleagues and all but a hundred or so of the army were dead. The Mahdi had gained complete control of the Sudan.

The Egyptian gendarmerie under its new leader Colonel Valentine Baker, a brother of the explorer and former Governor of Equatoria Sir Samuel Baker, next appeared in the Sudan. With 3,800 men, Baker landed at Suakin to relieve the garrison at Sinkat, some miles from the coast, which was besieged by supporters of the Mahdi. Cromer, who had briefed Baker in Cairo before he set off, wrote that 'It was with the utmost hesitation that I consented to the despatch of General Baker's force to Suakin. I was under no delusion as to the quality of the troops which he would command. Moreover, I feared that Baker Pasha would be led into the committal of some rash act.' To prevent this, Cromer asked the Khedive to write to Baker insisting that he act with the greatest prudence. Like Hicks, Baker had no experience of the men or the country. Disaster struck this force at Tokar. When the Sudanese attacked, the Egyptian troops dropped their weapons and ran; 2,400 of them were killed before they managed to get away.

Two weeks after the battle, General Charles Gordon arrived back in Khartoum. Like Baker before him, Gordon was summoned to Cairo by Cromer. 'You will bear in mind,' the British Agent told him, 'that the main end to be pursued is the evacuation of the Soudan.' This involved getting the officials and soldiers out of the districts as well as sending back the garrisons from along the Nile. The secondary plan was to hand back power to the native ruling families whom Muhammad Ali had crushed earlier in the century. By pitting Sudanese against the Mahdi, the British hoped to undermine his support and create an independent, secular, friendly régime. 'It seemed to me,' Cromer wrote afterwards, 'that it would be a wise policy to establish a "buffer state" in the Soudan, which would hold much the same relation to Egypt as Afghanistan holds to British India.' Perhaps Cromer had forgotten the cost to Anglo-Indians of two wars to win over Afghanistan. Anyway, here lay the flaw in his plan, for the Mahdi was more popular than even Cromer had assumed and the Egyptian government had very little to offer the old ruling families – Gordon could only really give them titles, certainly not power. However, Gordon still had the possibility of fulfilling the main aim of his mission, to evacuate the Sudan, although even on this point there were difficulties: Gordon insisted that he himself should remain 'until everyone who wants to go down [the Nile into Egypt] is given the chance to do so.' In the furthest garrisons, for instance in Gordon's old province of Equatoria, those who wished to leave were no longer in a position to do so, and for the same reason that Gordon was unable to rescue them: the Mahdi was in the way.

In September, by which time Gordon had been in Khartoum for seven months, it was still considered possible for the capital itself to be evacuated. Thank God for the steamers he had brought up-stream. On the 10th of that month, Gordon was able to send his second-in-command, Colonel Stewart, down the river with the British and French Consuls and more than forty other passengers. Gordon himself still would not leave. A week after the departure of the steamer, when it had passed Abu Hamed and was making its way around the great bend in the river, it foundered on a rock and the passengers were obliged to land. While they were on the shore, a Bedouin sheikh came up to them wearing the trousers, Stamboulieh coat and tarboosh of a local official. Stewart was reassured by his manner and appearance and accepted an invitation to visit his house, where he and all of the other passengers were killed.

In March, when escape from Khartoum was still possible, Gordon had felt no need to leave the capital. His work was not finished and besides, of the 34,000 people in the town, 8,000 of them were soldiers. They had over 2,000,000 rounds of ammunition and a factory which could produce more. Surrounding them were over 30,000 of the Madhi's troops, who sat and watched and waited. Gordon, inside the walls, did the same. He had requested reinforcements from Egypt and from Britain and he really believed that they would come and that together they would 'smash' the Mahdi. Evacuating the Sudan without destroying the Mahdi, Gordon insisted, would mean that at a later date the Sudan would have to be conquered all over again and it would take many more troops to do it. Events proved him right, of course, but the British government did not want to be dragged into another African war, which was where they thought Gordon was leading them. Meanwhile, Gordon waited in Khartoum, sometimes with hope, standing on the roof of his palace and looking out for the arrival of reinforcements up the river. At other times he decided that there were no troops on the way and then he wrote that 'I have the strongest suspicion that tales of troops at Dongola and Mero are all gasworks and that if you wanted to find Her Majesty's Forces you would have to go to Shepheard's Hotel, Cairo.'

The British government had first discussed the idea of sending an expedition to rescue Gordon and the garrison as early as April 1884, just eight weeks or so after he had arrived in Khartoum, but the order to prepare to move troops up the Nile was not given until August. The orders that Lord Cromer did eventually issue on 8 October to Lord Wolseley, the victor of Tel el Kebir and commander of this new force, were explicit: 'The primary object of the expedition up the valley of the Nile is to bring away General Gordon and Colonel Stewart from Khartoum. When that object has been secured, no further offensive operations of any kind are to be undertaken.' This was clear enough, although by the time Wolseley and his staff left Shepheard's Hotel, Stewart and the consuls from Khartoum were already dead.

The Gordon relief force advanced with caution. Wolseley had been forbidden to lead the force into action himself – too many 'names' had already been lost in this wilderness of a country – although during the very first assault on the force that marched across the Nubian desert another 'name', the second-in-command, Colonel Burnaby, was killed. The *Egyptian Gazette*'s obituary concluded that 'Probably no man in the army or out of it took such infinite pains to get killed as Burnaby did.' Then, on the following day, Sir Herbert Stewart, the next-in-command, fell and the command was now assumed by Sir Charles Wilson. He reached the Nile on 19 January and met the four steamers sent down-river by Gordon two days later. But instead of turning these around and making straight for Khartoum, Wilson spent the next three days reconnoitring the area. When he finally boarded the boats, they made slow progress, for the river was high and the current strong, and the Sudanese fired at them from the banks. The closer they got to Khartoum, the heavier the attacks and when they finally reached the capital on 28 January, the day of Gordon's fifty-second birthday, they were fired on by both rifle and artillery. 'An eager search was made through glasses,' Cromer reported, 'to see whether the Egyptian flag was still flying.' It was not. Gordon had died two days earlier. Unable to bring either Gordon or Colonel Stewart out alive, the relief force – and with it, both England and Egypt – retreated from the Sudan and abandoned it to the Mahdi.

However, Egypt still held on to Suakin. Emin Pasha was holed up in Equatoria, where Gordon had sent him as Governor in 1879 – 'I am still waiting for help and that from England,' Emin wrote in July 1886 – and from where Stanley 'rescued' him in April 1888. The Mahdi died six months after Gordon, in 1885, and was succeeded by a disciple, the Khalifa, whose troops kept pressure on the Egyptian garrison on the border at Wadi Halfa. All this and the feeling, both in Cairo and London, that Gordon had been badly treated and unnecessarily sacrificed, kept the Sudan in the public mind. It was seen as a dangerous and abominable place which by its very presence threatened the decency of western civilization. The Khalifa wrote a letter to Queen Victoria in which he explained that 'if thou wilt not yield to the command of God, and enter among the people of Islam and the followers of the Mahdi – grace be upon him, come thyself and thy armies and fight with the host of God. And if thou wilt not come, then be ready in thy place, for at His pleasure and at the time that He shall will it, the hosts of God will raze thy dwelling and let thee taste of sorrow.' Nothing could have been better aimed to guarantee the return of the Queen's soldiers.

★

Towards the end of 1885, the year in which Khartoum fell, Dr Liddon arrived in Egypt with his sister Mrs Annie King, a niece, and a dragoman by the name of De Nicola. Dr Liddon, a famous English preacher, was travelling on account of his health, for the climate in Egypt was supposed to be beneficial for him; Mrs King explained that this was 'the one long holiday he allowed himself in his life of serious work.' They intended to hire a dahabieh and to sail up as far as Abu Simbel, but even before they landed in Alexandria they realized that Egypt had become more of an army camp than a touring ground. 'Everybody anticipates the Nile will be more than usually pleasant up to the First Cataract, as the mass of tourists are frightened at the military preparations, that it would be fairly safe between the First and Second Cataracts, but so given up to the military that it would scarcely be pleasant.'

They decided to travel only as far as Philae. They would dearly have liked to see Abu Simbel, but what with the military considerations and their own timetable – they were going to 'do' the Holy Land as well – Philae was as far as they expected to go. They landed on Christmas Eve and immediately met Mr Charles Cookson, the British Consul in Alexandria and veteran of the 1882 riots where he was 'seriously wounded' – Baron de Kusel had recorded that Cookson 'had ventured out to use his influence in quieting the rioters in the Maltese quarter,

but received a knock on the head which nearly proved fatal.' Three
years later, this was the man who came on board the P & O steamer
as it docked in Alexandria, to introduce himself to Dr Liddon. They
had been friends during their university days, and the meeting was
a happy one.

Being led by their picturesque dragoman, De Nicola – 'You must
trost me, lady, trost me . . .' – they arrived at the Khedival Hotel, large
and comfortable and, of course, noisy. 'This hotel,' Mrs King wrote
to her family at home, 'was partly destroyed by the bombardment,
and is still being rebuilt.' They only stayed two days in Alexandria
before taking the ten o'clock train to Cairo and soon found some aspects
of travelling in Egypt exceedingly irksome: '. . . having waited an in-
tolerable time at the station . . . the train, finally starting when least
expected, left sundry of the passengers on the platform, whom we
could see helplessly gesticulating as we glided out of sight.' In Cairo
they stayed in Shepheard's Hotel, where at least half of the diners in
the vast dining-room, the noisiest Mrs King had ever been in, were
military men. The streets, too, were full of them. Here they met an
English lady and her two daughters – 'decidedly good-looking people',
Mrs King thought – who appeared to be determined to stay at Shepheard's until the daughters had found husbands. Their time was spent
'laying siege to the unmarried officers . . . one or more of whom dines
with them each day. So far as we can judge,' Mrs King decided, 'the
dinners have not yet produced the desired effect. Husband-hunting at
all your meals must be very fatiguing, not to say anxious work.'

When they set off up the Nile they met fewer attractive daughters,
but more military men. Telegrams arrived in Cairo, or word reached
them on the river of 'events' in the Sudan, but they heard no more
and Mrs King wrote to her daughter in England that 'probably you
know more about that than we do, as very little news is allowed to
filter through here.' Between Benisouef and Minia they passed a
steamer, full of sick and wounded soldiers, on its way down to Cairo.
The healthy ones passing up-river were sent by train as far as the railhead
at Asyut.

Two weeks later, when they had passed Sohag, their captain claimed
to have received reliable news of a terrible defeat for the British on
the border at Wadi Halfa, but when they reached Luxor a few days
later the British Consul assured them that the border was quite safe
and that they were even reducing the size of the garrison there. But
they were anxious all the same and Mrs King noted that 'last winter
travellers could not go a quarter of a mile from the river bank, as the
country was overrun by brigands, who robbed and murdered in most

of the towns along the Nile.'

Further up-river at Aswan, they encountered more activity. Two miles from the town they found the first military dahabiehs tied up and heard that at least two British regiments were stationed in the town. They sailed into Aswan in the morning with the sun low over the granite hills and the sunlight dazzling on the water and Mrs King decided that the military aspect added to the beauty and interest of the town. They anchored off Elephantine Island which 'gives a charming view of Assouan, the camp and all the traffic. It is a very busy scene in a pictur-esque spot, and at present a perfect climate.' Here their lives were run by the military. The train on the short line from Aswan to Shellal was used to take troops around the First Cataract. On the day Dr Liddon and his party planned to take the train, so that they could visit Philae, they were obliged to wait for two hours before the military would allow it to leave. Later, they dined with a Colonel G—, were taken to see the new excavations Professor Maspero was conducting with Egyptian soldiers as labourers, watched the officers play polo and took tea in camp.

Back in Shepheard's Hotel in Cairo more than a month later, Dr Liddon was introduced to the exiled Bishop of Khartoum. 'He spoke of Gordon as his dearest friend,' Mrs King wrote home, 'and a constant attendant at their services.' Gordon, the Bishop assured them, was 'the best and holiest of men, alike beloved and revered by Christians and Arabs.' They sat and listened to the old man's stories about the Christian martyr for so long that they had no time to sight-see on that day.

Finally, as they left Egypt via the Suez Canal on their way to the Holy Land, they crossed 'the battlefield of Tel-el-Kebir, now marked by a small English cemetery on one side of the railway, and large mounds of sand covering the Egyptian dead on the other side.'

Eleven years later, the *Daily Mail* correspondent G. W. Steevens saw a similar sight around Wadi Halfa when he was on his way into the Sudan, that 'man-eater – red-gorged, but still insatiable.' The town was the frontier post, but it 'has left off being a fortress and a garrison; to-day it is all workshop and railway terminus.' Here the railway across the desert picked up what the steamers from Egypt unloaded. Here, too, a little way out of town, was a cemetery. 'No need to dismount,' Steevens assured, 'or even to read the names – see merely how full it is. Each white cross is an Englishman devoured by the Sudan.' There would be more, too, for an Anglo-Egyptian army was being sent, as Gordon said it would, to reclaim the Sudan and to avenge Gordon's death. There would be little economic gain in it, for the Sudan had suffered from so many years of neglect that its farmland was now mostly uncultivated or uncultivatable. But that no longer mattered; Gordon's betrayal had to be righted. It was a public issue, although politically, too, the British could no longer afford to hold back in Africa – Uganda and Kenya had both become British Protectorates since the Sudan had fallen, and the British were now afraid that the Italians were encroaching on the Sudan from the east and that the French were moving inland from the west. In spite of their often-expressed reluctance to expand further, the British could not afford to allow anyone else to expand either.

The Anglo-Egyptian force advanced slowly and with care. The army of 10,000 soldiers was commanded by General Kitchener, a friend of Cromer's and of whom Gordon himself had written in 1884, 'The man I have always placed my hopes upon, Major Kitchener, RE, is one of the few *very superior* British officers.' Now here was the very man, with a well-trained force which included a young Winston Churchill, Lord Edward Cecil and Major Wingate, later Governor-General of the Sudan. Rather than trusting to the river, which had been so unpredictable in the past, Kitchener built a railway across the desert from Wadi Halfa to Abu Hamed, above the Fourth Cataract. This project showed the new determination in the British force. Under the direction of Bimbashi Girouard, who had built part of the Canadian Pacific Railroad, the Sudanese track was laid at a rate of over a mile a day, across a desert which was previously mostly uncharted and where water was always scarce. Also working on the railway was Captain W. S. Gordon, RE, a nephew of the dead general. Between 15 May and 31 October, 1897 – 169 days – more than 230 miles of track was laid and the railhead reached Abu Hamed on time.

Steevens from the *Daily Mail* was twenty-seven years old when he went up to Khartoum. Kitchener had made it clear that he did not want journalists on the expedition, but he had been given no choice by his superiors and even Churchill was under contract to a British paper. From Cairo, Steevens started out by train in a stuffy carriage piled high with 'a confusion of bags and bundles, of helmet-cases and sword-cases, of canvas buckets cooling soda, and canvas bottles cooling water.' Somehow the scene reminded him of going back to school. Some of the officers had been back to England on leave, but most had been discouraged because Kitchener did not want too many of his staff seen in London. They went to Turkey or Italy instead, or just hung around in Egypt. 'Thank the Lord, no more Cairo,' Steevens imagined them thinking, 'sweat all the night instead of sleep, and mosquitoes tearing you to pieces. Give me the night-breeze of the desert and the clean sand of the Sudan.'

Their servants spread out blankets on the hard leather seats in the carriage and they slept between Cairo and Luxor, where they then had to change trains, for the new track from Luxor to Aswan was built to a smaller gauge. There was no time to linger in Luxor however, nor any time to watch the river in Aswan. Shellal, the steamer station near Philae which Dr Liddon had used more than a decade before was 'one solid rampart of ammunition and beef, biscuit and barley; it clanged and tinkled all night through with parts of steamers and sections of barges. Stern-wheelers came down from the South, turned about, took in fuel, hooked on four barges alongside, and thudded off up-river again. No hurry; no rest.' One thudded off straightaway with Steevens on board. It took more than three days to cover the 200-odd miles to Wadi Halfa.

'Spring or summer, Halfa's business is the same,' Steevens wrote from the old border town, 'the railway and the recruits.' From Halfa he took the new Sudan Military Railway (S.M.R.) across the desert, travelling in 'a long double-bogie, with a plank roof, and canvas curtains that you could let down when the sun came in, and eight angarabs screwed to the floor. Therein six men piled their smaller baggage, and set up their tables, and ate and drank and slept and yawned forty-eight hours to the Atbara.'

Kitchener had reached Atbara with the advance part of his army at the end of March 1898, and had fought a battle for it on 8 April. He was sure now. The railway followed the troops through the long, hot summer and by the middle of August everything was ready for the final push on to the Khalifa's capital of Omdurman. The army, comprising a British and an Egyptian infantry division, one British regiment and ten Egyptian squadrons of cavalry, some artillery, camel corps, medical service and transport corps, was in fine form. 'There were not fifty graves in the cemetery,' Steevens noted happily, 'and most of the faces at the mess-tables were familiar.' The journalists were familiar faces, too, and one major in the camp explained that it was 'good to see all you fellows coming out again; means business.' As for the conversation around the mess-tables on those August nights when Khartoum was almost in sight, this was how Steevens recorded it: 'Going to the Gymkhana... Squat on his hunkers inside his wall... won't sell you a drop of milk, the surly devils, when we're saving their country... the houses at Omdurman are outside the wall, you know... not a bad notion of jumping, that bay pony... street-to-street fighting, we should lose a devil of a lot of men... did you hear the Guards cabled to ask what arrangements had been made for ice on the campaign?... but then he can't defend his wall; it hasn't got a banquette, and it's twelve feet high . . .' The battle was near. 'We were marching into lands where few Englishmen had ever set heel, no Englishman for fifteen years,' the correspondent wrote as the 20,000-strong army set out. 'We were to be present at the tardy vengeance for a great humiliation.'

The battle of Omdurman was a famous victory for Kitchener. The day before the battle, on 1 September, 1898, Steevens went out with a reconnaisance party to view the front of Omdurman. 'In front of the city stretched a long white line – banners, it might be; more likely tents; most likely both. In front of that was a longer, thicker black line – no doubt a zariba or trench . . . Only as we sat and ate biscuit and looked – the entrenchment moved. The solid wall moved forward, and it was a wall of men.' The following morning, that wall advanced towards Kitchener's army. Steevens called it the last day of Mahdism, and the greatest. White troops, he was certain, would never have withstood the fire that the Khalifa's men faced. When the battle was over – the Khalifa lost 11,000 men killed, 16,000 wounded; Kitchener's total casualties, killed and wounded, were said to be less than 500 – Steevens wrote sadly, 'Our men were perfect, but the Dervishes were superb – beyond perfection.' What the dervishes had achieved with their perfection was the hitherto unthinkable breaking of the British 'square', a solid phalanx of well-armed, well-trained soldiers. It was an event of such importance that Rudyard Kipling, the poet imperial, immortalized it in a poem entitled *Fuzzy-Wuzzy*, which ends:

> 'So 'ere's *to* you, Fuzzy-Wuzzy, at your 'ome in the Soudan;
> You're a pore benighted 'eathen but a first-class fightin' man;
> An' 'ere's *to* you, Fuzzy-Wuzzy, with your 'ayrick 'ead of
>   'air –
> You big black boundin' beggar – for you broke a British
>   square!'

Kitchener rode into Omdurman with his own red and white flag flying beside the captured black banner of the Khalifa. As he approached the entrance to the town, as Steevens tells it, 'an old man on a donkey with a white flag' came out to meet him.

'Would they all be massacred now?' the old man asked.

'No,' Kitchener told him, they would not.

The town then surrendered and the Anglo-Egyptian force marched in.

Two days later, on 4 September, Steevens crossed the river with Kitchener, his staff and detachments from the army, to Gordon's palace at Khartoum. 'You could see that it had once been a handsome edifice of the type you know in Cairo or Alexandria – all stone and stucco, two-storied, faced with tall regular windows.' From the flagpoles the Union Jack and the Egyptian flag were flown, the Guards' band played 'God Save our Gracious Queen', a river-boat fired its guns in salute, priests chanted prayers, Kitchener himself cried out 'Three cheers for the Queen!', helmets were thrown and it was felt that Gordon had been given a fitting tribute.

★

The year after Kitchener defeated the Khalifa, an Englishman by the name of Ewart S. Grogan arrived in Khartoum. By then there was nothing unusual in seeing an Englishman in the Sudan, but unlike another Englishman whom he met there, Grogan had not come up the Nile from Alexandria. Nor, like two other Englishmen also in Khartoum at the time, had he come across from the east, from the Red Sea coast. He also met three Frenchmen who had come over from the Atlantic coast. But Grogan's journey was even more spectacular – he had just completed the first overland crossing of Africa from Cape Town. When he reached Khartoum in 1899, Grogan was invited along with these six other European travellers to a 'great dinner' given by Kitchener, who had assumed Gordon's title of Governor-General of the Sudan. 'Our simultaneous arrival,' Grogan wrote, 'was an extraordinary coincidence, and that in what was almost the uttermost end of the earth.' During the dinner, Grogan was able to report that 'the name of an Englishman is held high throughout Africa, and the Union Jack is the surest passport in the land.'

After he had tasted the full pleasures of Khartoum's hospitality, Grogan set out for Cairo. A hundred and twenty years had passed since James Bruce went in search of the source of the Nile, to show 'to the world of what value the efforts of every individual of your Majesty's subjects may be...', less than fifty years since Flaubert and Florence Nightingale spent quiet months sailing up to the Egyptian border. But now for Grogan it was all very matter-of-fact. 'The Soudan railway soon carried us down to Wady Halfa,' he reported, 'thence a steamer to Assuan, and again the railway, and we once more stood in the roar of multitudes at the station in Cairo. And now it is over... Here I stand, in the land of certainty and respectability!'

PART TWO

SEEING THE SIGHTS

'... what is going on in all the *canges* that are fitted out like
ours? English ... gentlemen with ladies – albums displayed
on round tables – they will be talked about in green parks...'
Gustave Flaubert, *Travel Notebooks*, 1850

During the evening of 2 October 1872, Phileas Fogg, the eccentric hero
of Jules Verne's *Around the World in Eighty Days*, left his companions
at the Reform Club in London, took his *Bradshaw's Continental Railway
Steam Transit and General Guide*, collected his servant and a carpetbag
containing £20,000, and caught the 8.45 p.m. train from Charing Cross
Station. Crossing over from Dover to Calais, he then took the express
train to Brindisi via Mount Cenis, boarded the P&O iron steamer *Mon-
golia* and, only seven days after leaving London, arrived at the southern
end of the Suez Canal at eleven o'clock in the morning, exactly on
time. The steamer docked at Suez for a few hours and Fogg used the
time to go ashore and obtain a *visé* for his passport from the British
consular agent. Having fulfilled this formality, he returned to the wharf,
was rowed back to the steamer and waited for it to leave for Bombay.
'As to seeing the town,' Verne explained, 'he did not think of it, being
of that race of Englishmen who have their servants visit the countries
they pass through.'

Although Gustave Flaubert, when he declared that the temples bored
him, proved that even a man of learning and sensibility could tire of
seeing the sights in Egypt, many people who passed through the Suez
Canal did want to stop off in Egypt and, of those, most wanted to
do some sight-seeing. But in the second half of the nineteenth century,
the problem for the hurrying visitor wanting to go up to Aswan or
Abu Simbel was that the distances involved were formidable and the
available transport slow. So when the railway was opened between
Alexandria and Cairo, the old steamer route along the Mahmoudieh
Canal and the Nile was immediately abandoned by most travellers.
However, even starting from Cairo, where dahabiehs to let were tied
up along the quay at Boulak, Abu Simbel was still nearly 800 unpredictable miles away. The Egyptian season traditionally started in November
because not only was the weather just right – cool enough for Europeans
to travel in comfort and still much warmer than a northern winter

125

– but also, this was when the winds usually changed and began to blow from the north. Eight hundred miles with the wind and Allah behind you still took four to six weeks. But if the winds failed the boat had to be pulled or rowed up the river, at three miles an hour if the going was good. Obviously patience was an essential requirement for a Nile journey where the word *Inshallah* – God willing – was added to the end of each itinerary. So, although it was unheard of to have adverse winds for three consecutive weeks, it was obviously helpful to leave Cairo when the winds were behind you.

The first thing to be done, usually even before hiring a boat, was to find a dragoman. The word is derived from the Arabic *targuman*, which literally means 'interpreter'. The dragoman, however, was more than merely a linguist; he was also a guide and organizer. He knew better than his employers where they wanted to go and how they were going to get there; and along with the *rais* or captain of the boat he was the person who left the greatest impression on the traveller. A dragoman was usually indispensable, but the relationship between him and his employer was a delicate one: he had the knowledge but they had the money; they were the masters but he was their leader. Obviously it was important to get on with him from the start. Cook's *Handbook* for 1906 advised that 'It often requires considerable moral courage to keep these individuals in their proper places, for the more useful and capable they are the more easy it is for their employers to lose control over them.' It was essential to keep control of this man for he in turn usually kept the captain of the dahabieh in check.

Dahabiehs were one of the larger sort of Nile boat and, for a long time before Europeans visited the country were used by wealthy Egyptians and Turks to travel along the Nile. Rather like cars in our own time, dahabiehs were status symbols, a visible assertion of wealth, and a pasha would have at least one for himself and one for his harem. Later, dahabiehs were rented out to foreigners — Florence Nightingale's boat, for instance had never taken Europeans before, but had been for the exclusive use of a wealthy pasha's harem. Dahabiehs were also the most comfortable boats on the river at the time and when the Nile cruise became a popular and fashionable thing for Europeans and Americans to do, the number and variety available for hire increased greatly so that when Amelia Edwards arrived in Egypt for the first time, twenty-three years after Florence Nightingale, she had nearly 300 of them to choose from at Boulak. 'Now, most persons know something of the miseries of house-hunting,' she wrote, 'but only those who have experienced them know how much keener are the miseries of dahabeeyah-hunting.' The first problem was that they all seemed to look the same.

Some were a little longer and others a little shorter, some newly painted and others weather-worn, but their layout was usually the same. Even the crews tended to look alike to the travellers. A system of testimonials had been introduced whereby people who had previously hired a boat gave a written recommendation or condemnation to help future passengers, but even these – which every captain seemed to have – all appeared to be similar and sometimes were indeed the same sheet of paper passed on from one boat to another. 'All this is very perplexing,' Amelia admitted, 'yet it is as nothing compared with the state of confusion one gets into when attempting to weigh the advantages or disadvantages of boats with six cabins and boats with eight; boats provided with canteens, and boats without; boats that can pass the cataract, and boats that can't; boats that are only twice as dear as they ought to be, and boats with that defect five or six times multiplied. Their names, again – Ghazal, Sarawa, Fostat, Dongola – unlike any names one has ever heard before, afford as yet no kind of help to the memory.'

The dahabieh they eventually hired, which Amelia described as being 'more like a civic or an Oxford University barge, than anything in the shape of a boat with which we in England are familiar,' was a large one, 100 feet long, with eight sleeping cabins. 'These cabins measured about eight feet in length by four and a half in width, and contained a bed, a chair, a fixed washing-stand, a looking-glass against the wall, a shelf, a row of hooks, and under each bed two large drawers for clothes.' In addition, there was a dining saloon, a bathroom, and another small saloon in the stern which they used for storage. 'For the crew,' Amelia added, 'there was no sleeping accommodation whatever, unless they chose to creep into the hold among the luggage and packing-cases.'

Some dahabiehs were even larger than this, like the khedival boat at the disposal of the Prince and Princess of Wales when they toured Egypt in 1869, just before the opening of the Suez Canal. The fittings on Ismail's dahabieh were beautiful and expensive and the carpets were rare and thick. It was bigger than most Nile boats, too, and the Prince and Princess had a bedroom, two bathrooms and two dressing-rooms for their own use, and even the Hon Mrs William Grey, the Princess's companion who recorded their journey, had two cabins of seven feet by seven for herself and one each for her maid and her dresser. Because this was a royal party, locomotion was not left in the hands of the weather and, instead of unfurling the lateen sail, the royal dahabieh was towed up the Nile by a steamer, the *Federabanee*. This does seem to be missing some of the point of travelling by dahabieh, namely the sense of peace which settles over the boat as the wind fills the sail and passengers settle into armchairs under the awning on the upper deck, the land slipping past, scenery changing as gradually as the sun moving across the sky.

When a dahabieh had been chosen and a price agreed, a contract was drawn up which safeguarded both sides – foreigners could be sure that they would get to where they wanted to go and the crew knew they would be paid for taking them there. At first these were registered with the passengers' consulate, but as the number of foreigners in Egypt increased this became impractical and tourist agencies took over. Having arranged the formalities, the boat was taken across the river to the bank at Gezira or Giza where it was sunk to rid it of rats and whatever else was living on it. *Murray's Guide* stressed the importance of moving off that side of the river as soon as possible after the boat had been refloated, for otherwise the vermin simply climbed back on board and the process had to be repeated. After its submersion, the boat was dried, redecorated and fitted out with rugs, mattresses, bedding and whatever else the owners had agreed to provide. In the days before Cook's tours and travel representatives, it was as well to pay attention to these details at the beginning of a trip and make sure the work was done properly and that the boat was carrying the necessary equipment and stores. John Gardner Wilkinson, the Egyptologist whose guide to the country formed the basis for *Murray's Guide*, suggested a list of requirements which would fill the average modern home. Among the equipment he listed were mats, carpets, towels, sheets, cloths, pillows and cases, horse-hair mattresses, blankets and mosquito nets – preferably the invention of an earlier traveller in Egypt, Mr Levinge, who devised the curious hanging mosquito tent. This was considered indispensable, as were a national flag, pots, kettles, curtains, table and chairs, thermometer, two sheets of Mackintosh, a medicine chest, water filter and even a donkey, or at least a donkey saddle. The list of foods the passengers were advised to take with them was even more extensive. Of course, as more tourists went up the river, it became easier to procure the sort of provisions they would enjoy in towns along the way, but before that time it was necessary to make an expedition to the bazaars in Cairo, usually under the guidance of the dragoman.

'A rapid raid into some of the nearest shops, for things remembered at the last moment – a breathless gathering up of innumerable parcels – a few hurried farewells on the steps of the hotel – and away we rattle,' Amelia wrote of her departure from Shepheard's. With the dahabieh decorated and filled with their bags and provisions, all that was needed for them to start was a fair wind. Sometimes, if there was only a slight wind, the dahabieh was towed or rowed away from its mooring into the middle of the river before the great sail was unfurled. But if, as on this occasion, the wind was up, the captain stood on the upper deck, the steersman at the helm and all it took was a push from the sailors and the crowd which always gathered on the wharf when a boat was leaving. Their departure was then announced by several rounds fired from the dragoman's pistols. It was not a racing start, but a slow, sedate, stately progression.

★

The first part of a Nile cruise, now as then, was probably something of an anti-climax after the noise and excitement of Cairo. There were the Pyramids to look at of course, but they had probably already been visited from Cairo. Apart from them and the other pyramids at Sakkara, the most impressive antiquities were several hundred miles up-river. These first days, therefore, were a time to adjust to the slower tempo of the river and to living within the confines of a boat and a small cabin rather than a large hotel room. From a lounge-chair on the upper deck, the mosques and palaces of Cairo were seen slipping into the distance and although the Pyramids loomed impressively dark and mysterious on the west bank, less monumental sights – a farmer in the fields, birds on the banks, other boats on the river – also began to attract attention. One palm tree followed another and field after field slipped away. They lost count of it all, the dream sequence of the Nile began and it was not until the sun set on that first day that thoughts turned to food and the reverie was shattered.

Bedrashen, fourteen miles from Cairo, was often the stopping-point for the first night, a good place from which to visit the ruins at Memphis and Sakkara: Amelia Edwards arrived there by starlight. The cook had gone about his business in what was called the kitchen but was really a little shelter between the mast and prow. Further back, on the upper deck of the 100-foot boat, was the dining-room, 'a spacious, cheerful room, some twenty-three or twenty-four feet long, situated in the widest part of the boat, and lighted by four windows on each side and a skylight. The panelled walls and ceiling were painted in white picked out with gold; a cushioned divan covered with a smart woollen reps ran along each side; and a gay Brussels carpet adorned the floor.' The long dining-table was in the middle of the room around which hung gilt mirrors, with guns in the corner, hats on hooks between the windows and scarlet and orange curtains and hangings. The piano was to one side.

There was nothing for them to hurry their dinner, which was as slow and drawn-out as the progress of the dahabieh. But while Amelia and her companions were still seated around the dining table on their first night, they heard what she described as 'a prolonged wail that swelled, and sank, and swelled again, and at last died away.' It was quickly followed by other wails and then 'one long, still, descending cry, like a yawn, or a howl, or a combination of both.' Out on deck they saw their sailors sitting cross-legged in a circle on the lower deck, singing to a rhythm from a rosewood and mother-of-pearl tambourine and a clay and parchment drum. A lantern in the middle of the group added to the mood. Behind them were the Nile and the shadows of the Pyramids. The foreigners stayed out on deck. The stars were more numerous and hung lower than they had even seen before; the sound the sailors made was entirely unfamiliar to them and as jarring as the smell of tobacco and maybe of some hashish being smoked in a coconut and sycamore pipe, passed around the circle from hand to hand. On this first night on the Nile, under the stars, the magic of their tour began.

Dahabieh life was constricting for an active person and Florence Nightingale had found it very difficult to stay on board all day, which she was obliged to do when the wind was behind them. She was relieved when the sail dropped and she was able to walk along the bank. There was a great deal to do, however, if one was going to get the full benefit from the trip. There was always an extensive amount to be read about the tombs and temples, and about the exploits of other travellers on the river before them. Wilkinson in his guide reckoned that an essential library could only be cut down to about thirty volumes. In addition, however, there would have to be extra volumes for any special interests like bird-watching or shooting. On the other hand, if, like Charles Moberly Bell, *The Times* correspondent in Egypt in 1884, you felt like doing nothing, then that was exactly what you could do. Bell went up the river for a holiday with a couple of friends – Sir Edgar Vincent, Financial Adviser to the Egyptian government, and his brother Claude – and took with him only four books: one by Plato, the *Epic of Hades*, *John Inglesant* and Amelia Edwards's *1000 Miles up the Nile*. In between towns and temples they rested.

'You should see us,' the correspondent wrote home,
sprawling about the decks in the very lightest of attires [it
was June and they were going up as far as Wadi Halfa on
the Sudan border] . . . cool drinks and watermelons ready cut
into mouthfuls all around us – the only work we have to
do ourselves in the operation being the digestion . . . Servants
on the look-out for something to shoot, and when it is
found, the loaded guns placed in our hands, directed, and
nothing left for us to do but to pull the trigger, and not much use

doing that. If we want to look at anything someone is at
hand with the glasses, servants to whisk away the flies, and
to hold umbrellas over us. If, as rarely happens, we want
to go anywhere, we are lifted on to horses, umbrellas held
over us. I never was quite so lazy in my life.

Of course when they did stop along the way there was also some walking
to be done, but days were exhaustingly hot and they had little inclination
to see more than the absolute minimum.

Amelia Edwards had set off up the Nile in the cooler month of
December and was more energetic in her travels. Apart from seeing
almost all that there was to see at the time – and there was a great
deal of that – she fulfils the stereotyped image of Victorians by being
in a perpetual state of activity. She needed to be doing something,
to have something to show for her time. She read exhaustively on
the subject of Egyptology and observed the ways of the modern Egyptians as well. She painted scenes on the river and at the temples in
watercolours and she always carried a little sketchbook in her pocket
in case something caught her eye – todays's tourists carry pocket-sized
cameras with them for much the same purpose. Egypt was a mystery
to Amelia, a book to be read, she called it at one point, but one which
required a whole new vocabulary. 'We cannot all be profoundly
learned,' she explained, 'but we can at least do our best to understand
what we see . . .' If there were hills to be climbed, she would be amongst
those who were compelled to run to the top. There was an element
of competition in her as well, which came to the fore when they were
approaching Edfu alongside the *Bagstones*, a dahabieh hired by two English ladies whom Amelia had met on the steamer from Brindisi and
with whom she was now on friendly terms. There was also a third
dahabieh, an iron boat called the *Fostât*, and all three of them caught
the wind at the same time and moved off up-stream together. 'And
now,' Amelia announced, 'with that irrepressible instinct of rivalry that
flesh – especially flesh in the Nile – is heir to, we quickly turn our
good going into a trial of speed. It is no longer a mere business-like
devotion to the matter in hand. It is a contest for glory . . . In plain
English, it is a race.' Although all three were dahabiehs, they were
all different – the *Bagstones* was smaller than the *Philae*, while the *Fostât*
had the largest mainsail, but an iron hull – and they took turns to
lead the race. By the end of the day, dinner had been forgotten, to
sleep would have been difficult, the night's moorings were ignored
and even the crews entered into the spirit of the race. Winning was
a matter of pride.

At three o'clock in the morning they were awake to witness all three boats running aground on a sandbank. Amelia's boat, the *Philae*, was the first to be poled off and they made the most of this new advantage. The wind blew for the rest of the night and Edfu, Silsileh, Kom Ombo were all quickly passed. At seven o'clock in the morning, the *Philae* was only fifteen miles from Aswan, but it was losing ground and the other two boats were now in sight. This was too much for Amelia. She had to win the race. 'A guine'e for Reis Hassan, if we get first to Assûan!' she shouted. The small, powerful man was moved. His eyes glistened. This was his sort of sport, a matter now of pride and money. 'He touches his head and breast; casts a backward glance at the pursuing dahabeeyahs, a forward glance in the direction of Assûan; kicks off his shoes; ties a handkerchief about his waist; and stations himself at the top of the steps leading to the upper deck.' The sun rose higher, the day became hotter, the wind stayed constant and the two pursuing dahabiehs continued to gain on them. With five miles to go, only a matter of a few yards separated the three boats. Amelia's crew fell silent. By the time Aswan's minarets were in sight the *Fostât* was actually alongside them. They had come more than sixty-five miles and there was still nothing in it as they approached the final narrow channel which led into a tight bend and then straight up to Aswan through a passage which was only wide enough for one boat. The two of them approached it together, but then the *Fostat* made a mistake in adjusting its sail and the *Philae* went through first. Five minutes later, Amelia was in Aswan and her captain Hassan had a guinea in his hand.

In Aswan there was a town and marketplace to explore, and the Governor to entertain while waiting to be towed up the rapids of the First Cataract. When the *Philae*'s turn came to go up the cataract, one of the ropes that was being used broke; the Nubians who were pulling the boat saw this as a bad omen and left it tied up between the rapids. The next day the feeling was still all wrong and the *Philae* was moved no further even though they had paid the Sheikh of the Cataracts £12 for the service. At this point, one of the men in Amelia's party became so annoyed at the delay that he summoned the Sheikh and expressed his feelings in some well-chosen Arabic words. The Sheikh, Amelia reported, was rather upset and left them there and then. But the following day he arrived back with new ropes and about 200 men who hauled the *Philae* straight up the five miles of rapids.

Amelia could not stay to watch, however. It was against her nature to be so still and she set off into the desert and to the nearest villages with her sketchbook in her pocket. A few days later, having cleared the cataract, the *Philae* arrived off the temple of Abu Simbel by moon-light. Amelia thought that the four colossal statues of Rameses II outside the great temple were so fantastic that it was just possible that they might disappear with the moonlight and be remembered only as a dream. However, they were still there when she woke the next morning, as they had been for more than 3,000 years.

In 1837, a group of artists and Egyptologists accompanying Robert Hay had taken a cast of the face of one of the colossal statues (now in the British Museum). The casting process had left a coating of plaster over the face which a number of visitors had complained about, so Amelia and her companions decided to build a scaffolding around the face and to clean off the plaster. When this had been done, the newly exposed sandstone was a different tone to the rest of the statue, so they matched up the colouring by painting the face with strong coffee which the cook's boy brought them from the dahabieh. 'What with boating, fishing, lying in wait for crocodiles, cleaning the colossus, and filling reams of thin letter paper to friends at home,' Amelia wrote energetically, 'we got through the first week quickly enough – the Painter and the Writer [Amelia herself] working hard, meanwhile, in their respective ways...'

Forty miles further up-river they reached Wadi Halfa, the Second Cataract and the southernmost point of their journey: the rock of Abu-sir, the butt of a sandstone range which runs alongside the rapids for five miles or so. Amelia likened the rock to a cathedral front and climbed up it from the river bank. The top she described as 'a mere ridge, steep and overhanging east and south, and carved all over with autographs in stone. Some few of these are interesting; but for the most part they record only the visits of the illustrious-obscure. We found Belzoni's name; but looked in vain for the signatures of Burckhardt, Champollion, Lepsius, and Ampère.' From the summit she could see back as far as Abu Simbel and on up the river to the mountains of Dongola, 150 miles away. It was the most extraordinary panorama she had ever seen, especially the colours of the rock, the sand and water – pearl, pink, amber, purple. She could see far across the desert and thought that apart from 'the telegraphic wires stalking, ghost-like, across the desert, it would seem as if we had touched the limit of civilization, and were standing on the threshold of a land unexplored.' Ahead, also, was the great river, winding its way down through the desert. Although she had covered a thousand miles of it from Alexandria, its source was still literally unexplored. The view silenced her. She could not sketch. Words, she decided, could not convey this impression either. She would always remember it, but she would never be able to describe it. 'Nearly every traveller who has visited Abû Simbel,' *Cook's Handbook for Egypt and the Sûdân* (1906) advised, 'has been to this rock and inscribed his name upon it; the result is an interesting collection of names and dates, the like of which probably exists nowhere else.' Amelia refrained from adding hers.

Back on the *Philae*, the mainyard had been taken down, the mainsail rolled into a ball and stowed away, and a dozen oars fixed into runners on the lower deck. The boat's prow was turned to the north, to Aswan, Luxor, Cairo, Alexandria and home. The greatest excitements of their journey lay behind them; they now knew what to expect on their way back, although they were a little surprised to find five dahabiehs tied up at Abu Simbel. The day after their arrival, the *Bagstones* arrived in the company of yet another boat and for a few days the place was crowded with tourists busy with visits to the temples and to each other's boats. Then the others moved off and the *Philae* had the mooring to itself.

Some time after midday on Sunday, 16 February 1874, the boat's bell was rung as usual for luncheon and Amelia and her friends sat down to eat. Since the artist, Andrew M'Callum, did not appear, the bell was rung two more times; when he still did not come, Amelia assumed that he had wandered off to paint somewhere and maybe had even taken some lunch with him. They started without him and were in the middle of eating when one of the crew interrupted them to deliver a note which read: 'Pray come immediately – I have found the entrance to a tomb. Please send some sandwiches – A.M'C.' They immediately rushed off to find him and Amelia remembered that 'All that Sunday afternoon, heedless of possible sunstroke, unconscious of fatigue, we toiled upon our hands and knees, as for bare life, under the burning sun. We had all the crew up, working like tigers. Everyone helped; even the dragoman and the two maids. More than once, when we paused for a moment's breathing space, we said to each other: "If those at home could see us, what would they say!"'

She had probably read Captain Charles Irby's account of how he, James Mangles and Giovanni Belzoni cleared the sand away from the front of the Great Temple here, little more than fifty years before. The twenty of them now dug away at the side of the Great Temple with one fire shovel, one birch broom and a couple of baskets, scooping the sand away from the front of a wall which was decorated with figures and cartouches. It was undoubtedly of the time of Rameses II. If it was a tomb, therefore, it might possibly contain a mummy – maybe it would contain *the* mummy, the mummy of the great Rameses himself. They dug away at the sand until about six o'clock that afternoon, by which time they had cleared an opening about one and a half foot square, which was wide enough to send Mehemet Ali, one of the crew, inside to investigate. He came out quickly saying that it was beautiful and then Amelia went in and looked down

> from the top of a sandslope into a small square chamber...
> There was light enough to see every detail distinctly – the
> painted frieze running round just under the ceiling; the bas-
> relief sculptures on the walls; gorgeous, with unfaded colour;
> the smooth sand, pitted near the top, where Mehemet Ali
> had trodden, but undisturbed elsewhere by human foot; the
> great gap in the middle of the ceiling, where the rock had
> given way; the fallen fragments on the floor, now almost
> buried in sand.

They took it in turns to climb through the little opening into the chamber and then, when they had each taken a look, they covered up the entrance again in the hope of discouraging the crew from going in during the night and damaging the colours on the walls. Their satisfaction that night was great; their anticipation of the next day even greater. In the morning, the dragoman and Hassan, the captain, were sent to the nearest village to hire fifty labourers. Forty men arrived that afternoon and one hundred came the next day with their sheikh. While the English travellers entertained the sheikh, the men dug away at the sand until the entrance was uncovered, all but a large rock which had fallen from the mountain. They had cleared about three-quarters of the inside as well, but then they started leaning against the walls with their sweating backs and damaging the paintings, so Amelia decided that they had done enough.

As the true descendant of the sheikhs who had caused so much trouble for Belzoni, Rashwan Ebn Hassan el Kashef demanded much more than the agreed amount of money for the labour he had provided. He also wanted a pair of pistols and a game bag for himself. However, when he left, he took with him the prearranged cash sum of £6 for the men and a present to himself of jam, tinned sardines, eau de Cologne, some unspecified pills and half a sovereign.

What the party had uncovered was not a tomb but a small chapel built onto the side of the Great Temple. They spent the rest of that day and all of the next exploring it in their various ways. 'L. and the Little Lady took their books and knitting there, and made a little draw-ing-room of it,' Amelia wrote, while she sketched and copied the inscriptions and M'Callum measured the chamber and had a proprietor-ial look around the grounds. M'Callum then wrote their names and the date of discovery on a blank space just inside the doorway – as Belzoni had done at Thebes – and then wrote a letter to *The Times* announcing their discovery, after which they returned to the *Philae* and continued their way back north.

Sadly, within four years of their departure from Abu Simbel, before Amelia had even finished writing her account of their journey, the names inside the doorway had been defaced and the fresh wall-paintings had been damaged. 'Such is the fate of every Egyptian monument, great or small,' Amelia wrote in a burst of anger and frustration.

> The tourist carves it all over with names and dates, and in some instances with caricatures. The student of Egyptology, by taking wet paper "squeezes," sponges away every vestige of the original colour. The "collector" buys and carries off everything of value that he can get; and the Arab steals for him. The work of destruction, meanwhile, goes on apace. There is no one to prevent it; there is no one to discourage it. Every day, more inscriptions are mutilated – more tombs are rifled – more paintings and sculptures are defaced. The Louvre contains a full-length portrait of Seti I, cut out bodily from the walls of his sepulchre in the Valley of the Tombs of the Kings. The Museums of Berlin, of Turin, of Florence, are rich in spoils which tell their own lamentable tale. When science leads the way, is it wonderful that ignorance should follow?

In an effort to counter the effects of this sort of 'progress', Amelia founded the Egyptian Exploration Fund in 1883.

★

Snobbery, Amelia Edwards explained, was an essential part of what she called the *esprit du Nil* and she confessed to feeling it towards the common Cook's tourist as she sailed along in her boat, for the dahabieh was without doubt the most extraordinary and romantic means of travelling up the Nile. It was also the most expensive, which, in the way that prohibitive costs sometimes do, made it even more attractive to those who could afford it. One of the great advantages of travelling this way was that, winds willing, it was possible to proceed at one's own pace, sailing past towns that did not appeal and spending more time seeing things of particular interest. The timetable was flexible, unlike the itinerary that confronted another type of tourist who was, as Major Jarvis pointed out in his *Oriental Spotlight*, 'usually American

– that comes out in charge of a tourist agent's courier, and who has to see certain specified tombs, temples and mosques according to schedule, and at definite times, and is not allowed for one moment to do as he pleases. It is not certain,' the major concluded, 'if these people come out willingly or not . . .' Presumably, though, they chose to see the country this way because escorted tours became increasingly popular.

When James Bruce and the early nineteenth-century travellers sailed up the Nile, they were hailed from the banks of the river and invited to visit various sheikhs in their villages. These were more than just courtesy calls, though, for the sheikhs were autocratic rulers and had the power to delay or stop foreigners proceeding up the river. A hundred years later, however, Amelia Edwards's visits to native officials owed more to formality than necessity. As soon as the *Philae* reached Aswan after its race up the river, the painter Andrew M'Callum went to visit the Governor of the town, since it was he alone who had the authority to summon the Sheikh of the Cataract and to arrange to have the boat pulled up the rapids. The Governor was quick to return the Englishman's visit and within a few hours he appeared beside their dahabieh accompanied by the Mudir (chief magistrate) and Cadi (judge) of Aswan. During the rather difficult conversation that ensued in their saloon, Amelia offended the Governor by asking him where the slave market was to be found. Slave market? There was no slavery here, the Governor insisted, trying to cover the truth of the matter – there were indeed slaves for sale in the town – with his indignation. To appease him, they were obliged to play Verdi waltzes and Wagner's *Tannhaüser* on the piano.

Amelia found the visit instructive and entertaining, but ultimately trying. She thought that the problem with Oriental etiquette was that it 'is generally drawn out to a length that sorely tries the patience and politeness of European hosts.' The Governor stayed two hours on this occasion and then asked her to write down her name and address for him so that he could visit her when he came to England. There was very little chance of him appearing at her house in Westbury-on-Trym, Gloucestershire, because he had as yet never even been outside Aswan, but still she was not amused. She was, however, as courteous to the Governor as she had been to the sheikh at Abu Simbel whom she had unintentionally snubbed by giving him a knife and fork to eat with, since eating with his own fingers was beneath him and he had not brought his own attendant with him on that occasion. Consequently he was fed by one of the crew and then Amelia herself picked up pieces of food and put them in his mouth. This sort of entertainment, what travellers today could call a 'real experience', was not on offer to package tourists led around the country by a courier.

Thomas Cook himself had conducted the first group of tourists who came out to Egypt under the aegis of his company in 1869. They arrived too early to see the opening of the Suez Canal, but were in time to see the progress of the Prince and Princess of Wales, whom they appear to have followed (some would say chased) up the Nile. For this first 'Grand Tour of the East', Cook hired two Egyptian-built steamers, the *Benha* and the *Beniswaif,* and the tourists were divided into two groups of sixteen, but the separation was not too severe as they were nearly always in sight of each other as they made their rapid way up the Nile. Cook himself, firmly turning his back on those who travelled by dahabieh, wrote that 'Travelling by steamboat calls for the exercise of patience than exertion, and in this we had the advantage over the voyagers by the old Nile boats, whose patient endurance must have been very severely tested.'

For this first tour, Cook attracted clients who for the most part either would not or could not afford to travel independently, for although his tours to the Holy Land and Egypt were expensive – 150 guineas for a hundred days – they were much cheaper than organizing an individual trip. Cook's attention to his clients' comfort certainly extended to their dinner table and, although some tourists took their own supplies of tea and biscuits – just in case – they were served up huge quantities of English ham and Yorkshire bacon, tinned sardines and potted salmon from Liverpool, preserved fruits and marmalade from London, and Gloucester and Cheddar cheeses. Fresh meat, vegetables and eggs were bought on the way. Since Cook himself was an ardent supporter of the work of the Temperance Society, he only drank 'the sweet water of the Nile' during the trip, but it was always possible, as William Thackeray had discovered years before, to get hold of a bottle of Bass beer.

This first Cook's tour was a great success for the company and was no doubt also popular with the many Egyptians who supplied provisions or their own skills and labour. But some independent travellers regarded Cook's tourists with horror. After the first tour William Howard Russell of *The Times,* who had travelled with the Prince and Princess of Wales, accused Cook of hounding the royal party and of taking advantage of his position by organizing a tour for people who would not otherwise be allowed the privilege of seeing British royalty in action. The Egyptian monuments, Russell went on, seemed to be of secondary importance to these people whose primary aim was to rub shoulders with their future king and queen. He wrote that 'a cloud of smoke rises from a steamer astern' – the royal party were also being towed by a steamer, though – 'Cook's tourists have arrived! Their steamers are just below us in the stream. The tourists are all over the place. Some are bathing off the beaches: others with eccentric head-dresses are toiling through the deep sand after an abortive attempt to reach Philae. They are just beaten by a head in the race. Another day and the Prince and Princess would have been at their mercy!' It was of course unthinkable in the 1860s for a common subject to gain access to British royalty merely by paying money and making their choice. There were no such things as walkabouts then. The point that Russell was making, however, was that the tourist should have known better. Amelia Edwards in her daha-bieh, we can be sure, would never have pursued the Prince. She would have shown restraint, discretion, and above all would have had the breeding not to be so vulgar as to intrude. But Cook claimed that the river was open to everyone and that all he had done was to bring it within the reach of a new type of traveller. Travel, in this context, was most certainly a social leveller.

Thomas Cook complained about Russell's comments in a letter to the Prince himself, which he then published in his own travel paper, the *Excursionist*. There was more than just his name to clear. The Egyptian tour had been a success, but he knew that his hold on the new 'territory' could be damaged by the suggestion that his tours were common. The facts of the matter are more difficult to ascertain, but it seems clear that at one point the tourists did intend to approach the royal party, for Cook claimed that he had been told by Mustapha Aga, the British consular agent in Luxor, that the Prince would like to meet them. Cook explained away this misunderstanding in his letter: 'I will not say,' he wrote, 'that Mustapha Aga really meant what he said for the Egyptians have such a peculiar way of expressing themselves, that he might have intended the reverse...' Cook received no more than an acknowledgement of the receipt of his letter from the Prince, but a number of readers of the *Excursionist* were quick to support him. One of the tourists in that first party was a writer called George Rose, who had written a number of novels under the name of Arthur Sketchley. Rose produced an account of the journey partly through Sketchley's journal and partly through the narrative of another fictional character called Brown, a rollicking Cockney woman who did more than just drop her 'h's. It was Mrs Brown in particular who took Russell's attacks to heart.

> As to anyone a 'saying as I went to Egyp' a follerin' the
> Prince of Wales about, she claimed indignantly, I'd scorn

the action, as never was one for to intrude myself on no-one, and 'ave a 'usban of my own to foller, and foller 'im I will.' As to whether it would have been impertinent to have entered the royal presence, Mrs Brown fell back on a trusty old saying: 'Fiddle-de-dee. Impertinent indeed, "A cat may look at a king" as the sayin' is and I'm sure 'is Real 'Ighness would be glad for to fall in with some good honest Hinglish faces arter seein' nothing but there 'ere Turkey Blackamoors about.'

Whether the Prince of Wales would have done so or not is debatable, of course, since he did not reply to Cook's letter. But the danger of him doing so increased as each year passed, for in spite of the impressive list of royalty and nobility whom Cook's later escorted through Egypt, the bulk of their customers came from a different class of people and not all of them were 'honest Hinglish' either. This was a measure of the company's success, though, that they were able to attract all sorts of people to Egypt. Their tours were established on a regular basis and what they had to offer, which had not been provided before, was all of the wonder and most of the beauty of a Nile trip, with only some of the uncertainty, little of the difficulty and none of the danger. Travellers on dahabiehs and steamers had always been able to choose whether they would see the more unpleasant or impoverished side of Egyptian life or not; with Cook's the choice was already made. The boats became a little piece of the West floating along the African river. The dragoman knew from experience where these people would most enjoy visiting and understood just as clearly, since his job depended on it, where they would wish to avoid. The kitchens provided food which would not have been out of place in an English home. The Nile was tamed as never before and, by the turn of the century, it appeared to be entirely under Cook's control.

In an article in an 1888 issue of their *Excursionist* newspaper, Cook's announced that Egypt had become the mainstay of their world-wide business. The founder's son, John Mason Cook, a formidable business manager and a man of considerable physical presence – he once threw a dragoman off a steamer into the Nile for being impertinent – was renowned for the excellence of his organization and his energetic attention to detail. John Mason Cook became a mythical figure; from his head office beside Shepheard's Hotel in Cairo he opened branches in every main town in Egypt and established an organization which made the country accessible to tourists from all over the world. One traveller put it this way: 'Those donkeys are subsidized by Cook's; that little plot of lettuce is being grown for Cook, and so are the fowls; those boats tied up on the bank were built by the Sheikh of the Cataract for the tourist service with money advanced by Cook.' Cook's vouchers were honoured in all the best hotels. Their circular notes were more widely accepted than the English pound. Cook's ran the Khedive's steamer service on the Nile. Cook's won the Egyptian mail contract on the river. When General Gordon went up to Khartoum for the last time in 1884 it was on a Cook's steamer and, as a man who himself appreciated efficiency and attention to detail, it was praise indeed when he wrote to John Mason Cook to 'express to you my own and Lieuten-ant-Colonel Stewart's thanks for the admirable manner in which we have been treated while on your steamers,' adding rather poignantly that he hoped 'that I may perhaps again have the pleasure of placing myself under your guidance.' Later that year John Mason Cook was approached to transport the military expedition up-river to rescue Gordon 'for the simple reason,' Mr Cook explained in a speech to the Royal Normal College for the Blind in London in January 1885, 'that I had worked our Egyptian arrangements into such a form, that I had the monopoly on the passenger traffic on the Nile by steamer; and therefore the Government must buy me out or they must give me the work.' The statistics of the Gordon relief operation give some idea of the extent of Cook's services at the time: 50,000 fellahin operating 27 steamers and 650 sailing boats transported 18,000 soldiers, 40,000 tons of stores and 800 rowing boats up the Nile as far as Wadi Halfa.

Ordinary Nile steamer services were stopped during the campaign so that when Cook himself decided to go up into the Sudan, he had to hire a dahabieh from the Mudir of Dongola. He took his youngest son, seventeen years old at the time, with him on that occasion and the boat they sailed in was relatively small – only 24 feet long and 6 feet 6 inches wide; Cook renamed it the *Dog Kennel*. The door into the saloon was three feet high and the room itself was less than seven feet square. Above them in a coop, fifty chickens pecked at the deck. The water-filter broke almost as soon as they set sail and he was forced to drink water straight from the Nile. All this must have been extremely irritating for him, but there were some consolations. In spite of the cramped conditions and the fact that a campaign was being fought further up the river, he was well supplied with provisions for the journey. To last them for forty days, he took 40 loaves of bread, 400 eggs, 21 boxes of tinned sardines, 10 okes of rice, 15 lbs of cooking butter, six loaves of sugar, and a store of tinned meat, vegetables, condensed milk, packets of biscuits, macaroni, salt, capers, coffee, soup powder, sago, tea which he had brought out from England, and three tins of jam. 'Only three tins of jam for an expedition of 30 days!' he complained, a man of detail to the end. 'It may seem strange to you,' he told his London audience, 'but you can scarcely realise the value of jam to a man on campaign.'

The war effort clearly helped Cook's Egyptian business, as did the continuing presence of the British Army of Occupation. In 1889, *Vanity Fair* declared that 'The chief personage in Cairo is Cook.' They might have included the rest of Egypt as well. A story related by the *Daily Mail* correspondent G. W. Steevens concerns an incident during a tour of Upper Egypt on which John Mason Cook accompanied Lord Cromer, the British Agent and effectual ruler of Egypt. When they reached Luxor, the two Englishmen paid a visit to an old sheikh who lived on the edge of the town. The old man had obviously been rather protected from his country's recent history for he had no idea that the British Army was in occupation and had been for several years. This amazed Lord Cromer, widely known as 'the Lord', who asked the sheikh, 'Haven't you ever heard of me?' The sheikh, it appeared, had not.

So then Cromer asked him a second question and pointing at his escort asked, 'Have you ever heard of Mr Cook?'

'Oh, yes,' the sheikh replied. 'Cook Pasha – everybody knows Cook Pasha.'

*

What Cook's lacked in style, they made up for in the range of services they offered, with which no private boat-owner could compete. Douglas Sladen travelled with Cook's through Egypt in the opening years of this century and his account of the journey substantiates the company's claim that their steamers offered the very latest in comfort and that their tours brought the land of the Pharaohs and the cities of Islam within the tourist's reach. 'I have never enjoyed anything more than my voyage up the Nile in Cook's Tourist steamers,' Sladen wrote.

The tourist steamer he took from Cairo to Aswan was the middle range of boats Cook's offered at the time – they ran six steam dahabiehs, much smaller than the steamers and costing around £100 per person for a month's tour (the price includes sight-seeing, meals, in fact everything except alcoholic drinks.) The dahabiehs were exclusive boats for private hire, but Cook's also ran a fleet of express steamers from Cairo which took only five and a half days to reach Luxor and eight to reach Aswan, and ran twice a week during the height of the season. A first-class return ticket to Aswan on the express steamers for a nineteen-day tour which included four nights in the Luxor Hotel and three in the

Grand in Aswan, cost £25, while Sladen's trip on the tourist steamer, which was his floating hotel for three weeks, cost £50.

The cabins on the steamers were large and had enough space under the bed, for instance, to store a large Saratoga trunk. A steamer like the *Rameses*, one of the largest in the Cook's fleet, could sleep sixty-two passengers who, when they woke on their first Nile morning, would find a breakfast waiting for them in the dining-room which suggested that their eyes were mistaken either in the scenery beyond the cabin window or in the porridge, bacon and eggs, fish, ham, chicken, bread and marmalade and all of the other ingredients which went to make up the great British breakfast arranged on the table in front of them. Their eyes were not deceived in either thing, of course – this was the Cook's style, for reminders of home were important for less intrepid tourists; these familiar things reassured them. Sladen, however, was looking for excitement rather than reassurance. He had a cup of tea brought to his cabin at dawn which he sipped staring out of his window at the sun rising above the eastern desert. When they were passing something spectacular he took his tea up to the glazed sun gallery, wearing a big overcoat over his pyjamas. Then it was his turn for a bath in the white bathroom where the dark water pumped out of the Nile looked rather off-putting. 'But it does not make you muddy,' he reassured his readers; 'it has the same cleansing properties as other waters.'

From the water in the bathtub to the waters of the Nile via their substantial breakfast – between Cairo and Luxor, a typical itinerary for the steamer tourists included visits to the statue of Rameses II at Memphis (bequeathed to the British Museum by Caviglia and Sloane, who discovered it in 1820, but never taken to London) and from there to the Step Pyramid at Sakkara, both of which were reached from Bedrashen (fourteen miles from Cairo); the rock tombs at Beni Hassan (167 miles); the palace at Tel-el-Amarna (195 miles from Cairo, but usually seen on the return journey); the town of Asyut (250 miles), where the steamer also passed through the Asyut Barrage, restored by British engineers; the ruins of Abydos (345 miles, but also seen on the way back); and the temple of Dendera, 410 miles from Cairo and just forty miles from Luxor. But although the sites were magnificent, there were only four of them on the way up-river and two on the way back. This left a vast expanse of river and sand bank in between. There were of course plenty of villages where life was lived almost exactly as it had been recorded by travellers in the previous century. Feluccas and djerms, the larger cargo boats, sailed from one village to the next and, as Sladen wrote, 'you are passing something of interest every few minutes, whether it be a city, or a Nile village, or an exquisite palm grove, or picturesque incidents in native life, or the birds which turn the large shoals into a kind of zoological gardens, and seem to know quite well that no firing is permitted from Cook's steamers.' So, after breakfast, keen sightseers went to the sun gallery to sketch or take photographs of the scenery and maybe also to muse on the harmonious co-existence of the past and present. Less eager spectators went to the steamer's reading-room where, as on present-day Nile cruisers, they could refer to an extensive library of books connected with Egypt. Here also they read the newspapers, delivered each day with the mail, or wrote letters which could be sent from the steamer's postbox. Here at any rate there was peace. The lounge, on the other hand, situated in the centre of the promenade deck, spreading across the width of the boat and covered with a canvas awning, was occupied during the day by the least studious type of tourist. 'As it was full of easy chairs and tea-tables and wind-screens,' Sladen noticed,

> the idle and the unintelligent lounge about it all day long when they are not making excursions (which they like for the donkey rides), reading novels, or dozing, or playing bridge. Their day begins with afternoon tea, at which you have half Huntley and Palmer's productions instead of bread and butter. Special friends make up tea-parties, and the beautiful Arab servants, in white robes, and bright red tarbooshes, sashes and slippers, glide about, filling up their tea-cups as fast as they are emptied and bringing fresh varieties of Huntley and Palmer to compel people to over-eat themselves. This goes playfully on till somebody discovers that sunset is beginning.

On days when there was an excursion on shore, however, even this group managed to be more energetic. Sladen had chosen this particular Cook's steamer not because of the size of the rooms, the smoothness of the engines or the variety of biscuits on offer, but because of the reputation of the dragoman. Mohammed, whom Sladen calls 'the *doyen* of Cook's,' was a dragoman in the grand tradition – well-informed and witty, with an extensive repertoire of anecdotes about the past, about *dans le temps* when people travelled in a different style. As if to encourage the association between himself and those times past, Mohammed also had an extensive and elaborate wardrobe on board, had impeccable manners and real authority over souvenir hawkers and donkey boys. Indeed, it was certainly to a Mohammed in this mould, working on Cook's steamers in the 1890s, that one satisfied lady passenger penned the following poem entitled 'To Mohammed, by a lady admirer':

Who whipped the donkey when it fell,
and then the donkey boy as well
And dressed himself a howling swell

       "Mohammed"

Who led me to the ruined spot
Whether I wanted to go or not
and chid me when I called it rot

       "Mohammed"

Who sat so sweetly at my feet
With tarboosh red and slipper neat
and stirred my heart with many a beat

       "Mohammed"

Who taught us all and bossed the show
and made us listen, willing or no,
But always pleased us, made it go,

       "Mohammed"

And so when all this trip is done
The rides, the temples, tombs and fun
Forget it all I may, save one

       "Mohammed".

It was Mohammed, Cook's No 1 dragoman, who came into the dining-room each evening to announce the itinerary for the next day in his own idiosyncratic way – Sladen recorded word for word Mohammed's brief speech from the night before they reached Kom Ombo: 'Ladies and Gentlemen,' he began, clapping his hands to attract their attention. 'To-morrow, at ten o'clock, we arrive at Komombo; and in about five minutes walk to the Temple of Light and Darkness. Remember the very good light in the afternoon. Monument-tickets very much wanted! No donkeys to gallop!' – and it was Mohammed who was ready to lead them all off the steamer in the morning. The times mentioned in his speech were not approximations; Cook's did not operate by guesswork. At ten o'clock the gangway was out and ready to be descended just as the landing-stage was reached. Donkeys waited to be mounted at the foot of the gangway with donkey boys to watch over the riders, and policemen to watch over the donkey boys. Officials were ready to collect monument tickets. Dragomans were ready to explain to the tourists what exactly it was that they were looking at. The donkeys were still there when the tourists had seen enough, or when their itinerary dictated that it was time to move on. The tourists, who had been told exactly how much baksheesh to give their donkey boys when they returned to the steamer, then paid over that sum. A last look around, ship boarded, gangway pulled in and off they headed towards the next site.

It all sounds a little too regimented to be fun, but in a country where organization was previously unknown and where even today it is something of a rarity, this was indeed an achievement. It was a necessary one, too, for many of these new tourists in their puggarees and solar helmets, tweed suits or boating flannels, a cup, an opera glass and some matches in their pockets – the women in serge or linen skirts and jackets, felt hats, dark glasses, and a sun umbrella in hand. They were looking for edification, which they found in the history around them and which was reflected in the fervour with which they said their prayers and sang hymns during the religious services which were held on Sundays. Entertainments came out of the company's efficient service.

With the sight-seeing day over and the steamer underway, passengers had to choose which of the boat's facilities to make use of. They could sketch in the sun gallery, read in the library, sleep in their cabins, stroll on deck, write up their diaries, or maybe just have a much-needed wash and change of clothes. But whatever they did, all passengers wanted to see the sun set and the sky blaze with colours undreamed of in Europe or America. Sladen, who clearly enjoyed Cook's service as much as any of the people he shared it with, noticed that 'even the least intelligent people on the ship hurry to the side... and bring up ejaculations for a solid hour while the Egyptian sky proceeds with its marvellous transformation-scenes.'

With the sun set and the sky drained of colour, thoughts turned to dinner. With more than sixty people on board, the variety of dress and behaviour to be seen in the dining-room of a Cook's steamer was spectacular – Sladen was especially taken by a 'particular' young man in a silk suit, and a girl who seemed intent on emulating the well-dressed European women in Cairo with 'the gamut of summer extravagances. They have the moral courage,' he decided, 'for at least two different costumes between breakfast and dinner; and though a mere man is

Evelyn Baring, the Earl of Cromer (1841–1917). After the British occupation of
Egypt in 1882 he became Agent and Consul-General and instituted the 'Veiled
Protectorate' (*Hulton Picture Library*)

General Charles George Gordon (1833–85), Governor–General of the Sudan,
wearing the uniform given to him by the Khedive Ismail (*Hulton Picture Library*)

The first Thomas Cook office in Egypt, in the grounds of Shepheard's Hotel (*Thomas Cook Archive*)

Scottish troops at ease around the Sphinx after the Battle of Omdurman, 1898 (*Hulton Picture Library*)

A dahabieh on the Nile in the 1890s (*Royal Geographical Society*)

Tourists and dragoman at the Temple of Luxor (*Hulton Picture Library*)

A dahabieh off Abu Simbel – which was often the furthest that tourists would go up the Nile (*Henry Sotheran Ltd; by David Roberts*)

The port at Alexandria (*Private collection*)

The seafront at Alexandria, with the Cecil Hotel on the left (*Private collection*)

The old railway station in Alexandria, built by Robert Stephenson, from which travellers departed to see the sights of Egypt (*Hulton Picture Library*)

William Prinsep's painting of Victorian travellers visiting the bazaar in Cairo (*Martyn Gregory Gallery*)

Climbing the Pyramids – 'With the help of three Arabs', insisted Amelia Edwards, 'nothing can well be less fatiguing.' Clearly, not everyone agreed (*Hulton Picture Library*)

'Fourth Process: Cooling and Coffee' – William Prinsep's painting of the baths in Cairo (*Martyn Gregory Gallery*)

The entrance and terrace of Shepheard's Hotel, Cairo (*Thomas Cook Archive*)

limited to his theatre jacket for dinner, the irresponsible girl can dress as elaborately as she pleases for the evening, and the climate tempts her.'

Most tourists were tired by the time dinner was announced, for the days were hot and bright and it was as exhausting to sit on the steamer all day as it was to ride through the sand on donkeys. They ate a reassuringly familiar dinner, heard Mohammed or whoever announce the itinerary for the following day and then moved to the lounge for coffee and cigarettes. Only two clergymen and their wives played bridge on Sladen's steamer and so, clearly not too enamoured with many of the other passengers, he usually went to his cabin after coffee, lay on his bunk and read a guide book in preparation for the following day. At eleven o'clock, the electricity was switched off in the cabins and Sladen closed his eyes.

But not everyone wanted to sleep at that hour. There were plenty of passengers, lured to the Nile by its beauty, who thought it romantic to linger on deck under the starlit sky with the water glistening below them, a village in darkness or a ruined temple on the river bank, warm air blowing off the desert. It was enough to make them sing softly in the darkness. Forget the poverty of the village they were just passing, or the presence of British soldiers up and down the river. Forget all Egypt's social and political problems. Cook's protected its passengers from all of that and, apart from the rattle of the engine and the presence of the other passengers, the romantics among them were free to dream – of the *Arabian Nights*, of adventure around the source of the river, of Gordon and Britain's military heroes. All this, with the moon and the stars, the perfect weather, the rain and snow at home, a temple or tomb to visit tomorrow, the dinner jackets and the rustle of soft silk dresses, and the long Egyptian night ahead. Was it any wonder that Nile cruises were so popular with honeymoon couples?

★

Eustace Reynolds-Ball was unimpressed by the steamers that Cook's, and later their competitors, ran on the river. By all means go to Messrs Cook's or the Anglo-American Nile Steamer and Hotel Corporation, but hire a dahabieh. It was quite expensive, of course, but it really was the only way to see Upper Egypt and Nubia, have a holiday and restore one's health. Mr Reynolds-Ball also disapproved of steam dahabiehs which he thought were 'as incongruous a craft as a gondola turned into a steam-launch, and utterly opposed to the traditions of Nile travel – too reminiscent perhaps of Cookham Reach or Henley.' As for the tourist steamers, they horrified him, 'looking for all the world like a Hudson or Mississippi river-steamer . . . However, he noted with some relief in his guide book *Cairo of To-day*, 'this incongruous and insistent note of modernity is fleeting enough. Has not the appointed goal, some fifty miles or so higher up, to be reached by dusk, or the arrangements of the whole Nile itinerary, and the plans of hundreds of tourists, would be utterly upset?'

Whatever Mr Reynolds-Ball thought of the passengers who went on these steamers, it was infinitely more favourable than his view of tourists who combined travelling by steamer with the railway to cut down the cost or because they thought the Nile between Cairo and Luxor, for instance, was uninteresting. Thinking about them brought out that *esprit du Nil* that Amelia Edwards had noticed, that peculiar snobbery in him. He knew the rail-and-river tourists and he found them easy to dismiss: 'To one lacking in imagination,' he wrote, 'no doubt a great London highway like the Strand would be monotonous, while another would find the same fault with the Alps because each peak seems to him very like another.' But going up the Nile by railway was considerably cheaper and quicker, and it did become a popular way to travel. The world was speeding up and time seemed to be more precious. It only took a matter of hours rather than days to reach Luxor on the overnight express train, the famous Egyptian White Train, sleeping in a Wagons-Lits compartment. From Luxor one could then see a bit of the river by taking the mail steamer to Aswan.

By the time the much sought-after and recently reprinted 1929 edition of Baedeker's *Egypt and the Sûdân: Handbook for Travellers* appeared with its description of the Tutankhamun discoveries, the world had changed dramatically: the guide recommended complete tours through the country by railway for travellers in a hurry, although the editor did point out that the itinerary included stop-overs in towns which had the barest tourist facilities and 'is recommended to somewhat experienced travellers only.' The new Cook's steamers which appeared soon after 1921, when services were resumed after the First World War, had eighty or more berths on them; it was possible to travel 6,246 miles of the total 7,079 miles of Cecil Rhodes's dream route from Cape Town to Cairo by train and boat (Cook's had already conducted a special Cape-Cairo tour); and Imperial Airways had just begun their Anglo-Indian service with stop-overs in Alexandria and Cairo. Soon after that it was possible to fly up the Nile to Luxor and Khartoum.

ALEXANDRIA

'This is the news: he fishes, drinks, and wastes the lamps
of night in revel...'
                William Shakespeare, *Antony and Cleopatra* I, iii, 3–5

Few people enter Egypt through Alexandria now. They fly to Cairo
instead, or come overland from the south, or by boat through the Suez
Canal. From Cairo you can still get to Alexandria by plane – Air Sinai,
for instance, operates twin-engined Fokker Friendships and Egyptair
flies Airbuses on the route – or go by a variety of trains, or by car.
Going by boat, which was considered the only way for travellers to
make the journey between the two cities in the nineteenth century,
is no longer an option.

The railway line from Cairo still follows the single track laid out
in the 1850s by Robert Stephenson and his eighteen British engineers
and although the railway station they built in Alexandria was replaced
in the 1920s, the newer building still looks as though it was designed
not merely to put passengers on and off trains, but also as an expression
of the confidence and power of the people who conceived it – in this
case, the British advisers who effectively ran the Egyptian government.

Alexandria is, as it always has been, a city of contrasts. There are
the usual urban extremes of rich and poor, clean and dirty, new and
old; but there are also other contrasts of a different nature from those
encountered in Cairo, which are the more memorable. Cairo has the
look of an Arabian city invaded by the West while Alexandria is European at its centre, a centre which has now been reclaimed by the East.
The site of the original city founded by Alexander the Great is bordered
by the Mediterranean to the north and Lake Mariout in the south. The
new city has developed by spreading out east and west along the coast-
line, so that the tourist authority's brochures boast of twenty miles
of sandy beaches and fifteen miles of built-up coastal road. 'The Pearl
of the Mediterranean', the Egyptian tourist office calls it, perhaps also
recalling the colour of the marble with which the streets were paved
in ancient times. This is also the country's largest port, the centre of
the cotton trade where the close streets ring out with the call of cotton
brokers and the noise of old machines spinning through the day, of
boys pushing fabric-laden barrows and shouting out – '*ya! ya!*' – to
anyone who gets in their way.

Towards the end of May, with the close of Ramadan, the month of abstinence, in sight, Alexandria finds itself rich with expectation. This is evident along the rows of empty tables on the pavements outside the sea-front hotels and cafés, white cotton cloths clipped to the tabletops to stop them blowing away in the still-strong cold wind coming off the sea. Hotels and beach cabins have been freshly painted. The days are becoming the longer, hot, drawn-out affairs we expect of the Mediterranean. At night, the sight of Alexandrians promenading seems familiar to European eyes, but they are as different from Neapolitans, say, or Athenians, as Islam is from the Catholic or Greek Orthodox Churches. Within a matter of days the hotel rooms and dinner tables, empty now, will be filled as the Alexandrian season starts. The beaches, fetid with the smell of discarded crab shells, will be alive with laughter and music and shouting where now there is only the sound of large waves breaking on the shore and the scant comments from a line of men with fishing rods, out on the rocks up to their waists in water, trying to catch their dinner. But the season now is not the glorious affair it used to be and perhaps it is better to see the city like this, preparing, pretending, full of hope, than after, when not even the bravest face will be able to hide the truth of the matter.

The Cecil Hotel in the latest centre of the city, on Saad Zagloul Square and near the tram terminus at Ramleh Station, presents a few of Alexandria's contrasts. In the middle decades of this century, it was the meeting-place for the smart set. Lawrence Durrell had the narrator of his *Alexandria Quartet* meet the beautiful Justine here – 'In the vestibule of this moribund hotel the palms splinter and refract their motionless fronds in the gilt-edged mirrors. Only the rich can afford to stay permanently ...' – Princes (Radziwill, Galitzine), Archdukes and Dukes (Northumberland, Norfolk, Devonshire), the Earl of Errol, politicians and judges, writers including Somerset Maugham and Noel Coward, and a long line of generals (Monty was here, of course, and from 1936–44 this was part of the British Army HQ), have all distinguished the place. It was almost an honorary part of the British Empire, although the only visible reminder of this when Jan Morris visited it in the 1970s was an old English couple still resident here – 'relicts of the summery thirties – the wife blind and bed-ridden, the husband still sometimes to be encountered descending the dark staircase with a careful soldierly tread'.

If the Cecil was moribund in Durrell's day, it is most certainly so now. When I arrived, coming out of a brilliant summer day into the power-cut darkened interior, only the staff dressed in khaki were conspicuous. There were no smart couples sipping long cool drinks in the bar, no old soldiers shuffling across the lobby. There was just the staff's bright smiles and slow movements. That night at dinner in the considerable first-floor dining-room, I was the only guest present and after the waiter had served the first course of thin vegetable soup in a thick, white bowl, with a heavy spoon to drink it, he settled down in a chair in the corner and dozed off. Later, approaching my bedroom door with the hall lights back on, I noticed the plaque which wanted me to know that 'MOHAMMED M. KHALIL Stayed Here', and inside there was a light on by the telephone but all lines out of Alexandria, either south or north, were down. In the bathroom there was a shower and a bidet as well as a bathtub, but the water was off. Whatever European flavour this place used to have has now been heavily spiced.

★

There are still reminders all over the city that this was once part of the British Empire, for a short while officially a Protectorate. Outside the Cecil Hotel is the harbour which the British fleet bombarded in the last century and British engineers later restored, where Allied fleets docked during two world wars. Near the tram station there is the imposing old British Consulate, white-walled and red-roofed but empty now, weeds growing out of the rubble which blocks the path to its black front door, an outline still where the royal coat of arms used to hang, a bare flagpole jutting out a long way from the centre of its roof. The Union Restaurant around the corner from Tahrir Square (Place Mohammed Ali), along the street from the Union Club (defunct) and the Exchange Building (deserted), was founded in 1919 and only recently closed – officially just for refurbishment. When I went there it was still occupied by Mr Photios Photaros, the extraordinary maitre d' who remembered how it was in the '30s and '40s, always busy, when Sir Miles Lampson, the British Ambassador, used to pop in for a drink, when Montgomery conducted the Desert Campaign from a corner table, when there were five main chefs and eighteen waiters on the floor. Mr Photaros used to fly in pheasants and frogs legs from France, and pumpernickel bread from Germany, shellfish from Portugal, Cheddar cheese from England. He remembered that whenever Rita Hayworth and the Aga Khan were in Egypt, they came for dinner and always ordered the same dish – chicken flown in from Bresse – from the 480 items on the menu. He recounted all this as we sat on two simple wooden, Czech-made chairs, as old as the restaurant, around the only table left in the main dining room. Sunlight came in in a block under the half-closed shutters. Mr Photaros explained that he still came here every day to check up on the place, to plan, to feed the cats who kept out the rats which would be awkward to get rid

151

of later. He flicked through recipe books as though there was still a head chef to brief and as though planeloads of food were just about to arrive from Europe. Later, he placed the menu in front of me, half English, half in Arabic, with its twelve different ways with fresh crevettes, as though that too was still in order.

★

The passenger ships which do still call here now come from Italy via Piraeus and Haifa, loaded with cruise tourists who will see Alexandria in a day and maybe head for Cairo for another day, doing no more than dipping their fingertips in the font of history and leaving with little sense of the spirit of the place. They see the size and polished perfection of Pompey's Pillar, and will remember also the extent of the dilapidated houses and broken-down kiosks surrounding it. This is one of the single, striking impressions Alexandria has to offer, one of the easiest ones, too – but this has never been the way to see the city, even though Cook's and Baedeker used to suggest that you could do Alexandria in a day or two at the most. Modern visitors seldom get to see the Mahmoudieh Canal, for instance, which did as much as anything to revitalize the city in modern times by reconnecting it to the Nile. On the banks of this canal, as though in homage for the wealth it brought them, the city's rich pashas and leading merchants built villas along the canal and took their afternoon walk or drive along the avenue which ran beside it. A resident in the 1890s remembered the rich fig groves which ran right up to the canal's banks, and an old palace which she used to pass where a thirteen-year-old bride threw herself from a high window to escape the imprisonment of harem life. After her death the palace was closed up and abandoned. The tourist office discourages visitors to the canal now.

Alexandria is the offspring of many cultures. In the beginning there was Alexander the Great, twenty-five years old in 331 BC when he conquered Egypt and ordered the new capital to be built here on the Mediterranean coast, on the site of an older Egyptian fishing village. More important, there was a natural harbour here which looked out to Europe and which also had access to the Nile and to the interior Egypt. When Alexander conquered the country, the priests at the temple of Jupiter Ammon at the Siwa Oasis hailed him as a god, but according to legend, when he died of malaria in Babylon in 323 BC and his body was brought to Egypt to be buried, the High Priest at Memphis sent it back to Alexandria claiming that 'wherever this body must lie the city will be uneasy, disturbed with wars and battles'. According to the same legend, Alexander was buried in the Soma, a tomb beneath his temple at the main crossroads of the ancient city, but his body has never been found in spite of the claims of one dragoman attached to the Russian Consulate, who announced in 1850 that he had seen 'a human body in a sort of glass cage with a diadem on its head and half bowed on a sort of elevation or throne'. E. M. Forster, who recorded the dragoman's claim in his outstanding history of Alexandria, dismisses him as being 'probably a liar' and since no one else has claimed to have seen this same vision of Alexander on the site – now the Nabi Daniel mosque – he was probably right to do so.

The Greek community has always been large in Alexandria and it is still in evidence, most noticeably perhaps in the cotton and shipping industries, on the signs above numerous shops and in the names it has given to public places – the Antoniadis Gardens, for instance, given to the city on his death in 1922 by the wealthy merchant Anthony J. Antoniadis. There are Greek restaurants and cafés across the city, like the famous Pastroudis with its *art nouveau* décor and the gilt-friezed Athineos in Ramleh Square, more Greek than Egyptian. The Greek community has also given Alexandria a sense of its own identity through its writers, in particular through Constantine Cavafy (1863–1933), the 'old poet of the city' in Lawrence Durrell's novels and the man to whom Forster dedicated his guide and history of the city.

The Roman heritage is also strong in Alexandria. Its beginnings have come down to us most popularly through the tragedy of its early protagonists, Julius Caesar who was worshipped here as a god, Mark Antony and Cleopatra, seventh queen of that name and the last independent native ruler of Egypt before the present era. Like the Greeks, the Romans arrived in Alexandria as their power spread across the Mediterranean. They ruled Egypt for more than 400 years but, also like the Greeks, the monuments they constructed to their glory here in Alexandria have not survived with their legends. There are very few sights for the tourist in search of ancient Greece or Rome in Alexandria – outside the museum, that is. Octavian, who defeated Mark Antony and became the emperor Augustus, founded his own city, Nicopolis – 'City of Victory' – outside the Greek city, but all that is left of that is the name and whatever might now be buried beneath the modern district of Mustapha Pasha, near the Alexandria Sporting Club. There is still Pompey's Pillar to see, built in fact for the emperor Diocletian, and in our own time the discovery of a Roman theatre and baths near the Graeco-Roman Museum has greatly added to the attraction of Alexandria's antiquities. But they still do not amount to much.

Unlike its Roman-built neighbour Nicopolis, Alexandria did not disappear. It was well sited, at the pressure-point of the Mediterranean and Arabia, and its deep-water harbour and proximity to the Nile, qualities which attracted Alexander to the place, ensured its survival. According to legend, St Mark came here in AD 45, converted a Jewish shoemaker named Annianus (subsequently murdered) to Christianity and was himself martyred for objecting to the worship of the Alexandrian god Seraphis, in AD 62. According to Jerome, St Mark was buried in Alexandria, but unlike Alexander his remains were found and smuggled out of the Arab-controlled city in 828 in a crate of pork meat, to avoid inspection by the Muslim authorities. They now rest in the church of St Mark in Venice, but the saint's work in Alexandria was not in vain for the new creed took hold and the city became the third centre for Christianity after Rome and Constantinople.

There is more to Alexandrian history: waves of conquerors washed along the Mediterranean coast or flooded down the Nile. The great Arab general 'Amr ibn el-'As wrote to the Caliph Omar in 642 that 'I have taken a city of which I can only say that it contains 4,000 palaces, 4,000 baths, 400 theatres, 1,200 greengrocers and 40,000 Jews.' The sixteenth-century Turks who took the city had little interest in it and it suffered from their neglect, resembling more a town and then hardly even a village. Christians, too, were less interested in the place now that it no longer held the remains of St Mark and with the restraints imposed on them by the Muslims, they stopped coming here to worship. The learning, the great libraries and scholarship for which Alexandria had been famous in antiquity, had left the city as clearly as the spirit of confidence and humanity which had created it in the first place. When Napoleon Bonaparte invaded in 1798, the capture of Alexandria was an affair of little significance and also of little exertion, since there was not that much to defend. Alexandria surrendered knowing that Cairo, the centre of the country's wealth, learning and power, would fight on.

Under Muhammad Ali, the great pasha installed after the French and British forces had evacuated the country, Alexandria once again achieved new influence. Muhammad Ali built himself a palace at Ras el Tin, the 'Cape of Figs', a promontory by the eastern harbour, and in his audience hall his divan was so placed that from it he could watch the newly formed Egyptian fleet at anchor. Both the palace and the ships were signs of the growth of Egyptian power, for Muhammad Ali wanted to place himself on an equal footing with the Europeans in the Mediterranean. However, the capital was still in Cairo and the branch of the Nile which emptied near Alexandria had silted up since Alexander's time, so Muhammad Ali organized the digging of a 45-mile canal, the Mahmoudieh, which joined up with the Rosetta branch of the river.

Egypt's practical development in the modern era owed much to

influences from around the Mediterranean – even Muhammad Ali himself had come from Albania – and Alexandria, as the country's chief
port, was bound to benefit. The modern city grew rapidly and without
any real control. It was a messy city, and the only place worth mention-
ing, most visitors in the mid-nineteenth century agreed, was the Place
des Consuls, later called the Place Muhammad Ali and, briefly, the
Place Arabi (now the Midan Tahrir, 'Liberation Square') which has
at its centre a statue of Muhammad Ali on horseback, designed by
the French sculptor Jacquemart and cast in Paris. Even more confus-
ingly, it was often referred to as the Frank Square, the Grand Square
or more simply, as I shall refer to it, as the Square. Florence Nightingale's first impressions of the city were typical and she wrote, soon
after her arrival in November 1849, that 'There is nothing in Alexandria
but the Frank Square and the huts of the Alexandrians,' a slight exagge-
ration, perhaps, but certainly a compliment to the magnificence of the
Square which she thought was larger than any in London. *Murray's
Handbook* for 1847 explained that the 'Frank quarter stands at the extre-
mity of the town, farthest from the new port; which is in consequence
of the European vessels having formerly been confined to the eastern
harbour, and the consuls and merchants having built their houses in
that direction. It has, within the last seven years, greatly increased
in size by the addition of the large square ...' Within this square, the
guide explained, were the principal hotels and most of the consulates,
'and here the national guard are drilled soon after sunrise every Saturday
morning ...' The Square was the centre of the European quarter and
the hub of diplomatic life. The English community had been allocated
land to the north, where they built the Anglican Church of St Mark's
in 1855, and which became the focus for the British community; the
French and the Greeks were granted land to the south; the Armenians
and Italians built in the west. New public buildings were built around
the Square including the main theatre where touring companies from
Europe performed and where strangers visiting Alexandria were welcome without paying. At another corner there was a subscription library
and reading rooms. The Mixed Courts, the new legal chamber which
brought all foreigners, previously answerable only to their consuls,
under one law, were founded here in 1875. The élite Muhammad Ali
Club had its premises in the Square for a while and, at the southern
end, the old Palais Tossizza, once the home of a wealthy Greek merchant
who was also the first Hellenic Consul-General in Egypt, became the
Alexandrian *Bourse*. With the Cotton Exchange at one end of the palace
and the Stock Exchange at the other, this was the most important financial
institution in Egypt and 'the howls and cries that may be heard here

of a morning proceed not from a menagerie,' E.M.Forster explained, 'but from the wealthy brokers of Alexandria as they buy and sell.'

The work that Muhammad Ali put in hand to develop the city was continued by the Khedive Ismail, the profligate builder, who spent a fortune improving the harbour and docks. The opening of the Suez Canal was expected to damage the prosperity of Alexandria and it did divert much of the transit cargo, which no longer needed to be unloaded at Suez and carried overland. But Anglo-Egyptian and Mediterranean traders still used the older, well-tried route, and Egypt's exported goods, especially the valuable cotton trade, were still shipped from Alexandria.

*

Mabel Caillard was eleven years old in 1876 when her father was appointed Postmaster-General of Egypt and she and her family arrived in Alexandria, and she continued to live in or to visit Egypt until shortly before the start of the Second World War. Her family was not rich enough to buy a house in the centre of the city or among the pashas and millionaires who lived along the Mahmoudieh Canal, and initially the Caillards lived in one of the new sea-front hotels – the Hôtel des Messageries – where the huge rooms were cold in winter and the view over the grey-and-white Mediterranean was especially uninviting. Her mother disliked the city, the hotel, the food, even the novelty of it all, but Mabel was thrilled. She loved the activity and the contrasts in the city, the Europeans taking their afternoon strolls in the Square, the noisy cafés, the streetsellers and military bands, the mixed crowd of Arabs, Levantines and Europeans.

When they first arrived in Alexandria, new suburbs were beginning to be developed. One of these, Ramleh, about five miles to the east of the Square, consisted of sixty houses built without any particular order along the sands. The area was distinguished by the château that Ismail had built as his private residence on the coast. Ramleh was a quiet place and the air was much healthier than in Alexandria, and although there was no road across the sand, there was a new tram-line which made travelling easy. The community at Ramleh, as in Alexandria, was cosmopolitan, but when the Caillards took the tram out there for the first time, it was an Englishman whom they met first, who invited them to his house for tea, waving a parcel in front of them which, he explained with great excitement, contained 'Strawberry jam in a tin, brought all the way from England.' This, they later learned, was reason enough for his excitement and, perhaps reassured by a little touch from home, the Caillards decided to move to Ramleh.

Because the tram-line was the only thoroughfare at the time, the districts of the suburbs were created by the stations and were named after its inhabitants – Fleming and Bulkeley, Schutz and Bacos, all of whom were also members of the railway board. The narrator of Lawrence Durrell's *Alexandria Quartet*, remembering the clicking of the wheels of these little tin trams, thought that 'The very names of the tram stops echoed the poetry of these journeys . . .' Along the tram-line, the houses were simple, but painted in bright colours and, as so often with British expatriates, were surrounded by well-tended gardens. Mabel's mother wanted to live in a house painted in her favourite colour, blue, but none was free at that time so she settled for a pink stone bungalow with a small verandah and bright green shutters. Between the houses and Alexandria there was the desert, which they rode across and where, in the spring, the Bedouins ploughed the land and sowed corn seed. Towards the end of the last century, the inhabitants laid out terracotta tracks between the houses using fragments of broken pottery, some of them from Greek and Roman times, which were found in heaps around the city. When these tracks were eventually covered with tarmac, Mabel believed, it signalled the change 'from the old Ramleh, peaceful and picturesque, to the magnificent and vulgar place into which it has finally grown.'

The new foreign community in Alexandria and especially in Ramleh grew along the terracotta tracks and, as it spread, became more formal and split into cliques. The British were regarded as the most trustworthy and respectable by the others, although they were also rather exclusive. Mabel, however, remembered that they were 'friendly and pleasant. Everybody was young in those days and nobody was, as yet, very rich.' They organized themselves, as the British always did, and set up amateur dramatics groups, and held dances and recitals in a delapidated hall called the Sala Storari which were curtailed when it fell down. The Caillards mixed with people outside the British community, though, and on one occasion they were invited to dine at the house of a Turkish pasha. Dinner consisted of twenty-five courses served on a large communal copper dish and Mabel remembered many incidents from that meal –

> Mamma's surreptitious disposal under the table of
> undevoured dainties pressed upon her by an attentive host;
> my poor governess's nauseated efforts to swallow the
> succulent bits torn from a whole roasted lamb, which the
> eldest son of the house, with greasy fingers, popped into her
> mouth as a special mark of his favour; my father's dogged
> demolition of everything that was set before him, in the

desire not to offend by a refusal, and the attack of dyspepsia that subsequently crowned his sacrifice . . .

There was also the warmth of the welcome they received, the meeting with the women of the house in the harem quarters facing the sea, and the embroidery of roses which Mrs Caillard had admired and which was waiting in their carriage for them when they had said goodbye.

When her father had to go to Cairo on official business, Mabel and her sisters rode their donkeys with him up to Sidi Gaber station, where the Alexandria–Cairo train still stops. At other times, she went out riding along the coast with Hassan, her syce (groom), running beside her and telling her fantastic stories 'of which,' she regretted, 'I can recall only one – about a man who, having no land, built a house and planted a garden in his stomach.' But her blissful childhood did not last. One day when she was out riding she fell off her pony in an Arab village. Instead of running to help her get up, as she had expected them to do, the women of the village threw mud at her and she distinctly heard them call her 'Christian' with bitterness. Soon after this, the men of the foreign communities began regular rifle practice and finally, with a British fleet on its way and the Arabi uprising in the making, Mabel was sent back to England for safety in May 1882.

★

Since the Square was the official centre of European Alexandria and since the riots which followed the bombardment of the city by the British fleet in July 1882 were essentially anti-European, it is not surprising that the Square sustained the largest part of riot damage. With the new Khedive Tewfik in his palace in Ramleh and the rebel leader Arabi in Cairo, Baron de Kusel, the Customs inspector in Alexandria, landed with one of the first British marine detachments on Friday, 14 July. He was shocked by what he saw: '. . . there were dead bodies, telegraph wires and miscellaneous articles broken and thrown away. In some places the houses were still on fire or smouldering, and the thin columns of smoke curled up the blackened walls, as though mocking them . . . The Grand Square, which before the bombardment had been a source of pride, was now almost completely destroyed. The French and Italian Consulates had a few walls left standing, so had the British, but absolutely gutted.'

When the British troops regained control of the city, they imposed a martial law searching suspects and arresting looters and suspected murderers. Those people caught in the act were taken to the buildings of the Mixed Courts which, with the Anglican Church, were the only structures in the Square to survive the riots more or less intact. Lord Charles Beresford, commander of the British gunboat *Condor*, set up a drumhead court here at which de Kusel acted as an interpreter on several occasions. Those people found guilty of murder were marched out into the ruins of the Square – kept clear by a detachment of American marines – tied up against the acacia trees and shot. They were buried in graves dug around the statue of Muhammad Ali.

There was a great deal of controversy over these executions at the time, and also over the accusations that British troops – dear old Thomas Atkins, as he was patronisingly referred to – had also been involved in the looting. Even British officers were implicated as Mr Halton, a friend of the Caillard family who later became Egypt's Postmaster-General, discovered to his cost. Halton lived in a flat near the main railway station, which he had evacuated during the riots and which was subsequently broken into. Shortly after order had been restored in the city, Halton was invited to a dinner party, which he was obliged to attend in a dirty shirt, since his clean ones had obviously appealed to the looters and had been taken. One of these shirts, however, turned up that very evening being worn by a British officer.

After the landing of a British force in the Suez Canal in August and the decisive battle at Tel el Kebir in September, some sort of uneasy calm returned to the country. Although the uprising had been popular, it had been instigated by the army and had not had time to spread widely outside military circles. As Alexandria was rebuilt, the memory of the events which led to its destruction faded, although the resentment Egyptians felt towards the occupying British army did not encourage this. The new city which developed was even more heavily influenced by western taste and reflected the greater part that foreigners were now playing in the running of the country. The new régime, the 'Veiled Protectorate' instigated by Evelyn Baring, Lord Cromer, the new British Agent and Consul-General, brought with it a new group of western diplomats and administrators and when Mabel Caillard returned to Egypt in 1883 she found things very much altered. For a start, her father was now Director-General of Customs – Baron de Kusel's superior – and had rented Mr Fleming's house at Ramleh, a long low building with a turret at one end which Mabel, appropriately enough, thought resembled a railway train, since Mr Fleming had been a railway administrator. The reality of the house was a little less pleasing, though, for the roof leaked and rats ran around chewing pieces of mummies taken from the collection of Mr Amos, the next-door neighbour.

The house was not the only change in the Caillards' life, for the British Army was now in occupation – 'The general and his staff, austere colonels, quiet majors, dashing captains and young subalterns,' Mabel remembered with pleasure, as well as a group of officials formerly with the Indian Civil Service. After these people had settled in, Ramleh society became ever more formal, its entertainments extravagant and competitive. Dinners were lavish affairs of twelve or fourteen courses and even the after-dinner entertainments of *tableaux vivants* or recitals were taken very seriously. All this, fortunately, was something that Mrs Caillard relished and, according to her daughter, she was a notable hostess and enjoyed a challenge – when Judge Hills laid out the first Ramleh tennis court, the Caillards were quick to follow, rolling the sand outside their turretted house as hard and smooth as they could manage to make their playing surface. Lawn tennis then became an important part of their social life and 'At Homes' were now affairs to which guests brought a tennis racket and ball.

As Ramleh society became more sophisticated, some old practices were left behind. The donkey that Mabel used to ride out across the sands to the Spouting Rocks was replaced by a horse, called a pony after the Anglo-Indian fashion. A hunt was established in Ramleh by officers from the new British garrison and a pack of fox-hunting hounds were brought over from England. But unfortunately for the hunters, Ramleh and the land to the east of Alexandria did not live up to their expectations and there was no kill at the first hunt. But as with many sporting events, the aprés-sport was as big an attraction for some as the sport itself. Extravagant hunt breakfasts were held after the riding was over at which men in heavy riding boots and women in hunting dress ate game pie and cold hams and knew that the servants thought they were a little odd. The original reason for the hunt might have been diversion and fun – the soldiers had little to do in the barracks – but for Mabel's mother it was also part of her daughter's education. The mother had hunted as a girl in Leicestershire and she believed that young girls should hunt, or at any rate ought to be able to hunt, and Mabel's opportunity came in Ramleh. But the hunting did not last. For a start there was not much wildlife which needed to be hunted with horse and hound and then the hounds disliked the climate, fell ill and were sent off to Cyprus to recuperate. When they returned to Alexandria and died, the Ramleh Hunt seemed to die with them.

Mrs Caillard's prime concern for her daughter was that she should be prepared for her social initiation, her 'coming out' in society, which could be as traumatic as a blooding at a first hunt kill. It made little difference to the mother that her daughter was living in Egypt. She still took her lead from England. That way, even if the girl never got to use her skills in Egypt, she would not be at a disadvantage when she went back to England, for – and this was at the centre of her thinking – there always was an England and a home to return to, however far away. So on the night of Mabel's 'coming out', a ball was held for her and two other debutantes in the ballroom of a local house. The weather that night was very English – wet and with a gale-force wind blowing – and she had to put on a mackintosh and ride her pony over to the ball. Apart from this, and the fact that most of the guests had come on the tram or had walked across the sands, the ball went off as it would have done in England, with Mabel looking very much the part of the young deb in a stiff tulle balldress.

Although the Caillards had lived in Egypt for a long time now, their Englishness was brought forcibly to Mabel's notice one day when Sir Donald Currie, cruising around the Mediterranean with some friends, requested through John Mason Cook to be introduced to an English family who had 'made their home in the East'. Sir Donald and his friends were invited to the Caillard house for tea one day and, although the precise number of his party was unknown, Mr Caillard thought that there would probably be five or six of them. But he had miscalculated the size of Sir Donald's yacht and as the party approached the turretted house across the sands, Mr Caillard saw that there were twenty-eight of them coming for tea. 'My mother,' Mabel very reasonably explained, 'was nonplussed.' She had nowhere near enough food in the house to feed that many guests and there were no stores or markets nearby for her to rush out to. But she was determined not to be looked down upon and so she sent messages to her neighbours, asking for their help and for the contents of their pantries. The afternoon, Mabel announced with relief, was a great success. But what really mattered was the way Mrs Caillard refused to be seen as an official's wife stuck in a hick town in some God-forsaken place. She was an Englishwoman. 'In Egypt one had a house,' she explained; 'one's home was forever England.'

*

Baron de Kusel did not feel quite the same way about this when his employment as Controller-General of Customs was so abruptly terminated with the arrival of Cromer's new staff. He felt very much a part of Egypt, but the new administration could find no suitable post for him. 'With all haste in the world,' he wrote bitterly, 'in their thirst for economy, those in power appointed new-comers who, strangely enough, were their own friends and relations.' Instead of a pension, de Kusel received a golden handshake and was awarded the 4th Class of the Imperial Order of the Osmanieh. He spent several more years in Egypt, looking after a cotton factory in which he had an interest and at one time standing in as acting-Consul for the United States, before returning to England and settling in Surrey. His *Recollections* were published in 1915 and he died two years later, at the age of sixty-nine.

Even the newly founded English-speaking newspaper, the *Egyptian Gazette*, which was published out of Alexandria, thought it was odd that a man with as fine a record as de Kusel's should be replaced, but then maybe not even they understood how big a change had taken place within the Egyptian Service; the right sort of patronage counted for a great deal with Cromer in the British Agency in Cairo.

Ronald Storrs was one of the new breed of Englishman who benefited from the right sort of introduction. Son of the Dean of Rochester, educated at Charterhouse and Cambridge – where he was part of the John Maynard Keynes-Lytton Strachey circle – Storrs was accepted for the Egyptian Service by Sir Eldon Gorst, later Cromer's successor as British Agent. Storrs arrived at Port Said on board the P&O steamer *Arabia* on 5 October 1904, and took up his first post at the Ministry of Finance in Cairo. He was keen to make something of himself in the service, but he found that the work was less than taxing and when Lady Cromer, to whom he had letters of introduction, asked him whether he liked the work he was doing, he told her 'that I couldn't say because I didn't have any'. Within a couple of days, he was moved to a new department.

In the summer of 1905, his first in Egypt, Storrs left Cairo for Alexandria as part of the annual migration of ministerial staff – in his *The Leisure of an Egyptian Official* Lord Edward Cecil recorded that at a government meeting to discuss their summer quarters, one minister insisted that 'Undesirable people of both sexes live in hotels. It is not fitting that the seat of Government should be in such a place.' But each year they failed to agree on how else they might accommodate themselves. From his own experience, Storrs would have agreed with the outraged minister that it was not right for the government to work out of a hotel. He was given a room in the fashionable, white-washed Casino Hotel at San Stefano, halfway along the Alexandrian corniche between the city centre and Montazah and he did the little work that there was for him to do sitting on his balcony. Below him 'there was the perpetual din of dining and dancing at night, children playing and screaming in the forenoon, *consommations* in the afternoon, and marble-topped tables being cleared, cleaned, and rapped to call up a corps of Europeans and Berberin waiters'. As new to his job as he was to the town, Storrs was lonely in Alexandria. He walked along the shore or by the canal and went swimming or riding – 'once combining both in an experimental gallop naked to see what it was like, and proving it to be better adapted for bronze or marble than for human contours'. It was not until later, when he was Inspector of Customs Administration in the city, that he came to realize that 'Alexandria is not an obvious city; she requires, before revealing herself, time, study and love.'

The Customs Service in Alexandria brought in a large amount of revenue for the government, for import duties were charged at eight per cent of the value of cargo. Cargoes were valued by the customs officials themselves, which provided them with plenty of scope for backhanders and pay-offs. In the past, the service had been run by less scrupulous inspectors who had taken full advantage of these opportunities, as the so-called 'Manchester House' indicated, which was a fine villa built by a customs official with the bribes and extra payments he had received from undervaluing consignments of cotton goods. But under the new Director-General, Sir Arthur Chitty, known as Chitty Bey, the service was acquiring a new reputation for fair dealing.

Storrs thought that the Customs Service was a microcosm of the city itself – half a dozen British officers, a couple of Muslims 'of good family', some Copts who antagonized them – 'the over-work, dear Sir,' one of them complained to Storrs, 'from these pimps of Pilgrims!' – Syrians, Turks, admirers of Edward VII and a former Private Secretary to the Habsburg Empress Elizabeth of Austria. Storr's day started at around eight in the morning when he went on his rounds of the sheds and quays in the customs area. Some mornings he then sat in on the Menufih, the auctions that the Customs Service held of the goods confiscated from importers who either could not or would not pay their dues any other way.

'The glare, the dust and the rattle of the mule carts and the long paved quays, were equally hard on eyes, ears and feet,' Storrs wrote of his daytime work. Also, for four nights each month, he was on nighttime inspection duty, dealing now with drug smugglers instead of tax evaders. It was against the law to import or possess hashish in Egypt which, almost inevitably, made the drug much sought-after and always obtainable. The extent of the police and customs' failure to stop the drug being imported was highlighted by Storrs's claim that 'you had only to tell your servant to bring you a few piastres' worth for him to return in a couple of minutes with a reeking specimen in his hand.' The drug smugglers were inventive in the ways in which they brought hashish into the country and it was found hidden in almost every sort of cargo, 'as well as in unbelievable fastnesses of the human form'. People brought in many other things secreted about their persons – one day a French steamer arrived from Lebanon and a Syrian couple disembarked. The woman was so heavily veiled that not even her eyes were visible, but something about her caught Storrs's attention. She was wearing green silk gloves, he remembered, and stockings with a tartan check. At one point the woman bent over to get some money from her bag and Storrs watched her, thinking that she would look so much better in black silk hose. Then he noticed that there was something thick and solid and very unfeminine pointing down her leg and he had her searched by one of the female officials, who discovered that the woman was carrying a loaded revolver and three fierce-looking knives tucked into her garters. But there was nothing more criminal about it than her husband attempting to avoid paying the duty on his arsenal.

When Storrs first arrived in Alexandria, the British had been in occupation of Egypt for twenty-three years. It was also twenty-three years since Arabi's uprising, which is a long time for one country to be controlled by another without protest. But there were objectors and weapons turned up regularly in the customs shed in Alexandria; every now and then Storrs loaded up the official launch with these and other confiscated items, the usual list of 'books, postcards and pictures *contre les moeurs publique*' and threw the lot into the sea. But weapon smuggling and the underworld life of Alexandria were not the commonplace for him. Days were more usually spent checking forms and filling in reports. Storrs spent two years in Alexandria before being moved to another ministry in Cairo and in that time he became very fond of the city. He saw similarities between the Rue Sherif Pasha, which led off the Square, and Bond Street in London. He was excited by what he called the 'sinister rowdiness' of the port, which was matched by his own life, which was physically hard and unsparing, although not without its consolations. For three pounds a month he rented a small coastguard's cottage at the eastern end of Stanley Bay in Ramleh, which was then the favourite bathing beach for the British. He liked the house rather than the beach and enjoyed being right out on the promontory 'half surrounded by the sea and never silent from the roaring of the waves,' although he spent little time there. On the evenings when he was not working he invariably went to the Zizinia Theatre where, as opera critic for the *Egyptian Gazette*, he had free access to the ambitious productions of *La Bohème*, *Tosca*, *Lohengrin* and the more severe *Valkyre* and *I Maestri Cantori di Norimburga* of Wagner. After the show he wrote his reviews in a café nearby and then rushed to the station to catch the 1.30 am tram, the last one which made the twenty-five minute journey out to Stanley Bay.

Major C. Jarvis, whose *Oriental Spotlight* in the 1930s took a cynical view of Egypt and the English, observed from experience that Alexandria was very jealous of Cairo, for although Alexandria was Egypt's main port even after the opening of the Suez Canal, it was very much the second city. It might have been the official seat of government for a few months each summer, but the government was really on holiday then. When the summer ended, the diplomats and politicians went back south to Cairo, the beaches and cafés emptied and the racing season ended at the Sporting Club. When Storrs first heard that he had been posted to Alexandria's Custom Service, he was horrified. He thought of it as a punishment for poor work; he had been banished from the inner circle, the 'Cabinet-atmosphere' of Cairo, and sent to search through passengers' underwear and cigarette cases. It was not quite as he had imagined and he enjoyed his time on the coast, but he was happy when he was moved back to Cairo as Private Secretary to the British Financial Adviser in 1906.

Sir Thomas Russell Pasha, who served with the Egyptian police force from 1902 to 1946, was also posted to Alexandria at the beginning of his career. Russell, who arrived as Assistant Commissioner of Police, is linked more closely than anyone else with the crackdown on the drug trade in Egypt at the start of the century. The problem was certainly extensive; as *Cook's Handbook* for 1906 rather crudely put it: 'One of the greatest enjoyments of many classes of the modern Egyptian is to do nothing, especially if he has sufficient means to provide himself with coffee, and with some narcotic in the form of tobacco, opium, hashîsh ...' They reported that in 1903 about 24,349 kilos of hashish were seized by officials (British Customs seized a total of 16,277 kilos of cannabis in 1987) that the courts closed down twenty-two cafés owned by Europeans and 1,681 by Egyptians where the drug was sold, and that of the 366 patients admitted to the lunatic asylums, sixty-seven were diagnosed as being insane due to hashish smoking. Clearly, with such a popular habit, Russell had his work cut out. He enjoyed it, though. On one operation in 1911 he came up against one of the most notorious smugglers of the time, 'Abd el-Qadir el-Gailani. The operation began when Russell and the CID received reliable information that a large consignment of hashish had been delivered by a cargo ship and was lying in waterproof sacks just off the coast, waiting to be landed. Russell kept the tip-off secret and hid himself with a handful of men near the beach at nightfall; on the second or third night of his vigil he was rewarded with the arrival of a string of empty carts heading for the waterfront. With Russell that night was Bimbashi Ingram, the head of the Alexandria CID. They waited for the carts to come up from the beach before they moved in on them, but as they were coming up to them Ingram realized that the carts were still empty and they let them go past undisturbed. They decided that, being an old hand at this, 'Abd el-Qadir was taking precautions in case he was being watched by the police. This was the trap he had set for his trappers. Russell and Ingram sat back and watched the carts disappear above the beach.

A few nights later, Russell was off-duty and Ingram was alone with the men at their hiding place near the beach when the carts reappeared. This time, when they came back up from the beach, they were fully loaded. Again Ingram decided to let them pass, this time to see where the smugglers were going to hide the drugs. Also, he had spotted a Greek fisherman hanging around who was also showing an interest in the carts and Ingram wanted to see what he was up to before making his move. Ingram sent a man to Russell's house to tell him what was going on. Russell was getting ready to go to bed but, throwing a Burberry trenchcoat over his pyjamas, he left immediately for the beach where he found Ingram in disguise as an Arab. The smugglers meanwhile had taken the carts up to a house next door to the Governor of Alexandria's villa and were hiding the drugs in the stables. Ingram and Russell briefed their men and led the attack on the smugglers. 'We broke in and held everyone covered,' Russell explained coolly. There they found not only 700 kilos of hashish, enough to make the headlines of national newspapers today, but also the great 'Abd el-Qadir himself. 'What then was our astonishment,' Russell explained, 'to see the Greek fisherman with a party of ruffians closing in at the same moment from the opposite direction.' The undercover policemen prepared themselves for another fight, but then they saw that the Greek was none other than Bimbashi Giovanni, the Italian chief detective at Alexandria CID, who had also been tipped-off about the shipment and had also been staking it out undercover.

The haul was a sizeable one even for Alexandria's busy police, but smaller ones happened all the time. Russell explained that 'raiding hashish-smoking dens could be organized any night when one had time and took the place of rat-catching of one's youth; actual danger there was little, as fists did more work than fire-arms, but an occasional drawing of a knife and the risks of a broken neck as one scrambled over roofs in the dark gave plenty of zest to the chase.' With such enthusiasm for his work, it only took Russell two years to be transferred to Cairo as Assistant Commissioner of Police.

Russell took a historical view of the civil unrest in Alexandria. 'Since the time of the Romans,' he pointed out, 'Alexandria has been notorious for its disorderly mobs.' When he was there the tension between the communities was often palpable in the streets, with Egyptians demonstrating against the British occupation, Muslims and Copts quarrelling with each other, Greeks and Italians shooting it out – it took so little to spark off another riot, as, for instance, in 1911, his first year on the coast, when a report from the Italo–Turkish war announcing that Tripoli had been retaken by the Turkish army was enough to send a few thousand Muslims from the dock area up into the centre of the city and the Christian quarter, chanting in celebration. To start with, the crowd was more elated than aggressive but when they reached the Hamamil quarter, 'inhabited,' Russell explained, 'largely by low-class European prostitutes and their Greek bullies', the climate changed. The Greeks appeared on balconies and in upper windows and started shooting into the crowd. To calm them down Russell sent plainclothes men into the houses. The crowd then reached the Manshiya quarter and smashed every window and street lamp that they passed, but when they finally arrived in the Square they encountered Russell's mounted police. Here the crowd became violent and fighting broke out. Russell noticed that pistols were being fired and table-tops hurled from one particular café and, gathering a few of his men together, he stormed the place. Inside, he reported, 'I then found myself facing an enormous Sudanese armed with a chunk of marble table-top, and I landed him one on the jaw, with the result that I dislocated my hand, and finally laid him out with a good Whitechapel upper-cut with my knee in his groin.' The rest of the riot took rather longer to control.

Thinking back to these earlier days of rioting, Major Jarvis in the 1930s wrote that 'if Cairo has a riot in the streets Alexandria always has a bigger and better one the next day; there seems to be more building going on in Alexandria and therefore a better supply of bricks and stones to throw at the police. Also Alexandria has more Greek grocers to be looted and beaten. The present commander of police, however, unfortunately lacks the competitive spirit and has done a lot to pull Alexandria's average down, which is a great pity as it used to be one of the finest towns for a riot in all the world.'

★

Mabel Caillard came back to Alexandria in the summer of 1914 and rented a large villa at Ramleh, paying for it by taking in distinguished lodgers. The Cotton Exchange was closed for the summer and the city was as quiet and stagnant as the desert air. Friends and guests came out to the villa to pass the time. The German Chargé d'Affaires, who was staying in the villa, was having lunch with Mabel and two British engineers and had just declared that 'We are all friends here,' when he heard the news that France and Germany had gone to war. Britain, of course, they were all sure, would stay out of it. The Baron von Richthofen came to lunch with the German official and Mabel on

2 August and announced that he was returning to Germany to volunteer his services and then the next day the Chargé d'Affaires arrived back with tears in his eyes and told her that he would be moving out of the villa to a hotel in Alexandria, to be nearer the legation. But in spite of all these preparations, Mabel was surprised when that night, at midnight, Britain declared war on Germany.

Sir Herbert Kitchener, the British Agent in Egypt at the time, was on leave in London but Milne Cheetham, the acting Agent, gave assurances that Egypt would not be brought into the war. However, that situation changed when Turkey, still the sovereign power in Egypt, entered the war on the German side and the Egyptian Khedive Abbas II appointed a pro-German prime minister. British officials explained that this was not acceptable, but the Khedive ignored their warnings; the British then reacted quickly by declaring Egypt a British Protectorate, deposing Abbas and appointing his uncle Prince Hussein Kamel in his place as the newly styled Sultan of Egypt. British and allied troops made for Egypt, particularly to protect the Suez Canal, while Egyptians provided a range of ancillary services for their war effort through the Egyptian Labour Corps.

The war transformed life in Alexandria. A rigid press censorship was imposed and suddenly 'blankness enveloped us,' Mabel Caillard wrote, 'like a fog that leaves near objects clear and blots out the rest of the world with baffling completeness. We could see as far as the horizon ...' Martial law was also declared and gatherings of more than five people were made illegal unless officially sanctioned; this put an end to any chance of nationalist demonstrations. A new tax was levied on the European inhabitants by which they were made to pay for their own security forces. Enemy subjects were interned or deported and Mabel was shocked to learn that some of her German neighbours had been spying against the British. There was panic buying of food which then led to a food shortage and an increase in the price of even the most basic market goods. Every day, it seemed, there was a new turn to events. Then the British regiments were ordered to the European front and the Alexandrian barracks were emptied, leaving British residents feeling unprotected. Mabel Caillard looked out to sea, and wondered what would happen if the Turks decided to invade. She was reassured by the news that Indian troops would be arriving in Alexandria within a fortnight, but those two weeks passed without them appearing and so did another month. Then when they did arrive, they were sent off to Europe almost immediately. The order and predictability which had hitherto been at the centre of her existence had disappeared. A French contingent arrived and also left almost straightaway. And then, on one of the hottest days she had ever known, the Lancashire Territorials landed and the Mustapha Pasha barracks were occupied once again.

Events moved even more quickly now. Little was heard in Alexandria of the Turkish attack on the Suez Canal, or of the repulse, but Australian and New Zealand troops, the ANZACs, began arriving in the city and Alexandria became the centre of operations for the Gallipoli campaign. Many of the ANZAC troops camped out at Ramleh and Mabel saw them riding bare-back past her villa on the way to swim in the sea. Hector Dinning was with the Australian force and he remembered his stay in Alexandria before Gallipoli as a happy time. The harbour and the sea outside the breakwater were filled with transports, supply vessels and battleships. Small local boats sailed gently between the ships and the quays, loaded with ammunition or men. Dinning's evenings off-duty gave him time to look around the centre of the city, where he thought the people were more remarkable than the place. The centre was mostly crowded with men in khaki and women in the red and grey of nursing uniforms, but he got away from them and found some Egyptians to talk to. 'The best way of seeing them as they are is to take two boon companions from the camp, ride into town, and instal yourselves in an Egyptian café for the night, containing none but Egyptians, except yourselves; invite three neighbours to join you in coffee and a hubble-bubble. They'll talk English and are glad of your company. At the cost of a few piastres (a pipe costs one, and lasts two hours, and a cup of coffee a half) you have their conversation and the finest smokes and cup after cup of the best Mocha. This is no mean entertainment.'

Before the Australians left on active service the new season opened at the Alhambra Theatre near the tram terminus and for five piastres Dinning and his friends several times took seats in the gods. 'The gallery is always interesting, even in Australia,' he conceded, 'but where the gods are French, Russian, Italian, English, Jewish, Greek, and Egyptian, the intervals become almost as interesting as the acts . . .'

When the order came for the ANZACs to board ship for Gallipoli they left quickly and with high hopes. Mabel Caillard remembered them promising to be back in a matter of weeks – 'It was going to be a picnic.' Many of them did come back a few weeks later, but they were either the mutilated, grown older through their first, sudden experience of war, or the dead. Once again Alexandria was in chaos. The city was unprepared for the scale of the calamity: Victoria College was not yet transformed into the RAMC hospital unit; the Anglo-German hospital was short-staffed since many of the German nurses had been dismissed for singing *Deutschland Uber Alles*; the Indian Medical Service had only just installed themselves at San Stefano. Then just as quickly order was restored and the Red Cross flag was flying from a depressing number of villas and buildings in and around the city, with the palace at Montazah being declared the favourite convalescent home. Some of the patients who were well enough to walk used to stroll around Ramleh in their white prison jackets, the only clothing available when the regulation blue uniforms of the hospitals ran out. Staff from the new hospital units came to live with Mabel in her villa, including Major Horsley, a famous physician in peacetime, his wife and daughter, and another surgeon called Tubby.

Hector Dinning came back to Alexandria, too, travelling from the Suez Canal via Cairo by train. For more than three hours after leaving the capital he had been watching the flat delta land slip by with its palms and villages and stagnant canal. 'You tire of the regularity of recurrence. There is a hankering after the quiet stir and variety of the city of Alexandria.' The city was a welcoming sight indeed for him. He had come through the Gallipoli campaign unhurt and was resting between spells of active service and nowhere, he was to decide, could one rest better than in Alexandria. He walked around the city, noting what had changed and what had remained the same, like the most avid sightseer, and he brought an unexpected, wartime reminder of the world of tourism.

His days began happily enough 'at some hour later than *réveille*' when he had a bath and dressed at leisure. A visit to an Italian restaurant around ten o'clock set him up for the morning, for a visit to the Graeco-Roman Museum perhaps, which he liked because it was 'small, but highly charged with meaning', in spite of the fact that the newly compiled guide book was in French only and the Sudanese 'conductors' were 'English-less'. No matter, he had only come to browse at leisure, briefly and certainly without effort, before heading back towards the source of his present inspiration, the Square. Everywhere he went about the centre he saw nurses, no longer rushing around at work, but with time on their hands, time, too, for entertainment. Hector saw them in small groups making their way all over the city, 'in the cafés, the Oriental shops, the cars, the post office, the mosque; on the esplanade, on the outlying pleasure-roads of Ramleh, the golf-links, the race-course; the Rue Cherif Pacha teems with her, shopping or merely doing the afternoon promenade. She is sprinkled among the tea-parties at Groppi's; her striking red and grey adds colour to the Square of Maho-met Ali, to Rue Ramleh, and the Rue Rosette.' He had had a hard, lonely, fearful, all-male time of the war and in Alexandria he found relief at every corner, though not all of it in the shape of nurses. He was reassured that so much of the city's life continued as before. The Rue Sherif Pasha was still busy with French dowagers and their liveried coachmen. The prettiest women in Europe were walking along the same pavements as him. A group of young French girls passed him on their way to Mass. The red-tarbooshed fishermen were still to be found sitting on the harbour wall, smoking and laughing, their loose white robes blowing in the breeze. An old Russian aristocrat took the air in her open carriage. Nursemaids pushed prams along the front. This was the Alexandria he wanted to remember.

He walked to the Nouza Gardens, listened to the band playing and sipped a beer. Then he took a ride around the ancient Lake Mariout and the whole way through the Ramleh district – 'To drive through it in a gharry is to put yourself in the dress-circle' – in the hope that he would not make it back to the Square in time for the 6.30 organ recital at St Mark's, for the church would be full of khaki not tweed and the music, Handel and Bach, would send him back to his room with a heavy heart.

Having missed the church recital, he set off to see the Alexandrian night-life. There were two sides to the city at night. The fine side concerned the orchestra striking up at the theatre at 9.30, the cafés filling up, the opera-going crowd coming out at two o'clock in the morning for a late supper and a drive by the sea. Then there was the other side and, although he admitted that 'Alexandria cannot compare with Cairo in lasciviousness,' it had its own share of vices and the women were there to be had. In a café, with a piano and a few string instruments banging out *Tipperary*, the barmaids sat on the soldiers' knees while everyone sang and a group of Tommies called for more English beer – 'There is a simple crudity,' Dinning decided, 'in the man who persists in being an Englishman to the backbone in the land of Egypt' – and the Provost-Marshal came in with his whistle and baton to restore order.

At midnight, he inspected the Arab quarter. By now, this eager traveller had discovered the secret to sight-seeing in Alexandria: there are few monuments to visit and the museum, as he had already found out, is small, so consequently there is little that the sightseer is compelled to do. He has the time to sit and watch the Alexandrians. Dinning had the impression that there was little for them to do, either, since the cafés always seemed to be full and the people he watched encouraged the idea that they, too, had no work to do. Perhaps nowhere else in the world had he encountered such a serious and lasting enjoyment of idleness.

In one of the music-halls here he found 'one bloated, painted woman who screams an Arab rhythm at intervals under the influence of hashish,' to the accompaniment of an orchestra of pipes and drums. He noticed that there were no other women in the hall and so he decided that it must be the women who had the jobs which earned the livings which the men came here to spend. That, he was sure, was how it was. He, however, was different and he watched the men indulging themselves while keeping himself off narcotics and the evil-smelling alcohol. He drank coffee for the rest of the night.

'Somewhere in the small-hours a gharry comes for the lady, and the hall noisily gets emptied. And as you climb up to your room in the hotel opposite, you can hear the dispersing throng in argument and criticism far along the emptying street. Standing at your balcony door, it merges imperceptibly into the subdued murmur of the city, broken by a belated, wailing, street-cry.'

★

Alexandria was not the same after the soldiers and nurses left. An Englishman who lived in Egypt at the beginning of the century had noticed that the memories of foreigners who had lived in Egypt for some time were clearly divided by what they called 'the events'. 'It is an odd name, and I do not quite know how it grew up,' he explained, 'but that is how the revolution of 1882 was always referred to among us in Egypt. A thing had happened "before the events" or "after the events".' The war was viewed as another event by the foreigners who lived in Alexandria and it seemed to many of them that the best days for the British were now behind them.

A few years earlier, Constantine Cavafy, 'the old poet of the city', had written a poem about another foreign soldier who had come to the city, 'The God Abandons Antony':

> When at the hour of midnight
> an invisible choir is suddenly heard passing
> with exquisite music, with voices –
> Do not lament your fortune that at last subsides,
> your life's work that has failed, your schemes that have proved
>   illusions.
> But like a man prepared, like a brave man,
> bid farewell to her, to Alexandria who is departing.

CAIRO

'There was nowhere in Cairo where one might take a lady without affronting her modesty. The kind of veiled – and often unveiled – indecency is no stranger in music halls in England, but it must be admitted that Cairo went a shade or two further.'

Sydney A. Moseley, *With Kitchener in Cairo*

Cairo does not look its best from the air, especially at night, but this is the way that my companion and I approached it and it was a disappointing first sighting. The sun had gone down magnificently below a bank of cumulus cloud as we left Europe and started out across the Mediterranean, and its departure encouraged a rather sombre sense of passing-over which at the time seemed an entirely appropriate way to approach Egypt, passing into another time band and into a place more different than the four-and-a-half-hour alcohol-free Egyptair flight from London suggested. When we began our descent into Cairo, a hush came over the passengers and even the captain was silent. Then we saw it, a galaxy of pin-point street lamps glowing like stars in an English sky, so faint in the dust-enriched atmosphere that I thought at first that the window had steamed up. That was fine, but then we dropped down further and these street lights showed up well-planned broad avenues, very exact and regimented, and, moving along them, a few ordinary brand-name cars, the same sort of cars that we had just left behind. Hotels and restaurants advertised themselves in multi-bulb or neon signs, just as they did in New York, London, Paris, Rome. But where, I wanted to know, was the Cairo we had prepared ourselves for? The Cairo of broken-down houses and famously overcrowded streets, where minarets were as common as TV aerials and life was an exotic mixture of oriental nights and sharply-lit days, of barter, bugs, belly-dancing and baksheesh. That was what we had come for. But what we were looking at was very different.

Heliopolis is a wealthy suburb of Cairo and home of its airport since 1921 when the RAF began flying the desert mail route from here across to Baghdad, and Imperial Airways opened its Cairo to Karachi service. This Heliopolis was a sort of colonial Milton Keynes, an Egyptian new town, and although everything has a story to it, even Heliopolis, Egypt is so rich in history that it dismisses as minor or not sufficiently rewarding what other countries put on their postage stamps. All that remains of note from the ancient city of On, where the sun god Ra-Harakhte was worshipped and which the Greeks therefore called Helio-polis, city of the sun, is a single standing obelisk. There are two others, made of red granite, which used to stand beside it in the reign of Tuthmosis III (c. 1468 BC), but they were moved to Alexandria by Augustus Caesar to stand in front of the temple of the deified Julius Caesar. Then in the last century they were both given away: one was moved to the Victoria Embankment of the Thames in London, the other to New York's Central Park. (In his acceptance speech at the presentation ceremony on 22 February 1881, the US Secretary of State, William Maxwell Evarts, noted that great powers in antiquity – the Assyrians, Romans and Byzantines – had each removed obelisks from Egypt. Would France, Britain and the United States, who had each removed obelisks in the present one, achieve such greatness?)

A few miles from the remaining obelisk at the ancient site of Heliopolis, there is a sycamore tree known as the Virgin's Tree. Legend has it that the Virgin Mary and her son rested beneath this tree during their flight from the agents of Herod. Well, not under this exact tree, for the present one was grown from a shoot of another tree which, suffering from age and perhaps also the zeal of religious souvenir hunters, had collapsed in 1906. But even that tree was itself a replacement for one which had fallen in the 1670s. But the factual genealogy of the tree is less important than the legend – here rested the Holy Family.

It might be pure coincidence that the previous sycamore collapsed at the same time as this new town of Heliopolis was being built. The town was planned by a Belgian company, the Cairo Electric Railway and Heliopolis Oasis Company, which had been awarded a concession to build in the desert to the north-east of Abbassia and the British barracks, due east also of the royal palace at Qubba. The suburb was planned as an independent unit; it came ready-made and had its own Palace Hotel – intended to rival the Casino in Monte Carlo until the authorities enforced Egypt's anti-gaming laws – Sporting, Racing and Polo Clubs, churches for the Anglican, Greek Orthodox and Catholic, Roman Catholic, Muslim and Maronite creeds, and a monument to a Frenchman called Louis Mouillard who used to fly his glider from the top of the Moqattam Hills, overlooking the old city, and still lived to his sixty-third birthday. The roads in the new city were named in French, still the official language of the court, and Heliopolis, which was also called Masr el Gadida or New Cairo, attracted wealthy Egyptians as well as the foreign communities, although with the barracks and later the aerodrome nearby, the British were particularly conspicuous in the more modest apartments.

Mabel Caillard had called Heliopolis a place without a soul and we were inclined to agree with her as we flew into Cairo International Airport for the first time. We had hoped for a glimpse of some grand and romantic historical spectacle – illuminations at the Pyramids, perhaps – for which Egypt is so famous. The well-planned vision which greeted us in its stead, the conception of a Belgian baron who built himself a house here modelled on an Indian temple, was as unromantic as the outside of the international terminal. Inside the building, however, we had our first experience of a different order.

There is a row of narrow kiosks immediately in front of the terminal entrance labelled Bank of Alexandria, Banque Misr, Thomas Cook. Cook's always used to advise travellers to bring plenty of money and it is soon apparent why they did so. The tellers called out to us – *hello*, *welcome*, *change*, *doll-ars* – and smiled in the knowledge that all international arrivals have to change the equivalent of $150 before they are allowed through immigration. This is a hard and fast rule. Everyone, even people staying overnight en route to somewhere else, has to change their money. We didn't, though. Like tourists earlier in the century, we were taken in hand by the representative of a travel company, a tall, slim Egyptian in his mid-twenties called Ahmed who, in spite of the heat, was dressed in sweater, shirt and tie, as if ready for an early autumn evening on a 'preppie' American university campus. Ahmed smiled our way past the bank tellers, past an immigration officer who sat impassive, behind a large desk, black cap on his head, eyes staring in the direction of the passport pages which passed in front of him. After that, our luck ran out and the customs official wanted to see and to feel the contents of suitcases, wash-bags, toothpaste tubes until I discovered one of the advantages of travelling with an attractive blonde woman – she smiled and he waved us on.

In the last century, travellers arriving in Cairo were invariably struck by the chaotic energy of the place. When Florence Nightingale stepped off the boat at Boulak, the old dock in Cairo, on 26 November 1849, she needed a servant to keep back the crowd of porters and hawkers. Within an hour of her landing, she remembered, 'with our baggage on camels, ourselves with the Efreet running before us, the kourbash cracking in his hand (it is impossible to conceive anything so graceful as an Arab's run), we had driven up the great valley of acacias from Boulak to Cairo to the Ezbekeeyeh . . .' Forty years later, arriving from Alexandria by train, Mabel Caillard needed less protection from the crowd, but was still forcibly struck by her first moments in the city. 'When you came to Cairo it was as if you had entered upon another world. You were in the East – nay, more than this: Cairo was the East, its substance and its essence. The first whiff of it (a mixture of old dirt, incense, spices and bad drains) apprised you of the fact as soon as you drove away from the railway station . . .'

Outside Cairo International Airport on the night of our first arrival in Egypt, the smell of aviation fuel and petrol fumes was most prominent. The driver of a black, stretched Mercedes, also provided by the travel service, had backed up the car as close as he could to the exit of the terminal. As we came out into the hot night, several men came to help, to watch or to advise on the loading of our two suitcases into the car, all of whom then wanted to be rewarded. This moment, like the assassination of President Kennedy, will live forever in my memory – a first demand for baksheesh.

With Ahmed up front with the driver, we sat in the car for the hour or so that it had taken Florence Nightingale to reach her hotel. Certainly there had been enough activity around us to suggest that that was how long we had to wait for the yellow tour bus, which was blocking our way, to move off. A group came and loaded their luggage into and onto the bus. Then they opened the big windows as the temperature rose inside. We heard that we still could not leave the compound because the bus itself was blocked in by a fleet of taxis which were in turn cut off by another bus whose driver was missing. Where had he gone? To pray or smoke or whatever. This was the first time we heard the word *Maleesh*, never mind. A network of connections was spread across the forecourt of the terminal and everyone had their own, strongly-held opinion which they aired. Each driver also used his horn. The prevailing smell was still of fumes – of car and aviation fuel and now of cigarette smoke, too.

When we finally left the airport compound and passed through another security check where a bored policeman asked the driver which hotel he was taking us to – why? – we at last caught a whiff of the rich, dark smells of Cairo, the constantly regenerating city. The driver was happy behind the wheel of the big Mercedes for in Cairo it is immediately obvious that size, speed and wealth count. The Mercedes had them all and, with gusto, the driver accelerated past old taxis with doors held on by rope and donkey carts whose boy-drivers screamed at him. Later, when we came close to joining a pile of broken glass and rusted metal on the wrong side of the road, Ahmed also spoke firmly to him.

Our hotel was part of an international chain, a new concrete tower standing like the mast of a Nile-boat on the southern tip of the island of Zamalek, which the Egyptians just call *Gezira*, the island. In London it had been suggested that this place combined the excitement of the East with the comforts of the West, but it had a lot to live up to; Cairo's hotels were world-famous for over a century before the revolution. Baedeker's *Handbook* for 1929 called them excellent and smart and warned that in first-class hotels evening dress was *de rigueur* for dinner. 'Even the second-class hotels are well fitted up,' the editor reported, 'nearly all having electric lights, baths, etc.' Cairo then was also just as famous for its visitors as for the hotels they frequented. Earlier this century, Lord Edward Cecil, Financial Adviser to the Egyptian government, noted that 'Egypt is also a not uncommon resort for those who have good reason to refrain from stopping in their own country; so there is also a certain element of romance about these people, if one has a touch of imagination.' More recently this has continued to be true and Egypt has offered asylum to King Saud of Saudi Arabia when he was deposed in favour of his brother Faisal; to King Idriss of Libya when his army officers seized power; and to the Shah of Iran after Ayatollah Khomeini returned to Teheran. And in 1985, President Nimeiry of the Sudan was conveniently already on a visit to Egypt when he received news that he, too, was not welcome at home.

If this 'certain element of romance' and the true sense of the East were present in our hotel, we failed to notice it as we checked in and went up twenty-something floors in an air-conditioned elevator to the sound of mid-Atlantic musak. A porter displayed the functions and features of the room – shower, bath, wardrobe, fridge, TV and radio, telephone, desk and writing paper, laundry service, shoe shine, room service menu – and held out his hand for a tip in much the same way as any of his colleagues around the world. Then we stepped out onto the balcony. Even being more than twenty floors up we were surrounded by the dark and noise and dust and a hint of the fertile smells kicked up by the constant motion along the river and its banks. We did see some of that imaginary city. Lights from the restaurants on the corniche, from cars going across the bridges and boats gliding on the warm night breeze, played on the water. We looked along the trunk of the Nile, up past the island of Roda where the main Nilometer was built in 716 and still stands, obsolete now that the river is dammed. We looked up towards Africa.

In the morning we woke as though into a dream in which a mu'adhin called Muslims to prayer from his minaret – 'Allah Akbar, Allah Akbar, Allah Akbar' – and as he recited the next part of the call we heard his words echoed by other mu'adhin in other minarets across the valley just as in valleys to the north of the Mediterranean we had heard the silence of a new day break with the peal of bells from the hill-top convent and the rattle of rusted tin bells around the necks of sheep coming down the hillside to graze.

The view from the balcony in the early morning was as much as any tourist could ask of his first glimpse of a city. With full white sails unfurled, feluccas moved across the dark Nile. Traffic on the corniche roads was still light and we could pick out individual sounds of people calling to one another, of a car's horn, and then of a woman singing. Later they all mixed together and formed the city's distinctive roar and rumble. On the horizon to our right, beyond the extensive jumble of roofs and towers on Cairo's west bank, across one half of the Nile valley, the three main Pyramids of Giza shimmered – a mirage made perfect by the distance, a hazy continuation of a dreamlike view. To the left, past Garden City, we looked across the heartland of Islamic Egypt. In there was the mosque of 'Amr, the General of Mecca and friend of the Prophet Muhammad himself, who founded the city of Fustat, the Camp, in 640, and the university mosque of Al Azhar which was built by the Fatimid general Gawhar in 970 and was the beginning of the city of el Kahira, the Victorious, Cairo. On the horizon, at the other side of the Nile valley, was the citadel of Saladin and the mosque of Muhammad Ali whose tall, thin minarets were dismissed by Victorian travellers as being vulgar and too much like patented propelling pencils.

Baedeker thought that Cairo's European quarters, when mixed with the picturesque medieval Arab quarter, made 'one of the most attractive cities in the world'. That was in 1929. When I went looking for the remains of the European influence, I found that it was most noticeable in the old hotels and palaces like the one which Ismail built for the Empress Eugenie on Gezira in the style of her own suite at the Tuileries, which is now the Cairo Marriott Hotel. There were plenty of roads and bridges, laid out, designed or built by Europeans, like the hydraulically-tilting Boulak Bridge (now renamed the 26 July Bridge) which I was told was built around 1910 by the son of Gustave Eiffel of Parisian fame. The story in Cairo is that when it was discovered that the bridge would not open, Eiffel threw himself from its railings and drowned in the river. If this was true then he jumped in vain, for there are photographs of the central span of the bridge aloft. Also reminiscent of that earlier era were the English and Kasr el Nil Bridges and the English country house which was the British Embassy – missing the final stretch of its garden which used to run down to the river and across which the Egyptian government built a riverside road soon after the revolution of 1952. The Gezira Sporting Club and Automobile Club were still running, as was the American University, the Institut d'Egypte and the British Council. The districts of Ismailia, Abbassia, Garden City, Maadi and Helwan still existed, although many of the grand, Europeanesque buildings were crumbling or changed and were now less a memorial of a foreign past and more a part of the living city, almost as Egyptian as the Pyramids.

★

Of all the institutions created for foreigners in Egypt, none stands out quite like Shepheard's Hotel, which can trace its history right back to the 1840s, to Thomas Waghorn and the development of the Overland Route to India. Samuel Shepheard was another Englishman who came to Egypt in the 1840s. He was employed by Messrs Hill & Co, Thomas Waghorn's rivals, as manager of their British Hotel in Cairo which faced a plot of land called the Ezbekieh and was situated in an area that was popular with Europeans and was therefore called the Frank Quarter. By the 1840s, this area had been enclosed and was reached through gates which were guarded by day and locked at night. The seclusion also helped to protect the foreigners against the frequent outbreaks of plague or cholera. But its character was not exclusively European – the British Hotel stood beside one mosque and in front of another so that the predominantly western feel inside the building was in contrast to its immediate surroundings. Acquiring a reputation for being well-run and conveniently situated, Shepheard's Hotel became as popular with passengers travelling between England and the eastern empire as it was with the growing number of tourists who came to Egypt. In September 1848, for instance, Samuel Shepheard recorded that 'The English passengers arrived last night at one o'clock and I am happy to say I have my house full. The only distinguished family is that of Sir Arthur and Lady Bullen who is going out as chief judge of Calcutta. The others are all colonels, majors, etc. etc. but as they all pay alike for their accommodation they are all served alike.' These judges and majors and Egyptian tourists were as different from the people around them as the hotel itself was from its neighbouring mosque. In 1850, Florence Nightingale described the scene outside the hotel on the Ezbekieh in this way: 'I am sitting at this moment with open windows, six o'clock in the morning, three minarets and a palm visible above the trees of the Ezbekeeyeh; the beloved Nubian, old friend of a sakia, going under the windows, and all kinds of Eastern groups under the trees.'

In the 1840s and 1850s, the British Empire expanded in the East and created a boom time for the transit trade in Egypt. There was fierce rivalry between the various transit companies: Hill & Co took over

Waghorn's operation and then the Egyptian government took over Hill's, creating the Egyptian Transit Administration. But by this time, Shepheard already had his own name up over the hotel's entrance and the responsibilities of the house were his. It was by no means the only hotel in Cairo and, although the English and Americans seemed to like it, the French and Italians preferred the Hotel du Nil or the de l'Europe, or even the Giardino. Apart from the hotels, Osman Effendi's houses could still be rented, as Murray's 1848 *Guide* noted, although the proprietor was long since dead. For a longer stay in Cairo it was definitely worth considering taking a house or rooms, since board and lodging at Shepheard's at the time cost forty piastres per person per day, while a set of rooms – bedroom, sitting room, kitchen – in one of Osman's houses cost only five piastres per day, and to rent a good house in the Frank Quarter cost less than 250 per month. Of course what the hotels could offer that a rented house could not was a sense of community and therefore also of security.

In spite of his success, Shepheard had to work hard to keep his hotel running, something which his family in England clearly did not understand. In a letter written to them in 1848, he complained that 'you little think how often we cry bread and cheese in England is better than a luxurious living here. It is all very well for you, who are at home, to think what an easy thing it is to be abroad and coining money, but I should like a few to come out here and see what we have to put up with to get a living even!' Part of his problem was that although guests in the hotel wanted to see 'local colour', they were less enthusiastic about having to live with it in the hotel, and the comments they made about the way the waiters dressed or the efficiency of the reception desk would have been more fitting to a London hotel. They wanted a familiar and safe base from which to make excursions; they wanted Shepheard's to be a little piece of England, like the British consulate. In the end it did become a cocoon for them in the heart of Cairo, just as Cook's steamers later became on the river. They expected a European menu in the dining room and a bottle of claret or port on the table. They were prepared to pay well for all this, of course, and Shepheard charged as much for the claret as he did for a room for the night. There was money to be made in the hotel, but it needed his constant attention, and his time and energy to arrange.

When Abbas Pasha, Muhammad Ali's grandson, became ruler of Egypt in 1849, the British Consul-General Charles Murray arranged an interview for Shepheard at which the Englishman requested the lease of a larger building around the corner from his present hotel for a new establishment. The new site was an old palace overlooking the

Ezbekieh which had originally belonged to Muhammad Ali's Mameluke rival, Elfi Bey and had later been used as Bonaparte's private quarters in 1798. It was here that the general had first been unfaithful to his future empress Josephine, in a liaison with Marguerite Pauline Bellisle, the wife of a lieutenant of the French Chasseurs who had broken the campaign ban on bringing women with the camp by dressing her in uniform and smuggling her across from France. When Bonaparte saw the beautiful woman, he sent the husband back to France with what were appropriately called urgent despatches and invited her to a dinner at the palace on the Ezbekieh at which, it is claimed, he resorted to the obvious but effective tactic of spilling a drink over her dress. Insisting that he must clear it up himself, the young general led her to his bedroom where he spent an hour atoning for his clumsiness. The following day La Belliote, as she was called, was dressed in a general's rather than a lieutenant's uniform.

When Bonaparte was in residence, the Ezbekieh in front of the palace was still connected to the Nile by a channel so that when the river flooded, the square became a lake. But Muhammad Ali had the channel blocked and the swamp drained, and new gardens were then laid out. The palace in front of them was given to his daughter, Princess Zeinab, but she in turn handed it over to a religious institution. However, when Shepheard explained his plan for a new hotel, Abbas agreed to let him have use of the palace.

All colonial communities had at least one central meeting place, a focus for travellers and expatriates. Within a stable community, this was often a club or consulate. In Cairo, where foreign residents mixed with passengers hurrying between England and India, and tourists out for the Nile season, it was a hotel. The old Shepheard's had been successful and popular, but the new one became an institution. It was *the* place for a rendezvous in Cairo, situated on what became the divide between the European and Arab quarters; for many people this was where their Egyptian journey began and as early as 1857 the *Illustrated London News* reported that 'Shepheard's has long been known as the fashionable resort of the Egyptian tourist as well as the great halting place for the Indian passenger en route for our great Eastern possessions. Perhaps in no hotel in the world do you find such an assembly of the people of rank and fashion from all countries as are found daily sitting down to the table d'hôte in the grand salon of this establishment.' In Shepheard's, as the writer Anthony Trollope commented, 'the English tongue in Egypt finds its centre'. It was also the centre of a growing number of what we now call service industries, attracted by the hotel's guests: Anglican church services were held every

Sunday morning in a house near the hotel; bookshops, gunsmiths, outfitters opened nearby; and stores like Turnbull's, which supplied tourists heading up the river with tea, sugar, jam, lemonade and other English goods which they had not brought with them but were unwilling to live without, were just around the corner in Frank Street. Later, Thomas Cook & Son, the ultimate colonial travel agent, opened their first Egyptian office in a corner of the hotel's grounds. By 1861, when Samuel Shepheard sold the hotel for £10,000 and went home to England, he had done more than just ensure a secure future for him and his family – for many travellers, his name stands beside Badrutt and, later, Ritz, as synonymous with a style and scale of service which seemed to disappear when the grand age of touring also ceased.

Rather than suffer from the departure of its founder, Shepheard's continued to grow in size and reputation. The Khedive Ismail succeeded his uncle Said Pasha in 1863 and among the many improvements he encouraged or financed in Cairo were the remodelling of the Ezbekieh gardens and the widening of Ibrahim Pasha Street which ran in front of the hotel's terrace. Ismail also encouraged others to build and the whole area was redeveloped, so that Shepheard's was surrounded by European-style villas. But another of Ismail's 'improvements', the Suez Canal, which was opened in 1869, seemed likely to have serious consequences for business in Cairo and especially for its hotels and shops. With the canal open, it would no longer be necessary for people travelling between the Mediterranean and the East to pass through the Egyptian capital. But would they come anyway, people in Cairo wondered. They need not have worried, for by the time Ismail had completed his preparations for the reception of his royal and noble guests in Cairo, he had transformed the city and the new facilities were so attractive that many transit passengers now insisted on breaking their journey between England and India. How pleasant to take a week or a month's holiday in luxurious Egypt on the way through.

Ismail's building and renovation plan was as ambitious as his debts, later, were extensive. Because so much was done to create an impression on his visitors, the improvements were equally enjoyed by tourists and travellers who came after them. The focus of Ismail's attention throughout the celebrations was the French Empress Eugenie who, as a cousin of Ferdinand de Lesseps, had agreed to open the canal and with whom, it was rumoured in Cairo, the Khedive was in love. For her he built an elaborate palace on the eastern side of Gezira, decorated in the style of her own apartments at home, but which also showed the influence of Islamic architecture in the use of marble and mushrabiya work; gardens were landscaped along the river bank facing back into

Cairo proper. But there was no point in building a palace on the island for the Empress if the only way of getting there was by ferry, so Ismail had a temporary bridge built over the Nile from beside the Kasr el Nil palace to the southern end of Gezira, while plans were drawn up for a more permanent bridge with massive bronze lions at each end, which was completed in 1871. On the other side of the Nile, though, one significant improvement was ready in time for the canal celebrations. Everyone, including empresses, went to Giza to see the Pyramids when they were in Cairo, but the journey, although picturesque, was also notoriously uncomfortable and even difficult, as William Thackeray discovered. 'The journey,' he wrote, 'I find briefly set down in my pocket-book as thus:- Cairo Gardens – Mosquitoes – Women dressed in blue – Children dressed in nothing – Old Cairo – Nile, dirty water, ferry-boat – Town – Palm-trees, town – Rice fields – Maze fields – Fellows on dromedaries – Donkey down – Over his head – Pick up pieces – Howling Arabs – Donkey tumbles down again – Inundations – Herons or cranes – Broken bridges – Sands – Pyramids.' Clearly all risk of going 'Over his head' had to be avoided for the Empress, so Ismail ordered a solid road to be built from the west side of the Nile out to the Pyramids (which lies under the present Pyramids Road) and along which Eugenie is said to have planted acacia trees, part of a line of them which provided shade across the valley. She is also said to have made good use of the road during her visit to Egypt, riding out to the Pyramids each day that she was in Cairo. After the celebrations for the Suez Canal, Eugenie did not return to Cairo until 1909, by which time both her husband, Napoleon III, and the Khedive Ismail, had been deposed and were dead. On that occasion, the eighty-three-year-old woman did not ride out but was driven along the Pyramids Road. There were tears in her eyes as she passed along the avenue of trees which she had planted and which had now grown tall. At the foot of the Pyramids, the old royal lodge which had been put at the disposal of the Empress and her party in 1869 had been turned into the Mena House Hotel and welcomed anyone who could afford the prices.

In Cairo, Ismail also had plans to develop the district between the Ezbekieh and the Nile which was to be known as the Ismailia quarter. He even offered free plots of land to anyone who was prepared to spend 30,000 francs or more on building a house; at that price, there was a good chance that he would succeed in his intention of making his capital look something like the European cities which had so impressed him. The mile-long straight line of the Sharia Muhammad Ali was laid out from the south-east corner of the Ezbekieh right up to the front of the mosque of Sultan Hassan and the main gates of the Citadel. Another road named after the French physician Clot Bey, who had built up the Kasr el Aini hospital during Muhammad Ali's reign, was laid from the central railway station to the Ezbekieh, which had now become the modern centre of the city.

Of all the buildings founded by Ismail, none shows the extent of his impossible flirtation with the West better than the Opera House he built on the other side of the Ezbekieh to Shepheard's. Facing west, it was one of the centrepieces of his preparations, but like so much else it was built quickly – in about five months – and with more attention to appearance (its design was greatly influenced by the Paris Opera House) than to strength, although in the end it survived for more than a hundred years. Inside, it was decorated with rich crimson hangings and golden brocade. The royal box was fitted out with red brocade and the boxes for Ismail's harem were carefully screened off from the rest of the audience. On 1 November 1869, the first opera was performed in the new auditorium – not the *Aïda* that Ismail had commissioned from Verdi, for that was not completed for another two years, but instead the same composer's *Rigoletto*. The performance was a success, as Ismail had ensured it would be, but perhaps the audience itself provided a greater spectacle than the performers. The Empress Eugenie sat in the royal box between Ismail and the Emperor Franz Joseph of Austria; around them were a crowd of other titled guests and the leading figures of Cairo's international community. Few Egyptians were invited, but through the screens of the harem boxes the audience caught the glint of gold and of diamonds.

But who did Ismail expect to use the Opera House after its glorious opening? There was no tradition of opera in Egypt and European singing was as far removed from the Arabic idea of melody as white tie and tails were from the native jellabiya. But it was a good way of providing entertainment for an international audience, for an understanding of the language was not essential. So the Cairo Opera became a favourite haunt of the international community and was one more place where they were able to cocoon themselves from the country they lived in and watch Italian or French companies perform operas they had probably already seen in Paris or London or Milan.

Soon after the opening of the Opera, the focus of the Suez celebrations moved to the canal itself and Cairo's palaces and hotels were left empty. For a while there were no more royal processions, no more arrivals of illustrious people with their entourages. But Ismail's extravagance paid off, for although Cairo did lose some of the old transit trade, the coverage of the canal celebrations tempted a new kind of tourist to Egypt and the 1870 season was just as well attended as the royal 1869 one. John Mason Cook, who was running the firm's office near Shepheard's Hotel recognized that there were now two things which attracted tourists to Egypt. First, it was a country of educational, religious and historical significance; Cook pointed out that 'there is one prominent feeling of interest that underlies all our visits to these lands and waters of biblical history, i.e. the abiding impression that we are travelling amongst and gazing on scenes with which we have been familiar of our earliest recollections'. Second, Egypt was now also a country in which tourists could indulge themselves in any way they chose. So long as they could pay the price, anything could be bought in Cairo, from the services of Ethiopian slave girls or young boys in the public baths, to the most beautiful antiquities in gold, silver, precious stones, or old rugs and even genuine mummies. Tourists could feast on a lamb slaughtered and cooked on a spit in front of them, or attend a dinner where they would be served roast beef and a bottle of cold English beer. It had become a city of variety which catered for all sorts of tastes because, as Amelia Edwards noticed as soon as she stepped into Shepheard's Hotel in 1873, it was visited by widely different groups of people.

> It is the traveller's lot to dine at many tables-d'hôte in the course of many wanderings, but it seldom befalls him to make one of a more miscellaneous gathering than that which overfills the great dining-room at Shepheard's Hotel in Cairo during the beginning and height of the regular Egyptian season. Here assemble daily some two to three hundred persons of all ranks, nationalities, and pursuits; half of whom are Anglo-Indians homeward or outward bound, European residents, or visitors established in Cairo for the winter. The other half, it may be taken for granted, are going up the Nile. So composite and incongruous is this body of Nile-goers, young and old, well-dressed and ill-dressed, learned and unlearned, that the new-comer's first impulse is to inquire from what motives so many persons of dissimilar tastes and training can be led to embark upon an expedition which is, to say the least of it, very tedious, very costly, and of an altogether exceptional interest.

★

British troops reached Cairo on 15 September 1882, two days after the defeat of the Egyptian Army at the battle of Tel el Kebir. The first thing to be done was to arrest the leader of the uprising, Colonel Arabi. The second, effected on the 19th, was to disband the Egyptian Army. British troops were installed in the barracks and palace at Kasr el Nil (the site of the present Nile Hilton Hotel) where Arabi's troops had been stationed, and where they later held some famous regimental balls. They were also stationed in Abbassia and up at the Citadel, accepting the lessons of history that Cairo could be dominated by a few guns placed on the heights. The status of what was now called the Army of Occupation was as inexact as that of Evelyn Baring, later Lord Cromer, who arrived in Cairo a year after Tel el Kebir. The army was in Egypt to secure the rule of the Khedive even though he had not actually invited their protection, and Cromer was there as the British Consul-General and Agent. This at least was the official explanation. Practically, though, the British Army occupied Egypt because the British Government believed that it was the best way for it to guarantee passage through the Suez Canal for its shipping, and Cromer was there to run the country and therefore ensure its stability after the military uprising and the financial chaos of Ismail's reign. This new unofficial rule became known as the 'Veiled Protectorate' and there was no other country capable of interfering now. The French and Turks both protested, but the French warships off Alexandria had withdrawn when the British fleet bombarded and Turkey, who still claimed Egypt as its own sovereign territory, was both diplomatically and practically powerless.

Egyptians and Europeans called Cromer 'the Lord', which was apt since he was the most powerful man in the country and, although there were sheikhs up the river in Luxor who had never heard of him, everyone in Cairo knew exactly who he was. Cromer was forty-two years old when he came to Egypt as Agent, and was a member of the Baring family, which owned the bankers, Baring Brothers. As well as wealth, Cromer also had good connections; when his cousin, Lord Northbrook, became Viceroy of India, Cromer went out with him as his private secretary and it was from India that he reached Egypt in 1883.

Cromer was the perfect imperial administrator. Blunt and imposing, he was a skilled diplomat, reflective, well-read and extremely well-organized. If he appeared cold and reserved, he was also loyal and believed that he was fair. He confessed to having a great deal of understanding and compassion for Egyptians, especially for the fellahin, but he believed unalterably that they were not capable of governing themselves and that the job – what he called 'the mission' – of guiding them had fallen to the English and to him. The Englishman, he wrote, 'was convinced that his mission was to save Egyptian society, and, moreover, that he was able to save it'. Seeing his work in terms of a mission, he was obliged to devote his energy to it and, in longevity, his 'reign' was second only to Muhammad Ali's in the history of modern Egypt. To fulfil his mission, Cromer believed that he must stand back from the people who needed his help, just as he believed that the British Army of Occupation and the British officials must keep themselves aloof. 'If a French army had been in Egypt,' he wrote, 'the officers would have fraternised with the European residents. They would be sitting outside every café.' This is very much what the French had done under Bonaparte. Although Cromer conceded that this created a greater sympathy than existed between the British officers and the people around them, it also led to quarrels and that was something he insisted that they must avoid. They were to be respected, he decided, not loved.

But imagine how it appeared to the Egyptians and the other foreigners in Egypt to have this Englishman – who was extremely visible with his turbaned Indian servants and whose Arab syces ran in front of his carriage waving their sticks to clear the way, but who was also inaccessible – governing the country while claiming that he did not, who hid behind the 'Veil' and whose authority was reinforced by the presence of the British Army. Cromer never learned to speak Arabic properly because he did not want to be able to communicate with Egyptians; instead he learned some Turkish so that he could talk to the old officials and he also spoke French, which was still the language of the court. He might have been respected, as he hoped, but he certainly was not liked and, as the occupation continued, he came to be despised. The nationalists disliked him especially, of course, and when at the beginning of this century he wrote about the difficulties of preparing Egypt for self-government, nationalists in the *Egyptian Standard* wrote that the greatest problem facing their country was that 'one alien race, the English, have had to control and guide a second alien race, the Turks, by whom they are disliked, in the government of a third race, the Egyptians'.

International politics brought Cromer and the British Army to Egypt; internal politics would bring about the necessary reforms whereby they would eventually be able to leave. Careful handling of the country by British officials advising Egyptian ministers would bring about the recovery of Egypt. This, bluntly stated, was Cromer's view. Naturally the Egyptians wanted him and his forces out; Cromer claimed that he would like to go, but that the country just was not ready for it yet. 'The Egyptians,' he wrote, 'should only be permitted to govern themselves after the fashion to which Europeans think they ought to be governed.' On these terms, it was doubtful whether Egypt would ever be ready for self-government.

The new British officials created a new society. There had been an evacuation of Europeans, especially the British, from Cairo during the Arabi rebellion and even the hotels had closed, with the exception of the Hotel Royal to the north of the Ezbekieh which, according to one guide book, could then 'be said to have some claims on the gratitude of Englishmen,' for it alone was ready to serve their officers when they marched into the capital. Lord Cromer, in a moment of humor, quoted Lord Curzon's sharp observation on the habits of the British abroad: 'From my experience, I would say the first thing an Englishman does in the outlying portions of the Empire is to make a racecourse. The second is to make a golf course.' A polo pitch was usually added soon after. In Cairo all this was done on a plot of land just behind the Gezira palace which they were given by the Khedive and the resulting Gezira Sporting Club, with its race course and 18-hole golf course became another important focal point for the growing British community. The club was founded in 1882 and modelled on the Hurlingham Club in London. It even looked like an English sporting club with its red-brick, tiled clubhouse and flower beds on either side of the straight driveway. Like English clubs, although it was a sporting institution – no gambling or games of hazard were allowed – membership implied status. One was a member of Gezira twenty-four hours a day, as Rule 51 of the club's charter clearly stated, giving the committee the power to expel, 'If the conduct of any Member either in or out of the Club's premises shall . . . be injurious to the character and interests of the Club.' No doubt some members did conduct themselves in such a way as to be injurious, but that is not what is remembered. Unusually for Cairo, subscriptions to the club were not too high and if one had the right introduction, admittance was not a problem either. The Gezira Sporting Club served as Cairo's country club and was the meeting-place for the ruling classes since its membership included British Army officers, British Agency officials, and British administrators working for the Egyptian government as well as the family of the Khedive, the wealthier Egyptians and most foreign residents in Cairo – even tourists with letters of introduction could take out temporary membership. While riders and mounts kicked up the dust along the race track or dug up the turf on the polo lawn, representatives of Cairo's 'best people' watched from the shade of well-watered trees.

At the beginning of the century the club was officially renamed the Khedival Sporting Club – until the Khedive was deposed by the British government – and one observer noted that, although the cricket, tennis, croquet and riding were fine to watch, the club 'would be charming even if it had no sports for its wealth of flowers, its broad stretches of turf, its southern trees and beauty'. Major C. S. Jarvis, himself a member of the Egyptian Service, took another view entirely and thought that, although the club provided facilities for most sports, 'from plutocratic racing and aristocratic polo to mid-Victorian frivolities like croquet and plebeian pursuits such as bowls and hockey,' they were not always played in a sporting spirit. For instance, he noticed that there were two types of tennis to be watched at the club, the 'non-competitive' and the 'intensely hostile'. The latter he observed was usually played when the leading ladies held their tournament: '"words" fly across the nets faster and harder than the balls, and large crowds attend the Ladies' Singles – not because they are particularly interested in the game, but because they want to see a really good scrap with 14-oz. racquets.' The club was no holiday-home for the men either, if Jarvis is to be believed, for it was here that their futures were decided. 'It is on Gezira polo grounds,' Jarvis wrote, 'that the officers of the Cavalry Brigade are tested for their military efficiency and fitness for command, and on Gezira tennis courts that examinations are held as to the desirability or otherwise of retaining in the service the British officials of the Government. Exceptional skill at the game means not only the permanent employment of the official in question, but also ensures promotion and increase of pay.'

If the Gezira Sporting Club was an essentially foreign enclave, the Turf Club, which was founded in the early 1890s, was exclusively British. Its clubhouse on the Sharia el Maghrabi (now Adli Street), next door to the monumental Sephardic synagogue, had been the British Agency building until Lord Cromer commissioned a new house down by the river, where the Agency moved in 1893. The Turf Club was perfectly located in the centre of the European city within walking distance of the Ezbekieh, the British Agency, the British Army HQ on Sharia Kasr el Nil and the other European consulates and public buildings. Although it was a residential club, the accommodation was bad and in season there were never enough rooms to go round, so most members rented rooms nearby. Still, as one visitor at the turn of the century forgivingly remarked, at least if it was overcrowded during the season, it was overcrowded with the 'right' sort of man – 'almost every Englishman in decent Society belongs to it'.

The clubs were an easy way for the growing number of British in Cairo to meet each other and to get to know new arrivals. Ronald Storrs joined both the Gezira and the Turf Clubs as soon as he arrived in Cairo and it did not take him long to discover how disapproving his countrymen could be: 'It was difficult for foreigners to be elected and not easy for Egyptians even to make use of either club,' he remembered, so when he arrived to play tennis at the Sporting Club with one of the fellow-Egyptian members (a man who later became Prime Minister of Egypt), he was met by a decidedly cool reception. Storrs at this point was a junior member of the Finance Department and new to club life. He called the Turf Club 'the fenced city of refuge of the higher British community', where most members spent a few hours each day, having a drink or reading *The Times* or the *Vie Parisienne*. The doorman at the Turf Club was a Montenegrin 'of distinguished melancholy', the waiters in the dining-room were Greeks and the head waiter was a man called Socrates whom Harry Boyle, the Oriental Secretary and the man whom Storrs succeeded in 1909, had renamed Alphonse because he insisted that Socrates 'was not a possible name for a waiter'. Lord Edward Cecil, who was the only Englishman present at the Council of Egyptian Ministers and therefore the most powerful British official in the Egyptian Service, could be equally pompous in his attitude to the staff at the club. Cecil lived in rooms in the city, but always went to the club for breakfast. And since each morning for more than ten years he had always had a dish of cold meat and omelette and a cup of coffee, he had only to walk in and demand 'Breakfast quick' for his food to be brought to him. He described the dining-room as being more like a foreign railway station than anything else since everyone was always in a hurry to eat. 'The waiters go about at a trot, bang down the wrong dish in front of you, and rush away before you can object. The noise and clatter are terrific, but it is the only place where one can get decent food at a price less than that paid at a Monte Carlo restaurant.' The parallel was not such an idle one either. They frequented their own clubs rather than bars and restaurants in the city because these other facilities, especially around the Ismailia and Ezbekieh districts were notoriously expensive, intended primarily for wealthy tourists rather than European residents. John Mason Cook's advice that his clients would need to take plenty of money with them to Egypt was still relevant and in 1929 *Baedeker*'s reckoned that Egypt was more expensive than most European countries. In Cairo especially one needed money, the want of which was keenly felt by many British officials. Hence the appeal of clubs, for evenings as well as during the day, for here food was cheaper and drink dependable.

'It is the custom,' Lord Edward Cecil explained, 'that before dinner every one should come to the club and have a drink and a talk with his friends.' They talked about business and politics, sport of course, plans for future social engagements and then the latest scandals. Social circles in Cairo were small and personal behaviour was not always as impeccable as might be assumed from the picture so far. Often rumours were unfounded and simply malicious, borne out of idleness or boredom, but they would still be believed. Cecil, who visited the Turf Club two or three times each day, held the view that more harm was done in the hallway of the club than in any other 'British' room in Cairo: this was the place to be seen, or else risk being talked about.

These clubs and the other meeting-places established after 1882 helped the British to do Cromer's bidding and stay aloof. But anyway there was something inherent in many of these latter-day Empire-builders who, when deposited in a place in the sun and handed a certain amount of power, kept themselves apart from other foreigners. Perhaps it was because, wherever they were, they did not recognize themselves as foreigners; their British characteristics, instead of being assimilated or compromised by contact with a new environment or different culture, were accentuated. The hollyhocks growing at the Gezira Sporting Club and the oak tree on the lawn outside the British Agency bear witness to this. Grass does not survive in the Egyptian climate without the greatest care and almost constant watering, but the British insisted upon lawns at their establishments.

Within this male side of the expatriate British society, there was a strict hierarchy; they might all be Best People, but some were better than others. One day, while waiting for his golf partner to arrive at the Sporting Club, Cecil considered the truth of this. The golf links were common ground for club members, as was the clubhouse itself, but although all these people walked across the links together, they were divided by an intricate arrangement of taboos. 'There is the swagger military set; there is the smug military set. There is the Egyptian Army set; there is the smart official set; there is the smug official set. There is the smart professional set; there is the smug professional set, and so on.' Most important, however, one might have access to any number of these sets, but one only belonged to one of them, a state of affairs which was clearly borne out by the story Major Jarvis told of two young Englishmen who had gone to the same school and university in England and had come out to Egypt together. One of them was chosen for the most prestigious department, Finance, while the other joined the Ministry of Education, known rather disparagingly as P.I. (Public Instruction).

Finance, having grasped the situation in all its clarity, failed to see Education for several months, but one day they came face to face outside the Club and recognition was unavoidable.

'Hullo,' said Finance heartily; 'I'd no idea you were out here. What Department are you in?'

'Well,' said Education meekly, 'as a matter of fact I'm in the P.I., But I don't want you to mention it to anyone at home as I have told my people that I am playing a piano in a brothel.'

The most prestigious set of all to belong to in Egypt was the British Agency; this was the real seat of power. From his large wooden desk in the office between the Agency's drawing room and billiards room, looking out onto the crested wrought-iron gates and the garden where Lady Cromer had planted her oak tree, the British Consul-General and Agent ruled Egypt, and the new British Agency building in the Kasr el Dobara quarter (now Garden City) was a symbol of his ascendancy. The decade of the 1890s was perhaps his greatest, for the British administration seemed to be producing results and the Egyptian economy, which Cromer himself had declared bankrupt in the 1870s, was buoyant. The country appeared to be more settled than it had been since the early days of Ismail's reign, although there were still calls for Egypt for the Egyptians, and while the British government insisted that their army was only here as a temporary measure, Lord Cromer knew that withdrawal was impossible.

Officially Cromer was just an ordinary diplomat although, as Dean of the Diplomatic Corps in Egypt, he took precedence over the consuls of the other represented nations. When Colonel Thomas Skelton Harrison arrived in Cairo in November 1897, as the new Diplomatic Agent and Consul-General of the United States, it was to Lord Cromer that he applied concerning the correct form for presenting himself to the Khedive and it was Lord Cromer whom he visited first. Harrison liked the Englishman, calling him 'a friendly, plain, outspoken, gentleman. He seemed to me to be about sixty years of age [he was in fact 56 at that time], tall, with a round, clean-shaven face, and a good-natured English countenance.'

Harrison and his wife Louise were living in a first-floor suite at Shepheard's while the American Agency was being redecorated for them and, twelve days after their arrival, they were invited to a Tuesday 'At Home' at the British Agency. They left Shepheard's at 10.15 pm and found about forty guests already at the Cromers'. 'The house is spacious and elegant,' wrote Harrison, who had a good eye for detail, in his diary, 'with some rich and appropriate furnishings. At first, we assembled in the drawing-room; afterwards in the ballroom and music-room, a large square apartment, with glaring white walls and ceilings, unrelieved by gilding or any colour; the furniture, too, was of white wood-work and the stuffs with which it was upholstered lacked character. The lights were electric – and the whole was very trying to the women.' He was particularly sensitive to what the women might find trying because his wife had already caught a 'Shepheard's cold', which resulted in him going alone to the Cromers' dinner on the following Saturday night. There were only a dozen people present on this occasion, among them Cromer's niece, a German official called de Mohl and his wife, and Major-General Sir Herbert Kitchener, now Commander-in-Chief of the Egyptian Army, whom Harrison described as 'a superb-looking, soldierly man, at least six feet tall, and weighing at least one hundred and ninety pounds, and about forty-five years old'. Harrison approved immensely of this gathering. He had already been to one of the grand state banquets at the Abdin Palace, in honour of the visiting King of Siam, where electric lighting was used for the first time and where, inevitably, the power was cut off. At the British Agency, of course, the power did not fail. At dinner, Harrison, who has left long descriptions of his more memorable dinners in Cairo, sat between Miss Baring and Lady Cromer and he was clearly charmed by them, too. The table linens and decorations he thought were exquisite, the glass was especially elegant, the two Indian servants in white and gold livery and turbans were efficient. The food 'was more than excellent,' he recorded with the relish of a gourmet. Although the menu was modest compared to the fifteen courses he had been served at the Khedive's banquet, at least here 'everything that should have been hot was so. First, a clear, golden soup, with small green balls of something soft' – eggs and cornmeal, most likely; then an *entrée, en timbale*; then what seemed a *fricandeau* of veal and a variety of decorative vegetables around the dish; then cold breasts of wild ducks, I think with meat jelly; an aspic and a potato mayonnaise salad were served at the same time; then an ice and a pastry; but just before this, a cherry bounce from Norway; again, either a crisp cake or pastry – no cheese.' During all this Harrison talked to Lady Cromer, who explained to him how Europeans lived in Egypt and what they got up to. She told him about flower shows and horse events and then advised him on the hiring of domestic servants. They could, it seems, have been anywhere in the world; certainly the house and the dinner owed more to English than to Egyptian influence, more to Victoria than to Abbas Pasha. When they finished their dinner, the ladies left the men to their claret, port and cigarettes and it was then that a little reminder of where they were arrived in the form of coffee – 'Turkish'.

Although Harrison found the Cromers excellent hosts, there were many people in Cairo who thought that Cromer himself was a cold and despotic man who lived up to the soubriquets he had earned when he was plain Sir Evelyn Baring – 'the Great Bear' and 'Overbaring'. Mabel Caillard, who was a familiar figure in Cairo during the winter seasons of the 1890s, remembered several incidents which confirmed this impression of Cromer. Although dinners and balls at the British Agency were the most important occasions for the British community and more difficult to get invited to as an outsider than the Khedive's parties, she found them dull and overly formal. The atmosphere in the house was depressing. But some of the balls, she remembered, 'if you could survive the early crush and the official chill of your reception, were quite enjoyable'. It was clear, however, especially towards the end of his 'reign' when his health failed, that Cromer did not enjoy this part of his duties. Among the numerous stories which circulated about him, there was one which concerned two young men who arrived at an Agency ball with a great appetite. Form dictated that they wait until supper was announced before making their way from the white ballroom to the dining room, so in the meantime they propped up the walls and looked expectantly towards the doorway. When the supper-room was at last declared open, they were the first to hurry down the long corridor. But before they reached the food, they encountered their host and, as Mabel explained, 'in "the Lord's" mind their air of joyful satisfaction could bear but one interpretation. "Going?" he asked them, a look of sympathetic understanding dawning on his face. He conducted them to the door, genially wished them good-night, and saw them off the premises.'

*

Major Jarvis described Cairo in this way: 'The city consists of some shops and hotels, the Turf and Gezira Clubs, and about ten thousand Government offices. To the north is Abbassia where the soldiers live, north again is Heliopolis where enormously wealthy retired Egyptian officials have palaces, and the Royal Air Force small flats, and south is Maadi where some highbrows addicted to gardening dwell. They also read poetry and write books. There are some Pyramids and a Sphinx to the west, and duck shoots to the north-west and south-west. East there is nothing except the Citadel where Saladin used to keep a part of his army.'

In the same manner, the major divided the Egyptian year into four seasons: the first from December to February was for the shooting of duck and snipe; from March until June was spent preparing for the summer leave; from July to September there was the husbands-only season for the 'finding of and improving of acquaintance of "summer friends" and October and November was the season for the wives to return and see off their husbands' "summer friends"'. This last, the major thought, 'is the most sporting season of the four as if the "summer friend" is a veteran at the game she puts up a very good run for her money, and all Cairo has bets on the result'. He might have written 'all European Cairo', for the city he describes is so completely lacking in Egyptians that it does not even include those parts of the city which existed before Europeans arrived. But there was really no way that foreign residents could successfully pretend that 'Egyptian Egypt' did not exist. For a start there were the regular visits to the Khedive and his court for Lord Cromer and the other foreign representatives. Although perhaps not as extraordinary as James Bruce's meeting with Ali Bey and his son-in-law a hundred years earlier, they were still impressive and conducted according to oriental form.

The visits of the official wives to the Khediva in her harem apartments at the Abdin Palace sound a little more exciting. Lady Cromer, for instance, used to take a different group of English ladies for an audience once a fortnight. On the day that Mabel Caillard was invited, the ladies formed up a cavalcade of carriages outside the British Agency and set off in formation. At the palace, the Englishwomen were introduced by the English First Lady who was herself invited to sit beside the Khediva on a gilded settee; the others were shown to a row of gilt chairs covered in green velvet. Slave girls in bright silk gowns brought them all coffee in gold filigree holders which were studded with jewels, or sherbet in gilded glasses, which the women drank in silence. When the girls had cleared away the glasses, the Khediva addressed each woman in turn, talking in French, but usually saying no more than 'Vous allez bien, madame?' Clearly the spectacle was more important than the discussion, although after she had finished her rounds, the Khediva spoke to Lady Cromer for a few minutes and then the audience was concluded with each of the Englishwomen in turn curtseying and walking backwards out of the room, since it was considered an insult to turn one's back on royalty. But the behaviour of some of the women often provided enough gossip for the ride home – one woman, for instance, arrived in a serge skirt and a sailor's hat, the outfit in which she had been riding that morning; the Khediva made it clear that she was not amused. On another occasion, someone went up and shook the royal wife's hand and then turned around to walk out. These breaches of palace etiquette were not appreciated and it was left to Lady Cromer to explain this to the visitors.

The class system which divided British officials in Egypt was equally rigid amongst the women. At the top of the social pyramid towered a trinity of ladies: the Agent's wife, the wife of the Sirdar or commander of the Egyptian Army and the wife of the officer commanding the British Army of Occupation. Even between these three there was rivalry. The Agent's wife was 'First Lady', but the two military wives fought across a battlefield of balls and dinners to establish their claim to the title of 'Second Lady'. After Kitchener reconquered the Sudan the fight was won by the Sirdar's wife since her husband then also became Governor-General of the Sudan, a post which seemed to be a precursor of the job of Agent and Consul-General in Egypt.

For a while there was also a Ladies' Club in Cairo, which was ruled over by the top women, but the ranking system defeated it. The problem was that there were not enough top women to fill the membership of a club and so they had to rely on juniors to make the thing viable. Realizing their power, the juniors insisted that they should exist on an equal footing with the leading ladies, at least inside the club. But the senior ladies protested; if Lady Cromer, for instance, came into contact with Mrs –, then it would be Mrs – who would benefit, for in her conversation for the next few weeks the phrase 'as I was saying to Lady Cromer' would crop up as often as credulity would allow. Mrs –'s friends would then consider it unjust that the First Lady had spoken to her and not to them. In a way, they might just as well have been in Reigate or Cheltenham from the way they behaved and their club collapsed under the weight of these apparently insoluble social problems.

Englishmen seemed to administer the country in spite of, and often in complete ignorance of, the obstacles in their way. When Ronald Storrs was working in the Finance Department, he was surrounded by Egyptians but he had almost no contact with them. The system of administration and the social facilities available to him meant that, apart from those Egyptians who served him at home and in the clubs, and Egyptian officials in his office, he was most likely to form his impression of the character of the people from shopkeepers and cab-drivers. However eloquent and interesting they were, they were hardly likely to provide an adequate picture. Storrs described a typical day in Cairo in this way – after a morning in the office, during which he saw rather than spoke to his Egyptian officials, he rode or drove to the Turf Club or back to his flat for lunch and then spent the rest of the afternoon out at the Sporting Club playing tennis or golf. He then popped into the Turf Club again on the way home for an evening drink to catch up on the news and gossip and then he either went out to dinner or to the opera, or back home to his flat and his enthusiastic servant. He might have been observing Cromer's wish that a British official should be seen and not known – Major Jarvis noticed that these officials 'have a heavy, silent manner and refuse to express an opinion on anything' – but he was also successfully cutting himself off from the people whose lives he influenced. When they finally rose against him, the strength of their opinion came as something of a surprise.

The British did not always remain apart from other Europeans, though, and in the big hotels especially they mixed with one of the most cosmopolitan crowds in the world. Nowhere was this clearer than at Shepheard's Hotel which seemed to reflect in its own development and expansion the growing foreign influence in Egypt. It was no longer the hotel of the Overland Route; by the turn of the century, the old hotel, added to bit by bit, had finally been knocked down and was replaced by a new four-storey building with imposing mouldings and folding slatted shutters in the continental style around the windows. The name of the hotel was arced in electric lights in the centre of the roof and really only some of the elaborately patterned railings and a tall palm tree in the front garden suggested the location of the hotel. Without these, it could have been an imperial hotel in Venice or Vienna, Paris without the mansards, or even London. The Khedive Ismail had wanted to take Cairo into Europe, but what the Europeans had done was to build a little piece of Europe within Cairo, almost sealed off from the rest of the capital.

Shepheard's Hotel was constantly popular and busy, but it was no longer the most élite hotel in the community. Since the society was so stratified, the 'best people' favoured places where the crowd either would not or could not follow. Lord Edward Cecil, who as senior official and also a son of the British Prime Minister existed in a rarified atmosphere, advised that although all of the big hotels gave at least one ball a week – so that it was possible to attend one every night – 'the smart ones, to which all the *Best People* go, are the Savoy and the Semiramis'. ('Who constitute the *Best People*', Cecil observed, 'is a matter of opinion except, of course, in the cases of yourself and the person to whom you are talking.') Shepheard's, he thought, only ranked as the fourth hotel in Cairo before the First World War. It had still attracted Henry Stanley, though. The day that he came back from the interior of Africa – without Emin Pasha but with the expedition's doctor, Dr Parke, and one of its assistants, Mr Jephson, it was, as one bystander put it, 'quite a memorable event'. The day he came to the hotel was one of the wettest on record in the city and the streets outside Shepheard's were under two feet of water. Planks were laid out from his carriage across to the steps leading up to the hotel's terrace where a crowd waited to greet him, and to pass comment. The artist E. M. Merrick, for instance, confessed that she was 'a little disappointed to see how short a man Stanley was'. His reputation was so impressive that she expected it to be matched by his stature.

Stanley found the crowd lounging in wicker chairs on the terrace more than he could cope with. They were talking about him certainly and he was sure that they were being critical. He wrote that 'to have escaped their censure, I ought to have worn a parchment band on my forehead, bearing the inscription "Ladies and Gentlemen, I have been in Darkest Africa for three continuous years, living among savages, and I fear something of their spirit clings to me; I pray you have mercy"'. They probably would have criticized the band, though. These people in turn received plenty of criticism from their fellow-guests. Edward Lear had written that 'On the whole this Shepherd's [sic] Hotel ... is more like a pigstye mixed with a beargarden or a horribly noisy railway station than anything I can compare it to.' The railway station image was quite apt, for still one of the most conspicuous groups of guests staying in the hotel were passengers en route to India or going back to England. The arrival of one group was described by someone else in the hotel in this way: 'In they swarmed, men with pith helmets and women in indescribable costumes – a compromise between a bedgown and a bathing-dress – to take forcible possession of any rooms that might seem to be vacant.' Amongst them were certain young women of the Ladies' Eastern Fishing Fleet who were going back home without a husband and were unkindly referred to as 'Returned Empties'. The most striking contrast, however, was between the young women on their way out East in search of a husband and the wives returning home at the end of a period of service, the 'two currents of the living tide, setting in from or to India,' as one guest observed. 'The sallow, haggard-faced women from India ... the fresh-faced, blooming, shrinking English maidens...'

For girls going East with serious ambitions, however, Cairo was an important landfall, the first place for them to try out their skills, for the young men were just as dashing in Cairo as in Calcutta or Simla, in fact more so if we are to believe Ronald Storrs, who noticed that 'An ordinary young man fluent in Arabic, no less at home in the desert than in the bazaars is already half a hero to an unknown goddess descending fresh from Europe in the latest Paris fashion.' There was also a better chance of meeting young men from other countries here, Egypt being nearer Europe and more popular with Americans. Being on the India route, it had the added advantage of attracting a number of young officers also on their way out east for the first time. But

Storrs did not hold out much hope for this sort of liaison. It was fine so long as they stayed out in the colonies, but 'if they settle down in England his accomplishments are at a discount and her elegance by no means unique, so that either and sometimes both are liable to a rancorous devaluation'.

It was in Cairo also that many new arrivals from home discovered for the first time that there was a great rivalry between the various colonial and imperial services. They might all be Englishmen but, as Lord Edward Cecil pointed out, 'We in Egypt profess to despise Anglo-Indians as people who are out of touch with Europe and essentially provincial, whilst they, on the other hand, talk with contempt of our size and village politics. One method of showing this lofty hostility is to pretend not to understand anything about the other's country or language.' This meant that a young English girl passing through Cairo for the first time on her way out east needed to add diplomacy to her other accomplishments if she was to avoid being cut out of important social circles.

*

A great number of travel narratives were published in the first half of the nineteenth century which described Egypt as a country in transition, where influences from the West were coming into contact with the world of Islam. The magnificent ruins of ancient Egypt were also there to be found and the published adventures of travellers who went looking for them, or just stumbled upon them or, as in the case of Irby and Mangles, were enlisted to help clear them, also made exciting reading. Egypt then appeared to be on the frontier of western civilization and travellers had only to pull themselves away from bars or dining-rooms, hang their dinner jackets in their wardrobes and leave the hotels to find themselves in a world which was made familiar through the *Arabian Nights*.

According to these earlier accounts, eastern life could also be observed from the terrace of Shepheard's Hotel, but by the turn of the century, the picturesque Nubians working water-pumps, whom Florence Nightingale had observed, had long since disappeared and been replaced by hawkers, donkey-boys, dragomans and performers, all of whom were barred from coming up the steps by the hotel's imposing Montenegrin doormen in scarlet-and-white uniforms, daggers or revolvers pushed into their waistbands. At the beginning of this century, Douglas Sladen recorded that as soon as he stepped out of the hotel he was invited to buy:

> postcards, local and foreign newspapers, hippopotamus-hide
> whips, roses, carnations, mushrabiya tables and photograph
> frames, stuffed crocodiles, live leopards and boa-constrictors,
> sandalwood work-boxes, Turkish delight, Persian embroideries,
> Sudanese beads made in England for the natives of the Sudan,
> Nubian daggers, Abyssinian war-maces, Japanese fans and
> postage stamps, Smyrna figs, strawberries, tarbooshes, scarabs,
> and little images of gods and men made in various materials three
> thousand years too late to go into the Tombs of the Pharaohs.

Mixing with the vendors were conjurors, acrobats, baboon-keepers and
Egyptians offering a number of other services including that of romantic
escort which became especially popular after Rudolph Valentino paraded his Arabesque robes and flashed his eyes in front of the movie
cameras. Tourists who wanted to see this Egypt of their romantic imagination needed the man in the flowing robes and head-gear, the sheikh,
or as Major Jarvis spelt it, the 'sheek', to complete the illusion. The
problem with this was that real-life sheikhs were few in number, and
large in stature and dignity, unlikely to parade themselves in front of
Shepheard's. A stand-in was found amongst a particular group of young
men in Cairo who were, Major Jarvis reckoned, 'by trade either a boot-
black, seller of fly whisks, or cigarette-end collector for some secondary
tobacco company'. If their looks matched the tourists' image – tall,
with a hooked nose and dark, flashing eyes – then they 'are fitted out
with the robes that their position demands and are sent to provide a
long-felt want at the portals of Shepheard's and the Semiramis in Cairo,
Mena House Hotel at the Pyramids, and the Winter Palace at Luxor.
Here they are available to give the finishing touch to the desert scenery,
and for a very few piastres extra are willing to walk arm-in-arm with
their patronesses at sunset.' Some would go even further. Bimbashi
McPherson, who was a teacher in the Khedival School in Cairo – which
he described as 'a sort of Eton of Egypt' – came across one of these
men on Christmas night, 1901, and wrote to his brother Jack that 'Many
of the lady visitors are pretty hot and one wonders sometimes whether
they are attracted most by the antiquities or the iniquities of Egypt.
On Christmas night, when Hamid and I rode out to the Sphinx we
saw in the moonlight in the sandhollow a colossal bedouin and from
beneath him appeared a little feminine attire, so little that it would
not have betrayed its wearer, but that a little voice said in English:
"Mind tomorrow night". When we called for our bikes at the Mena
House Hotel a little gentleman was looking for his wife and fearing

she would catch a cold through her stupid habit of wandering "alone" in the moonlight.'

Although the 'Sheeks' and hawkers invariably did a good trade in front of Shepheard's, a better trade was done by the dragomans, for everyone who came to Cairo had to see the sights and these men offered guided tours to the Pyramids at Giza, to the collection of real antiquities in the Egyptian Museum and through the mediaeval part of the city. The rivalry between them was fierce, for the rewards were often very large. In season, a crowd of guides gathered around the steps of Shepheard's at the beginning of each day, although only two of them were allowed to approach the steps at any one time. If a guest wanted to hire a dragoman, then the porter informed the doorman who in turn chose the dragoman, in the process probably collecting his cut. Because these doormen had power over the dragomans, if one of them annoyed him, they would not be offered any work. But all morning the doorman was harried by the dragomans and on the morning of 30 January 1902, it became too much for one particular Montenegrin, Youssef Agha. As soon he took up his post that day, the usual crowd began pestering him for the favour of the first client of the day. It was a normal start to an unexceptional day. But among the crowd, Youssef noticed one Mohamed Hassan Attwara, a dragoman who had lived in India for many years and in this way had become a British subject. Attwara had benefited by his status and had been dragoman to Sir John Aird, the British engineer, but he had recently fallen out with Youssef Agha and so had been banned from touting for business at Shepheard's. When the crowd of dragomans began pestering Agha, the Montenegrin picked on Attwara and told him to go away. Attwara refused and an argument ensued. There were a few guests out on the terrace by now, so there were plenty of witnesses when Agha pulled out what everyone had always assumed was a purely decorative six-chambered revolver, waved it at the men in front of him, shot point-blank at Attwara and then fired a few rounds into the crowd.

'This terrible tragedy,' the *Egyptian Gazette* reported that day, 'taking place on the very steps of the hotel at a frequented hour of the morning, has created a profound sensation in the Capital.' The police, apparently, were 'quite paralysed by the horror of the situation'. At first it was believed that Attwara had died from his wounds and that another dragoman, Ahmed Imam, had also been seriously wounded. Youssef Agha was charged with murder and handed over to the Russian Consulate to be sent back for trial in Cettinge, his country's capital. But on 3 February, the *Gazette*'s reporter revealed that, far from being dead, he had found Attwara alive and happy in the Deaconesses' Hospital in Cairo, 'making a hearty luncheon, flanked on one side by a bottle of wine and on the other by a case of cigarettes. He cheerfully and with pride displayed his wounds, and descanted his emotions . . .'

Although the victim survived and Youssef Agha was packed off to his home town, the management of the hotel were clearly anxious about the effect the incident would have on their business and a note appeared in the *Egyptian Gazette* to say that His Imperial Highness the Grand Duke Boris of Russia, who was in the hotel at the time, had expressed the greatest satisfaction with Shepheard's. In other words, he was not frightened of being gunned down on the hotel's steps. But the management need not have worried; it was all good local colour for the tourists, and right in the middle of the season, too – the Long Bar was busy and, to get a table at Shepheard's restaurant for some time after the shooting, reservations had to be made several days in advance.

But events at Shepheard's or any of the other grand hotels were not often as colourful as this and engaging a dragoman for the day was usually a less dramatic affair. It was still possible to ride out to the Pyramids, as visitors had had to do in the nineteenth century, but by the early 1900s there was also a tram which ran from the Ezbekieh Gardens and followed the Pyramids Road right to the foot of the monuments. (A public notice in the *Egyptian Gazette* early in the century alerts 'lovers of romance' to the fact that there was 'an extra service at "FULL MOON" to allow of tourists visiting the spot by moonlight'.) Cars were also becoming a more common sight in Cairo and in 1901 the *Egyptian Gazette* noted that 'The advent of automobiles to the streets of Cairo in considerable numbers is a characteristic of the present season. One or two were to be seen last winter, but this year they seem to have become fashionable, and a day seldom passes but a wayfarer sees at least four or five.' However altered the mode of transport, the experience of a visit to the Pyramids had not changed since the days when Belzoni had broken into the chamber of Chephren's Pyramid and Edward Lane had spent his weeks in a tomb nearby. There were still Egyptians offering their services or goods, only now there were more of them selling to an increased number of tourists. Camels and donkeys could also still be hired, just as they can be now. The Pyramids had become one of the greatest attractions of the tourist trade in Egypt and Douglas Sladen wrote at the beginning of the century that 'The jumping off place for the Pyramids is one of the most bustling spots in Egypt. The tram pulls up in the shadiest bits of the avenue . . . The camels make a splendid background and the foreground is sketchy with tourists of all ages and conditions in special desert dress.'

It is wonderful to consider how many people have been photographed standing, kneeling, sitting, astride camels, horses or donkeys, in front of or on top of the Pyramids and the Sphinx. Film-processing businesses in Egypt must be among the safest in the world. Before the invention of the photographic image, this same compulsive behaviour was exhibited by artists of all calibres, although the scale and complexity of the view from the top of the Second Pyramid usually defeated all but the best. Still, getting to the top of the Pyramid was just as popular as when Thackeray and Twain accomplished the feat. In the 1870s, Amelia Edwards reported that 'The ascent is extremely easy. Rugged and huge as are the blocks, there is scarcely one upon which it is not possible to find a half-way rest for the toe of one's boot, so as to divide the distance. With the help of three Arabs,' she reckoned, 'nothing can well be less fatiguing'. But not everyone agreed with her and one Englishman who came to Egypt to recover from an attack of typhoid fever in December 1888 announced that, although he was used to walking about twenty miles each day, climbing the Pyramid was the most fatiguing exercise he had ever undertaken. When he finally reached the top, his clothes were soaked through with perspiration. He was also unable to speak for some considerable time. But probably even if Amelia Edwards had shared his feelings, visitors would have wanted to climb to the top and, once up there, to pull out their sketchbooks or cameras, to look and point and discuss the view. The strange thing about it is that the view is entirely predictable. There is Cairo and its minarets. There, on the other side, is the desert. Just below is the edge of the Nile valley, exactly where you would expect it to be.

William Thackeray who was always inventive in his descriptions of Egypt – he called the Pyramids 'Two big ones and a little one' –

! ! !

– likened the Pyramid he was climbing to Waterloo Bridge in London, 'a building as vast and as magnificent, as beautiful, as useless, and as lonely ...' When he finally reached the top, he looked around and reported that 'If the forty centuries *are* on the summit of the Pyramids, as Bonaparte remarks, all I can say is, *I* did not see them.' Leaving a poster of *Punch* tucked under a stone on the summit, he returned to earth. Others before and since him have left other things: their refuse and uneaten lunches, and their names carved into the rock.

From the top of the Second Pyramid, tourists also looked down on one of the best hotels in Egypt, the Mena House, which had been

Ismail's hunting lodge until it was bought as a private house by an English couple, Ethel and Hugh Locke-King, in the 1880s. The Locke-Kings, who also started a motor racing track at their home in Brooklands, Surrey, in 1907, were attracted to Egypt by its climate. But they could not find a hotel in Cairo where they would enjoy spending several months each year, so they decided to buy the old royal residence. They were not only extremely rich but also had great taste, and they redecorated the house with works of art and mushrabiya carvings inlaid with ivory and mother-of-pearl, salvaged from dilapidated houses in Rosetta and Damietta. They found old tiles and mosaics, carved-wooden doors and brasswork and their massive dining-room, in the style of Islamic architecture, was lit by a galaxy of antique lamps. The house was Arabesque in design, but when the Locke-Kings decided to open it as a 'First Class Family Hotel', the spirit of the place was most definitely British: an Anglican chaplain held services for the guests three mornings each week. There was a golf course with real grass onto which, according to legend, the Prince of Wales drove a golf ball from the summit of the Second Pyramid in 1915. The Mena House also had a terrace which could seat a hundred people at a time, and some of the terrassiers from Shepheard's were also seen out here in their sun hats and dark glasses, taking tea in the presence of the Pyramids. Certainly neither Edward Lane nor Florence Nightingale would have approved, but the Khedive Ismail might have felt that his wish had come true. Here was the modern, western world, sitting in an Egyptian hotel in the shadow of the Pharaohs.

Pharaonic influence on the terrace at Shepheard's was limited to the stone sphinxes which sat on either side of the main entrance, but the Arabic influence was more pronounced and certainly more vivid. British officials might refrain from too close a contact with Egyptians, but there was nothing to hold back other foreigners in Cairo and the Arabian city presented itself to them in a number of immediate guises. There were the sellers of souvenirs, objets d'art and dirty postcards. There were the girls who shook their hips apparently in invitation on the stages of the El Dorado café down in the fish market, at Madame Badia's Casino de l'Opéra and at the numerous other cafés around the Ezbekieh – none of which according to *Baedeker*, were 'suitable for ladies'. The city could be both sacred and profane – sacred in the guided tours around the mosques and tombs of Islamic Cairo, most notably in the famous tours conducted by a Frenchwoman and a learned Orientalist called Mrs Devonshire, profane in the salacious entertainments for which it also became famous.

Mrs Devonshire was already an elderly lady when Freya Stark stayed with her in Cairo in 1937, but she explained that she had arrived in Egypt as a young woman, a widow with two daughters and no money. She studied Islamic history and architecture, which was a wise thing to do considering the city she was in, and from her tours and her published guides she made enough of a living to bring up her two daughters and to support herself. Her groups were small to start with, usually just a few keen Orientalists and maybe a professor or two from Europe. She took them to parts of the city which were well off the tourist route, and the Egyptians in these places, who 'did not often penetrate into modern Cairo', as one of her admirers put it, were amazed at the sight of the French lady in her black cape and felt cap with a few academics and an officer or two in uniform. Some of the children in these out-of-the-way places ran after them and called out 'Nasrani! Nasrani!' – Nazarenes, or Christians – but they were chased away by the special policeman who also accompanied her groups. The commotion must have been mortifying for her.

Mrs Devonshire's followers had an insight into Islamic art which was far beyond that of the average visitor walking through the arched doorways of the mosques of Sultan Hassan or Ibn Tulun with their dragomans or Baedekers. For instance, when Freya Stark was in Cairo in 1934, she tried to visit an out-of-the-way tomb on her own, but when she got there she was turned away by the sheikh of the place. The next day she told this story to Mrs Devonshire – she described her 'with gloved hands and an ebony cane, her walk stiff, her hat a little unlike anyone else's, evoking an atmosphere of distinction and femininity not visible any longer, but real, like a pressed rose' – and a day later she found herself in a two-seater car with the old lady and a young Frenchman, tearing through Cairo's backstreets on her way to the tomb. When they reached the place, the men came out to greet her. 'The sheikhs all knew Mrs Devonshire,' Freya Stark recorded, 'and gathered in a friendly way.'

For many tourists, however, it was the living Arab world moving across this background which attracted them, the Oriental scenes of veiled women and lordly men, of bargaining in the khan for rugs, or silver, jewellery and copper bowls, for lapis lazuli from the Sinai desert with its flashes of gold. This was the Cairo that the Prince of Wales, later Edward VII, saw during his visit in 1889. Accompanied by Harry Boyle, the Oriental Secretary, the Prince arrived in the carpet bazaar in less than regal attire. Clara Boyle, the Secretary's wife, recounted that 'As they entered the bazaar, the Prince of Wales said to my husband: "Pitch into me as a miserly old hunks as much as you like; it won't break my bones. But I want those carpets at reasonable prices." Harry threw himself into the part. He did not spare His Royal Highness and explained to the dealers that "this poor gentleman can't afford luxuries, moreover, he is a miser, and it would therefore be quite useless to ask for their usual inflated prices."' The Prince then bought the carpets at a 'reasonable price,' but later that day the hall of the Agency was packed full of the bazaar's dealers who had found out who the 'miser' really was and who were naturally rather upset. So upset, in fact, that Boyle was barred from their bazaar 'and as a result,' his wife complained, 'I have now not a single memento, neither carpet, rug, or anything else, which might have come from the Cairo bazaars.'

Another Prince of Wales, later Edward VIII and the Duke of Windsor, also came to Cairo. He arrived in 1915 and, because of the war, his visit was conducted in secrecy. But Ronald Storrs, who by then had replaced Harry Boyle as Oriental Secretary, had known that something was up because the High Commissioner (the British Agent and Consul-General had changed his title when Egypt became a British Protectorate) had actually deciphered several telegrams himself, an occurrence previously unknown. Like his predecessor, Storrs was assigned to take the Prince, travelling incognito, through the bazaars and mosques, 'and never,' Storrs wrote deferentially, 'have I piloted any person who entered more swiftly into the spirit of the place'. In the carpet bazaar, they stopped in front of a stall where the Prince saw a Qubba rug that he liked. In his 1916 guide-book to Cairo, Eustace Reynolds-Ball explained that making a purchase in the bazaars was still an elaborate and delicate matter of negotiation and altercation, and that 'negotiations are hedged round with an amount of ceremony that recalls the stately fashion in the *Arabian Nights*, when the purchase of a brass tray or an embroidered saddle-cloth was a solemn treaty . . .' Storrs had advised the Prince to offer the dealer one-tenth of the asking price, for prices in Cairo had escalated alarmingly since the beginning of the war. The Prince was told that the rug he liked would cost him £50, but Storrs interrupted and said that it was worthless. The Prince offered £4. Then, Storrs recalled, the dealer 'let himself go; it was all very well for Mr Storrs to criticize the stock, but if every subaltern in the British Army – then really –; the Prince listening spell-bound by the invective'. However, the Prince did buy the rug, for an undisclosed final price and, like his grandfather, his identity was discovered by the dealer, who was again upset. This time, however, the dealer made the most of the situation and when Storrs next went to the bazaar he found a rug bound and wrapped and addressed to the Prince of Wales at Buckingham Palace. It was good for business, the dealer explained.

The more profane side of Oriental life was sometimes glimpsed in the hammam, what is known as the Turkish bath. By the time of the Prince's visit most hotels in Cairo had their own bathrooms and the public baths were an object of curiosity rather than necessity. Fifty or sixty years earlier, however, there had been no choice. In 1843, Mrs Sophia Poole, the sister of the Orientalist Edward Lane, visited the baths in Cairo and wrote a letter to a friend in England in which she commented that 'bathing in the Eastern manner is to me extremely agreeable'. There were about seventy hammams in Cairo at the time and her brother, in his *Modern Egyptians*, to which she refers her reader, had explained that 'Bathing is one of the greatest luxuries enjoyed by the people of Egypt.' Wealthy Cairenes had their own private baths inside their palaces and villas, but most people went to the public baths which were usually open to men in the mornings and women in the afternoons; confusion was avoided by tying a piece of cloth on the door when women were using the baths.

Inside the building, the floors were laid with black-and-white marble and the two central chambers had domed roofs pierced by a number of small windows which let in fingers of sunlight through the steam and smoke. Each of the main chambers and the series of smaller rooms leading off them were of a different temperature so that bathers could increase the level of their perspiration. Later, an attendant came to manipulate them, cracking each joint of the body in turn; 'the neck is made to crack twice, by bending the head round, each way, which,' Lane noted from his own experience, 'produces a sensation rather alarming to an inexperienced person'. Even the ears were thoroughly twisted and turned. Although it involved a certain amount of pain, relief soon followed when the attendant began to shampoo, soap and rub down the bather's body. Then came the relaxation. According to Lane, 'a mattrass is spread, for the bather, on the mastab'ah, covered with napkins, and having one or two cushions at one end. On this he reclines, sipping a cup or two of coffee, and smoking, while a láwingee ['a boy, or beardless young man, who attends the bather'] rubs the soles of his feet, and kneads his body and limbs.' This, Sophia Poole declared, was a luxury.

The hammams had no parallel in the West and nowhere at home would foreigners have seen so many naked or partially clothed people. When Sophia Poole went to the hammam, she was accompanied by three female acquaintances – one Englishwoman, one Abyssinian and one Syrian – and although she enjoyed the sensation of the bath and massage, she was less enthusiastic about the people she shared the bath with. 'On entering,' she wrote of the steam room, 'a scene presented itself which beggars description. My companions had prepared me for seeing so many people undressed' – Lane himself had written that 'Many women of the lower orders wear no covering whatever in the bath; not even a napkin round the waist: others always wear the napkin and high clogs' – 'but imagine my astonishment,' his sister continued, 'on finding at least thirty women of all ages, and many young girls and children, perfectly unclothed. You will scarcely think it possible that no one but ourselves had a vestige of clothing. Persons of all colours, from the black and glossy shade of the negro to the fairest possible hue of complexion, were formed in groups, conversing as though full dressed, with perfect *nonchalance*, while others were strolling about, or sitting round the fountain.' Here were the fleshpots of Egypt, depraved and disapproved of, where women lounged around smoking and eating, completely naked – 'the eyes and ears of an Englishwoman,' Sophia insisted, speaking with confidence for her own sex, 'must be closed in the public bath in Egypt before she can fairly enjoy the satisfaction it affords'. It was a question of propriety, of what was correct both in behaviour and in morals, and clearly Sophia found something very incorrect in the baths.

Sophia Poole's warnings would have been enough to convince even the most reluctant of hedonists that the hammams in Cairo had to be seen. To a sensualist like Gustave Flaubert, who was, however, unlikely to have read her letters, visiting the hammams took on something of a religious imperative. He had already been several times to the bath near the Hotel du Nil and had found himself attracted to one of the young attendants – 'Here it is quite accepted. One admits one's sodomy,' he assured his friend Louis Bouilhet, 'and it is spoken of at table in the hotel . . . Travelling as we are for educational purposes, and charged with a mission by the government, we have considered it our duty to indulge in this form of ejaculation. So far,' he admitted, 'the occasion has not presented itself.'

Presumably getting tired of waiting for this occasion, Flaubert went in search of it and paid five francs to reserve the entire bath where the young attendant whom he fancied worked. Unfortunately, on the day that he went, the boy was not working and his attendant was an old man. 'Hot water flowing everywhere,' Flaubert wrote to Bouilhet; 'stretched out indolently I thought of a quantity of things as my pores tranquily dilated. It is very voluptuous and sweetly melancholy to take a bath like that quite alone, lost in those dim rooms where the slightest noise resounds like a cannon shot, while the naked *kellaas* call out to one another as they massage you, turning you over like embalmers preparing you for the tomb. That day . . . my *kellaa* was rubbing me gently, and when he came to the noble parts he lifted up my *boules d'amour* to clean them, then continuing to rub my chest with his left hand he began to pull with his right on my prick, and as he drew it up and down he leaned over my shoulder and said "*baksheesh, baksheesh.*" He was a man in his fifties, ignoble, disgusting ...' Flaubert pushed him away and then, patting him on the shoulder, laughed loudly, the sound echoing through the empty chambers of the hammam.

Sex, baths, boys, steamy chambers filled with naked women – these were powerful images and were bound to appeal to the imagination of some visitors in Cairo. One reaction, like Sophia Poole's, was of outrage. Others considered that this was the centre of a web of depravity which had spread the whole way across Egypt and which they had probably first come into contact with in Alexandria and Port Said when someone tried to sell them postcards. Yet others found the whole thing very appealing indeed – here was the bait which Thackeray assumed had trapped his friend J. F. Lewis. Women in captivity, the harem, an unlimited number of wives and, somehow linked to all this in the minds of so many foreigners, pimps and violence, extortion, the underworld of gambling, drinking, drug-taking, prostitution – for some, Egypt appeared to have it all.

Because foreigners regularly came looking for illicit pleasures in Cairo, those who provided them were attracted to the European quarter; the area behind the Ezbekieh became the prostitute quarter, which the policeman Russell Pasha called the Red-Blind district. Many of the un-licensed but tolerated brothels in the Wagh-el-Birka, to the north of Ezbekieh, were run and worked by European women, sliding down the scale which started in Paris, Marseilles or Naples, and which would end further east in Bombay or beyond. In the area around Derb-el-Wasa'a, which ran into the Wagh-el-Birka, and where the Coptic Church of St Mark held services every Sunday, there were Egyptian, Nubian and Sudanese women for hire. Russell Pasha described it in the 1910s as 'a zoo, with its painted harlots sitting like beasts of prey behind the iron grilles of their ground-floor brothels, while a noisy crowd of low-class natives, interspersed with soldiers in uniform and sight-seeing tourists, made their way along the narrow lanes'.

This area, situated between the Ezbekieh and Cairo Central Station, became as much a part of the Cairo tour for some foreigners as the Egyptian Museum and the Giza Pyramids. Others must have got the idea that women and young men could be obtained anywhere in Cairo, as Harry Boyle discovered. Although he was an official of the British government, Boyle did not fit into Lord Cromer's mould for servants of the Empire. He spent more time with Egyptians and Levantines than with the Agency or Palace set; he was extremely well-read; and he paid little attention to the way he was dressed. One day he was taking his tea on the terrace of Shepheard's Hotel, ignoring Sir Thomas Lipton, the tea magnate who wanted Boyle to find a post for his nephew and who was sitting at a table nearby. Boyle had not made any special effort to dress for tea – according to Ronald Storrs, Boyle's usual appearance was exceptional enough: 'His coat was old, his trousers bagged at the knee and sagged at the waist, his boots were almost medieval in their turn-up. On his head a battered straw hat; rather beyond heel a mongrel but *sympathique* cur: the whole enclosing a man of genius.' Sir Thomas Lipton, however, a tall and muscular man, had paid a little more attention to his appearance that day.

Perhaps because of the way he was dressed, it was to Boyle that an American tourist addressed himself that day.

'Sir, are you the Hotel pimp?' the American asked him straight out, explaining that he wished to be introduced to what he called 'a personable young man.'

'I am, Sir,' Boyle replied smartly, 'but the management, as you may observe, are good enough to allow me the hour of five to six as a tea interval. If, however, you are pressed perhaps you will address yourself to that gentleman' – he pointed to Sir Thomas Lipton – 'who is taking my duty; you will find him most willing to accommodate you in any little commission of a confidential character which you may see fit to entrust to him.'

While the American went over and approached Lipton, Boyle paid his bill and hailed a taxi at the bottom of the hotel's steps. As he climbed in, he heard, as Storrs tells it, 'the sound of a fraças, the impact of a fist and the thud of ponderous body on the marble floor'.

★

Cairo was transformed in 1914. The heat wave that summer, the hottest in twenty years, was a presentiment of what was to come, and the iron of the Kasr el Nil bridge expanded so much that it was impossible to open it to allow river traffic through. By the end of the year the Egyptians had a new ruler, Hussein Kamel, with the new title of Sultan of Egypt, who replaced the deposed Khedive Abbas. A new senior British representative, Sir Henry MacMahon, replaced Kitchener 'Rex' as Consul-General with the new title of High Commissioner. And Britain took Egypt into its empire by making it a Protectorate. Germans and Turks disappeared or were interned and, as in Alexandria, British, Imperial and Allied troops flooded into the city.

The Mena House Hotel, in the shadow of the Pyramids (*Royal Geographical Society*)

The British Agency in Cairo, commissioned by Lord Cromer, now the British Embassy (*Hulton Picture Library*)

The entrance to the Continental Hotel, Cairo – the rival to Shepheard's, across the Ezbekieh Gardens (*Hulton Picture Library*)

The tomb of Rameses VI in the Valley of the Kings. Before electricity was installed torches were needed to light the interiors. A painting by William Prinsep (*Martyn Gregory Gallery*)

Seeing the sights in Luxor – Cook's tourists view the ruins of the Ramesseum (*Thomas Cook Archive*)

A little piece of England – the Winter Palace Hotel near the Temple of Luxor (*Hulton Picture Library*)

Howard Carter's guests, including Lord and Lady Allenby, taking refreshments in the Valley of the Kings on the day that he opened the Golden Shrine inside the tomb of Tutankhamun in February 1923 (*Times Newspapers Ltd*)

Carter's discovery of the Tutankhamun tomb has ensured Luxor's reputation as a treasure-trove (*Times Newspapers Ltd*)

A Cook's steamer below the Cataract Hotel in Aswan: the hotel's popular terrace, or belvedere, can be seen on the right (*Thomas Cook Archive*)

The opening of the original Aswan Dam in 1902, attended by the Duke and Duchess of Connaught, HH Abbas Helmy Khedive and Lord Cromer (*Hulton Picture Library*)

An unusual way to see the Dam was to go by trolley from Aswan (*Hulton Picture Library*)

In the Canal Zone, after the Second World War, the British were increasingly isolated, and many servicemen and their families experienced a very different Egypt (*Hulton Picture Library*)

After President Nasser nationalized the Suez Canal Company, the British forces invaded Egypt, but this time were quickly obliged to withdraw (*Hulton Picture Library*)

The practicalities of war were felt in Cairo as in Alexandria. Here, too, the press was heavily censored and martial law was imposed which put an end to the visible manifestations of what was becoming an irresistible movement towards national independence. More than 20,000 Egyptians were employed, willingly or not, in the Camel Corps, of whom 220 died in action and a further 4,000 died in hospital from their wounds. A German army under General von Kressenstein threatened Egypt across the Suez Canal and, in 1916, a German plane bombed Cairo killing one woman, her dog, and two cab horses near the Eastern Telegraph Company's office, to the west of the Ezbekieh and a block away from the Turf Club, although much nearer the abandoned German Consulate.

Cairo, as a neutral city, also attracted its fair share of enemy spies who were encouraged by Egyptian discontent with British rule and who also hoped for scraps of information from careless, off-duty soldiers. Storrs was on leave in England when war was declared, but when he returned to Cairo he took with him a Browning pistol and a hundred cartridges, 'thinking how foolish it would feel to be held up, unarmed, by some enemy agent in a backstreet of Cairo'. Back in Cairo and still officially the Oriental Secretary, Storrs was involved with the efforts of the Arab bureau to foster the idea and practice of the Arab revolt in Turkish-held territories. T.E. Lawrence, whom he called 'my little genius', worked with him. Lawrence himself described Storrs as 'the most brilliant Englishman in the Near East'. Storrs by this time fulfils one image of the archetypal Englishman abroad, tall, energetic, with short-cropped dark hair, an abbreviated wing-commander's moustache, hiding his revolver inside a double-breasted suit with generous, pointed lapels. He had more work to do than time to do it in, but somehow he still found time between waking up at 6.30 am and leaving for work to read Homer, or the autobiography of Haydon. Gertrude Bell was also in contact with Storrs and working with the Arab Bureau. She was staying in Shepheard's, where she discovered that, although there was a war going on, Cairo was still its usual extravagant self. 'It is heavenly weather – almost too nice for wartime I feel,' she wrote to her mother. Hotel life was just as glamorous as well and, although clearly preoccupied with her war-work, she still confessed that 'I rather wish I had brought out more clothes. Could you possibly send out to me the blue shot silk gown with a little coat and its own hat trimmed with feathers...'

This was not the experience of the average soldier in Cairo, of course. Hector Dinning, who was on leave in Cairo before Gallipoli, noticed that 'It is at Shepheard's that officers most do congregate. According to a sort of tacit agreement – extended later into an inescapable routine order – none lower in rank than a Subaltern enters there.' But there were more than enough officers to fill the place – after the evacuation of the Dardanelles it was claimed that there were 200 generals in Shepheard's – and more in the other grand hotels. As Storrs noticed, the race meetings at the Gezira Sporting Club were still well attended, the tennis courts were full and it was almost impossible to get a table at the Turf Club. Cairo was a favourite place to spend leave because, in spite of the ever-present khaki uniforms, it was at least possible to escape wartime rationing. One wing commander who made a point of booking his room at Shepheard's well in advance, described his leave in much the same way as tourists did before and after the war. 'I would arrive in the evening and have a drink at the Long Bar,' he remembered. 'After a bath – and what large old-fashioned deep baths Shepheard's had – I would dress for dinner and join a party of my friends to dance and dine until early morning. As the dawn came up we would ride out to Mena House for an early morning swim in the swimming-pool, then go into the hotel for a large breakfast before going out to the desert to shoot. I would ride back to Shepheard's for lunch and then take a siesta. I would awaken to find a *safragi* by my bedside with a refreshing tray of tea, then I would go sightseeing for an hour or so before starting the same round all over again.' Not everyone at Shepheard's was quite so energetic. For the first few days of his leave, Martin Briggs, an officer with the Sanitary Section of the Royal Army Medical Corps, spent most of the time between meals in the bath, savouring the difference between 'these marble halls, with their herds of bowing attendants, and the cheap *pensions* or *bourgeois* hotels that have usually housed me'.

For the other ranks, life on leave in Cairo was entirely different. No grand hotels or dinner-dances for them and although they rubbed shoulders with officers in Groppi's café, they were more likely to be surrounded by Egyptians in the bazaars and less salubrious bars and music-halls across the city. They were billeted in makeshift camps, or in barracks on the Citadel, at Kasr el Nil or in Abbassia where, as Briggs observed, the new buildings 'suggest that Britain has sat down very deliberately and heavily in Cairo'. When soldiers arrived in Cairo, they received the back-pay they were owed for their service and perhaps nowhere in the world was it easier for them to spend it. Prices rose to meet them.

Australians and New Zealanders were particularly noticeable around the city, although many of the ANZAC troops were stationed in a camp behind the Mena House Hotel. When they came into Cairo on the tram they made for the bazaars – Hector Dinning was dazzled by the street of the Muski. 'Rich colour is splashed over the stalls and the throng,' he wrote: 'there is music in the jingle of wares and the hum of voices; and the sober and graceful mosque, its rich colour gently mellowed by centuries of exposure, lifts a minaret above the animation.'

Not everyone was struck by the beauty of the architecture. Some were stung by the cheap alcohol, much of it home-brewed, and had eyes only for the available women. There were more than 3,000 licensed prostitutes in Cairo and an unknown number of unlicensed ones. At the same time, there were more than 30,000 ANZACs billeted in and around the city, many of whom found their way to the brothels. When Guy Thornton, a chaplain-captain with the ANZACs, drove around the quarter behind Shepheard's and the Ezbekieh, he was horrified by what he described as 'the shrieks of invitation, the coarse clamour, and the unspeakable sights of that veritable hell on earth'. It was undoubtedly a depressing place, for the arrival of soldiers back from service with their pay in their pockets and looking for a woman had resulted in a big increase in the number of women for hire. Hector Dinning, echoing the sentiments of many of his colleagues, wrote that 'All the pollution of the East would seem to drain into their foul pool.' But in spite of Thornton's night-time visits to the brothels to dissuade soldiers from entering, and in spite of the Cairo police force's efforts to control it, the trade continued. When Russell Pasha arrested the main pimp of the district, a man called Ibrahim el Gharbi – 'Dressed as a woman and veiled in white, this repulsive pervert sat like a silent, ebony idol' – it resulted in a group of lesser pimps taking over the running of the business. There was a price to pay, however, and in 1916 it was estimated that twelve per cent of the Expeditionary Force were suffering from venereal diseases. The knowledge of that, and the extortionate treatment they received at the hands of many of the city's dealers, obscured the memory of the sunshine, the extraordinary habits and activities, the beautiful buildings and ancient relics that they also saw in Cairo. The dream was over. 'The alleged romance of Cairo is alleged only,' Hector Dinning wrote with sadness. 'Cairo is not romantic; it is picturesque, and picturesque beyond description.'

*

Major Jarvis wrote that 'It was a pity the Australians had to go back to Australia after the war. It was so dull without them.' But it was not just the absence of ANZACs that was different about Cairo in the 1920s. Cromer and Kitchener had gone and there was a feeling that the best days of the British occupation were over. The country was becoming politicized in a way which was unthinkable a few decades earlier. Egyptians hoped that all these ruling foreigners would leave with their armies and the British knew it. When General Allenby defeated the Turkish army in Palestine in September 1918 and ensured the British hold on Egypt, he returned in triumph to Cairo. But because British officials wanted to avoid offending Egyptian sentiments – after all, Turkey was another predominantly Muslim country – it was decided that there would be no big parade to welcome him back. Mabel Caillard, however, was determined to go along and cheer him. As she set out for the Continental Hotel, across the Ezbekieh from Shepheard's and with a better view of the general's route, she noticed that, in defiance of the recommendation, some foreign residents had hung their national flags in front of their houses. The Continental was not particularly crowded – Mabel remarked that 'I had seen a greater crowd of spectators at the passage of the funeral of some local functionary' – and when the general passed in front of the hotel, she and a few others waved from the terrace. A fire-engine outside the Opera House clanged its bell and the RAF staged a fly-past. But that was all. Mabel then noticed two Egyptian men who had also come to see what they had assumed would be a victory parade – after all, Egypt was now part of the empire and the British and their allies had won the war. When the general's two cars and their outriders had passed by, Mabel was standing close enough to these men to hear one of them ask, 'What do you say? Does this man carry victory in his hand?'

'Never!' the other answered emphatically.

LUXOR

> 'It is very hard to be all day by the deathbed of the greatest of
> your race, and to come home and talk about quails or London.'
> Florence Nightingale in Luxor, 11 February 1850

Most towns in Egypt have well-defined districts to them – the newest developments, the European-inspired tourist or residential quarter and the older 'Arab' town. But tourism is so much at the heart of Luxor that the dividing lines are hard to find. At night, poor Egyptians stretch out to sleep on the verges between the two-lanes of the Sharia Nahr el Nil, the corniche road. They lie between the big hotels and moorings for the Nile boats, their white robes spread out like tablecloths on the grass. Budget tourists sleep at the back of the town and away from the river in what might be the 'Arab' part where cheap, run-down pensions have no lifts or restaurants, where they sweat through still nights without air-conditioning or electric fans.

During the daytime, the town only seems to have one thought in its head and that is tourism. It doesn't matter where you are, in bars, in the street, in the bazaar, the pleas abound – 'Have you been to – did you want – can I take you – please – please?' To see is all here, and both foreigners and Egyptians come to see Luxor's tombs and temples. There is a newish museum of ancient art, but it is not on the scale of the Egyptian Museum in Cairo, where most people have already been by the time they get to Luxor, and it only opens in the dead, drinking hours at the end of the day between sight-seeing and dinner. The bazaar cannot compete in size, variety, picturesqueness or price with the Muski or the Khan el Khalil in Cairo. There really is little to do but to consider what has to be seen, to see, and to worry about whether there will be enough time to see whatever is left. There is no escape and even across the waters of the swimming pools in the Etap or Winter Palace hotels the talk is of heat and hieroglyphics and it is hard to feel entirely at ease about squandering time in such an irresponsible way. At night, most of the restaurants pack up early and lights in hotel bedrooms are seldom on late, for visitors like to get out to see the sights before the sun gets too hot. The point of all this activity is to learn about and be impressed by the remains of a dead civilization, to walk through deserted temple buildings and the plundered tombs of pharaohs and nobles who lived three or four thousand years ago. Inevitably this induces meditations on the transience of life and on the skill of these long-dead people. In one sense, Luxor exists in a time warp, for the town *is* the temples; whatever is built up around them exists in an inferior relation to them, even though the modern town has now completely encircled the east bank sites. But it little matters whether it is nineteenth-century mud houses or twentieth-century concrete hotels, the temples make the town and the more that is discovered about the lives of the ancient Egyptians, the more the monuments that have survived them come to life. Cairo might be Egypt's modern capital, but Luxor is still its spiritual centre.

'Go there and spend time at the temple of Amun in Karnak,' an Egyptian told me in Cairo. 'Do this for me. Not just an hour, but day after day. Go back to it as often as you can and you will understand something about us Egyptians.'

Another Egyptian had invited me to his home for lunch before I left the capital for Luxor. He lived on Zamalek, the smart district just along from the Marriott Hotel, in a between-the-wars block which looked out across the Nile to the centre of the city. A row of these apartment blocks with names – that have not been changed – like Park Lane and Dorchester House, all near the Gezira Sporting Club, was another reminder of the British occupation. The building is inevitably a little drab and dirty on the outside, for it seems that more sand and dust and fumes descend through the atmosphere onto Cairo than any other city in the world. But being dirty is not necessarily a sign of decay and, inside, the building was immaculate. The broad white marble flags of the staircase gleamed and the brass and woodwork had a rich patina to it. My host was a man in his seventies with a colour to his skin which north of the Mediterranean would be called a 'rich' tan. He was successful and wealthy and the living and dining rooms of his flat overlooking the Nile were decorated with great care. European antique furniture was mixed with expensive Egyptian tables, a collection of antique silver – small boxes and dishes – an eclectic collection of paintings, Oriental rugs on the floor. He had started out with very little and had made good. His servant brought us pickled cucumbers and limes, served his master a bottle of local beer and poured me a can of imported lager. It was 38°C outside, but the air-conditioning kept the place cool – and then he pointed to a cabinet in the archway between the two rooms, at the centre of his home. Behind a glass door was a figure of Anubis, the jackal god, god of the dead, with his long sleek body and tall, alert ears. There were also several smaller figures and statuettes of gods and people, all of which were genuine – 'Look,' he insisted, 'Look!' They were of importance to him beyond their value, for they were a link back through his family, from whom he had inherited them, to his past.

Later that day I took the train from Cairo Central Station up to Luxor, the Wagons-Lits train. The track as far as Asyut, 233 miles from Cairo, was built as part of the Khedive Ismail's development scheme, but it was not until Kitchener advanced on the Sudan in the 1890s that the line was completed to Luxor and a regular service was operated. The Compagnie Internationale des Wagons-Lits Egypte pour le Tourisme was founded in 1898 as an offshoot of the European company which already had a reputation for making railway travel comfortable on the continent. The new services was an immediate success in Egypt and transformed travel along the river. Instead of the days that it took even the most express of Nile steamers to complete the journey, the train took a little over twelve hours to get from Cairo to Luxor and in a sleeping car you could leave Cairo late one afternoon, have dinner alongside the river, go to bed and wake up to find breakfast waiting for you on the table and Upper Egypt outside the window.

Douglas Sladen travelled with the Egyptian Wagons-Lits in 1904 and was most complimentary about the six-year-old service. 'The dinner is very well done and the new sleeping-cars of the *wagons-lits* are admirable; the rooms, which contain two berths each, are arranged in pairs, with an excellent dressing-room and lavatory between each pair. The beds are very comforable' – not everyone agreed with him – 'the rooms with their plaited cane walls (which are covered with leather screens in cold weather) are very cool and pleasing to the eye; and there is comparatively little vibration, so that it is easy to sleep.'

But before sleep, there was an evening out on the train. G. W. Steevens, the *Daily Mail* correspondent, had ridden on this railway line in the year that the Wagons-Lits were started and he noticed two distinctly different types of travellers. First there was the group who had just decamped from Shepheard's and the Continental, the Savoy-Gezira-Mena House-Grand Hotel crowd – he calls them 'the Bel Alp in winter quarters' – people 'who know all lands but no languages, who have been everywhere and done nothing, looked at everything and seen nothing, read everything and known nothing – who spoil the globe by trotting on it.' For them the new overnight express allowed them to 'do' the land of the Pharaohs in double-quick time, to dictate the pace at which they saw it. Another thing about the train was that it was safe; it carried them beyond the lives of Egyptians who lived along the river, whereas the boat took them through the valley at a pace which was often not much faster than the lives around them. This constant, busy, railway motion, the continuous noise, the urgency of the rhythm of the train on the tracks symbolized the difference between these two peoples.

The other type of traveller most in evidence on the train, Steevens noticed, was the 'Imperial Englishman' with his fair hair, blue eyes, square shoulders and even squarer jaw, a look about him that was as solid as he believed his empire to be. He also had a self-reliance which made him stand out from other nationalities. At night on the train, this 'precise, imperturbable, Imperial Englishman takes off all his clothes, and goes to bed cleanly in his pyjamas; he bathes standing up, and shaves religiously each morning, and carefully brushes his clothes.' In the club car or smoking room, the Englishman is the most reserved of the group and 'appears to throw out his talk as a kind of afterthought and accompaniment to smoking.' And what floated out on his cloud of tobacco smoke? 'When he does talk,' Steevens reckoned, 'it is not of money, like the travelling American, nor of beer and time-tables, like the travelling German, but of sport.'

Steevens would have been surprised at the change that has come over the Wagons-Lits and its passengers since the turn of the century. The Imperial Englishman has gone, of course, although a new breed may yet spring up, and on the night I travelled there were more French than Germans, more Chinese and Japanese than Americans. The compartments, too, have changed since the 1890s: they still have two berths each, but the walls are covered with formica panels in place of cane and leather screens, and the luxury of a dressing room has been compressed into a small cupboard over in the corner by the picture-window, which conceals a wash-basin and mirror. Undoubtedly great care has gone into the positioning of this unit for, with a certain amount of dexterity and the help of a very safe safety razor, it is possible to shave and watch the river at the same time. The lavatory is now at the end of the corridor and, worst of all, there is no dining-car. This is a shame, for it was the pride of the old service and the cause of much interest, as Vita Sackville-West discovered when she took the train, for that night the dining-car caught fire and 'trailed after us like the tail of a comet down the line.' They stopped and tried to put it out, but they were half-hearted about it, being in greater fear of robbers in the night than of the comet-like fire. The train continued and in the morning the car was completely burnt out. Dinner nowadays is the railway's interpretation of an airline meal served in the compartment on a pull-down table, slightly bigger than the average 747's. I shared mine with a middle-aged Chinese engineer unable to attempt even the most basic conversation in any European language, while I in turn would not know the difference between residents from Chinese Kashgar and

Shanghai, even though they live further apart than people in London and Cairo.

But some things never change and Steevens would have been reassured by the conversation, later in the club-car, when a French group en route from the Manial Palace Club Mediterranée, Cairo, to the Akhenatun Club Mediterranée, Luxor, discussed beer and time-tables and sport.

★

Luxor, which is a corruption of the Arabic *el Uksor*, the palaces, was originally the name of a village of huts which leaned against the temple of Amun-Min, but now it has come to refer to the whole area of the temple complexes of Amun-Min and Karnak, the hotels and houses around them, and the west bank site of Thebes and the Valley of the Kings as well. When Lucie Duff Gordon made her winter home here in 1863, most of the temples were still up to their architraves in sand, tourists – who even then she accused of wanting 'to *do the Nile* as fast as possible' – moored their dahabiehs on the east bank or pitched tents nearby and the only contact they had with people from the village was when they needed food or donkeys. Lucie changed all that when she moved into the French House, which Mustapha Aga, the British Consul in Luxor, had had dusted and furnished with carpets and a divan in preparation for her arrival. 'The house is very large and has good thick walls,' she wrote to her husband in January 1864, 'the comfort of which we feel to-day for it is blowing a hurricane; but indoors it is not cold at all. I have glass windows and doors to some of the rooms. It is a lovely dwelling.'

As she became accepted by the community and especially by the Sheikh, Yussuf, the descendant of the holy Abu-l-Hajjaj himself, whose mosque was built on top of the temple, so the foreigners who came to visit her were also accepted and were treated in an entirely different way to the travellers who had come before them. The Arabs respected Lucie and called her Noor-ala-Noor, which she translated as 'God is upon thy mind, or Light from the Light.' Lucie's daughter, Janet, had married Henry Ross, a partner in the bank of Briggs & Co in Alexandria, where the couple had settled in 1861. However, five years later there was a financial crisis which affected most parts of the British Empire – what Janet called 'that famous "Black" Friday' – and the Briggs Bank crashed with many others. The Rosses decided to leave Egypt 'with what remained of Henry's hard-earned fortune,' and went to Luxor in a government steamer in March 1867 to say goodbye to Lucie. On the way up-river they had great difficulty buying food or coal from the villages. Wherever they went, they saw old women or young children who told them that they had nothing to offer them. But one of the Egyptians travelling with them realised what was happening – for the past few years, the arrival of a government boat had meant hardship, for they were collecting taxes or labour to build the Suez Canal. The villagers were scared, but the Egyptian explained to the villagers that 'the daughter of the *Sitt-el-Kebir* (the Great Lady) was on board, who, like her mother, loved the Arabs. The effect was magical,' Janet wrote to her father. 'Milk, fowls, lambs, etc., suddenly appeared at absurdly low prices, some were even brought as gifts... As we got nearer to Luxor, we found people waiting at the landing-places with presents...' When they finally reached Luxor, they found that their arrival had been anticipated, for a man, whose daughter Lucie had treated, had ridden the forty-five miles from Kenneh to Luxor to announce them.

Luxor was in celebration for them. Religious men brought flags; villagers decorated the entrance to the French House; and the water-carrier marked out a path of damp earth for the landing-stage to the front door. Later, Bedouin horsemen paraded in front of the house and the local magistrate gave an elaborate dinner, to which Lucie rode on her donkey, with Janet leading her and Henry Ross walking by her side. 'As we went through the little village,' Janet remembered, 'the people came out of their mud huts and called on Allah to bless us, the men throwing down their poor cloaks for my mother to ride over and the women kissing the hem of her dress.'

Two years later, Lucie Duff Gordon was dead and her daughter had gone back to England, but the Suez Canal was open and the first of many Cook's tours was on its way up the river. When Janet came back to Egypt in November 1903, she felt a stranger in the country – 'it seemed so odd to take tickets for Assouan – to get into a sleeping-compartment at Cairo in the evening and find oneself at Luxor next morning.' Travelling arrangements were made in bulk and the journey was a less personal affair; for someone who remembered how it had been, it was a depressing experience.

By the start of the century, the east-bank river frontage at Luxor had been transformed. The Luxor Hotel had been opened with the support of Thomas Cook's in 1877 and was fully booked for the whole of its first season, with most guests staying for an average of ten weeks. In 1883, M. Maspero, the conservateur of Egyptian antiquities for the government, began clearing the temple of Luxor, the smaller and less important east-bank temple, and the French House along with the other buildings around and on top of the temple were pulled down. The house of the British Consul, Mustapha Aga, lasted longer than most because the old man demanded a huge amount of compensation for the move. But even his house went and only the mosque of Abu-l-Hajjaj remained.

The particular attraction of this temple is its proximity to the river bank and after the centuries-worth of sand and human débris had been cleared away, it looked extremely imposing from the river. G. W. Steevens wrote in 1898 that 'When the boat pulls up at Luxor the landing-stage appeared to be a colossal temple... Arcades of huge pillars, some complete, some half broken down, some sprawling in hideous dislocation – they loomed grey and motionless and solemn in face of the ancient river and the flaming sunset.'

That same year of 1898 the railway was completed from Cairo to Aswan and the Wagons-Lits service made Luxor a popular place for a visit of a week or two. The *Egyptian Gazette*'s society correspondent notice this trend in a report on 5 January 1901: 'Luxor is in a transition state at the present time. Before the railway, people came up by boat and stayed at Luxor for some time. Now, this has been altered,' they explained with a note of despair, 'and at present it is quite impossible to gauge who is going to make a long stay and who is merely passing through.' The implication behind this was clear. More people moving through the town more quickly changed its character. 'We were numbers, not human beings,' Janet Ross complained about her journey, a sentiment which has been echoed many times since.

The Luxor Hospital which was officially opened by the Khedive Tewfik in January 1891 was another indication of the town's development. When the ailing Lucie Duff Gordon lived here, the villagers relied on her own slight medical knowledge to cure their sickness. 'My doctoring business has become quite formidable,' she wrote happily to her daughter in 1866. 'I should like to sell my practice to any "rising young surgeon." It brings in a very fair income of vegetables, eggs, turkeys, pigeons, etc.' In the 1880s when the 100-room Luxor Hotel was open during the winter season, the hotel's resident doctor used to minister to the sick villagers. But then in 1887 John Mason Cook began collecting donations for a native hospital from tourists who visited the town. This was philanthropy indeed and Cook himself guaranteed to make up any shortfall in the donations for the support of the hospital once it was opened.

With more tourists coming up the river by train, more hotels were built – the 72-room Savoy and the 220-room Winter Palace, which was opened in 1905, were both built near the temple and the landing-stage on the river front. Their guests could sit on the terraces and look across the river to the rich west-bank farmland and the hills of Thebes where the great Pharaohs were buried. In front of the terraces, the new Nile Street became the most popular place for a promenade and the horse-drawn open carriages which clip their way along it now are the same ones that used to make their way along it in the company of horses and donkeys – cars were not seen in Luxor until the 1920s. In the apparently golden years before the First World War, Dr Wallis Budge explained to tourists that the town they were staying in had, as recently as the 1880s, been 'nothing more than a cluster of poorly-built mud-houses...', but that it had been touched by 'the forces of civilization' and had become 'a clean, well-kept town, and the waste of time, fatigue, and annoyance which used to accompany a prolonged series of visits to the temples on each side of the river are now things of the past. Nowhere in Egypt can time more profitably or more comfortably be spent than at Luxor.'

Tourists used to cross the river in the early morning, when the winter sun still left a haze over the west-bank valley. Then, as now, there was a choice between crossing in a broad-sailed felucca or in a motor-launch, the slower sailing vessel being the cheaper. As the temple of Luxor and the modern riverside buildings merged into one block and the Winter Palace Hotel began to look a little like the temple's annexe, the width of the river became apparent, as also the extent of the east-bank site. It was over three miles from the landing-stage to the Valley of the Kings as the crow flies – the road, which led around the side of the hills, was considerably longer – and over two miles from the temple of Rameses III at Medinet Habu in the south-west, to the temple of Seti I at Qurna. Just getting from one temple to another on camel or donkey could tire out the faint-hearted sightseer, although sturdy men like the great *briseur d'obstacles*, Henry Morton Stanley, might 'do' the west bank in a day. Stanley was sent to Egypt as a correspondent for the *New York Herald*. Its proprietor, James Gordon Bennett, had met the twenty-eight-year-old reporter in Paris and instructed him 'to attend the opening of the Suez Canal and then proceed up the Nile. Send us detailed descriptions of everything likely to interest American tourists.' This he did and then proceeded, as instructed, to Jerusalem, Constantinople, Scutari, Teheran, Isfahan and across India. ('After that,' Gordon Bennett had told him, 'you can start looking for Livingstone. If he is dead bring back every possible proof of his death.')

Stanley's one-day tour of the west bank was energetic even by today's standards: 'We were occupied,' he wrote, 'in seeing the tombs of the kings, Asasif, Abd el Kurnah, the Ramasseum, the colossi of Memnon, Medînet Hâbu, and Dêr el Medineh.' These were the same sites that travellers had been visiting almost since Belzoni had finished his work in Egypt, although more tombs had been opened in the Valley of the Kings. Stanley recorded the existence of forty-seven tombs, of which only twenty-one had actually been discovered; Cook's *Handbook* for 1906 reported the discovery of another twenty; while twenty-three years later *Baedeker's* listed sixty-one opened tombs. A few more have been discovered since then. What was different for tourists on both sides of the river at the turn of the century was the state in which they found the temples and tombs. In 1870 Stanley complained that the temples of Luxor were being defiled by the villagers and that 'the close mass of Arab huts within the courts effectually prevent measurements, but by going in on all fours into these Arab huts, we saw a profusion of capitals which capped the columns that supported them.' The great explorer was horrified. 'Only utter barbarians would have dared to desecrate a temple of such splendour with mud huts. One wonders whether Ismail, the Khedive, knows of such things...' No doubt Ismail did know and, under his patronage, the conservation of many of the country's antiquities became possible, although it is likely that this was due more to the importance which foreigners attached to the relics than to any great interest shown by Egyptians. Archaeology was the child of the curiosity and activities of a number of people who had both leisure and money to devote to what was sometimes decades of expensive research and digging, decades which might reveal nothing more than a few shattered pottery fragments, a heap of corpses or architectural remains. Those Egyptians who could have financed such archaeological work in the nineteenth century had other things to spend their money on – decaying palaces and villas along the Nile are a reminder of that.

Even though so much of ancient Egypt was partly visible above the sands, there were very few Europeans who took up Wilkinson's suggestion that they should conduct their own excavations. Belzoni, Salt, Drovetti and the other leading figures in the drama which resulted in the rediscovery of ancient Egypt in the first half of the nineteenth century were either financed by wealthy patrons or paid for their labours from the sale of Egyptian antiquities to western collectors and to the new national museums. But there were lesser characters in the early nineteenth century like Dr Henry Abbott and Anthony Harris, who collected and studied antiquities and who also stimulated interest in ancient Egypt. They have themselves achieved a kind of immortality by giving their names to antiquities which have ended up in the great European and American museums. Stanley's attitude was rather different, and more typical of travellers in the second half of the nineteenth century. If the period up to 1850 was one of exploration and exploitation, in which it must be admitted they were encouraged by Muhammad Ali who gave away many of the country's most precious obelisks and statues; later visitors, like Stanley, were more concerned with conservation. In part this is explained by the fact that so many of the more portable objects had already been removed. European conservationists worked with the knowledge that a great many important pieces were already sitting in foreign collections.

The creation of the Antiquities Service in the 1850s by Auguste Mariette Bey also had a great effect on the preservation of Egypt's monuments. From now on, all new discoveries had to be submitted to the Service. They still allowed some antiquities to be exported, but an export licence was now needed. The Service even ran a sale room in the Egyptian Museum in Cairo where it was possible to buy items for export which the Service did not need. However, many foreigners now confined their collecting to smaller, more portable pieces, which could be smuggled out of the country if an official permit was not forthcoming. The majority of Egyptians still felt that there was something suspicious about foreigners' interest in their past. Dr Wallis Budge had expressed the view, in his *Handbook*, that Egyptians could not understand anyone wanting to excavate merely for 'the love of learning or the advancement of science' – and, he went on, 'the older generation regard all those who do work of this kind as wicked men.' But he was being disingenuous here, for experience had clearly shown Egyptians that, although some foreigners were interested in science, many who came to dig were motivated by the desire to improve neither knowledge nor science: they dug in search of wealth and fame. And from the columns, obelisks, sarcophagi with or without their mummies, the busts, statues, mastabas, papyri, jewellery and the whole range of other antiquities which Egyptians had either watched or helped foreigners take out of their country, these people had benefited very little.

Stanley's clear expression of outrage and righteousness was a common complaint at that time. Undoubtedly Egyptians did damage the temples and tombs by living in them, as a visit to the temple of Edfu today will show, where the bright colours of the walls and ceiling have been blackened with smoke. But now that the huts have been cleared away and the monuments cleaned and a good bit restored, it is clear that the most conspicuous damage from the nineteenth century was done by foreign visitors themselves. Early travellers used to carve their names on the pillars of temples or at the entrance to tombs along the Nile as an act of appropriation. Belzoni's name, put there in his own hand, is still visible at the entrance to 'Belzoni's tomb', No 17 in the Valley of the Kings. He discovered, or uncovered it, and he felt that he had a claim on it, just as he believed that he had a right to its contents. But that was Belzoni. Who, on the other hand, was John Gordon and what was his justification for carving his name on one of the pillars of the great hypostyle hall in Karnak? Like so many other visitors, he seemed to treat the monument as a visitors' book. Reading through the mass of names and dates carved all over the country is to encounter a who's who of foreign travellers, troops and tourists, many of whom have become what Amelia Edwards called the 'illustrious-obscure'. Not that this was anything new – the Greeks and Romans also left their marks here and the French troops of the 3ième Regiment of Bonaparte's army were continuing a long tradition when they engraved the tombs at Beni Hassan in 1800. Here also are the names of Robert Hay (1822), Hyde and Grosvenor (both 1829) and of M. Olivier (1846). In other places, the graffitti serves as a perpetual reminder of the nationalities who came here – Appleyard, Mangles, Salt, Delamain, Buvry, Wroblewski, Caulfield, Stanger, Littleton, Fernic, Levinge, Lyons, Hamdy Bey, Alexander 'cum gloria et felicitate Russ Imperavit.' These were noted down at random, but everyone who notices the defacement has their own special villain. I traced the itinerary of Charles Irby (1817) most of the way up the river, whereas Lucie Duff Gordon thought that 'worst of all Prince Puckler-Muskau has engraved his and his *Ordenskreuz* in huge letters on the naked breast of that august and pathetic giant who sits at Abou Simbel. I wish someone would kick him for his profanity.'

★

Before 1910, the only way of seeing the inside of tombs was to light flares or torches or, later, to take flashlights, but when electricity was installed in the desolate Valley of the Kings, tourists were able to see by the glare of electric light from 8 a.m. to 12 a.m. each day from the middle of November to the middle of April. At the end of the morning's sight-seeing, tourists had their lunch either in the Cook's rest house, topically named the Chalet Hatasoo, or else they ate in the tombs in much the same way as had the traveller Eliot Warburton in 1848. While he and his companion left their servant Mahmoud in one tomb to prepare the food and make their coffee, they went off to visit another, where they met a party of seven travellers – a Russian prince, a German, three Italians and two French – whom they invited to join them for their meal. Mahmoud was understandably upset at first, but he divided up the food and 'made things comfortable in the charnel-house; a fire was lighted, carpets spread, and coffee was already diffusing its fragrance.'

It is a particular excitement to eat in a tomb, sitting on the rock floor, dipping into a bowl and perhaps then noticing something, a detail of a wall painting perhaps, which has been missed before. 'The noonday sun now kept the outward world to himself,' Warburton remembered, 'while the tomb afforded us its friendly shelter before our time: many a pipe smoked incense to the spirits of the departed kings whose unconscious hospitality we were sharing in common with the bat, the scorpion, and the worm.'

Warburton's lunch party broke up at two o'clock and they then went on to see another temple, but he wrote that by the evening, 'exposure to the powerful sun of the Thebiad' made him grateful for the shelter of his tent. Many tourists later on had less determination and often by mid-afternoon the necropolis had been evacuated by the living who made their way along the path past the now-silent colossi of Memnon, whose shadows lay heavily across the green fields, to the feluccas and motor launch moored at the quay.

Most travellers admitted that they saw Thebes and Karnak and Luxor too quickly, but most of them also explained that their speed was encouraged by the desire to outstrip the souvenir-sellers who followed them everywhere. Apart from the sights themselves, the single most persistent impression they took away from Luxor was that the whole town seemed intent on selling them something. When they stepped out of their hotel or off the boat, dragomans, guides, boat-owners, donkey-boys and carriage drivers, and, inevitably, souvenir-sellers were waiting for them. The most obvious souvenir in the early days was a little piece of the past – a fragment from a mummy case, a piece of a mummy itself, a scarab or papyrus. *Baedeker's* was only repeating time-honoured advice when it warned the inexperienced tourist to 'confine his purchases to reliable dealers or to the sale room of the Cairo Museum; expensive objects should not be bought without previous consultation with a connoisseur.' But the temptation was too great for most people and consequently a thriving cottage industry sprang up in Luxor and in the west-bank villages to meet the new demand. Their products were often very convincing, too, and the scarabs which came from the village of El Tarif were particularly noted. Some of the things they offered were undoubtedly genuine, though. Henry Stanley wrote that 'If they but express a wish to buy, mummies by the wholesale, whole mummies, heads of mummies, hands, feet, limbs and trunks of mummies, human, animal, and bird mummies will be offered to them... The following,' he recorded with evident distaste, 'is an inventory of articles purchased by a gentleman in the portico of the Ramesseum and before the tombs of the kings: "Three men's heads, one woman's head, one child's head, six hands large and small, twelve feet, one plump infant's foot, one foot minus a toe, two ears, one part of a well-preserved face, two ibis mummies, one dog mummy..." Oh certainly,' he concluded, 'Thebes is the place to buy souvenirs; such that will make timid women pale and innocent children cry; such that will make old people think of their graves and Atheists thoughtful.' One cannot but help wonder what the gentleman was going to do with his preserved cadaver fragments when he got them home.

Whatever happened to them, the trade in relics from the past was a valuable one and although most mummies were genuine – there was a case of a tourist being sold a 'mummified' corpse which decomposed before he even had time to get it out of the country – many of the other items were most definitely fake. A couple of years after Stanley, Amelia Edwards commented that the work of production went alongside that of excavation; that some foreigners were wise enough to buy the genuine articles, while others were duped into buying reproductions at 'genuine' prices. The scale of the manufacturing industry, which was illegal at the time, was clearly illustrated by an incident which occurred one day when Amelia and a companion went to pay a visit to one of the consulates in Luxor. Unknown to her at the time, the consulate had been moved to another house, but when she knocked on the door of the original house, she was admitted by an old woman and shown into 'a large unfurnished room with three windows. In each window there stood a workman's bench strewn with scarabs, amulets, and funerary statuettes in every stage of progress.' They looked around at pots of colours which the forgers had been using, at their brushes and files and the magnifying glasses which allowed them to carry out the most delicate forgeries. 'That three skilled workmen furnished with European tools had been busy in this room shortly before we were shown into it,' Amelia deduced, 'was perfectly clear.' However, what was not clear to her at the time, in fact until a well-dressed Arab who was the head of these forgers came in and hurried her out of the door, was that this was no longer the consul's house. 'I met that well-dressed Arab a day or two after,' Amelia remarked, 'near the Governor's house; and he immediately vanished around the nearest corner.'

But although the largest part of this growing market was satisfied by well-made reproductions, there were some visitors who had sufficient knowledge to by-pass the hawkers and some of these people did still find genuine antiquities. During the 1880 season, for instance, a wealthy American collector, who had already been to the Cairo

Museum's sale-rooms and had decided that the objects on sale there were not of the quality he wanted, came to Luxor and bought a papyrus which, in terms of technique, colour and preservation, was the most wonderful piece he had ever seen. It could have been a brilliant imitation, but that was the risk one had to take when buying on the black market. The American was inclined to believe that it was the real thing and his excitement put him in no position to bargain, so he paid the high asking price and, being certain that he would never get an official export licence for it, he hid the papyrus in his travelling truck and smuggled it out of Egypt. While he was in Europe, the American went to see an expert Egyptologist to confirm his opinion and the expert told him that it was indeed an important piece, in fact from an unknown tomb. He asked him where he had bought it; the American was sufficiently flattered at having his opinion confirmed that he told the expert about a man he had met in Luxor, one Abderrassul – the expert passed the information onto the Service in Cairo.

The Abderrassul family were well-known in Luxor, coming from the village of Kurna and having often provided labour for the Antiquities Service. They had also made money selling antiquities which they found themselves, boasting descent from an unbroken line of tomb-robbers which could be traced right back to the thirteenth century. When they could not find new tombs, they made reproductions. But one day all that changed. Making his way across the mountain near the colonnaded temple of Queen Hatshepsut, known to the Arabs as Deir el Bahri or the northern monastery, one of the Abderrassul family noticed that part of the slope was covered over with sand and he and a few relatives decided to investigate. Of course they had no licence to dig and also of course they had no idea what they might find, but the plain below them was dotted with mortuary temples, the southern side of the Theban hills was the burial place of ancient queens and nobles, and just over the crest of the slope the Antiquities Service was working in the Valley of the Kings – so anything was possible. But there were no known tombs in that place. They had to work at night to avoid the suspicion of the Service officials and also of the other villagers, digging by the light of a cotton-wick oil lamp, just as their ancestors had done, and like their ancestors they found a tomb, one of the most spectacular and important finds of modern times. The Abderrassul family had no idea of the full extent of their success; they just knew that they had struck a rich seam, for mummies were piled up one on top of another. If they brought down too many items at one time, they knew they would be found out. But if they were careful and clever, they could all live off this find for many years to come. Accordingly, only the elders of the family were let in on the secret and at various intervals over six years they returned to the tomb, brought out items of gold or papyri, recovered the tomb and sold the pieces at good prices to foreign collectors. Then they sold a papyrus to an American collector who told the story to an expert in Europe; the Abderrassuls were arrested and the true story eventually came out.

When Emil Brugsch of the Egyptian Museum in Cairo heard the story of the Abderrassul family's activities, he was astonished. He was not a great field-worker like his brother, or the previous Keeper of the Museum, Auguste Mariette, but he knew enough about antiquities and about the burial methods of the ancient Egyptians to realise that they had stumbled upon something very special indeed. On the morning of 5 July 1881, he crossed the Nile with an assistant and the head of the Abderrassul family. He had been to the temple of Hatshepsut before, but he had never bothered to climb the slope above it. When he did so, the tomb-robber brought him to an opening cut into the hillside which was covered over with large stones. Rolling these away, Abderrassul dropped a rope into the hole and invited Brugsch himself to go down first. Leaving the assistant with Abderrassul, Brugsch lowered himself into the darkness. He could hear that the shaft was deep – if this was a trick then it was a very unpleasant one. He climbed down thirty-five feet before he reached the bottom and then, when the surface above him was just a thin saucer of light, he lit a lamp and proceeded along a passage which brought him into a chamber, an ancient morgue where sarcophagi and mummies were piled on top of each other or leant up against the walls. A few had been opened by the robbers and the mummies inside had been unwrapped to retrieve the offerings and papyri that had been interred with them to ensure safe passage and happy reception in the after-life. Others, which Brugsch examined, had survived intact. Jeremiah Lynch, another American visitor who met Brugsch during the winter of 1889–90 was told that at this point 'he was nearly overcome with emotion and had to go out in the sunshine for a couple of hours, before he could control himself sufficiently to re-enter.' What he had seen and touched were the mortal remains of some of the greatest rulers of ancient Egypt. The first mummy he came across was that of Seti I, who reigned 3,500 years before Brugsch found him and whose tomb Belzoni had opened and claimed in 1871. Then he found the mummies of Amosis, Amenophis I, of Tuthmosis III and of Seti's son, Rameses II, the great temple builder. They and the others – there were forty of them in all – had been moved to this tomb-pit above Deir el Bahri thousands of years before by temple priests to protect them against tomb robbers.

The writer C. W. Ceram, in his dramatic account of the story of archaeology, quotes one Egyptian ruler as complaining that, 'They who build
with granite, who set a hall inside their pyramid, and wrought beauty
with their fine work, their altar stones also are empty as are those of
the weary ones, the ones who die upon the embankment leaving no
mourners.' Tombs cut into the rock, they thought, would be safer.
But then as now, the valley tombs attracted robbers. Whereas latter-day
tomb-robbers were thwarted to some extent by the Antiquities Service,
in ancient times tombs were protected by priests. When there was a
chance that a tomb might be broken into, the priests moved the mummies to another tomb. Rameses II, for instance, was moved several
times – to his father's tomb and then to that of Queen Inhapi, before
he, too, was carried in secret out of the valley and over the crest of
the mountain to the tomb above Deir el Bahri. 'A count showed that
the assembled rulers numbered no less than forty,' Ceram explained.
'Forty mummies! Forty coffins containing the mortal remains of those
who once had ruled the Egyptian world like gods, and who for three
thousand years had rested in peace until first a robber, then he, Emil
Brugsch-Bey, had again laid eyes up them.'

That was on 5 July 1881. The problem then was what to do with
the mummies for there was no way, once the story was out, that they
would be safe where there were. Brugsch decided to move them and,
nine days later, the tomb was empty, the royal mummies loaded onto
a steamer and, along with Brugsch himself, on their way down the
river. Word had been sent ahead and a reception was awaiting them
in Cairo, but a more impressive spectacle was provided by the fellahin
along the Nile. Here in the countryside, travellers had always liked
to compare modern Egyptians with their ancestors as portrayed in
tomb-paintings. As the steamer passed along the Nile, fellahin walked
alongside it on the bank as they would have done if they were burying
one of their own. The men fired off their guns to salute the dead kings
and the women wailed, weeping and throwing dust or sand over their
faces and breasts. Mourners from one village passed on the care of
the mummies to a group from the next, but the lamentation was constant
for the rulers and for the greatness of their past.

*

The arrival of the royal mummies in Cairo, and the interest they
renewed, led, in 1889, to the long-overdue removal of the Egyptian
Museum from its temporary site in Boulak to the 500-room palace
of Giza on the west bank of the Nile, which Ismail had built for his
harem at a cost of 120,000,000 francs. Egyptology benefited from all

this, for it became fashionable and glamorous to show an interest in the Egyptian past in a way that had not been seen since Belzoni's time. Religious amateurs were stirred up as well, for here was Rameses II – had he actually looked upon the face of Moses, or was he the one who raised up Joseph? Nothing was certain still, but it was all in the air again and the debate brought an increased number of tourists to Luxor, who sat sipping drinks under the bougainvillaea on the terraces of the riverfront hotels and argued about it.

They also went to the bazaars and bought overpriced reproduction scarabs and funerary figures, or went to photographic shops like Antonio Beato's and bought large-scale prints of the sites. As in Cairo, there were also balls for these people to attend during the season, especially in the principal hotels, and usually the larger Cook's steamers held small dances for a few select guests. Luxor was then no different from any other fashionable holiday resort. During the day tourists enjoyed the facilities the town had to offer – here it was temples and tombs for the sightseer, a sporting and gymkhana club for the less enthusiastic. At night there were the activities which wealthy travellers could now enjoy almost anywhere in the world. But Luxor had one thing which nowhere else in the world could offer – a night-time outing to the magnificent temple of Karnak, by moonlight if you were lucky. It was the precursor to the present-day *son et lumière* show and Florence Nightingale described it in this way: 'Karnak by starlight is peace; not peace and joy, but peace, – solemn peace. You feel like spirits revisiting your former world, strange and fallen to ruins... It should always be seen in solitude and by night; one eternal night it should have, like Job's, and let the stars of the twilight be its lamps; neither let it be seen in the dawning of the day.'

Like any other resort, Luxor also felt the effects of events in the rest of the country: after the British bombardment of Alexandria and the invasion of 1882, fewer tourists came up-river, in spite of Cook's assurance in that September that 'We shall not... advertise any tour that will involve the slightest personal risk to any of our travellers. Two months later, as they announced plans for a new tour which would include a visit to the site of the Battle of Tel el Kebit, they explained that 'our position as Managing Agents of the Steamboat Service on the Nile throws upon us the responsibility of doing all we can to restore confidence in the minds of intending travellers,' although probably the presence of the occupying British Army was more successful at this than statements in the *Excursionist* magazine. During the various Sudan campaigns, Luxor was visited by more than its usual number of soldiers and their wives. The tourists came back in ever greater numbers in the first decade of this century, only to stay away again at the outbreak of the First World War. It was a cycle which has repeated itself as predictably as the flood of the Nile.

Martin Briggs, architect turned sanitary officer during the war, pointed out that even if there had been tourists, steamers had stopped running up the river and those soldiers who could be bothered to travel south on the 72-hour leave, came by railway. But even train services were badly effected: the Wagons-Lits were only running a few restaurant cars and the station buffets were far from reliable. In Luxor, where Briggs arrived on Christmas 1917, the buffet had sold out of everything that was edible – 'Not a piece of bread, not an egg, not a sandwich,' he complained, 'not even a bar of chocolate was available.' Clearly the town was expecting a very different sort of visitor.

The war exposed the true character of Luxor, for without tourists the new town was as dead as the old. The hotels closed down or, if they were lucky, were requisitioned as convalescent homes and the streets were filled with people in hospital uniforms, just like the gardens of Ramleh in Alexandria. The temples and tombs were still there, but few people visited them; cafés and bars were only patronised by visiting soldiers; the souvenir market shrank, guides had no one to escort, boatmen no one to ferry and the only businesses in Luxor which did do well were the photographic shops. 'The number of Kodaks in the E.E.F. is phenomenal,' Briggs reported. Officers used large-format cameras because their luggage was not too restricted, but even subalterns and privates carried 'V.P.K.s' and other small cameras and whenever they found themselves in front of a monument they took a picture. Luxor's photographic stores even managed to expand their range of services and branched out into mail-order developing for soldiers in Lower Egypt and the desert. But however well those stores did, the war was not good for the town; Briggs commented that it meant 'the substitution of a handful of military officers for a small army of millionaires.' Those Egyptians who had not volunteered or been 'persuaded' to join the Egyptian Labour Corps sat through those last two quiet winters of the war in relative idleness. The explosion of energy which had brought the foreigners, the hawadji, to their country a hundred years before, such a brief moment in this eternal place, appeared to have exhausted itself.

But across the river on the western shore, activities were underway which assured that foreigners would always return to this place in their veils and hats and dark glasses, climbing across the valley with a gleam in their eyes.

*

The activities of the Abderrassul family at Deir el Bahri and the return of Emil Brugsch and the royal mummies to Cairo proved two things to the Antiquities Service – that there were still more tombs to be found, and that it could now go some way towards stopping unauthorized people getting at them, for the network of Egyptologists around the world ensured that if a new find did appear on the market abroad, then Cairo would hear about it. The problem for the Service was that it did not have the necessary funds to carry out extensive digs itself, so it attracted private archaeological parties to carry out the work under its supervision. Whatever was found was split equally between the government and the archaeologists. This was not an ideal arrangement for the Service, but it at least meant that if anything was found the Service would receive a share of it. There was, however, one exception to this rule: if a tomb was found intact, the government insisted on its right to keep the entire contents. But as no tomb had ever been found with all of its funerary furnishings in place, none of the private archaeologists was likely to object to this.

In 1902, the Service awarded a licence to a well-known and wealthy American archaeologist, Theodore M. Davis. Davis was sixty-five years old at the time, but he approached the great Theban necropolis with energy and enthusiasm, although like the tourists he stayed away from Upper Egypt during the scorching summers and confined his operations to the winter seasons only. Davis arrived in Luxor at an interesting time. As the historian C. W. Ceram pointed out, the pioneer phase of archaeology was finished. Although the remarkable Belzoni in the early nineteenth century claimed that he prepared for his excavations with solid historical research, his methods are now considered primitive, and even destructive; modern archaeologists shudder at his account of walking over mummies in a Theban burial pit. By the start of the twentieth century, the trowel and brush were more likely to be found in the archaeologist's bag than dynamite or a sledgehammer. Davis approached his work with these more modern methods and they brought him rich returns: in his first winter he excavated the tomb of Tuthmosis IV in the Valley of the Kings; during the next winter, working with the English archaeologist Howard Carter, at that time an inspector with the Antiquities Service, Davis opened the tomb of Hatshepsut and found the sarcophagi of the great queen and her father, Tuthmosis I, although both of them were empty. (His mummy had already been found by the Abderrassul family, but hers has never been found.) The following year, 1904–5, Davis came across his greatest discovery, the tomb of Yuya and Tuya, the parents of Queen Thi, on a site to the north-east of the valley which had been marked out for him by Professor Maspero, the Director-General of the Service. The first indication that he had found a tomb was the uncovering of steps leading down into the rock. This was on 12 February 1905, and by the end of the day a doorway had been cleared and a small boy sent into the darkness. When he reappeared a few moments later, he was holding a staff of office and the gold yoke of a chariot. Davis himself climbed through the small hole next and discovered that there was a second flight of stairs leading to a second door. The tomb had obviously been broken into long ago and the objects scattered here must have been dropped when the robbers were disturbed in their work.

Davis left the tomb for the day and returned early the following morning with a group of important guests, including Queen Victoria's son, the Duke of Connaught. Invitations to be present at the opening of tombs had long been one of the perks for royalty or friends of the Khedive or the British Agent in Egypt. In the previous century, parties were sent out specially to find tombs or burial pits which could then be opened in the presence of the visitors. For some more gullible or less important guests, known tombs were resealed and covered over to guarantee a good show when they were so cleverly rediscovered. For the Duke of Connaught, however, Davis had found the real thing, a tomb which appeared to be more or less intact, apart from the one disturbed entry long ago. Breaking through the seal and entering the tomb, they stepped into a chamber of thirty by fifteen feet, which was eight feet high and completely undecorated, not even a single inscription on the wall. But they did not notice this at the time, for, as Dr Wallis Budge described it, 'those who were allowed to enter it saw the most envious and gorgeous funeral furniture which has ever been seen in an Egyptian tomb.' Gold-plated mummy cases, boxes and chairs, sealed jars of oil and wine, boxes of cooked meat wrapped in black muslin, chairs, a used bed, as well as the Canopic jars containing the intestines of the deceased – the tomb was filled with treasures which have in turn filled an entire gallery (No 13) of the Egyptian Museum in Cairo.

Davis's find could not have been better timed for the Luxor tourist trade and, as a result, the number of winter visitors increased and the town's image as treasure trove – re-established by the discovery of the royal mummies at Deir el Bahri – was further enhanced. There was gold in the ground and there were still more tombs waiting to be discovered. Why, even the gentle excavations carried out the following year when foundations were prepared for the new Winter Palace Hotel turned up some ancient flint implements, some of which were 15,000 years old. It seemed an appropriate place to build 'a bit of Europe in the heart of the East,' as one travel writer dubbed it a few years later, and to plant the bougainvillaea which seemed an indispensable terrace decoration.

★

Luxor was still popular as a health resort and invalids continued to follow Lucie Duff Gordon's lead and to winter in Upper Egypt. One Englishman who came here for his health was Henry Stanhope, the fifth Earl of Carnarvon, who arrived in Luxor in 1903, the year that Davis and Carter opened Queen Hatshepsut's tomb. Carnarvon was only thirty-seven years old when he came to Egypt, but two years earlier he had been injured in a racing accident and was advised by his doctor to spend his winters in a warm climate. One of the remarkable things about Carnarvon's racing injury of 1901 was that it was not sustained on a horse but while driving a car. He was an energetic and obsessive man who was fortunate enough to have sufficient funds to indulge his passions; Ceram records that in his college days at Trinity, Cambridge, he had the old wood panelling in his rooms restored at his own expense. When he came down from Cambridge, he earned himself a reputation as a sportsman – shooting, riding, and then sailing around the world in 1889. When automobiles came into production Carnarvon bought one – the third car to be licensed in Britain was his – learned to drive it and then, inevitably, wanted to race it. In 1901, when he was racing in Germany with his chauffeur, Edward Trotman, he crashed and injured his chest. Two years later, Carnarvon, who as Ceram puts it 'could have been produced nowhere but in England, a mixture of sportsman and collector, gentleman and world traveller,' arrived in Luxor. He returned the following winter and was in town when Davis discovered the tomb of Yuya and Tuya; Carnarvon's interest in Egyptology was stimulated. He was an ill man, but he still had an urge for risk and excitement, and he still liked to collect – digging into Egypt's past would allow him to indulge himself.

Carnarvon was granted a licence to work on a site near the village of Sheikh Abd El Qurna in 1907, but after six exhausting weeks he had met with little success and, unlike Davis, only had one mummified cat to show for his labours. He was not discouraged, though, and the next season he decided to hire an assistant to help him; Maspero in the Antiquities Service recommended Howard Carter. Although he had most recently been making his living as a painter, Carter was well qualified to help Carnarvon: he had worked on a series of excavations and restorations in the Theban hills, both for Maspero and for wealthy patrons; he had cleared the tomb of Seti II at the expense of a Mrs

Goff; and, most important for Cararvon, he had worked with Davis.

Carnarvon employed Carter in 1907 and by the time the First World War broke out, they had excavated tombs in Thebes and at two sites in the Nile delta. They had also published an account of their work, *Five Years' Explorations at Thebes*. But although they had found a large number of small items – some of which have recently been rediscovered in the Carnarvon family home, Highclere Castle – these were scarcely recompense for the effort, or for the large sums Carnarvon had invested and, later, Carter labelled many of then 'uninteresting'. However, if after seven years Carnarvon's enthusiasm was flagging, there was soon a compelling reason for him to continue: in 1914 Theodore Davis fell ill and Carnarvon bought his licence to work the main site of the Valley of the Kings. Davis had made rich finds in the tomb of Yuya and Tuya, the most extensive collection unearthed in Egypt, but both Carter and Carnarvon were convinced that there were even richer tombs still to be discovered in the valley. Davis's tomb was only that of the parents-in-law of a pharaoh; imagine what wonders might be found in the tomb of a pharaoh himself.

We do not have to imagine, for the story is well-known, told by Carter himself, of how after working in the valley for another seven winters without finding their tomb, the English aristocrat decided to give up his licence to excavate; how Carter persuaded him to dig for just one more season; and how having returned to Luxor on 28 October 1922, he arrived at the new site they were working on a week later when 'the unusual stoppage of the work made me realize that something out of the ordinary had happened.' A step cut into the rock had been uncovered. Two days later Carter sent a telegraph to his patron who was still in England, announcing that 'At last have made wonderful discovery in valley; a magnificent tomb with seals intact; recovered same for your arrival; congratulations.' Sixteen days later, with Carnarvon and his daughter Lady Evelyn behind him, Carter walked down the sixteen steps and for the first time examined the seal on the door. It was a royal seal. Behind the doorway, however, they only found rubbish, a few small items from the reigns of a number of kings, and another passage leading them to another door.

When they had cleared their way to this second door, slowly and with care, Carter made a breach in its top left-hand corner and, pointing his light, looked inside. 'Surely,' Carter wrote later, 'never before in the whole history of excavation had such an amazing sight been seen as the light of our torch revealed to us.' Carter, Carnarvon and Lady Evelyn each looked in on a remarkable collection of jewels, furniture, animal heads and provisions, a sight intended to please divine eyes.

What they were looking into was the antechamber of the tomb of Tutankhamun, a room 26 feet 3 inches by 11 feet 9 inches, which had another two doors leading off it, also with royal seals; as there was no mummy or sarcophagus to be seen in this chamber, obviously it would be found in one of the others.

Carter claims that that was all they achieved on 26 November and that the following day they returned with an electric light. With this, they realized that a hole had been made into one of the inner doors and, peering through it, they saw that it, too, was filled with 'wonderful things,' but that it had been disturbed by tomb-robbers. However, although many of the items in the chamber had been thrown around, it seemed that very little had been removed. Carter's claim that the tomb had been broken into before and therefore was not technically intact was a crucial one, for, according to the terms of their licence, they would have to hand over the contents of the tomb if it was intact. A legal case was made of this and in 1924 the Egyptian Government won the right to retain its national treasures, which now fill a dozen galleries in the museum in Cairo.

But the matter is still not settled. Both Carter and Carnarvon were secretive about their exact activities and although they claimed not to have entered the tomb on that first day, 26 November, subsequent reports stated that they entered both the antechamber and the burial chamber. It seems unlikely that after fifteen years' digging they would have been able to resist going in and having a look around on this first day. It seems very improbable that they decided to go home and wait until the morning, and according to a recent report in *The Times*, 'Objects from the tomb have cropped up in American museums, indicating that some were removed unofficially.' It is possible that they were removed on that first day.

Carter and Carnarvon reported their find to the public three days after they first entered the tomb. They had agreed to tell their story exclusively to *The Times*, which announced on 30 November 'what promises to be the most sensational Egyptological discovery of the century.' By only talking to *The Times* and by keeping other reporters away from the tomb, they added a touch of mystery to the find. What was it all about? Why was Carter arguing with the Antiquities Service? Was he really found trying to sneak out a wooden figure of Tutankhamun in an empty crate of Fortnum and Mason's red wine? The story was perfectly timed to capture the world's imagination: the Great War was over and a new period of prosperity had begun; radio broadcasting, the increased distribution of newspapers and even the start of Imperial Airways had brought the world closer to Tutankhamun, and brought

Egypt within the reach of a new breed of tourists.

Like so many sensations in other fields, the discovery of the tomb might have become dead copy after a while, just as the Abderrassul finds had been. But the tomb of Tutankhamun was different. The tomb in Deir el Bahri was cleared in nine days, but there was so much material in this new tomb that a guide-book published as late as 1927, five years after the initial discovery, explained that the mummy case had still not been opened. Nor had what was known as the Treasure House or the Annexe been put on show to the public. By then, of course, the story had a new twist to it and newspapers had a strong human angle with which to sustain the public's interest – Lord Carnarvon had died.

In March 1923, four months after the initial discovery, Carnarvon had been bitten by a mosquito in the Valley of the Kings. A few days later, he cut himself while shaving and the bite began to bleed, became infected and then developed into an inflammation called erysipelas. He also had blood poisoning by this time, so he went back to Cairo, to the Continental Hotel on the Ezbekieh, from where *The Times*, still retaining their exclusive rights, reported regularly on his condition. On 24 March he was 'showing a definite if not great improvement.' A few days later his condition was 'complicated' when he developed pneumonia. And then at 1.45 a.m. on 5 April, he died.

His death, at the age of fifty-seven, would alone have been enough to spark off a newspaperful of 'Curse of the Pharaohs' copy, but there were a number of curious coincidences which supplied the fact-starved rivals of *The Times* with plenty of news. At the same time as Carnarvon died in the Continental, there was a power cut and – significantly? – the lights went out; no logical explanation was ever found. Back in Britain, on that same April night, the earl's favourite terrier which had itself been to the valley, suddenly fell down dead. Here begins a long chain of curious and not-so-curious events stretching over more than a decade: Carter's secretary, Richard Bethell, was found dead and the cause of his death was never ascertained; Bethell's father, Lord Westbury, committed suicide by jumping from a seventh-storey window in a London apartment block; then Carter's partner, Arthur Mace, and a French Egyptologist died – both had been into the tomb; Archibald Reid died in London as he was about to X-ray another mummy; and Lady Elizabeth Carnarvon and the fifth earl's two half brothers, Aubrey and Mervyn, also died. It made great newspaper copy which was occasionally backed up by evidence from experts. The Egyptologist Arthur Weigall confirmed his belief in the curse of the mummy's tomb just in time for him to become what newspapers labelled 'Victim No 21'

– he died from an 'unknown fever'.

These stories were good for business in Egypt, and Luxor in particular was flooded with tourists as well as experts, all burning with a feverish desire to explore the unknown. In three months during the 1926 season, for instance, 12,300 people came to look over the tomb, to stare down at the remains of the king behind the legend, and to dream – as Carnarvon must have dreamed – of the treasures that had been interred with him. Of the group of guests who went in with him when he first saw Tutankhamun's funeral shrine, Carter wrote that 'Each had a dazed, bewildered look in his eyes, and each in turn, as he came out, threw up his hands before him, an unconscious gesture of impotence to describe the wonders that he had seen.' In our own time, visitors must go to the Egyptian Museum in Cairo to see the treasures and then travel to Luxor to see the place where they were found, but although the details of the curse may have finally receded into memory, the image of this particular pharaoh has remained with us and become a single, unifying link between Egypt's past and present, lying untouched and unseen in its triple coffin for more than 3,000 years until an English archaeologist revealed the golden face to the public in Egypt and to newspaper readers around the world – 'the unity of past and present,' Carter wrote wisely, 'is constantly impressed upon the archaeological adventurer.'

*

Early one May morning, I met an Egyptian sitting outside the Thomas Cook office in the arcade beneath the Winter Palace Hotel in Luxor. His name was Tadros Botros, more commonly known as Mr Peter, the Chief Guide at Cook's. He was an elderly man, a Copt, and was dressed in a loose white jellabiya with a white scarf wrapped several times around his neck, a pair of sunglasses hiding his eyes from the sharp morning sun. Mr Peter had been with Cook's for more than forty years and was a guide for at least a decade before that, but, most important, he was with Howard Carter when he found *the* tomb. He said that he was twelve years old at the time – in which case he was born in 1910 – and that he worked as a sort of clerk right through the winter seasons up to 1926. As he was telling me his story, he paused to draw on his cigarette and to recapture some of the exact details – that was all such a long time ago, after all, and some of it had escaped him and disappeared as finally as the smoke he blew from his mouth. Just then one of the younger guides walked past and said, 'Tell him we call you "the King Beater".'

'Mr Carter,' Mr Peter told me emphatically, as though I might disagree, 'was very nice, very polite, very honest, very kind to all his labourers.'

There were so many foreigners who had come to Luxor since then and employed Mr Peter's services – he remembered Bernard Shaw with a smile and he said that he thought the British in particular used to make very good tourists – but most of all he remembered Carter and his kindnesses, Carter who took him away from Luxor where he had been born and brought up, where they rode asses and sailed feluccas, Carter who took him to England for a four-month holiday in 1927 where cars were fast, the streets were crowded and where there was rain, a rarity, and snow, literally unheard of.

Since then, apart from a period when he trained to be a guide and another time, in 1940, when he worked for the Egyptian Labour Corps, building a road across the desert from Luxor to the Red Sea coast, Mr Peter had been at the other end of that archaeological link of dead-buried-preserved-forgotten-rediscovered-studied-shown. He has kept it alive, too, through the advent of the motor-car and the lean war years, through the revolution, the deposition of the king and the departure of the British, through the tourist boom of the '60s, the tension between Muslims and Copts, between the Arabs and Israelis. He was not very concerned about the way the British or French, Americans or Italians behaved here. He would have dismissed it in similar words to Flaubert's – 'a mini-life amid the débris of a life that was far grander...' He did talk briefly about the assassination of Sadat and the performance of Mubarak, but he always came back to his work, to Tutankhamun and Carter, as though the place we were sitting in somehow existed outside that other present-day world.

'Fifty years as a guide,' he announced slowly, proudly, lighting another cigarette, 'and I'm still learning, still studying. But one thing I know for sure is that there are more tombs from the list of the pharaohs still to be found in the Valley of the Kings.'

It would be foolish to disagree with him. When Belzoni left the valley with the sarcophagus of Seti I, he announced that there were no more tombs to be found. When Carnarvon was given his licence to dig in the valley, Maspero of the Antiquities Service told him that really it was a waste of time, that there were no more tombs to be found now. History mocks us in Luxor.

ASWAN AND THE
SUDAN

'This is no longer Egypt; it is negro, African, savage – as
wild as the other was formal.'

Gustave Flaubert, 9 March 1850

In London, the Egyptologist I sought out for advice was a model
of academic reserve and serious intent while we discussed finds in Luxor
and the museum in Cairo. But later, when I mentioned that I was
also going to Aswan, he smiled, sighed, clucked.

'Ah,' he told me. 'You are lucky. You must try to save as much
time as you can for Aswan. It is the St Tropez of Egypt.'

When I arrived in Aswan, I quickly realized that he didn't mean
that the river bank was lined with naked and partially-clothed sun-
worshippers. It would be hard to know who in Aswan would be on
the scene first to correct such impropriety, although it probably would
not be the police. But Aswan did resemble St Tropez in the atmosphere
around the moorings of dahabiehs, feluccas and tourist steamers tied
up at the end of their run up the river and preparing to go back down
to Luxor or Cairo.

Aswan is in part a holiday town, for when it is cold in Alexandria
it is still hot here. Several tourist booms have left an odd assortment
of hotels and restaurants dotted along the river front, the most recent
one creating what is probably the biggest eyesore in the country: the
towering Oberoi Hotel. There was another boom in the early 1960s
which resulted in a series of almost identical, austere buildings appearing
throughout Egypt, most properly represented by the box-rooms and
balconies set in the exposed concrete frame of the New Cataract Hotel.

As the flotilla of boats moored on the river suggests, Aswan is also
a frontier town: beyond here is a different land. It even looks like
a frontier, for the wide-open plains which spread around Cairo and
Luxor have been left behind and Aswan is hemmed in by dark, granite
hills which drop down close to the river's edge. There is little room
for it to flood here. The Nile, mother and father of Egypt, is almost
confined at the bottom of the First Cataract where it bends and slows,
its flow broken by a series of cobbled rocks and islands in mid-stream.
The largest of these is called Elephantine on account of the way the

water has shaped the rocks which fringe its water-line, which do look like wading elephants if you squint a little. This island was the site of the original settlement in the time of the pharaohs, but the few standing columns of a ruined temple on the southern tip of the island, worked and reworked by Egyptians, Greeks and Romans, are all that remain of it now.

As a frontier town, Aswan was the starting point of the caravans heading into Nubia and the Sudan, and the place where traders coming back from the south entered Egypt with gold, ivory, gum-arabic, animal skins – and, of course, valuable black slaves. James Bruce considered that he was safe when he reached the town after travelling to what he thought was the source of the Nile. Forty years later, Jean Louis Burckhardt, in his disguise as Sheikh Ibrahim Ibn Abdullah, took three weeks to cross the Nubian desert from Aswan to Berber in the Sudan with a caravan of traders. They were a miserable bunch: having fought off an attack by Bedouins, they resorted to stealing from each other and quite a few of them and their camels were left for dead in the desert before the caravan once again caught a whiff of the deep, vital scent of the Nile. As Egypt became stronger and richer under Muhammad Ali, it attracted more trade and the route from the south flourished: Aswan became a thriving marketplace. Although politics and the creation of the Sudan's own seaport have more or less stopped the trade that used to pass through to the Mediterranean, the bazaar is still a lively place of dust, donkeys and barter, especially in the tourist season.

The building of the Aswan High Dam, which began in 1960, changed the town considerably, for it brought a crowd of labourers and engineers to the area. When it was finished, the resultant flooding of the Nile valley for several hundred miles above the dam destroyed a number of villages and many of the displaced Nubians have been resettled here. But, however much its population has changed, most of the original attractions have survived intact. The river, controlled above this point, still flows in swirls and eddies around the rocks. Feluccas glide between the islands and the shore, their white lateen sails picking up a gust of wind, pushing them forward briskly, too briskly into a lull behind another island. The canvas flaps against the mast and the boatmen row out into mid-stream again in search of a following wind. The climate is still warm and dry in winter and the usual, blistering, road-melting affair in summer. But most of all it is the air that is the same, as pure as ever, coming sand-blown and scorched across the surrounding deserts to remind the visitor that Aswan is an outpost, for it brings a far-away frazzled scent with it, totally unknown in Europe. Here you really are in the middle of nowhere, in a caravanserai at an oasis on the Nile.

*

A French force arrived in Aswan on Friday, 1 February 1799, under General Desaix, Bonaparte's much-travelled second-in-command. They had been ordered to pursue and to capture or kill the Mameluke leader, Murad Bey, Ali Bey's son-in-law, who had escaped from Cairo after the Battle of the Pyramids. But by the time the French reached the First Cataract, the Mamelukes were already on their way across the Nubian desert. Desaix called a halt in Aswan. The French built a fort and garrison, with facilities for their own entertainment – cafés and restaurants. They wandered over the ruins on Elephantine Island and went up the cataract to the island temple of Philae which, like the temples in Luxor, were being used for shelter by the villagers. Indeed, the French enjoyed the full range of activities which were available to tourists fifty or almost a hundred years later. They lay in the shade and drank the local beer. They gambled and smoked and sailed on the river. They watched Nubians shooting the rapids on logs. The philistines amongst them carved their names on the pillars of the temples in just the same way, as Alan Moorehead points out, as had Roman soldiers centuries before them – in just the same way, also, as tourists who came after them. The more artistic among them mused on the beauty of the river or, like Baron Vivant Denon, one of Bonaparte's *savants*, made sketches of the ruins and islands. Their reactions to what they saw were also similar to the foreigners who came after them. Some, like Denon, thought the Nubians were barbaric, which they believed was shown clearly enough in the way they dressed: the men were naked apart from a scant loin cloth and women wore the shortest of leather girdles. Others found this appealing.

When Florence Nightingale arrived at Elephantine, fifty years later, she, too, was met by what she calls 'Troops of South Sea savages'. Back across the river at Aswan she found traders who had only recently come up from the Darfur province, south-west of Khartoum, with cargoes of animal skins and slaves. 'The skins were heaped up under the palms,' she wrote, 'and so were the slaves, most of them girls of about ten or fifteen, with beautiful little hands, making measures of meal, kneading it, and making cakes in the hearth.' Later, above the cataract at Philae, she saw an English artist drawing the temple, 'and is a picture himself; he always wears the Turkish dress – a blue gubbeh, white kaftan, red turban'. One night, when she and her companions, Charles and Selina Bracebridge, were invited by this artist and his wife to dine in their tent, they took their own chairs, carpet and cushions from the dahabieh and scrambled across the sand and rocks to their hosts' camp. 'The dinner,' Florence explained with the sarcasm with which she usually described social engagements, 'was very much like a London dinner: Mr.— was fine and courteous; Mr.— was stupid and silent; Mrs.— was nice and *naïve*.' To her horror, therefore, when she had been up the river as far as Abu Simbel and was on her way back down the cataract, she discovered a whole fleet of English boats at Aswan including the Consul-General Mr Murray's – 'it was exactly like a wood-cut in one of Captain Cook's voyages,' she wrote, 'the savage scene, the neat English boats and flags in the little bay'.

If Aswan made Florence think of Captain Cook, the activities of Gustave Flaubert who arrived in Aswan a month after she had left for the north, bring to mind a later visitor to the South Seas, Paul Gauguin, with his images of reclining nudes and their 'long-lost barbarian luxury'. Flaubert describes this place of dark rocks and bare hills as a negro landscape. In a shop here he meets Azizeh, an almeh – 'tall, slender, black' – who takes him and his companion, Du Camp, to a mud hut, removes her loose robe, replaces it with a European-style cotton dress and dances for them. Her movements are firm and fast. 'This is no longer Egypt; it is negro, African, savage – as wild as the other was formal.' Here, also, he meets a 'little girl spawned by some Englishman' in the brothel, buys a silver ring from a woman selling bread, and eats delicious fresh fish and dates in a café.

This, then, was what Aswan had to offer its visitors – a perfect climate, if a little too hot in summer, beautiful light, an immaculate temple, the violence of the river at the cataract and the peace of the river-reach at Elephantine, a good market, a brothel and a pretty mixed group of inhabitants. There was the old granite quarry, too, where the Pharaonic Egyptians had cut stone for their statues and obelisks. Lucie Duff Gordon visited this quarry in January 1863 and called it 'that most poetically melancholy spot'. Returning to her boat she also met slave traders on their way back to the Sudan. They had just loaded their camels with the goods they were taking to sell in the south – soap and sugar, fabrics and weapons perhaps – and were ready for the desert crossing. They invited the Englishwoman to join them for a meal, 'and oh!', she remembered, 'how delicious it felt to sit on a mat among the camels and strange bales of goods and eat the hot tough bread, sour milk and dates, offered with such stately courtesy'. Later she reported that she had eaten many strange dinners 'with odd people in queer places' in and around Aswan. Like Flaubert, she also thought it would be worth making the journey there just for the girls, whom she described as being as innocent in the face as they were perfect in body.

By the late 1860s, Aswan, with its caravanserai and adobe houses, had a population of almost 10,000 Arabs, Turks, Berbers, Abyssinians and Nubians. But soon after this, Cook's steamers began to moor off the town with increasing regularity and the sight of Europeans and Americans also became unremarkable. As always happened along the tourist route, the town itself began to change. Its inhabitants realized that regular steamers meant regular money to be made providing food, souvenirs, donkeys and camels for the tourists to ride around the cataract to the shore opposite Philae, proving the truth of what Lucie Duff Gordon wrote after her first winter in Egypt: 'The English have raised a mirage of false wants and extravagance which the servants of the country of course, some from interest and others from mere ignorance, do their best to keep up.' At Aswan there was also good payment for pulling the *hawadji* boats up the cataract or for providing amusement for the passengers by shooting the rapids on logs. In 1875 Cook's took one more step along the river by opening the first regular steamer service between Aswan, or Shellal as the upper station was called, and the Second Cataract at Wadi Halfa. It is likely that General Gordon used this service on his way to and from the Sudan. I mention his name here because it was on account of his power as an embodiment of what the British public considered to be the virtues of the Victorian age – strength, justice, compassion, Christianity, fearlessness – that so much was done to try and save him. After his death, it was the power of his legend as the Christian martyr that continued to focus attention on north-east Africa. We can forget the Suez Canal and the route through to India and Australia for now – that was secured by the British invasion of 1882. The reconquest of the Sudan by the British and Egyptian force under General Kitchener was part of another quite separate move, although one which can also be traced back to James Bruce, and which was furthered by the expeditions of explorers like Richard Burton, Speke and Grant, Baker, Stanley and Livingstone. This was the European powers' scramble for new colonies in Africa.

On 17 September 1898, Cecil Rhodes, the most energetic and powerful supporter of the scheme to build a railway from Cape Town to Cairo through all-British territory, made a speech in Port Elizabeth, in what was then the Cape Colony, in which he stated: 'As you know, Sir Herbert Kitchener only started the other day, and we can fancy we see them marching tonight towards Khartoum. We are coming up from the South, and we are going to join him as sure as I am standing here ... What was attempted by Alexander, Cambyses, and Napoleon, we practical people are going to finish.'

In fact Khartoum had fallen on 2 September and Kitchener had already held his memorial service for Gordon. The Mahdi's body had been dug up and thrown into the Nile, while his skull had been saved and was being sent down to Cairo. But Rhodes was correct in thinking that Kitchener was on the move. He had received reports of a European force at Fashoda, 459 miles further south on the White Nile, a forlorn and unfriendly place which Alan Moorehead describes as 'a miserable collection of square, flat-roofed houses on the riverbank'. Romolo Gessi, Gordon's deputy, had written some twenty-five years before Kitchener left for Fashoda that 'It is said anyone sent to Fashoda never returns. The climate is unhealthy, the air pestilential . . .'

Kitchener was within sight of Fashoda on 16 September, the day after Rhodes had made his speech. Why had he hurried to a desolate town of so little strategic importance? Why had he not stayed in the north to enjoy his victory? The reason lies in the way that new African colonies were being claimed by the Europeans. Sometimes it was enough just to establish a garrison and raise a flag to claim sovereignty for your country. The reports that Kitchener received suggested that someone had done just that. In fact the place had been occupied by a French force of a hundred men under a Captain Jean-Baptiste Marchand. They were not strong enough to seize the Upper Nile, either against the native tribes or the British force, but that was not their intention. They had marched the 3,000 miles from Brazzaville in the Congo, across the Equator and through some of the most inhospitable country in Africa, just to fly their flag and claim their rights. If they achieved that, they would consider the two-year journey worthwhile.

In an earlier era – since, as Gessi pointed out, Fashoda was an unwelcoming place to live – they might have got away with it. But technology was tied up with the new expansion. This was the age of engineering wonders. In order to get his army to Khartoum, for instance, Kitchener had built a railway right across the Nubian desert and there was no reason, as Cecil Rhodes knew, why it should stop there. The British engineer Sir Colin Scott Moncrieff realized the importance in those times of the British holding the upper waters and the recently discovered source of the Nile, since they also wished to hold Egypt. 'A civilized nation,' he explained, 'would surely build regulating sluices across the outlet of the Victoria Nyanza and control that great sea as Manchester controls Thirlmere. This would be an easy operation. Once done, the Nile supply would be in their hands.' The implications were clear to him: 'if poor little Egypt had the back luck to be at war with these people in the upper waters, they might flood Egypt or cut off the water supply at their pleasure.'

Kitchener's five boats arrived at Fashoda on the morning of Thursday,

19 September, with two battalions of Sudanese troops and a hundred Cameron Highlanders. Captain Marchand, who had been in Fashoda since 10 July and had received a note from Kitchener the day before, joined the general on his steamer at half-past ten. The two men were cautious, even hostile towards each other at first. A British major, Smith-Dorrien, watching the meeting through his field-glasses from another boat, wrote: 'After much bowing and scraping and saluting, what I suppose was a map was spread out on the table, then followed much gesticulation and apparently angry conversation. Distinct signs of hostility on both sides.' But then they calmed down, congratulated each other on their achievements – the Frenchman on his march, the Briton on his victory at Omdurman – and each suggested that the other should withdraw his forces. Both, of course, declined and it was decided that they would leave it up to their respective governments to settle the dispute. A tray of whisky and soda was brought in and, with what the Frenchman called 'this awful smoked alcohol', toasts were drunk to the British Queen and the French President.

At three o'clock that afternoon, Kitchener returned the courtesy of Marchand's visit, landing with a detachment of men who pitched camp under an Egyptian flag right beside the French garrison. Leaving this force, Kitchener returned to Khartoum and was back in England by the end of October, where a considerable crowd came to greet the victor of Khartoum – according to Lord Edward Cecil, who had been with Kitchener at Fashoda, the general, 'owing to the mismanagement of the police, had the greatest difficulty in getting away from Victoria Station'. Marchand left Fashoda soon after Kitchener to receive his new instructions in Cairo, where he learned that his government had decided to abandon the garrison. They really had no alternative. A hundred men without allies in a hostile land surrounded by a larger and better equipped force – it sounded like Gordon at Khartoum all over again. On 10 December 1898, the French officers of the Fashoda garrison were invited to a luncheon in the English camp and that evening the English officers dined in the French garrison. The following morning the French tricolor was lowered with great ceremony and the British guns fired in salute as Marchand and his force withdrew and moved eastwards towards Abyssinia, the Red Sea and the unexpected completion of their trans-African journey. The British, by this action, secured control of the entire course of the Nile from its source in Uganda, through the Sudan and Egypt to the Mediterranean near Alexandria. Soon it was possible to travel the length of the Nile by railway and river steamer, to send telegraphic messages from one end to the other and then even to follow the new railway line – the 'Lunatic Line' as it was commonly called – from the river's source down to Mombasa on the Kenyan coast. The threat of Sir Colin Scott Moncrieff's 'easy operation' to control the Nile at its source was no longer necessary since the British also controlled the lands which the sluices would hold to ransom.

★

As early as 1886, Mrs Annie King, in Egypt with her brother Dr Liddon and their energetic dragoman De Nicola, wrote from Aswan that 'We hear there are at least two regiments encamped here, but they are sending many men down, as there is a great deal of fever amongst the troops.' A few days later, she and her party went to look around the military camp on Cataract Hill, south of the town beside the river. There they had tea with the officers. The Egyptian frontier at that time was established at Wadi Halfa near the Second Cataract, but the reserve force was stationed here in Aswan. When the British Government decided on the reconquest of Sudan, more troops moved south and there was an even greater build-up in the town. But when the railway was completed right through to Shellal, it was no longer necessary to come up from Cairo or Asyut by boat, which then had to be hauled over the cataract by the men of the Sheikh el Shellal. The alternative to this had been to leave one boat below the cataract and move the luggage by camel or donkey around the cataract to another boat, perhaps Cook's *Prince Abbas*, which would then take the traveller into Nubia. With the new railway, it was necessary to change trains at Luxor, to go along the narrow gauge railway to Aswan and then change again for the short ride to Shellal. When Cook's began their regular steamer service on the Nile, dahabiehs which had previously been the only viable riverboats for Europeans took on a new image. They were now for wealthy travellers who could afford to see the Nile at a leisurely pace. When the railway was opened right the way through the country, even the steamers, which Florence Nightingale for instance had objected to so strongly – 'I would not go in a steamer on the Nile, if I were never to see the Nile without it!' – acquired a new kudos. G. W. Steevens of the *Daily Mail*, on his way through to the Sudan, came up to Aswan by steamer on 12 February 1898, 'a lazy afternoon, too late for coffee, too early for tea'. By then the town had several good hotels, the premier of which was the riverside Grand, opposite Elephantine Island and near the Tribunal Court. Like the Winter Palace in Luxor and perhaps also Shepheard's in Cairo, the Grand became a rallying point not only for passing foreigners but also for the businesses which they found useful: Thomas Cook's and their rivals, the Anglo-American Nile and Tourist Co, both had offices in the Grand, as did the Sudan Government

Steamer Authority, when it was established. There was also a chemist, the Savoy Pharmacy, P. Gondopoulo's Royal Photo-Book Stores and MacGillivray's photographic shop nearby.

But Steevens had no need of Aswan's tourist facilities, for a friend of his had hired a dahabieh from Cook's and moored it just off Elephantine Island. A boat with six oarsmen met him at the steamer landing-stage and took him around the island to the bay where the dahabieh was tied up. 'Where was I?' he wondered when he caught sight of six dahabiehs, all flying the Union Jack. 'At Henley or in Oxford for the Eights?' He thought the dahabiehs, with their lateen sails furled and their woodwork painted white, looked just like houseboats on the Thames, an idea which was reinforced when he stepped aboard and went into the saloon. 'Many people would be only too glad to have that saloon, lying placidly six hundred miles from the nearest possible upholsterer and decorator, for their drawing-room at home.' It was decorated with the finest furniture, a library of books, pictures on the walls, even a piano – an appropriate setting, he thought, for what he called that crowning blessing of civilization, the English lady. His hostess, who was a lady herself, sat with him at dinner that night around a table covered with a fine cloth, with food from in and around the Nile, as well as tins and preserves brought out with them from Europe or Cairo. The wine was good, the service impeccable. Really, it seemed that even here in wartime Aswan, halfway between the exoticisms of Cairo and the savagery of the Khalifa's Sudan, the British managed to preserve their way of doing things. Their expectations of life were constantly fulfilled.

However, before they had finished their civilized dinner that night, a 'discordant yell surged through the glass doors'. They carried on eating, but someone referred to the commotion by explaining that there was to be a 'fantasia' and that clearly it had just begun. After dinner, when they went out onto the upper deck which was forbidden to the crew, they saw that the outline of the boat, the awning posts and even the massive mast had been decorated with white, green, red and blue lanterns and that stalks of sugar-cane had been tied all around the railings. Crowded onto the low forward deck were about 120 Egyptians. They had already eaten the sheep which tradition demanded they be given for reaching Aswan and Steevens reports that there 'was also hasheesh and brandy – they called it brandy – and, perhaps, they too are not without their share of the credit for the entertainment'.

Steevens had never seen anything like it and probably neither had his hosts, although this was a regular feature of the Nile journey before Cook's introduced the package tour. His descriptions are coloured by that, for he was clearly surprised and amused and, in a way, also at a loss to explain it; 'we all seized the nearest support,' he wrote, 'and tried to hold ourselves upright while we laughed at the crew.' All of the crowd below them were making some sort of noise and he divided them up into an outer ring – 'its quality of sound is best described as the voice of a camel crossed with a bagpipe' – and the inner ring of dancers and musicians. Of the dancers he noticed one in particular, one of the men who had rowed him to the dahabieh that afternoon, who now had a stick of sugar-cane in his turban and the butt of a cigarette in his holder, clenched in the corner of his mouth. He was obviously drunk or drugged or both. 'Every limb and every gesture spelt a mixture of insane fury and imbecile good-fellowship,' Steevens wrote. It also spelt the boatman's adherence to his own traditions. With a British army controlling his country, a British adviser ruling his ruler and a British company employing him to look after this small group of British abroad, the fantasia was as much an assertion of the boatman's traditions as the dinner Steevens had enjoyed in the dining-saloon had been of his British habits. They were both stubborn and resilient and tried to resist the changes which contact with each other forced upon them.

The fantasia was over before midnight, which was late enough in Aswan where people woke with the sun, but for hours after the dancing and singing had stopped – by which time Steevens himself was in bed – he heard 'a crunch, crunch overhead as they chewed at sugar-cane. The crew were eating the decorations.'

Three days later, Steevens left Aswan by the 'dusty, ramshackle, seven-mile railway' to Shellal, where he was to board the Cook's steamer, *Prince Abbas*, which would take him as far as Wadi Halfa. At Shellal the military were in even greater evidence. All along the jetty there were tall rows of crated bully beef and sacks of flour and, marching up and down between them was a British Army subaltern, a short, dusty man, whom Steevens had met once before and who had impressed him. He was shouting out orders, 'energetic, ready, and resourceful, with no theory, but any amount of practice – a pocket edition of the British Empire.'

★

Steevens reported that the 1897–8 season had been the most brilliant Egypt had seen. 'Some people say there have been 50,000 visitors though that seems impossible yet the hotels of Cairo will hold, I suppose, nearly 2,000 visitors, and they change continually.' Fifty thousand visitors from almost all over the world. He remembered meeting Swedes, Portuguese, Siamese and Brazilians just in one day and, although there were more British and Americans than anyone else, there were also plenty of French, Italians, Greeks – and Germans 'in huge helmets, with huge puggary, huge blue goggles, knickerbockers, and chess-board stockings; women in the same helmets and goggles, vast blue veils, sunshades, short skirts, and vast hands and feet; both sexes crested with Meyer or Baedeker rampant...'

The success of the Sudan campaign brought more foreigners to Egypt and therefore also to Aswan where, in common with other Egyptian towns, the foreign community was a transient one. Cook's predicted that Aswan, with its warm winter climate and 'other attractions', would become one of the most popular winter resorts in the world. In their *Excursionist* magazine of 2 September 1899, they announced that 'the accommodation at the "Grand Hotel" has proved quite inadequate during the last few seasons. We have therefore arranged for the erection of a large new establishment to be called "The Cataract Hotel".' The Cataract was built on a promontory a little way outside the town in what was then the desert, just opposite the southern tip of Elephantine Island. An English architect resident in Aswan designed a three-storey building with two symmetrical wings, an uncomplicated structure painted in red-brown, with window openings and its name highlighted in white. Inside, the hotel was fitted to the highest standards: filtered water on tap, electricity throughout and an English housekeeper who rushed across the polished wooden floors. Only two years had passed since Steevens marvelled at the décor on his friend's dahabieh. There was also an English doctor on call and a clergyman came to hold regular Anglican services.

The Cataract Hotel was opened in January 1900, the month in which Steevens died of enteric fever in Ladysmith. On 11 January, the *Egyptian Gazette* reported in its new regular feature entitled 'Assouan Notes' that 'Over 100 persons sat down to table at the Grand Assouan Hotel last night, and I doubt if any Cairo hotel could shew as many. Assouan is certainly increasing in popularity.' Then only a week later it announced the opening of the Cataract: 'A large number of residents responded to the kind invitation of Mr. Pagnon [the lessee] to the inaugural dinner given by him at the new Cataract Hotel ... All the local officials, including the Commandant, Sub-Governor and Mamour of Aswan were present. The Government engineers and Messrs. John Aird & Co.'s staff were also very strongly represented. There was no lack of good things for dinner...'

The new hotel was a great success, as was the Savoy which opened soon after it on Elephantine Island; the Grand was already beginning to look old-fashioned. The writer Douglas Sladen, visiting the town a few years later, noticed that 'It is a curious fact that Assuan, one of the most beautiful places on the Nile, should of all others be most dependent on its hotels. If you are not going to the "Cataract," or the "Savoy," you may just as well not go to Assuan at all. The people who go to Assuan are, in ninety cases out of a hundred, attracted solely by the gaiety which is to be found at the "Cataract," or in a quieter way at the "Savoy", with its pleasant tropical gardens.'

Within the space of a few years, foreigners, and especially the British, transformed this part of Aswan. The Duke of Connaught, who was staying in the town, laid the foundation stone for a new Anglican church in March 1899, to which Queen Victoria herself donated a font. A telegraph line linked the town to the capital, running alongside the railway track on which the Wagons-Lits service was now operating. New shops and hotels, like the St James, continued to open. The Camel Corps had a barracks just outside the town. Various missions to the Sudan, including a Catholic and a German Pioneer Mission, also had bureaux here. The indispensable Sporting Club was founded and held race meetings during the season; it prided itself on its camel races. There was also a golf course, and tennis and sailing clubs. A museum was opened on Elephantine in 1912 which displayed a collection of antiquities which had been found in the area and on the far side of the island there was Kitchener's Island, given to the general on his victorious return from Khartoum and Fashoda, which he in turn donated to the Egyptian nation. It was already rich in palm, pomegranate and banana trees, as well as oleanders and roses, but more trees and shrubs from tropical Africa were planted as the foundation of the present botanical gardens. There was still the native town with its government offices, where the market still operated on Thursdays. There was the bazaar and the Bishareen camp in a Muslim cemetery about a mile to the east of the town which were still popular with the tourists. But as a trading town, Aswan had ceased developing. The new Anglo-Egyptian government in Khartoum built a railway from the Nile at Atbara, about 200 miles north of the capital, to the newly created Port Sudan on the Red Sea, which was opened by Lord Cromer in January 1906. After that, goods for export outside Egypt no longer needed to come down the Nile. Cattle and camels were still imported through Aswan and the bazaars were filled with Sudanese crafts as well as silver and gold, whips and sticks made out of rhinoceros horn or hippopotamus hide, ostrich feathers and stuffed crocodiles. It was also claimed that as late as 1920 it was possible to buy black slaves in Aswan's bazaar, although the government strongly denied it.

For a few months each year, generally from November to March, the population and disposable wealth in Aswan was increased considerably by the arrival of foreigners, escaping northern winters. During these months, the centre of this society was the belvedere of the Cataract Hotel, a covered terrace open to the south and west, filled with wicker chairs and tables. This was a perfect place from which to watch the Nile and the sailing boats around Elephantine and even the most energetic sightseer, Sladen reported, 'usually, sooner or later, comes into line with the loafers who begin to assemble in the belvedere of the "Cataract" about four o'clock for afternoon tea, and sit over their tea for the rest of the afternoon, looking out from that point of vantage on the best sunsets in all Egypt'.

Luxor had been an unexpectedly colourful place: the fields in the countryside around the town and across the river were rich green, the earth a deep brown. Even the sand was brightly coloured. These colours and the blue of the sky were also found on the walls of the tombs in the valley. The vibrant daylight which is a feature throughout Egypt, a light which is clear and sharp but which seems almost to have a texture to it, is more powerful in Luxor than in Cairo. But its vitality seems modified by the colour of the countryside. In Aswan, however, there is little apart from the palm trees to detract from the sky. A couple of thousand years ago when Aswan was the Greek town of Syene, there was a well into which, one observer noticed, the sun's rays descended perpendicularly at midday on the summer solstice. This, it was therefore deduced, meant that Aswan was on the line of the Tropic of Cancer. Although the tropic has since shifted a few degrees to the south, in the middle of the day in Aswan, even now, the sun seems to descend straight down and with dazzling intensity so that sand and rock and Syenite stone shimmer in its light. But when the sun drops behind the western hills, the valley is filled with colour, with browns and purple on the islands and the western shore. The sky is rich in colours which really do quicken the pulse and which very few artists have managed to capture. The refracted light on the river's surface makes the water seem dense like mercury, and quite as dull. Then the sky parades a series of distinct colours above you – orange, pink, crimson, scarlet, puce. This is the famous Egyptian afterglow and nowhere is it more spectacular than above Aswan. Winston Churchill, who had received his first commission in the 4th Hussars only three years before, in 1895, was twenty-three when he accompanied the army to Omdurman as a lieutenant and a special correspondent for the *Morning Post*. 'The banks of the Nile, except by contrast with the desert, display an abundance of barrenness,' he wrote in *The River*

War, which was published in 1899.

> Their characteristic is monotony. Their attraction is their
> sadness. Yet there is one hour when all is changed. Just
> before the sun sets towards the western cliffs a delicious flush
> brightens and enlivens the landscape. It is as though some
> Titanic artist in the hour of inspiration was retouching the
> picture painting in dark purple shadows among the rocks,
> strengthening the light on the sand, gilding and beautifying
> everything, and making the whole scene live. The river,
> whose muddy windings give the impression of a lake, turns
> from muddy brown to silver-grey. The sky from a dull blue
> deepens into violet in the west. Everything under that magic
> touch becomes vivid and alive. And then the sun sinks
> altogether behind the rocks, the colours fade out of the sky,
> the flush off the sands, and gradually everything darkens and
> grows grey, like a man's cheek when he is bleeding to death.
> We are left sad and sorrowful in the dark, until the stars light
> up and remind us that there is always something beyond.

For the British, one day in particular brought out their national character away from home and that was Christmas. At home it was so
rich in tradition and ritual, a marker for each year, that they were loath
to forget it when they were away. In Aswan, the British began their
Christmas celebrations as they would have done at home, by attending
the morning service in the local Anglican Church. But after the service,
events took a more sporting turn – a donkey gymkhana was held in
the Cataract's grounds, as well as a donkey polo competition played
with an Eton football. There was croquet on the lawn and tennis in
the courts. Then in the evening guests dressed in uniform, dinner jackets
and long dresses watched the sun set from the belvedere before going
in for the gala dinner. The dining room was a model of Islamic architecture, with deep arches, a domed central ceiling and intricate mushrabiya
work. In one corner the hotel's band played European tunes. Dinner
was served by the Egyptian staff dressed in long white robes and broad
red sashes, but it was no Egyptian dinner and with the Christmas tree,
the roast beef, plum pudding and mince pies, with Scotch whisky,
French wines and English beer, the guests would have been forgiven
for imagining for a moment that they were back home. Then, after
the tables were cleared and the music played out, there was the view
from the belvedere and the Nile-side balconies to remind them of where
they were, for the sky in Europe does not have this vibrant quality

and its stars are merely pricks of light, not these blazing fires, its rivers do not look as powerful or dramatic as this one, nor does its air carry that constant reminder of the hot, harsh, lonely desert which surrounded them.

★

The choice of name for this hotel, the Cataract, was a poignant one, for by the time it was opened work had begun on an engineering project which effectively did away with the First Cataract. The Aswan Dam came into existence after the Egyptian Government commissioned the British engineers, Sir William Willcocks and Sir Colin Scott Moncrieff – of whom Lord Cromer later wrote, 'No Englishman employed in the Egyptian service did more to make the name of England respected' – to report on the most effective way of controlling the Nile within Egypt. There were already barrages across the river near Asyut and Cairo, and across the Rosetta and Damietta branches of the river north of the capital, but in the momentous year of 1898, Lord Cromer was still forced to write that 'The most crying want of the country at present is an increase in the water supply.'

The idea of building a dam was a logical one for when the Nile swelled with the annual rainwater from the highlands of Ethiopia and Uganda, it broke its banks in Egypt and flooded the valley; for the rest of the year the countryside was dry. There were irrigation channels and primitive pumps which fed off the river and redistributed some of the water as the river rose and fell, but the whole thing was left too much to chance for the liking of the practical European mind. If there was a good flood and a high Nile, there followed a good harvest, plenty to eat and cotton to export. If there was a low Nile, there was famine. By building a dam and a reservoir behind it, it should be possible to regulate the flow of water to provide a plentiful and predictable supply throughout the year. In a country where more than ninety per cent of the land was uncultivated and barren, new water levels would create the opportunity to reap the maximum harvest from existing farmland and even to reclaim new land from the desert.

The contract to build the dam went to a British engineering firm, Messrs John Aird & Co, who had already carried out restoration work on the Nile barrages. Using Italian and Egyptian labour, work started in the summer of 1898 and the foundation stone was laid by the Duke of Connaught on 12 February 1899. The foundations of the dam were completed two years later and the visible masonry work by June 1902. That December, the Duke and Duchess of Connaught returned to Aswan to open the dam. An inscription on the side of the wall which

255

runs along the top of the dam (which is now guarded by nervous Egyptian soldiers who discourage pedestrians by aiming loaded machine guns at their heads) records the fact that: 'This stone was laid, to complete the dam, by H.R.H. The Duchess of Connaught on the 10th December, 1902, in the 11th year of the reign of H.H. Abbas Helmy Khedive.' The Khedive and Lord Cromer were also present at the ceremony and both felt a sense of satisfaction that it was their countries which had brought about this wonder of the modern world.

The new dam produced instant results and although there was an unusually low Nile during the years of construction which led to a poor harvest and a belief amongst the fellahin that somehow this was all due to the work going on at Aswan, Lord Cromer wrote that the dam 'is by far the most popular step we have ever taken, all the more so because we have done it ourselves, without French or other co-operation'. The effects of the dam on agriculture are reflected in statistics: between 1881 and 1911 almost a million extra feddans (a feddan was just over an acre) were farmed, bringing the total cultivatable area to more than 5,500,000 feddans; for an initial outlay of £E2,340,000, the annual rental value of the lands which benefited from the new irrigation system was reckoned to have increased by about £E1,553,000 within four years of the dam's opening; the increased saleable value of this land had increased by almost £E16,000,000. Cook's *Handbook* for 1906 reiterated Cromer's doubt that 'in the records of engineering work, another instance can be quoted of such results being achieved with so relatively small an outlay of capital'.

The dam became as important a tourist attraction as anything else in Aswan, although of course it was the British who expressed pride in the work. Scarcely forty years before, the source of the river had still been a mystery, but now it was tracked, charted in places and finally controlled. It was a monumental construction, running straight across the river for one and a quarter miles. In places it was over 100 feet high and its base was almost as thick on the river-bed. Most poignantly, it had been built out of granite from the quarries in Aswan, the same quarries from which the ancient Egyptians had taken stone for their temples and monuments; this provided a useful parallel which was not lost on its British supporters. 'American experts,' Douglas Sladen reported somewhat deferentially in 1908, 'have said that the erection of the Pyramids was nothing, as an engineering feat, compared to the erection of the Assuan dam, which they consider the greatest of the marvels in Egypt.' The artist R. Talbot Kelly, writing in *The P&O Pocket Book* that same year went even further, suggesting that the dam had begun a great new era in Egypt, 'the massive structure of the dam itself, controlling the mighty river and the thousand miles of fertile land below demonstrates to the world that, great as Egypt *has* been, greatness in her rulers had not been buried with her past. Equal to her most glorious period is her present day, and who can say what her future may be?'

There were drawbacks, of course, and not everyone was so enthusiastic. The dam worked in the following way: when the level of the Nile began to rise towards the end of July, the dam's 180 sluice gates were left open because the first water was thick with silt and, more important, because the farmland needed as much water as possible in the summer. On 1 December, by which time the river was carrying less silt and the Nile below Aswan was well into its flood, the first sluice gate was closed. The others were gradually closed after this so that between December and February the reservoir above the dam, at first capable of storing more than 37 billion cubic feet of water, was filled and a lake was created which stretched back over a hundred miles into Nubia. Between March and July, when the river was at its lowest level, the gates were opened and the countryside irrigated.

The two main objections to the dam came from very different quarters. Some engineers, including Sir William Willcocks who had drawn up the original plans which had subsequently been modified, insisted that the dam as constructed was inadequate for the country's needs. The other, more vocal objection, came from Egyptologists and amateurs of ancient Egypt who were outraged by the fact that when the reservoir was full, the temple of Philae was submerged almost up to the capitals of its columns. The conservationists claimed that this was a crime against history and beauty, for the Philae temple had always been considered one of the most perfect in Egypt. The argument became a public one in which science was portrayed as cold, insensible and damaging to the environment. But in the end neither side was satisfied, for although the conservationists did succeed in having the original design modified, the dam was later enlarged.

In 1904 Janet Ross, the daughter of Lucie Duff Gordon, arrived in Aswan for a holiday. She had been away from Egypt for more than forty years and coming by train from Luxor – where her mother's old house had been pulled down and her friend 'Sheykh Yussuf' no longer known – she wrote that 'That journey was hotter and dustier than I could have imagined anything, even in Egypt, could possibly have been, so the pull across the river from Assouan to the island of Elephanta was delightfully refreshing.' She had taken rooms in the quieter Savoy Hotel, which was famous for its extensive gardens. Looking out of her window at the Savoy, Mrs Ross caught a cheering glimpse of the place she remembered. 'We were early travellers,' she wrote. 'The brown earth was being sown and watered several times a day, and in an incredibly short time the whole place was green and the grass ready to mow. The river was sinking fast, and every morning the Arab women from the village behind the hotel dibbled seeds into the strip of mud off which the water had receded in the night. Every evening we watched the wonderful afterglow – no words can describe it – as though all the jewels of the world had been showered over an opal sky.'

But Aswan was not as it had been in the 1860s and the most significant change was the dam itself. One morning 'a pleasant Scotchman', the head of the works at the dam, sent his steam launch down to bring Janet Ross to visit the construction. She was clearly impressed by it – 'I could not help thinking how jealous the old Pharaohs would have been of that mighty work,' she wrote – and then they rowed across the rising waters of the lake-reservoir to the island of Philae. 'I confess,' she wrote after that visit,

> that in spite of my admiration for the colossal barrage, and the knowledge that it had brought food and prosperity to thousands of *fellaheen*, and would prevent seasons of scarcity or of devastating floods such as I had seen in bygone years, the first sight of Philæ was really painful. The waving palm trees were all dead and stood out yellow-brown against the blue sky; the *sunt* bushes were dead, a tangle of withered branches wrapped in withered weeds left by the receding waters of last year; the beautiful temples no longer stood high on a green island, the water nearly touched their steps, and in a few weeks would rise and rise and cover them nearly to the roofs.

She landed on the island and walked around the temple which her mother had visited – in May 1864, having come up from Aswan on a donkey in the company of Omar, her servant, and some English friends. Then, they had decided to spend the night there and the women had settled down in the Osiris chamber of the temple, with Omar sleeping across the doorway to protect them. 'I could not sleep for the heat in the room,' Lucie wrote to her husband, 'and threw on an *abbayeh* (cloak) and went and lay on the parapet of the temple. What a night! What a lovely view! The stars gave as much light as the moon in Europe, and all but the cataract was still as death and glowing hot, and the palm-trees were more graceful and dreamy than ever. Then Omar woke, and came and sat at my feet, and rubbed them, and sang a song of a Turkish slave.' Now her daughter walked across the temple with her mother's words in her mind. The palm trees were dead, the sight of Europeans in the summer was no longer as surprising as 'swallows in January' and the temple, strengthened and shored up, was submerged for several months each year. 'Philæ, beautiful, wonderful Philæ, was no more,' Janet wrote. 'For a few minutes hatred of the utilitarian science which had destroyed such loveliness possessed us.'

★

Damage to the island of Philae was not the only price of progress, as Janet herself noticed on that journey. Earlier in the nineteenth century, the Nile valley had supported an abundance of wildlife, but so many travellers came to shoot for sport that less and less of the sought-after species were found along the popular run between Cairo and Aswan. Janet remembered that 'When in 1867 I was at Assouan, pelicans, wild geese and ducks, and all kinds of plover and small birds abounded,' but by 1904 there were few birds to be seen except hoopoes and grey kingfishers. She was told that 'the Italians, who had been employed in thousands to build the great dam below Philæ, had shot them all'. Italians, English, French (including Flaubert), Germans, Americans – it really did not matter what nationality they were, most men took guns with them up the Nile and very few could resist taking a shot at the wildlife from the deck of their dahabieh or steamer.

Of course the western sportsman could shoot plenty of birds in Europe, albeit of a different species – the occasional eagle or vulture which was still seen along the river made a prize shot – but of much greater interest to them were the large animals and the game. In ancient Egypt, elephants, rhinoceroses, hippopotamus and even lions lived along the river, as tomb paintings show. They were also considered suitable sport for a pharaoh or nobleman and so they began to move south. For the modern visitor, the crocodile seemed to excite the greatest interest. Lucie Duff Gordon had been eager to see one and had written that 'As to crocodiles, Inshallah we will eat their hearts, and not they ours,' but only twenty years later a Cook's tourist had complained about the lack of these animals, even as far up as Aswan. 'Cook ought unquestionably to have a few stuffed ones placed on sandbanks,' he suggested. Dr Wallis Budge reported in Cook's *Handbook* for 1906 that: 'Until a comparatively late period this creature frequented the Nile so far north as the Delta, but steamers and sportsmen have, little by little, driven him southwards . . .'

In a report on African game, Lord Cromer reckoned that one of the reasons wild animals were so abundant in the interior was that wars between rival tribes devastated large areas of the countryside which then became a sort of no-man's-land. On this land, wildlife flourished. 'The *Pax Britannica* can never do for African game in the future,' Dr Wallis Budge admitted, 'what the Zulu Impis, the Masai Moran, the slave-raiders, and the Dervishes have done in the past.' On the contrary, the *Pax Britannica* brought with it the sportsman and hunter. But the British in the Sudan, or rather the Anglo-Egyptians, for the country was officially jointly ruled by Britain and Egypt from 1899 and their two flags flew side by side, introduced game licences and new laws designed to protect endangered species and to control the number of other animals that could be hunted. Under these regulations, English cartridges for instance, were banned from being imported into Egypt, although perfectly satisfactory replacements could be bought in Cairo from Cook's, who were agents for the Nobel company. British Army standard issue .303 rifles were also prohibited, but there was still plenty of opportunity for a good bag – in 1905, for instance, 2,101 head of game were recorded as having been killed in the Sudan by residents, officers, officials and visitors. The list included gazelle, buffalo, cheetah, elephant, giraffe, hippopotamus, leopard, lion, rhinoceros, antelope and a whole range of other animals including wild dogs, asses and boars.

The centre of the revived Anglo-Egyptian Sudan was, appropriately enough, Khartoum. The Mahdi had established his own capital at Omdurman, opposite the official one, and after Gordon's death the Mahdi's successor, the Khalifa, had had Khartoum evacuated and more or less destroyed: only Gordon's palace and the Austrian Mission Church survived from among the larger buildings. The ruins were abandoned to the desert sands and a few vagrants. Now, with the British and Egyptians in control, Khartoum was once again the seat of power. This had been hard enough to imagine when G. W. Steevens crossed the river with Kitchener in 1898. 'When Allah made the Sudan,' the journalist wrote, quoting an Arab saying, 'he laughed.' Steevens saw little advantage in the place and, considering the campaign of reconquest, he wrote: 'Count up all the gains you will, yet what a hideous irony it remains, this fight of half a generation for such an emptiness ... a monotone of squalid barbarism ...: it has neither nationality, nor history, nor arts, nor even natural features. Just the Nile – the niggard Nile refusing himself to the desert – and for the rest there is absolutely nothing to look at in the Sudan.' The best that could be hoped for what he called this 'God-accursed wilderness, an empty limbo of torment', was that it would be administered by a few British officials under a military law and that it would be quiet and would eventually be able to support itself. There was no great prospect, he was sure, for cultivation,' for if you drained off the Nile here, it would affect the harvest in Egypt. The other, greater provider of revenue in the past was the slave trade which the British had tried so hard to abolish. There used to be a good trade in ivory, too, but that had almost come to an end. 'Gum-arabic and ostrich feathers and Dongola dates,' he reckoned, being practical about it, 'will hardly buy cotton stuff enough from Lancashire to feel the difference.' In terms of benefit to Britain, you could forget about the Sudan.

But there was still something powerfully emotive about the place and Gordon, who had tried to do so much for the Sudan, was at the centre of it. One contemporary journalist called him 'the only white man of modern times whom all would place in the lower heaven'; the reconstructed capital at Khartoum would be a monument to him and Kitchener was the man who began it. Lord Edward Cecil, with Kitchener in 1898 after the battle at Omdurman, remembered that 'I had the good luck to go over alone with Lord Kitchener to Khartoum . . . He was certainly moved by the historical associations, taking trouble to identify the place where Gordon actually fell . . . but his mind was really in the future. He was already rebuilding the capital of the Sudan . . .'

Kitchener himself designed the new centre for the capital, or rather he made the decision to lay out its broad new streets according to the pattern of the British flag. This served two purposes: not only was it patriotic, but also it made the place easy to control with a few well-placed machine-guns. It was indeed to be a reminder of Gordon. The reconstruction started immediately and a new palace was built for Kitchener – who had been appointed Sirdar (Commander-in-Chief of the Egyptian Army and Governor-General of the Sudan) – on the site of Gordon's palace. Where the martyr had been killed, the very spot on which he was supposed to have been speared, which had become a hallway of the new building, was decorated with Sudanese spears and swords, rifles, helmets and a single cannon – a military shrine with a plaque which stated bluntly: 'Charles George Gordon. Died 26th January, 1885.'

'Best of all,' Douglas Sladen wrote in 1908, 'in the public gardens behind the palace, high over the plumes of palm and plantain, thrust into the mercilous sunshine so typical of the mercilous desert races with which he strove, is the statue of Gordon on his camel,' a replica of one outside the Royal Engineers HQ in Chatham, England. Sladen reckoned that 'The American riding along the sandy road beneath it feels, as instinctively as the Englishman, that he is in the presence of a hero . . .'

Britons around the Empire also paid homage to the hero, or appeased their guilt at having abandoned him, by donating generously to a fund that Kitchener set up to build a college in Khartoum to Gordon's memory. The Gordon Memorial College, which opened in 1902, took in 370 or so Sudanese students and brought them up according to the British public school tradition. Under the guidance of its first Principal, James Currie, an Oxford Blue and a Scottish international footballer, students were trained to fill the less important posts of the country's new administration.

Foreign society which developed in the Sudan after its recapture was a different affair to the social complications and sophistications of Egypt. The Sudan was removed from the south/north and east/west crossroads, which had created the diverse and constantly changing communities in Cairo and Alexandria, and the Sudan official's existence was often a bachelor and a solitary one; his experiences had more in common with imperial administrators in other 'far-flung' parts of the empire, with whom he was often compared. 'The Indian Civil Service,' Major Jarvis of the Egyptian service explained, 'we know is patchy, and the Egyptian Government very much what you would expect, but immediately you cross the Sudan border you feel instinctively that you are coming into contact with a hundred per cent cock-angels and nothing else.' This was remarkable, the major felt, because the service was so new. It had attracted what he called 'practically all the male paragons of virtue in the Empire'. But it was precisely because the Sudan's administration was new that it worked so well, for the system that Gordon had attempted to establish in the 1870s had fallen apart under Mahdist rule and the new Anglo-Egyptian government was able to start afresh. The Sudan Political Service became one of the most élite civil services in the world. It was able to attract the majority of its recruits from Britain's top universities by offering them a large salary and the chance of running a province the size of England, which was more than some young men could resist. The drawback to the service was the climate: officials were obliged to retire between the ages of forty-eight and fifty-two, though after an extended period in tropical Africa they were likely to look and feel much older.

Both this new breed of administrator and a rugged type of tourist were attracted to the country because it seemed to offer a new frontier, although the entry into the country was anything but strange. The Sudan Military Railway ran from the steamer station in Wadi Halfa across the Nubian desert to Khartoum. The fawn-coloured trains were considered the most luxurious in the world and by 1908 a regular sleeper service was in operation. The running of the dining-car was sub-contracted to a Greek firm whose picturesque attendants were compared to harem attendants – in the 1950s, one visitor likened a Sudanese major-domo serving him a seven-course meal on the train, to 'Mr. Henri Soulé at Le Pavillion'. Passengers on the sleeping-car were served a full English breakfast, lunch, tea and a dinner which was 'moderately well-cooked,' according to Douglas Sladen, 'and with hardly anything over-hung.' There were a few touches of home, too, with English mar-malade at breakfast, Huntley and Palmer biscuits, Worcestershire sauce and plenty of Scotch whisky and English beer. If there was a shortage of wine, at least the mineral water was served iced.

The train from Wadi Halfa terminated at Halfaya, the station across the Nile from Khartoum. As there was no bridge when Sladen visited it, it was necessary to take a steam launch over to the hotel. But there was a hitch when he arrived – mail bags had been loaded on top of his luggage and he had to wait for over an hour before they were removed. It was irritating, but, he confessed, 'We did not like to say much because there was such a very impressive man walking about and eyeing us all – he had a white suit and white tennis shoes, a pink collar, a Cambridge-blue tie, and a crimson tarboosh.' Sladen thought he was grand enough to be a khedive, but he turned out to be the Cook's representative in Khartoum who 'pestered us to book for Cook's excursion to the city of Omdurman, and Cook's excursion to the battle-field of Omdurman, and Cook's excursion to the Blue Nile, and Cook's personally conducted tour round the sights of Khartoum. For the ordin-ary tourist Cook runs Khartoum.' Along with the Cook's representative came 'another grand person in a white frock coat with a green velvet band round his hat,' which, when he turned round, revealed that he was from the Grand Hotel, where Cook's had opened their office in the 1901–2 season. The services they offered were all part of the redevel-opment which had made Khartoum a more attractive centre for the intrepid traveller or sportsman; almost each year of the first two decades of this century saw improvements to the town's facilities, although even in the 1950s there was still no sewage system in Khartoum and 'night soil', as it was called, was still collected by camel-drawn carts.

Bimbashi D. C. E. ff. Comyn was an officer with the 'Black Watch' regiment until he decided to leave what he considered were the confines of regimental soldiering and to join the Egyptian Army – 'the plum of extra-regimental employments abroad,' he thought. The Egyptian Army provided officers for the Sudan and Comyn was sent to Khartoum to take up his first post – as commanding officer of No 1 Company of the Camel Corps, Describing Khartoum as he saw it at the turn of the century, Comyn wrote:

'Of the public buildings the palace, war offices, and post-office alone stood. The little villas along the river front, with a few shops in rear, formed the four-year-old town. One ploughed one's way about, ankle-deep in sand.' But four years later, on his way back to Egypt, he came across what he called a mushroom city. 'Palace and villas had been added to out of all recognition. Elegant walls replaced those of green brick; new buildings were erected everywhere, including a magnificent mosque. There were two fine hotels; the streets were lighted with electricity; the river front was, owing to the embankment, no longer a mean path, but a fine esplanade.'

It was, he thought, just like a European city, but right in the heart of Africa, although perhaps his opinion was coloured a little by the demanding conditions he had been living under.

From his service experience, Comyn divided postings for British officers in the Egyptian Army into several categories. First there were the Cairo posts which were certainly no hardship: 'One patronises balls and other gaieties, polo of the best, golf, rackets, &c. But who has not heard of the Khedival [Gezira] Sporting Club? The season over, one endures for a couple of months, with an occasional (or is it weekly?) week-end at San Stefano, and then – the three months' leave that follows the nine of work.' The second possible post was in Khartoum or one of the stations between the two capitals where officers lived an office life from nine to two. 'There, too, are polo and all the sports afforded by a well-run club. The society of the gentler sex is as yet limited. Home leave, as in Cairo, is as regular as the hour-hand.' But the third group, who took up posts south of Khartoum had a very different experience of service life. Those officers posted to the Nile stations or the major provincial towns were linked to the capital by the weekly or fortnightly mail-boat or by the telegraph wire but it was only when tourists or fellow-officers passed through that they were able to get up a game of tennis or a chukka of polo. 'At the worst there is a white man once and again to talk to,' Comyn explained, and there was always the annual leave to look forward to. Meanwhile, if anything went wrong, they had only to send a wire and support arrived. The telegraph was literally their lifeline – if someone was ill, a wire brought help; if they ran out of food, drinks, soda water or whatever, supplies arrived at the receipt of a message. Their bungalows were comfortable enough and generally protected them against the weather, although their life was hard. They were well paid for their work and, having little to spend it on while they were up-river, they usually managed to save money for when they resigned their commissions or retired. Indeed, if you were the right sort, it was a good life, although the main draw-back, the mosquitoes, was one which Comyn thought, from his own experience, should be spelt out in capital letters. 'Mosquitoes in tens, in hundreds of thousands of millions by night. Any one who has dinner in the open after dark in these parts is perhaps a pachyderm, and certainly a lunatic.'

The final category was the officers who were sent to the out-stations beyond the river and the easy reach of the telegraph wire. They were called the 'Bog Barons' and lived in circumstances which were not that different from those endured by the African explorers, just the other side of their own society's reach. For them, an officer's house was a native mud hut. He ate tinned food from his store while it lasted and then lived off fresh food from the market and whatever he managed to shoot for himself. If he was ill, he would probably have to rely on the local people to look after him. His leave, which was the only time he was sure to see other Europeans, was entirely dependent on when he could safely leave his district. For these posts, officers and officials were more likely to be chosen for their attitude and athleticism than for any academic prowess. Indeed, the high number of varsity sportsmen who were selected for the service earned them the comment that they were the 'Blues who beat the Blacks.' As one senior official in the Sudan Service put it, 'Of course we sent the *clever* lads to the northern provinces. The south is no place for a *clever* man. Anybody clever would go crazy. For the south we had to have stolid chaps, but, by Jove, what good chaps they were!'

Comyn spent four years on service in the southernmost provinces of the Sudan as a police officer, a magistrate, inspector and at one time also as Acting-Governor of a province; both the service and the country were still unsettled after the Mahdist rule. In some villages, the Sudanese had never seen a white man before and Comyn learned that suggesting rather than demonstrating his power, that making a show with a large escort so that he would be seen to be powerful, was the most effective way of displaying his authority. Also, in the early days of the Service, it was regulation for officers in the field to dress in full uniform, with boots and spurs, whatever the weather – most often his struggle was against the weather and not the people. He rode his camel or pony across fearful countryside full of lions, crocodiles, snakes and a host of malarial insects and other dangers. He lived amongst sand-drifts and mirages in the desert and the creeping dangers of the swamp. When he was on the move he pushed himself hard, rising at three in the morning at which time his servant brought him a cup of sugared cocoa. He left the camp fifteen minutes later and went on ahead with an orderly and a guide, while the rest of the men packed up camp. At sunrise he took off his warm clothing, which he left on the path for the bearers to pick up and bring on, and he put on his topi. Then at nine o'clock he stopped and found some shade to sleep in, was woken a couple of hours later when his servant brought him a meal of antelope steak or chicken, with some biscuits and tea, had a bath and then went back to sleep until three in the afternoon. He then rode for another three hours or so, ate another helping of antelope or chicken, only this time with some soup as well, and prepared for the night. The camp was made up as a square, with his camp-bed, covered by the indispensable mosquito net which also kept the crawling insects off him, making up one side. His bearers slept on beds of cut grass and built fires to keep themselves warm, while the other two sides were taken up with the armed men.

Comyn's life was dominated by the climate and the countryside. Sometimes it was so hot that he hardly had the strength to climb up onto his camel and he perspired freely without even moving. The terrain was rugged and practically uninhabited. This was the boundary of the British Empire, although not so far away from the Ugandan protectorate or from the French Congo. The great explorers like Bruce, Speke, Grant and Baker, and Stanley only thirty years before him, had come this way in search of answers to the questions about the Nile and the nature of the African interior. Now Comyn was ruling it as the last effective link in a chain of command which stretched the whole way back to London. His journey out to the frontier was a social progress through the functions which were a necessary part of life in Cairo, Upper Egypt, Khartoum and even El Obeid. But out on the frontier he was alone with his Egyptian and Sudanese men, administering the lives of primitive people. It seems a little strange that an amiable Englishman should choose to work under these conditions and so far from his fellow-countrymen and women, away from a society which understood him. But Comyn and the other 'Blues' and 'Bog Barons' around the headwaters of the Nile invariably chose far-off postings in preference to service in the capitals or the Egyptian provinces. They were the 'stolid chaps', better suited to this sort of life. 'If the intending bimbashi can be "choked" off,' Comyn advised, 'far better that that should happen in England.' If they did go ahead, however, the rewards were great: 'they see big game and shoot it if their eye is straight. They see countries and people. They administer large districts. Very often they wander in those most fascinating tracts of the world – the blank places of the cartographers – the *unexplored*. In a word, they make Empire.'

OUT OF EGYPT

'He who follows not custom in the East is a fool'
Lord Edward Cecil, *The Leisure of an Egyptian Official*

Consider some of the foreigners in these pages: the withdrawn English officer or official in Cairo spending more time in the club than the office; the 'frontier Blue' in uniform, boots and spurs whatever the weather; the early explorers in search of knowledge and wealth; the later, wealthy tourists in topis and puggarees in search of distraction and entertainment; sensualists out for pleasure; women in sun-veils trying to look dignified on an ass; Christians out for elevation; scholars looking for proof – but however long the list gets, very few of these people wanted to know, or were able to know, the Egyptians. Instead, they came in search of their own particular version of the country, glimpsed from hotel terraces and city bazaars, from steamer moorings or railway platforms, government offices, military parade-grounds and club-house windows. Egyptians with whom they came into contact – boatmen and dragomans, porters and vendors, taxi-drivers and petty officials – hardly represented the Egyptian people, the majority of whom were to be found in villages along the Nile and in the delta, where foreigners seldom ventured. The British, especially, were élitist and reclusive. Lord Cromer had pointed out that 'in default of community of race, religion, language, and habits of thought, which ordinarily contribute the main bonds of union between the rulers and the ruled, we must endeavour to forge . . . artificial bonds between the Englishman and the Egyptian . . .' But what could these artificial bonds be?

Both nationalities were veiled: the Englishman hid behind his natural reserve and an inbred sense of superiority; the Egyptian was kept apart by his different customs as well as by his resentment at being ruled by an alien race. Few foreigners bothered to look for the real Egyptian behind the stereotyped image of fat pashas and lazy workers, sharp dealers, poor soldiers, down-trodden peasants. Although people like Lucie Duff Gordon did make the effort to lift the veil, most found it easier to accept these received impressions and to dismiss Egyptians, as one lady put it at the start of this century, as being 'so brutish, so insensitive, so mentally deficient'. It was not only the Egyptians who received this treatment, for other 'alien' nations were viewed in a similar way and the French writer A. B. de Guerville noticed when he was in Egypt in 1905 that, 'extraordinary as it may seem, Englishmen, intelligent, educated and charming, will speak of a Greek as "that black man" or "that nigger"'. Egyptians, Turks, Sudanese, Nubians all received the same treatment. The cosmopolitan crowds in hotels and on the river were not always so extreme, but their prejudices were formed by the same attitudes.

As for Egyptians, they were most likely to regard foreigners and especially the British in one of two ways. Those Egyptians who came into contact with tourists regarded them, as Baedeker had pointed out, 'as a Croesus, therefore as fair game,' and felt justified in 'pressing upon him with a perpetual demand for bakshish ...' The editor then recommended a few words which would be effective as a way of handing over this gift – *imshi* ('be off') being the most common. An Egyptian coming into contact with British officials would often express respect for their attitude towards their work – they were usually fair and diligent – but the problem was that they were *there*.

In October 1897, Thomas Skelton Harrison, the United States Consul-General, wrote in his diary that 'The evacuation of Egypt, either diplomatically or by force, will mark the beginning of England's lost prestige.' This was hardly a unique insight, but it proved to be true. In spite of the Englishman's reluctance to have anything to do with Egyptians themselves, Britain needed to hold Egypt, not only as a piece of its African empire but, more important, because of the Suez Canal. The British government was still making money out of its forty-four per cent shareholding in the Suez Canal Company, but the value of the canal to its shipping was far greater; it has been accurately called the lifeline of the empire, the imperial jugular. But when Britain annexed Egypt and made it a protectorate in 1914, it severed the link which had held Egypt to the Turks for more than 400 years. Egyptians finally believed that they could be free and this led to the creation of the first official Nationalist party, the Wafd, which literally means the delegation, in 1918. From then on, the British were confronted with increasing force by nationalist groups and they retreated both literally and politically towards the canal. The uprising of 1919 and the passive resistance which Zaghlul led against British rule in 1921, modelled on Gandhi's civil disobedience in India, brought an end to the protectorate and the country was granted a semi-independence – the Sultan Fuad became King. Then in 1936 a new treaty was drawn up which was intended to give Egypt complete independence. The British High Commissioner became a mere ambassador and British troops were withdrawn from the capital, but, although these were important steps, Egypt was still not free. As the American writer John Gunther remembered on his trip through Egypt in 1953, 'In the 1930s and during the war fashionable Cairo had practically the texture of a British town. There were all manner of Oriental trimmings, to be sure, and East met West in a maelstrom of conglomerate internationalism, but the basic overlay was British.' If nationalism was gaining a hold, it was also clear that old habits died hard.

In 1929, the twenty-six-year-old Evelyn Waugh took a pleasure cruise in the Mediterranean. During the cruise, Waugh met a young English couple and while on board, the wife, Juliet, developed pneumonia. When they reached Port Said, it was decided that she should go to the British hospital, and Waugh accompanied her and her husband, Geoffrey. They were met by the usual crowd on the quayside, they took Juliet to hospital, they had a drink on the terrace of the Casino Hotel where a 'gully-gully' man came to do his tricks for them and, later, they booked into Bodell's Hotel, which was run by a retired English officer and his wife. On the sand along the sea-front, a group of young Egyptians in green-and-white kit were playing football and each time they kicked the ball, Waugh reported, they shouted out ''ip-'ip-'ooray'.

Major Jarvis, a few years later, commented that although in 1860 Port Said was nothing but a mound of sand, by 1890 it was notorious for vice and evil and was known as 'the wickedest town in the East'. However, he lamented, 'a long line of British Commandants of Police have ruthlessly swept all this away and utterly spoilt the old-world charm of the place'. He even went as far as to complain that it now had a puritan air about it 'that vaguely suggests the interior of a Wesleyan chapel'. The interior of Bodell's Hotel seemed to have been a little like this. It was recommended to Waugh as the only hotel in town where one was guaranteed not to meet Egyptians – they were actually referred to as 'gyppies' – but all of the Englishmen-abroad in the place were there because one of their relatives had just been rushed off to the British hospital. Finding this waiting-room atmosphere more than they could bear, Waugh, Geoffrey and a young lawyer 'just down from Cambridge' went in search of Port Said's famous vices, having prepared for the outing by leaving watches, tie-pins and rings behind in the hotel. But all they found were a couple of brightly lit, stucco-fronted brothels called the Maison Dorée and Les Folies Bergères. At the back of the Maison Dorée, they came across another brothel, called the Chabanais, but when they went in they realized that it was the former establishment under another name and entered from the back door. Clearly, in Waugh's experience, the pleasures of Port Said had been over-rated, and yet this was the one town that was known to every British soldier in the canal zone. Later, it came to play a special role in the history of the British in Egypt.

When Juliet was well enough to travel, she, Geoffrey and Waugh took the train to Cairo and, deciding that they needed to cheer themselves up after her illness, booked into the Mena House Hotel. Here they engaged in a full round of tourist activities: they swam in the pool, rode camels out around the nearby villages, looked for souvenirs, attended luncheons packed out with Americans, Englishmen, Australians in jodphurs and – here was the difference – 'very smart Egyptian officers with vividly painted motor cars and astonishing courtesans'. They took tea on the terrace overlooked by the Pyramids – 'it was like having the Prince of Wales at the next table in a restaurant,' Waugh decided, 'one kept pretending not to notice, while all the time glancing furtively to see if they were still there'. On Easter Monday the hotel held the traditional gymkhana but it was badly attended and only consisted of camel and donkey races, one for each of the different classes of entrants – gentlemen, ladies and Arabs. 'All the prices were raised for that afternoon,' Waugh reported. 'Apart from this it was not really a success.' The place had lost its old sparkle and the foreigners who went there were a different set from those before the war.

As he steamed out of Port Said a few days later, travelling second-class for once, Waugh found himself in the company of some latter-day 'Overlanders', who had left the ship at Suez, gone to Cairo and then caught up with it again in Port Said. Over coffee and a sandwich they talked about their two main impressions of Egypt: the Pyramids and the exorbitant prices at Shepheard's Hotel. 'Two pounds ten, simply for a single bed and no bathroom. Think of that!'

*

The Second World War came slowly to Egypt. In May 1940, when Europe was already tearing itself apart, Alan Moorehead arrived in Egypt as war correspondent for the *Daily Express*. He found the place anything but at war and wrote, 'I flew on to Cairo where we bathed in the pool of the green island, Gezira, in the Nile, or watched the cricket. The Turf Club swarmed with officers newly arrived from England, and a dozen open-air cinemas were showing every night in the hot, brightly-lit city. There were all the left-overs from the dollar years when all Egypt swarmed with rich American tourists. 'We had French wines, grapes, melons, steaks, cigarettes, beer, whisky, and abundance of all things that belonged to rich, idle peace.' These included the ritualistic sports of golf and polo too. As with the First World War, foreigners in Cairo continued to enjoy themselves and were criticized for doing so while their countrymen elsewhere were fighting and dying. In particular officers seen in the big hotels were singled out. In her book on Shepheard's Hotel, Nina Nelson quotes a poem that was popular in Cairo at the time:

> We never went West of Gezireh
> We never went North of the Nile
> We never went past the Pyramids
> Out of sight of the Sphinx's smile.
> We fought the war in Shepheard's
> And the Continental Bar
> We reserved our punch for the Turf Club lunch
> And they gave us the Africa Star.

By the time Alan Moorehead reached the Sudan in 1941, however, there was no escaping the war, even so far south. On an earlier trip to Khartoum, which he called 'a well-run Empire country club,' he remembered staying at the Grand Hotel. 'Here on the terrace,' he wrote, 'which is perhaps two degrees cooler than the smiting sunshine outside, you meet ivory hunters and coffee planters from the Congo, cotton growers from Gezira, and district commissioners from Juba and Wau up the river. On that terrace I was introduced to the pleasant custom of taking a bottle of iced beer for breakfast. From there I saw my first wild hippopotamus floating down the White Nile.' But in 1941 the hunters and planters and growers had been replaced by soldiers; staff cars were parked in front of the Grand Hotel and Tomahawk fighter aircraft flew overhead.

By the summer of 1943, when Noël Coward arrived in Egypt to perform for the Allied troops in Egypt, Montgomery had already won his famous battle out in the desert at El Alamein, to the west of Alexandria, and the German and Italian forces had evacuated north Africa. There had been a very real threat that both Cairo and Alexandria might fall – when Alan Moorehead reached Alexandria, for instance, he had been cut off in the Cecil Hotel after the headquarters had retreated to Cairo. 'We got rooms easily,' he reported with some despair. 'The bar was half empty . . .' But all that was in the past and, by 1943, as it had been towards the end of the 1914–18 war, Egypt was the place to come to on leave. The Australians and New Zealanders were back, prices had risen and some Egyptians were becoming very rich again. Complaints about 'Gyppoes', 'Gyppy tummies' and bilharzia were common talk and the girls at Madame Badia's café still attracted the crowds.

Noël Coward stayed in the British Embassy when he came to Cairo, since he was a personal friend of the British Ambassador, Sir Miles Lampson. On his first day in the capital he took his breakfast on the balcony of his room, overlooking the Nile, and then before lunch he went to meet an old friend, Wing Commander the Earl Amherst, who, Coward points out, had arrived in Egypt in 1940 as a major in the Coldstream Guards but had somehow won his wings. They sat on the terrace at Shepheard's, and later he wrote in his diary that

> The restrictions of wartime are unknown; people sat there sipping Gin-Slings and cocktails and chatting and gossiping, waiters glided about wearing Fezzes and inscrutable Egyptian expressions. There were uniforms everywhere of all ranks and services and nationalities including Constance Carpenter in a natty shark-skin two-piece with E. N. S. A. on her epaulettes. These uniforms indicated that perhaps somewhere in the vague outside world there might be a war of some sort going on. This place is the last refuge of the soi-disant 'International Set'. All the fripperies of pre-war luxury living are still in existence here; rich people, idle people, cocktail-parties, dinner parties, jewels and evening dress. Rolls-Royces come purring up to the terrace steps; the same age-old Arabs sell the same age-old carpets and junk; scruffy little boys dart in between the tables shouting 'Bourse! Bourse!' which when translated means the Egyptian 'Times'.

It was reckoned that at least 2,000,000 troops visited the country during the war and the impressions that most of them took away were as extreme as those of the ANZACs in 1918. It was wartime and they were away from home in a country where they were often not appreciated and where they did not speak the language, did not under-stand the customs, did not enjoy the climate, were often badly accom-modated and badly treated; they were loud in their complaints. The local 'colour' which had amused tourists for years was a source of irri-tation to them. As James Cameron explained many years later, 'Few British ever tried to know Egypt. Thousands of them, with baffled memories of base-camps and shoeshine boys think they did, yet their impressions were almost always coloured with various resentments of compulsion.' In this case they were compelled to be in Egypt because of the war. And although there were compensations in the beauty of the country and the warmth of the climate, the foreigners on the land-scape still tended to get in the way. One night in August 1943, Noël Coward dined with the American Minister on the roof of his house near the Pyramids, lounging on divans with a coffee and a brandy, and later he wrote that 'The whole setting was enchanting. A sky blazing with stars, the lights of the Cairo blackout twinkling in the distance, the moon slowly coming up and silvering the Pyramids and the desert hills stretching away into the distance. An authentically romantic atmosphere in the finest Egyptian tradition shattered beyond redemption by the flat-footed arrival of the visiting American Senators.'

★

The war went away, but the British did not. In September 1945, an Egyptian delegation went to London to negotiate the withdrawal of British troops. The British response, delivered four months later, was that it had now authorized its ambassador to start preliminary negotiations. This was not good enough for the Egyptians. Egypt had been an internationally acknowledged independent state since its admission into the League of Nations in 1937. If it was independent, why should it still be occupied? A general strike in February 1946 led to rioting and the destruction of British property; the time for passive resistance was over. The British position became increasingly untenable and when the British government finally agreed to withdraw all British troops to the canal zone, there was some feeling of satisfaction in Egypt. But the facts spoke out against it: in 1903 there had been 5,000 British troops in Egypt; before the Second World War there were reckoned to be twice that number; by the 1950s, British strength in the canal zone had risen to 88,000 troops. They had built up a fortress there. The canal camp was one of the largest overseas military bases anywhere in the world, covering 9,714 square miles, built at a cost to the British government of £500,000,000 and running two-thirds of the length of the canal. It was obvious that they did not intend to give it up. What was left of the British Empire depended on it. But the British garrison was hemmed in and was an easy target for anyone who wanted to go out and throw stones or bombs or shoot at them. British officers still got off to Cairo for weekend leave and were seen in the clubs and the big hotels, but they were no longer safe and a sort of niggling, vicious guerrilla war developed between British troops from the east side of the canal and Egyptians over on the west. In January 1952, this 'war' escalated.

On 25 January, in response to attacks on their own positions, British troops moved along the canal and into Ismailia, surrounded the police barracks and gave the 800-odd Egyptian auxiliary policemen inside one hour to surrender. Had this happened fifty years earlier, they probably would have done just that. But some of these men were well-trained, the stations were in contact with Cairo by telephone, and the order they received from the Minister of the Interior, Fuad Serag ed-Din, also the Secretary-General of the Wafd party, was that they should resist the British force. By the end of the day, forty-one Egyptians had died attempting to carry out this order and another thirty were lying in the British military hospital. The following day, 26 January, is known as 'Black Saturday'.

In the morning there were large demonstrations in the centre of Cairo. Egyptians were angry at the events in Ismailia and chanted anti-British slogans. As the retired police chief Russell Pasha had observed in his memoirs six years earlier, it only took the smallest incident to turn one of these demonstrations into a riot. By midday, this demonstration was indeed a riot and guests on the terrace of Shepheard's Hotel could see smoke rising above the trees of the Ezbekieh, the Opera Square; Madame Badia's was on fire. The Turf Club was being attacked, too. Service continued as usual in Shepheard's and pre-lunch drinks were still enjoyed on the terrace, but during lunch more rumours spread around the dining-room, in particular that Groppi's café had been smashed up and that the Parisiana restaurant was on fire, as was the St James'. To those at the tables in Shepheard's, it seemed that the whole European quarter of Cairo was now in danger.

Mr C. Churchill, a retired brigadier who was the manager of Cook's office beside Shepheard's Hotel, was in his rooms in the nearby Victoria Hotel during that lunch hour. When he saw what was happening in the street, he decided to leave his room and return to the office. He would be safe there. He left the Victoria just as rioters started smashing up the furniture and burning carpets and, without being spotted, for he thought that the crowd would attack a foreigner, he made for Shepheard's. But when he turned the corner into the Sharia el-Maghrabi he saw that he was too late; Shepheard's was in flames. In the first attack, a grenade and several petrol bombs had been thrown into the lobby by the chanting crowd, but these had been dealt with at once. Then the electricity had failed and the next group of incendiaries was more successful. Joe Scialon, the barman in the Long Bar, continued serving generous drinks on the house, but smoke was soon drifting through the hotel's corridors and guests were being evacuated. By three o'clock the upper floors of the hotel were in flames. At four, a detachment of police arrived and escorted the hotel's guests through the crowd and later on to the Palace Hotel in Heliopolis. Two people had died in Shepheard's and no one now tried to put out the fire.

The destruction in Cairo was directed at all obvious foreign landmarks, particularly at the British, and Shepheard's hotel, 'where the

English tongue in Egypt finds its centre,' as Trollope had written almost a century before, was too good a target to miss. Cairenes had wanted the removal of the British and, three years after Black Saturday, John Gunther commented that they were indeed no longer there. 'The cafés and bars are packed with Egyptians,' he wrote, 'not Englishmen.' But they were still to be found elsewhere in the country and Gunther also wrote that the main concern of Egyptian foreign policy was 'the double problem of getting the British out of the Sudan and Suez. This,' he concluded, 'will be finally achieved by 1956.' His words were prophetic for, on 31 March 1956, the last battalions of British troops, Life Guards and Grenadier Guards, regiments whose ancestors had fought at the battle of Tel el Kebir in 1882, embarked on the troopship *Devonshire* at the Abbas quay in Port Said. India was already lost and Britain now abandoned its Egyptian base.

As though to confirm Thomas Skelton Harrison's prediction sixty years before, that the evacuation of Egypt would be the confirmation of Britain's loss of prestige, British troops attempted to re-invade Egypt that October in response to Nasser's nationalization of the Suez Canal Company. This time they arrived in concert with the French and Israelis. The *Egyptian Gazette* of 1 November reported that British jets had bombed Cairo, Alexandria, Ismailia, Port Said and Suez. It quoted British nationals, resident in Egypt, as being horrified and ashamed. Shame was a justified response.

The British Army had first arrived in Egypt during a war – with the French – it had re-invaded several times since then and now it took another war, if that is what the six-week long shambolic Suez campaign can be called, to make sure that they stayed out. It was indeed confirmation that Britain could no longer impose its rule on another country either through diplomatic or military threat. The British Empire was seen to be lost at Suez; after the invasion, British nationals were expelled and reminders of the British era were removed – for instance, the Union Club was closed, the Lady Cromer Dispensary was renamed the Egyptian Red Crescent, there were no more society pages in the newspapers, and Victoria College in Alexandria, perhaps Britain's most important contribution to Egyptian education, was significantly renamed Victory College.

*

Memories linger long. I had been in Upper Egypt and I arrived back in Cairo too late to attend the British Ambassador's cocktail party in honour of the Queen's birthday, which was held in the solid white house that Cromer built. I was leaving Egypt too soon to attend the

British community's ball at which they celebrated the same occasion, only this time with sausages and mashed potatoes flown in especially by British Airways. It takes place every year, but every year there are fewer people amongst the dinner jackets and long dresses who remember the seasons and the coming-out balls of the '20s and '30s in what was then the 'Residency', which has what was once described as 'the finest sprung dance floor in the East'.

My diary for my last few days went something like this: morning, British Council; afternoon, British Embassy; evening, Mena House Hotel; next morning, Anglican church; lunch, Anglo-American hospital; afternoon, Gezira Sporting Club. I was staying at Shepheard's Hotel, too, but this was not pre-revolutionary Egypt. A plaque inside the entrance of Shepheard's explained that it had been founded by Mr Samuel Shepheard of Preston Capes in 1841, entirely rebuilt in 1891, enlarged in 1899, 1904, 1909 and 1927. It was entirely rebuilt again after Black Saturday and the Egyptian revolution, but this time on a new site overlooking the Nile, a few blocks away from the British Embassy and from where the Kasr el Nil barracks used to be. It was a dull and depressing place in the summer that I was there, for it was once again being renovated and most of the floors were closed off or gutted. The management were delighted to see me. Flowers and chocolates up in my room on the eighth floor – 'For you the most special room in the hotel!' – with a fine view out over the Nile and the new Semiramis Hotel next door, especially of the blue waters of its swimming pool, a facility Shepheard's has never offered its guests.

During the day the hotel was filled both from within and without by the sounds of construction work. At night the dim yellow-lit corridors were silent apart from the odd snatch of an argument, or an incident on television, that came rattling down from a far-off room. They told me at the desk that the hotel would be very good when the refurbishment was completed. The head man smacked his lips and smiled a wonderful, broad, convincing smile as he explained how the fridges in the rooms would work, the numbers would no longer fall off the doors, the airconditioning would not rattle, the basins no longer leak, and, no, he knew nothing more about the history of the place than what the plaque up there on the wall across the lobby had told him.

I had met Egyptians in and around the hotels and tourist offices, people who served me, taxi-drivers and shop workers, as well as others just living around me, wealthy Cairenes, and poorer Cairenes who could not afford to drink in Shepheard's and who would not want to anyway. I met army colonels and privates, police officers, teachers, farmers and engineers in Upper Egypt. In one village, where the main street was a dust track busy with donkeys and carts, I was approached by a young man called Mahmoud who invited me to his home. He wanted me to see it. Electricity was old hat, but the alley was only now being dug up to lay sewage pipes. Some boys at the end fed rubbish into the black-edged flames of a fire. Mahmoud left me alone for a few minutes in the sitting-room of his first-floor apartment. It was painted a tobacco-coloured gloss, with blue paper above the picture rail; on the walls hung two large monochrome photographs, one of a military man in uniform, the other of an elderly gentleman in a dark suit and a tarboosh, both a little faded. I could hear women talking softly in another room, but I never saw them. He returned with a tray – a cup of tea, a bowl of sugar and a glass of water – and watched me drink it. Then he disappeared and came back with an electric fan. Later, while he beat me at chess, he asked me if I knew or had met Michael Jackson.

Earlier, I had met an Egyptian whose mother was English. She had lived in Cairo for most of her life, had been married to an Egyptian, who was dead now, but she had always seemed to her son to live a sort of Tunbridge Wells-existence. It was not just that she had chosen to live that way. Egyptians, he thought, were resistant to outsiders. They were now so used to being visited that while they held your hand in the street and opened the doors to their homes for you, they still kept something of themselves back. They beckoned from behind a veil.

In the smouldering ruins of Shepheard's Hotel on the morning after Black Saturday, the structure around the hotel's entrance was found to be intact and words inscribed on the lintel were still legible. *Quis aquam Nili bibit serum bibet*, roughly translated, means that whoever drinks the water of the Nile will drink it again. This is an Egyptian superstition. In a tomb at Beni Hassan, overlooking the dazzling sun-white valley and surrounded by vivid tomb paintings, I had been invited to eat with two Egyptians wearing blue jellabiyas and white scarfs, who were preparing their luncheon on the floor. I squatted down alongside them and dipped pieces of bread into a dish of foul and another of salad. Then one of them handed me a tin which contained water from the Nile. I hesitated, for I had heard plenty of tales about its emetic qualities, but my hosts laughed at me and gestured that I should drink. The tin had originally contained baby-food, but it was now old and rusted. While I drank, both men watched me and, later, shook my hand. In the evening, after I had left them, I was ill.

A few days later, when I left Egypt, I was driven out to the airport by a tall, elderly man with thick spectacles and thinning hair, who insisted that I sit up front with him. 'We talk.' It was a public holiday and the city was deserted; only the dust and sand and tourist buses hurried around us in the heat.

Ali, like so many other men I had met in Egypt, told me that he had fought with Monty in the war. Oh, yes, he liked the English all right. He filled in the silences by singing 'aye-aye-iddee-iddee-aye' over and over again.

Then I told him about my lunch in the tomb at Beni Hassan and that I had drunk the local water.

'Good, good,' Ali said, 'English are good. You drink Nile water, you come back. I like English.'

Later I asked him what the public holiday was for and, after thinking about it for a bit, he told me that it was to celebrate the evacuation of the British troops from Egypt.

'But no,' he said, slapping my knee, 'no. You English, you come back.'

BIBLIOGRAPHY

1 First hand accounts of Egypt:

(The editions of the letters, journals and autobiographies listed here are the ones from which I have quoted.)

D'Athanasi, Giovanni: *A brief account of the Researches and Discoveries in Upper Egypt, made under the Direction of Henry Salt, Esq.* (John Hearne, London, 1836).

Baldwin, George: *Political Recollections Relative to Egypt* (Cadell & Davies, London, 1801).

Barker, Edward B.B. (ed.): *Syria and Egypt under the last Five Sultans of Turkey* (Samuel Tinsley, London, 1876).

Belzoni, Giovanni: *Narrative of the Operations and Recent Discoveries in Egypt and Nubia* (John Murray, London, 1820).

Bevan, Dr Samuel: *Sand and Canvas, a narrative of adventures in Egypt* (London, 1849).

Blixen, Karen: *Out of Africa* (Century Hutchinson, London, 1985).

Briggs, Martin: *Through Egypt in War-Time* (Fisher Unwin, London, 1918).

Bruce, James: *Travels to Discover the Source of the Nile in the Years 1768, 1769, 1770, 1771, 1772 and 1773* (Longman & Rees, London, 1804).

Burckhardt, Jean Louis: *Arabic Proverbs, or the Manners and Customs of the Modern Egyptians* (John Murray, London, 1830).

Burckhardt, Jean Louis: *Travels in Nubia* (London, 1819).

Caillard, Mabel: *A Lifetime in Egypt, 1876–1935* (Grant Richards, London, 1935).

Cameron, James: 'Egypt' in *Travel in Vogue* (Macdonald, London, 1981).

Cecil, Lord Edward: *The Leisure of an Egyptian Official* (Hodder & Stoughton, London, 1921).

Churchill, Winston Spencer: *The River War* (Longmans Green, London, 1899).

Comyn, D.C.E. ff.: *Service and Sport in the Sudan* (John Lane, London, 1911).

Coward, Noël: *Middle East Diary* (The Right Book Club, London, 1945).

Cromer, Evelyn Baring, The Earl of: *Modern Egypt* (Macmillan, London, 1908).

Dinning, Hector: *By-Ways on Service, Notes from an Australian Journal* (Constable, London, 1918).

Duff Gordon, Lucie: *Letters from Egypt* (Virago, London, 1983).

Durrell, Lawrence: *The Alexandria Quartet* (Faber & Faber, London, 1968).

Edwards, Amelia: *A Thousand Miles Up the Nile* (Tauchnitz, Leipzig, 1878).

Fane, Henry Edward: *Five Years in India* (Henry Colburn, London, 1842).

Fay, Eliza: *Original Letters from India* (The Hogarth Press, London, 1986).

Flaubert, Gustave: *Flaubert in Egypt*, translated and edited by Francis Steegmuller (Michael Haag, London, 1983).

Gérard de Nerval: *Voyage en Orient* (Charpentier, Paris, 1851).

Hill, G. B. (ed.): *Gordon in Central Africa* (De La Rue, London, 1881).

Grey, Catherine: *Journal in the Suite of the Prince and Princess of Wales* (New York, 1870).

Grogan, Ewart S. and Sharp, Arthur H.: *From the Cape to Cairo* (Hurst & Blackett, London, 1900).

Halls, J. J. [ed]: *The Life and Correspondence of Henry Salt, Esq.* (Richard Bentley, London, 1834).

Harrison, Thomas Skelton: *The Homely Diary of a Diplomat in the East, 1897–1899* (Houghton Mifflin, Boston and New York, 1917).

Irby, The Hon. Charles Leonard, and Mangles, James: *Travels in Egypt and Nubia, Syria and the Holy Land* (John Murray, London, 1844).

Jarvis, Major C. S.: *Oriental Spotlight* (John Murray, London, 1937).

King, Annie: *Dr. Liddon's Tour in Egypt and Palestine in 1886* (Longmans Green, London, 1892).

Kinglake, Alexander: *Eothen* (William Blackwood, London, 1889).

de Kusel, Baron Samuel Selig: *An Englishman's Recollections of Egypt, 1863–87* (John Lane, The Bodley Head, London, 1915).

Lane, Edward William: *An Account of the Manners and Customs of the Modern Egyptians* (Ward Lock, London, 1890).

Legh, Thomas: *Narrative of a Journey in Egypt and the Country Behind the Cataracts* (John Murray, London, 1816).

Lynch, Jeremiah: *Egyptian Sketches* (Edward Arnold, London, 1890).

McPherson, Bimbashi: *The Man who loved Egypt* (Ariel Books, London, 1985).

Merrick, E. M.: *With a Palette in Eastern Palaces* (London, 1899).

Moberly Bell, E. H. C.: *The Letters of C. F. Moberly Bell* (London, 1927).

Moorehead, Alan: *African Trilogy* (Hamish Hamilton, London, 1944).

Morris, Jan: *Places* (Faber & Faber, London, 1972).

Nightingale, Florence: *Letters from Egypt, a Journey on the Nile, 1849–50*, edited by Anthony Sattin (Barrie & Jenkins, London, 1987).

Poole, Sophia: *The Englishwoman in Egypt* (Charles Knight, London, 1844 and 1846).

Ross, Janet: *The Fourth Generation* (Constable, London, 1912).

Russell, Sir Thomas: *Egyptian Service, 1902–1946* (John Murray, London, 1949).

Russell, William Howard: *My Diary in India in the year 1858–9* (Routledge, Warne & Routledge, London, 1860).

Sackville-West, Vita: *Passenger to Teheran* (The Hogarth Press, London, 1926).

Sladen, Douglas: *Egypt and the English* (Hurst & Blackett, London, 1908).

Southey, Robert: *Letters from England* (Longman, Hurst, Rees & Orme, London, 1807).

Stanley, Henry M.: *My Early Travels and Adventures in America and Asia* (Sampson, Low, Marston & Co, London, 1895).

Stark, Freya: *The Coast of Incense, autobiography 1933–1939* (Century Hutchinson, London, 1985).

Steevens, G. W.: *Egypt in 1898* (William Blackwood, London, 1898).

Steevens, G. W.: *With Kitchener to Khartoum* (William Blackwood, London, 1898).

Storrs, Ronald: *Orientations* (Ivor Nicolson & Watson, London, 1937).

Thackeray, William: *Notes of a Journey from Cornhill to Grand Cairo* (Chapman & Hall, London, 1846).

Thornton, Guy: *With the ANZACS in Cairo* (Allenson, London, 1917).

Twain, Mark: *The Innocents Abroad* (Chatto & Windus, London, 1897).

Tytler, Harriet: *An Englishwoman in India*, edited by Anthony Sattin (Oxford University Press, Oxford, 1986).

Warburton, Eliot: *The Crescent and the Cross, or Romance and Realities of Eastern Travel* (Henry Colburn, London, 1845).

Waugh, Evelyn: *When the Going Was Good* (Penguin, London, 1951).

2   Histories:

Peter Mansfield's and P.J. Vatikiotis's books have both provided sound bases for the historical background, while Alan Moorehead's accounts gave valuable insight into the spread of the West along the Nile.

Bates, Darrell: *The Fashoda Incident of 1898 – Encounter on the Nile* (Oxford University Press, Oxford, 1984).

Beatty, Charles: *Ferdinand de Lesseps* (Eyre & Spottiswoode, London, 1956).

Bird, Michael: *Samuel Shepheard of Cairo* (Michael Joseph, London, 1957).

Boyle, Clara: *Boyle of Cairo* (Titus Wilson, Kendal, 1965).

Ceram, C. W.: *Gods, Graves and Scholars, the story of archaeology* (Penguin, London, 1984).

Chapman, Caroline: *Russell of the Times* (Bell & Hyman, London, 1984).

Connor, Patrick (ed.): *The Inspiration of Egypt, Its Influence on British Artists, Travellers and Designers, 1700–1900* (Catalogue to an exhibition held at Brighton Museum, 1983).

Dawson, Warren R.: *Who Was Who in Egyptology* (Egypt Exploration Society, London, 1951).

Flower, Raymond: *Napoleon to Nasser, the Story of Modern Egypt* (Tom Stacey, London, 1972).

Gunther, John: *Inside Africa* (Hamish Hamilton, London, 1955).

Hoskins, Halford L.: *British Routes to India* (Frank Cass, London, 1966).

Mansfield, Peter: *The British in Egypt* (Weidenfeld & Nicolson, London, 1971).

Marlowe, John: *Anglo-Egyptian Relations, 1800–1953* (The Cresset Press, London, 1954).

Moorehead, Alan: *White Nile* (Hamish Hamilton, London, 1960).

Moorehead, Alan: *Blue Nile* (Hamish Hamilton, London, 1962).

Nelson, Nina: *Shepheard's Hotel* (Barrie & Rockliff, London, 1960).

Nelson, Nina: *The Mena House, 100 Years of Hospitality 1869–1969* (Cairo, 1979).

Poole, Stanley Lane: *Life of Edward William Lane* (Williams & Norgate, London, 1877).

Searight, Sarah: *The British in the Middle East* (East-West Publications, London, 1969).

Vatikiotis, P. J.: *The Modern History of Egypt* (Weidenfeld & Nicolson, London, 1969).

3   Guides:

I have included James Aldridge's book on Cairo, which he describes as a biography of the city, and E. M. Forster's book on Alexandria among the guide books because that is how I have used them. The classic handbooks here are still useable and useful – I travelled up the Nile with Budge's 1906 *Cook's Handbook.*

Aldridge, James: *Cairo* (Macmillan, London, 1970).

Baedeker, Karl (ed.): *Egypt and the Sûdân, Handbook for Travellers*, 8th Edition (London, 1929).

Budge, E. A. Wallis: *Cook's Handbook for Egypt and the Sûdân*, 2nd Edition (Thos. Cook & Son, London, 1906).

Forster, E. M.: *Alexandria, A History and a Guide* (Whitehead Morris, Alexandria, 1938).

Murray: *A Handbook for Travellers in Lower and Upper Egypt*, 8th Edition (John Murray, London, 1891).

Reynolds–Ball, Eustace: *Cairo of To-Day*, 9th Edition (A&C Black, London, 1916).

Wilkinson, Sir Gardner: *Hand-Book for Travellers in Egypt* (John Murray, London, 1847).

4   Newspapers and Magazines:

I have drawn on a number of newspapers and magazines, and the following were particularly useful.

Egyptian Gazette (Alexandria and Cairo)
The Sphynx (Cairo)
The Times (London)
The Excursionist (Thos. Cook & Son, London)

INDEX